third edition # Human Reproductive Biology

Sylvia S. Mader

McGraw Hill **Learning Solutions**

Boston   Burr Ridge, IL   Dubuque, IA   New York   San Francisco   St. Louis
Bangkok   Bogotá   Caracas   Lisbon   London   Madrid
Mexico City   Milan   New Delhi   Seoul   Singapore   Sydney   Taipei   Toronto

Human Reproductive Biology, Third Edition

8 9 0 QDB QDB 15 14 13 12

ISBN-13: 978-0-07-731355-5
ISBN-10: 0-07-731355-0

Custom Publishing Specialist: Shirley Grall
Production Editor: Tina Hermsen
Printer/Binder: Quad/Graphics

Brief Contents

Contents

Readings

Of Special Interest

Bioethical Focus

Preface

When I was an instructor at Massachusetts Bay Community College, the biology faculty was given the opportunity to initiate and create new courses that would be of interest to students. It occurred to me that college students would be particularly interested in a human reproductive course because many were just entering their reproductive years. Therefore, I decided to develop a reproductive biology course that would include human genetics, because young people are often unaware of the genetic implications of human reproduction. When I searched for an appropriate text, it was clear that, although many sexuality books were available, there was no suitable textbook for my course. Therefore, I decided to write one.

By now the course, Human Reproductive Biology, has been offered many times over at Mass Bay and around the country as well. The course and textbook are always well received by students, who are given the opportunity to fulfill their science requirement while learning applicable information that will enhance their lives. It is time—and indeed, past time—to bring out a new edition because of the many advancements in the field. This edition of the text has been thoroughly updated to make it appropriate for students in the twenty-first century.

The goals of the book remain the same, however: to provide students with a working knowledge of human genetics and human reproductive anatomy and physiology. I also aim to show that human reproduction is related to the fields of human evolution, human behavior, and environmental science. This book has three parts, one for each of its goals.

Part I, Human Inheritance, emphasizes that DNA is passed from one generation to the next during reproduction. DNA makes up the genes that lie within the chromosomes, and the chapters in Part I discuss chromosomal inheritance prior to genetic inheritance. Sexual reproduction ensures that the genotype of the offspring will differ from the genotype of either parent. The chances of an offspring receiving a certain combination of genes may sometimes be predicted, and this information is pertinent when the offspring could inherit a genetic disorder. Both theoretical scientists and medical practitioners are presently emphasizing that many genetic disorders can possibly be prevented. Techniques are available today—and perhaps more will be available soon—to control and to cure genetic disorders. The hope for cures lies in modern genetic research, including genomics, the application of molecular genetics to the human genome.

In Part II, Human Reproduction, Chapter 5 explains hormone action, and then Chapters 6 and 7 discuss male and female reproductive anatomy, physiology, and human sexual response in depth. In Chapter 8, following a description of fertilization, the major biological events of embryonic and fetal development are outlined. A discussion of birth control procedures and devices in Chapter 9 emphasizes the effectiveness and the side effects of each method. Infertility and assisted methods of reproduction are also discussed in that chapter. Finally, the signs, symptoms, and cures of the most prevalent sexually transmitted diseases are reviewed in Chapter 10, and Part II concludes with a special supplement devoted to AIDS.

In Part III, Evolution, Behavior, and Population Concerns, Chapter 11 reviews the principles of evolution before tracing the history of human evolution. This information serves as a basis for the next chapter, which relates human behavior to that of other animals and to human evolution. Finally, Chapter 13 emphasizes that human evolution has led to a very large human population, which places stress on the very environment that sustains it. Students need to be aware of modern ecological concerns before they can help alleviate them.

Third Edition Organization

Part I now has four chapters instead of five. As in the second edition, the first chapter is Chromosomes and Chromosomal Inheritance. The second chapter, now entitled Genes and Medical Genetics, covers both autosomal and sex-linked inheritance. The third chapter, DNA and Molecular Genetics, discusses DNA structure and function and also biotechnology as it applies to human reproduction. The fourth chapter is a new chapter entitled Genetic Counseling. This chapter considers all the methods a genetic counselor uses to determine the chances that a child will be free of genetic disorders that run in the family.

Part II again has six chapters. Chapter 5 was renamed Reproductive Hormones and Sexual Maturation because it now discusses all the hormones that pertain to human reproduction before considering the development of the sex organs and the secondary sex characteristics. Chapter 6, Human Reproductive Systems, now covers both the male and female reproductive systems. Chapter 7, Human Sexual Response, which is new to this edition, discusses this topic in some depth. The remaining three chapters in Part II cover the same topics as in the previous edition.

Part III again has three chapters. The chapters in this part have the same sequence as before, but Chapters 11 and 12 were renamed Evolution and Behavior, respectively, to reflect their more comprehensive content. Finally, while the last chapter has the same title as before—namely, Population Concerns—it discusses modern ecological problems in more depth.

Pedagogical Features

Readings are of two types: Of Special Interest and Bioethical Focus. Of Special Interest readings describe a particular topic in more depth and/or discuss modern technologies. For example, "Living with Klinefelter Syndrome" tells the experiences of a young man who has this syndrome. "Prenatal Genetic Test Analyzes DNA from Fetal Cells" explains how it is possible to test fetal cells in a mother's blood to find out if a fetus has a genetic disorder. "Preventing Birth Defects" emphasizes the steps that can be taken to help ensure a healthy baby. All readings are new to this edition.

We are faced with difficult decisions today, because most of the new reproductive choices available are surrounded by ethical controversies. Each chapter of this text ends with a Bioethical Focus reading that presents the various points of view about an issue and invites students to consider which course of action seems appropriate to them. The instructor can use the Bioethical Focus readings as the starting point for interesting and lively class discussions.

Illustrations particularly help students who are visual learners because of the care with which each illustration has been developed and executed. All illustrations are in full color, and most are new to this edition. To facilitate student learning, each illustration in this edition is on the same or the facing page to its reference. This is possible because software is now available that allows the author to page the book in her office.

Part Introductions highlight the central ideas of each part and specifically tell how the topics contribute to biological knowledge.

Boldface Terms are terms that are pertinent to the topic being discussed. They are defined in context, and all are defined in the glossary as well.

Chapter Summaries offer a concise review of the material. Students may read them before beginning the chapter to preview the topics of importance, and may also use them to refresh their memory later after achieving a firm grasp of the concepts.

Reviewing the Chapter allows students to assess their understanding of the information in the chapter. When they can successfully answer each question, they have mastered the content of the chapter. The questions are page referenced.

Additional Genetics Questions are included at the end of Chapter 2 to help students master their understanding of genetics. Answers to these questions are given in Appendix B.

Critical Thinking Questions are included because all persons need to learn to think critically. The critical thinking questions ask students to apply their recently acquired knowledge to new and different situations. Suggested answers appear in Appendix B.

Understanding Key Terms, a list that appears at the end of each chapter, contains all the boldfaced terms used in the chapter. Each term is accompanied by a page number indicating where it is introduced and defined.

Testing Yourself, found in Appendix A, is new to this edition. Approximately 15–20 multiple choice questions are given per chapter. This appendix can serve as a mini-study guide to help students prepare for multiple choice examinations.

Further Readings are provided in Appendix C for students who would like more information about a particular topic or are seeking references for a research paper. Usually the entries are books and *Scientific American* articles that expand on the topics covered in the chapters.

Glossary and Index. An end-of-text glossary and index are included. The glossary allows students to review the definitions of the boldfaced terms that appear in the text. The index helps them locate topics quickly.

What's New

All of the chapters have been completely revised and updated for this third edition. Nearly all of the tables and illustrations are new. The readings are new also.

Chapter 1: Chromosomes and Chromosomal Inheritance This rewritten chapter now more thoroughly discusses cell structure and the cell cycle. The discussion of meiosis now includes crossing-over. The coverage of chromosomal syndromes is more complete. Of Special Interest readings are "Reproductive Cloning" and "Living with Klinefelter Syndrome." The Bioethical Focus is "Choosing Gender."

Chapter 2: Genes and Medical Genetics This rewritten chapter now walks students through the process of gamete formation before discussing one-trait crosses. The chapter also covers the mechanics of two-trait crosses and then discusses dominant and recessive autosomal genetic disorders. The topic of polygenic inheritance leads to a discussion of multifactorial disorders. Coverage of pleiotropy includes an interesting examination of Marfan syndrome. Sex-linked inheritance is also included in this chapter, as are new discussions of sex-influenced and sex-limited traits. Of Special Interest readings are "My Genes Made Me Do It," "Barr Bodies," and "Living with Hemophilia." The Bioethical Focus is "Environmentally Induced Birth Defects."

Chapter 3: DNA and Molecular Genetics As before, the chapter covers DNA and RNA structure and their functions, but a new section on genetic mutations now follows. Biotechnology is discussed in this chapter, including an updated presentation of gene therapy, genomics, and molecular analysis of the human genome. The Of Special Interest reading is "New Cures on the Horizon." The Bioethical Focus is "Genetic Profiling."

Chapter 4: Genetic Counseling This chapter begins by explaining the use of amniocentesis and chorionic villi sampling coupled with karyotyping to discover abnormal chromosomal inheritance. There follows a discussion of the use of pedigrees to determine the inheritance pattern of a disorder and to calculate the chances of an unborn child having a genetic disorder. The chapter ends by describing modern methods of testing the fetus for genetic disorders and the new procedure of transferring to the uterus only embryos free of a disorder following in vitro fertilization. Of Special Interest readings are "Pedigree for Fragile X Syndrome" and "Prenatal Genetic Test Analyzes DNA from Fetal Cells." The Bioethical Focus is "Abortions."

Chapter 5: Reproductive Hormones and Sexual Maturation This chapter has been completely rewritten and reorganized. A more thorough discussion of the endocrine system, including the principle of feedback control, precedes consideration of the gonadotropic and sex hormones. The development of the male and female sex organs is tied to a discussion of the role of the Y chromosome and the *SRY* gene. The influence of testosterone on development extends to differences in the male and female brains and possible influences on sexual orientation. The secondary sex characteristics are more thoroughly explained and discussed in this edition. Of Special Interest readings are "Chemical Signals," "Pineal Gland," and "Dangers of Anabolic Steroids." The Bioethical Focus is "Hormone Replacement Therapy."

Chapter 6: Human Reproductive Systems This chapter has been rewritten and reorganized to present a more complete discussion of both male and female reproductive anatomy. Hormonal control of the female reproductive cycle is also reviewed. The Of Special Interest readings are "Prostate Enlargement and Cancer" and "Shower Check for Cancer." The Bioethical Focus is "Sex Education in Schools."

Chapter 7: Human Sexual Response This new chapter relates the male and female sexual response to the Masters and Johnson four-phase model. The chapter explains that models of sexual arousal based on internal and external stimuli are being formulated, and that so far, studies suggest more similarities than differences in males and females. The Of Special Interest reading is "Sexual Arousal and Response in Your Life." The Bioethical Focus is "The Study of Human Sexual Response."

Chapter 8: Fertilization, Development, and Birth This chapter has been completely rewritten and reorganized. The process of fertilization is illustrated with new art. Discussions of the processes of development and the extraembryonic membranes now precede an examination of the stages of development. The three stages of birth are illustrated with new art. A new major section explains and illustrates the effects on a mother during pregnancy. Of Special Interest readings are "Preventing Birth Defects" and "Deciding Between Feeding by Breast or by Bottle." The Bioethical Focus is "Maternal Health Habits."

Chapter 9: Birth Control and Infertility   This chapter has been rewritten and reorganized throughout. The section on birth control methods begins with the methodology for sterilizing males and females. Descriptions of the various birth control methods and devices have been updated, as has the discussion of abortion. The most current methods of assisted reproductive technologies are also discussed. Of Special Interest readings are "Endocrine-Disrupting Contaminants" and "Assessing Assisted Reproductive Technologies (ART)." The Bioethical Focus is "Assisted Reproductive Technologies."

Chapter 10: Sexually Transmitted Diseases   This chapter has been completely rewritten to include the most up-to-date information regarding the transmission and treatment of sexually transmitted diseases. A discussion of hepatitis B is new to the text. An explanation of the STDs from a bacterial source now precedes the discussion of STDs from a viral source and other infections. Of Special Interest readings are "Bacteria and You," "STDs and Medical Treatment," and "Preventing Transmission of STDs." The Bioethical Focus is "Identifying Carriers."

AIDS Supplement: This supplement has been completely rewritten and reorganized, with new art to illustrate the prevalence of AIDS, the phases of an HIV infection, and the HIV life cycle. The discussion of drug therapy for an HIV infection has been updated. The Bioethical Focus is "HIV Vaccine Testing in Africa."

Chapter 11: Evolution   This new chapter considers the origin of life before discussing the theory of evolution and the evidence that supports it. There follows an explanation of the evolution of primates, australopithecines, and finally humans. This chapter serves as a background for understanding human sexual behavior, discussed in the next chapter. The Bioethical Focus is "The Theory of Evolution."

Chapter 12: Behavior   Using other animals as examples, this chapter establishes that behavior, including sexual behavior, has a genetic basis but is modified through learning. Human culture, which arose during the evolution of humans, adds another layer to the learning experience of humans. Mating behavior, which centers around female choice and male competition, can also be seen in humans. Sociobiologists interpret behavior according to many of the same principles that apply to other animals. The Of Special Interest reading is "Courtship Display of Male Bowerbirds." The Bioethical Focus is "Animals in Zoos."

Chapter 13: Population Concerns   This chapter has been completely rewritten and reorganized. The growth rate of the human population is related to the contributions made by the more-developed and the less-developed countries. This chapter describes how the consumption of resources, such as land, water, food, energy, and minerals, leads to the pollution of the environment. Reduction in resource consumption and a switch to renewable energy supplies could eventually result in a sustainable society. The Bioethical Focus is "Oil Drilling in the Arctic."

Acknowledgments

Robert J. Caron
Bristol Community College

Kate Sullivan Collopy
University of New Hampshire

Johnny El-Rady
University of South Florida

Margaret F. Field
Saint Mary's College of California

Gertrude W. Hinsch
University of South Florida

LeLeng Isaacs
Goucher College

Joan Lorch
Canisius College

Alvin G. Massinger, Jr.
Herkimer County Community College

Nancy L. Pencoe
State University of West Georgia

Lawrence J. Wangh
Brandeis University

Mala Kruss Wingerd
San Diego State University

Scott D. Zimmerman
Universtiy of Wisconsin–Stout

About the Author

In her 20-year career with McGraw-Hill, Dr. Mader has written an impressive collection of textbooks. Aside from *Human Reproductive Biology*, now in its third edition, Dr. Mader has written *Understanding Human Anatomy and Physiology*, fifth edition; *Human Biology*, eighth edition; *Inquiry into Life*, tenth edition; and *Biology*, eighth edition. Dr. Mader became a textbook author when she discovered that the learning techniques she so successfully used in her teaching were also appropriate for biology textbooks. Dr. Mader's direct writing style and carefully constructed pedagogy provide students with an opportunity to learn the basics of biology, anatomy and physiology, and also human reproductive biology.

HUMAN REPRODUCTIVE
BIOLOGY

This individual has Down syndrome because he inherited three copies of chromosome 21.

PART

I

Human Inheritance

Sexual reproduction in humans requires sex cell formation, fertilization, and development. Each sex cell carries half the total number of chromosomes as the body cells, which are called **somatic cells.** This helps ensure that every child (except identical twins) receives a different combination of chromosomes. The genes are on the chromosomes. It is sometimes possible to determine the chances of an offspring receiving a particular chromosome and gene. Therefore, if the genetic makeup of the parent is known, it may be possible to determine the chances of a child inheriting a genetic disease.

Genes, now known to be constructed of DNA, control not only the functions of the cell but also, ultimately, the characteristics of the individual. **DNA** contains a code for the sequence of amino acids in proteins, which are synthesized in the cell. This is how DNA controls the makeup and functioning of the cell. In the past several years, knowledge of DNA structure and function has led to a new industry—biotechnology—which has contributed to advances not only in the fields of agriculture and medicine but also in human genetic inheritance.

Chapter 1

Chromosomes and Chromosomal Inheritance

1.1 The Human Cell

Every human being is made up of billions of **cells,** the basic units of life. Nothing smaller than a cell is capable of growth and reproduction. All human cells are bounded by a plasma membrane and contain a nucleus and cytoplasm (Fig. 1.1). The plasma membrane allows nutrients to enter the cell, where they serve as a source of energy and as building blocks for the synthesis of new substances to be used inside the cell or secreted for use elsewhere.

Nucleus

The **nucleus,** a centrally located structure, is the command center of the cell. The nucleus is bounded by the nuclear envelope, which is pitted with pores that allow movement of molecules from the nucleus into the cytoplasm and vice versa. It is of particular interest to us that the nucleus houses chromatin, long stringy material that condenses and coils just before cell division to become the **chromosomes.** Normally, humans have 46 chromosomes in each nucleus. Chromosomes

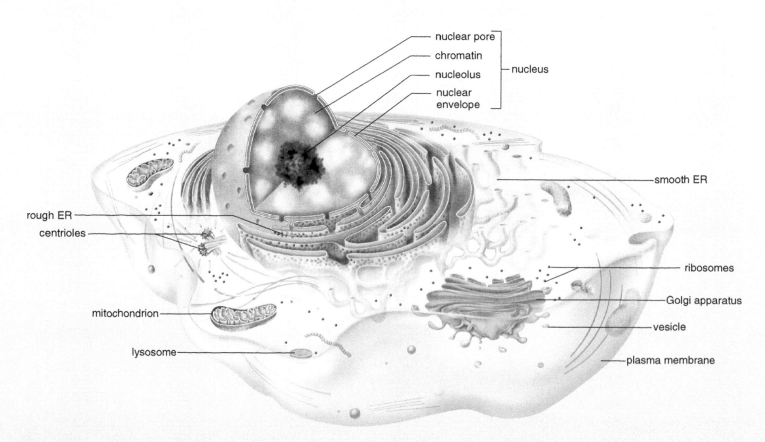

Figure 1.1 **Somatic human cell.**
The two major parts of a cell are the nucleus and the cytoplasm, the contents of the cell outside the nucleus. We are particularly interested in the nucleus because it contains the chromosomes. The chromosomes carry genetic information in the form of genes composed of DNA. DNA specifies the production of proteins; the organelles in the cytoplasm labeled here are involved in protein production and/or modification.

carry the **genes,** which determine what the specific cell is like and also what the individual is like. That's why the nucleus is sometimes called the command center of the cell.

The **nucleolus** is a special region of chromatin where the subunits of ribosomes are made. The subunits travel through the nuclear pores, and ribosomes are assembled and function in the cytoplasm. **Ribosomes,** as discussed in the next section, carry out protein synthesis.

Cytoplasm

The **cytoplasm** is the portion of a cell that lies between the nucleus and the plasma membrane. The cytoplasm contains various small bodies called organelles, and each organelle has a specific structure and function. Several organelles are involved in the production, modification, and secretion of proteins. **Proteins** have both structural and physiological functions in cells and in the individual. Some proteins are enzymes that speed chemical reactions, thus allowing the cell to grow and reproduce. We will see that several hereditary disorders are due to malfunctioning enzymes. This is because genes, the hereditary units of chromosomes, specify the synthesis of proteins at the ribosomes. Ribosomes can occur freely in the cytoplasm but often are attached to an organelle called the endoplasmic reticulum.

The **endoplasmic reticulum (ER)** is a complicated system of membranous channels and saccules (flattened vesicles) that can be quite plentiful in cells actively engaged in protein synthesis. When ribosomes are attached to endoplasmic reticulum, it is called rough ER, and when they are not, it is called smooth ER. You can imagine that proteins made at rough ER could enter its lumen (inner space), and this is exactly what happens. Once inside the ER, the protein is modified (Fig. 1.2). For example, when a carbohydrate chain is added to the polypeptide, it becomes a glycoprotein.

Small vacuoles (sacs) called **vesicles** bud off the ER and take the protein to the **Golgi apparatus.** The Golgi apparatus also modifies proteins and packages them in vesicles. Some of these vesicles take proteins to the plasma membrane, where they are secreted. Others are **lysosomes,** which contain very powerful enzymes that are capable of digesting large molecules taken into the cell and even parts of the cell itself. If lysosomal enzymes were to escape, the cell itself would cease to exist!

Mitochondria are energy-converting organelles. They take in oxygen and break down nutrients into a form of energy the cell can use to synthesize proteins, among other substances. Finally, the **centrioles** are active during cell division, which is our next topic. The pair of centrioles outside a nucleus (see Fig. 1.1) are a part of a granular region called the centrosome. A centrosome is necessary for the formation of a spindle apparatus, a structure that is intimately involved in the movement of chromosomes during cell division.

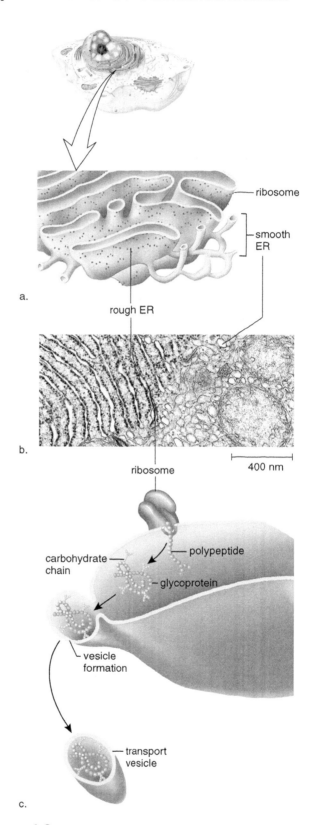

Figure 1.2 Rough endoplasmic reticulum (ER).
a. Rough ER has attached ribosomes. **b.** Rough ER appears as flattened saccules, while smooth ER is a network of interconnected tubules. **c.** A protein (polypeptide) made at a ribosome moves into the lumen of the organelle, is modified, and is eventually packaged in a transport vesicle that takes it to the Golgi apparatus.

1.2 Human Life Cycle

The human life cycle involves growth and sexual reproduction (Fig. 1.3). During growth, a type of nuclear division called **mitosis** ensures that each and every cell has a complete number of chromosomes. In order for sexual reproduction to take place, a type of nuclear division called **meiosis** occurs in the sex cells, or **gametes.** Meiosis reduces the chromosomal number by half, called the **haploid (n)** number of chromosomes; the haploid number in humans is 23.

Meiosis occurs in the sex organs, also called the **gonads.** In males, the testes produce sperm; in females, the ovaries produce cells that become eggs. The sperm and the egg are the gametes.

A **zygote** comes into existence when a haploid sperm fertilizes a haploid egg. Each parent contributes one chromosome of each type to a zygote, which then has the **diploid (2n)** number of chromosomes. As the zygote develops into an individual, mitosis occurs and ensures that each somatic cell has the diploid number of chromosomes.

Cell Cycle

The **cell cycle** consists of the three stages of interphase as well as the mitotic stage. Mitosis and cytokinesis occur in the mitotic stage. While mitosis is division of the nucleus, **cytokinesis** is division of the cytoplasm and organelles. The cell divides, and then it enters interphase before dividing again. Therefore, **interphase** is the interval of time between cell divisions. The length of time required for the entire cell cycle varies according to the type of cell, but 18–24 hours is typical. Mitosis and cytokinesis last from less than an hour to slightly more than 2 hours; for the rest of the time, the cell is in interphase (Fig. 1.4).

It used to be said that interphase was a resting stage, but we now know that this is not the case. The organelles are metabolically active and are carrying on their normal functions. If the cell is going to divide, DNA replication occurs. During replication, DNA is copied, and each chromosome becomes duplicated. Also, organelles, including the centrioles (see Fig. 1.1), duplicate. A nondividing cell has one pair

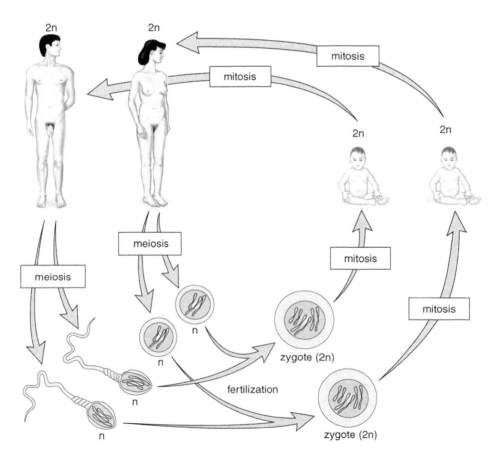

Figure 1.3   Life cycle of humans.
Meiosis in males is a part of sperm production, and meiosis in females is a part of egg production. When a haploid sperm fertilizes a haploid egg, the zygote is diploid. The zygote undergoes mitosis as it develops into a newborn child. Mitosis continues after birth until the individual reaches maturity, and then the life cycle begins again.

of centrioles, but in a cell that is going to divide, this pair duplicates, and there are two pairs of centrioles outside the nucleus.

As you can see in Figure 1.4, interphase consists of three stages, called G_1, S, and G_2. The S stage, of course, is when replication of DNA and duplication of chromosomes occur. While biologists originally used the letter G to stand for "gaps" before and after synthesis of DNA, it is better for us to think of G as standing for "growth" because during G_1, the organelles begin to duplicate, and during G_2, synthesis (production) of proteins occurs. These proteins are necessary to cell division, which will soon take place.

The G_1 and G_2 stages have checkpoints at which the cell cycle can stop if all is not well. For example, if DNA is damaged, as by exposure to solar radiation or X rays, stopping the cell cycle allows time for the damage to be repaired so that it is not passed on to somatic cells. If DNA cannot be repaired, the cell will undergo **apoptosis,** or programmed cell death.

The fourth stage of the cell cycle is the M stage, during which mitosis and cytokinesis occur. Mitosis requires a number of phases as will be discussed in section 1.3.

1.3 Mitosis

Mitosis *is nuclear division that produces two daughter cells, each with the same number and kinds of chromosomes as the parental cell, the cell that divides.* Therefore, following mitosis, the daughter cells are genetically identical to each other and to the cell that produced them.

When mitosis is going to occur, chromatin in the nucleus becomes condensed, and the chromosomes become visible. Each chromosome has duplicated and is composed of two sister chromatids held together at a **centromere.** The sister chromatids are genetically identical, meaning that they contain the same genes. At the completion of mitosis, each chromosome consists of a single **chromatid.**

Figure 1.5 gives an overview of mitosis; for simplicity, only four chromosomes are depicted. (In determining the number of chromosomes, it is necessary to count only the number of independent centromeres.) During mitosis, the centromeres divide, the sister chromatids separate, and one of each kind of chromosome goes into each daughter cell. Therefore, each daughter cell gets a complete set of chromosomes and is 2n. (Following separation, each chromatid is called a chromosome.) Since each daughter cell receives the same number and kinds of chromosomes as the parental cell, each is genetically identical to the other.

Mitosis occurs in humans when tissues grow or when repair occurs. Following fertilization, the zygote begins to divide mitotically, and mitosis continues during development and the life span of the individual. Also, when a cut heals or a broken bone mends, mitosis has occurred.

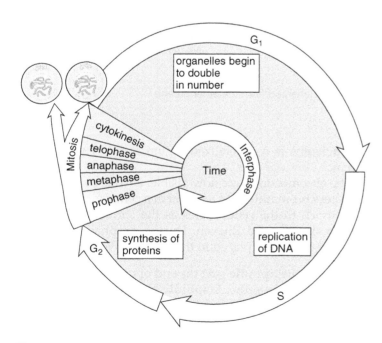

Figure 1.4 The cell cycle.
The cell cycle has four stages. During interphase, which consists of G_1, S, and G_2, the cell gets ready to divide, and during the M stage, nuclear division and cytokinesis (cytoplasmic division) occur.

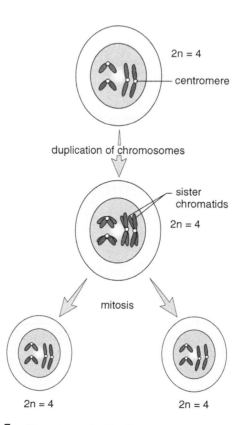

Figure 1.5 Overview of mitosis.
Each parent contributes one chromosome of each type to a zygote, which becomes the first parental cell. The blue chromosomes were inherited from one parent, and the red chromosomes were inherited from the other parent.

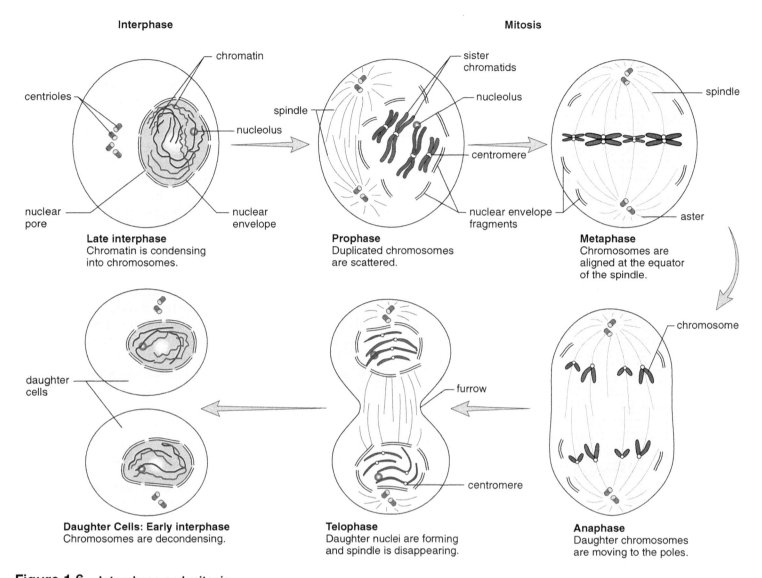

Figure 1.6   **Interphase and mitosis.**
The blue chromosomes were inherited from one parent, and the red chromosomes were inherited from the other parent.

Stages of Mitosis

As an aid in describing the events of mitosis, the process is divided into four phases: prophase, metaphase, anaphase, and telophase (Fig. 1.6). Although the stages of mitosis are depicted here as if they were separate, they are actually continuous, and one stage flows into the other with no noticeable interruption.

Prophase

During **prophase,** several events visibly indicate that the cell is preparing to divide. The two pairs of centrioles outside the nucleus begin moving away from each other toward opposite ends of the nucleus. Spindle fibers appear between the separating centriole pairs, the nuclear envelope begins to fragment, and the nucleolus begins to disappear.

The nucleolus is a specialized region of DNA within the nucleus.

The chromosomes are now visible. Each is composed of two sister chromatids held together at a centromere. Spindle fibers attach to the centromeres as the chromosomes continue to shorten and thicken. During prophase, chromosomes are randomly placed in the nucleus (Fig. 1.6).

Structure of the Spindle   At the end of prophase, a cell has a fully formed spindle. A **spindle** has poles, asters, and fibers. The **asters** are arrays of short microtubules that radiate from the poles, and the fibers are bundles of microtubules that stretch between the poles. The centrioles may play a role in organizing the spindle, but their location at the poles of a spindle could simply be to ensure that each daughter cell receives a pair of centrioles.

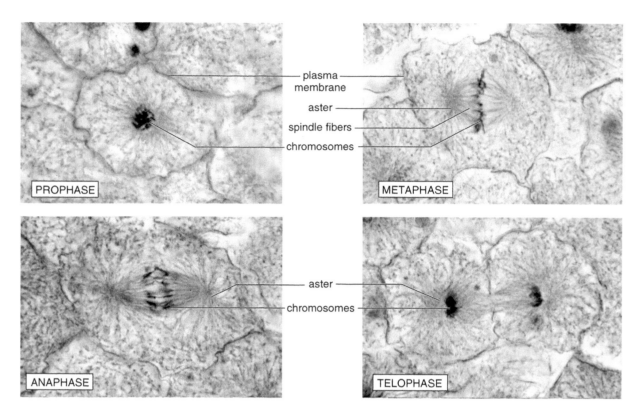

Figure 1.7 **Micrographs of mitosis occurring in a whitefish embryo.**

Metaphase

During **metaphase,** the nuclear envelope is fragmented, and the spindle occupies the region formerly occupied by the nucleus. The chromosomes are now at the equator (center) of the spindle. Metaphase is characterized by a fully formed spindle, and the chromosomes, each with two sister chromatids, are aligned at the equator (Fig. 1.7).

Anaphase

At the start of **anaphase,** the sister chromatids separate. *Once separated, the chromatids are called chromosomes.* Separation of the sister chromatids ensures that each cell receives a copy of each type of chromosome and thereby has a full complement of genes. During anaphase, the daughter chromosomes move to the poles of the spindle. Anaphase is characterized by the diploid number of chromosomes moving toward each pole.

Function of the Spindle   The spindle brings about chromosomal movement. Two types of spindle fibers are involved in the movement of chromosomes during anaphase. One type extends from the poles to the equator of the spindle; there they overlap. As mitosis proceeds, these fibers increase in length, and this helps push the chromosomes apart. The chromosomes themselves are attached to other spindle fibers that simply extend from their centromeres to the poles. These fibers get shorter and shorter as the chromosomes move toward the poles. Therefore, they pull the chromosomes apart.

Spindle fibers, as stated earlier, are composed of microtubules. Microtubules can assemble and disassemble by the addition or subtraction of tubulin (protein) subunits. This is what enables spindle fibers to lengthen and shorten and what ultimately causes the movement of the chromosomes.

Telophase

Telophase begins when the chromosomes arrive at the poles. During telophase, the chromosomes become indistinct chromatin again. The spindle disappears as nucleoli appear, and the nuclear envelope components reassemble in each cell. Telophase is characterized by the formation of two daughter nuclei.

Cytokinesis

Cytokinesis is division of the cytoplasm and organelles. In animal cells, a slight indentation called a **cleavage furrow** passes around the circumference of the cell. Actin filaments form a contractile ring, and as the ring gets smaller and smaller, the cleavage furrow pinches the cell in half. As a result, each cell becomes enclosed by its own plasma membrane.

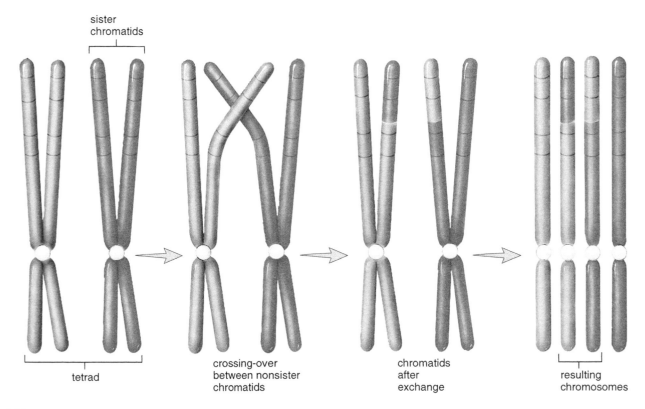

sister
chromatids

tetrad

crossing-over
between nonsister
chromatids

chromatids
after
exchange

resulting
chromosomes

Figure 1.8   **Crossing-over.**
When homologous chromosomes are in synapsis, the nonsister chromatids exchange genetic material. This illustration shows only one crossover per chromosome pair, but the average is slightly more than two per chromosome pair in humans. Following crossing-over, the sister chromatids may no longer be identical and instead may have different combinations of genes.

1.4 Meiosis

Meiosis, which requires two nuclear divisions, results in *four daughter cells, each having one of each kind of chromosome and therefore half the number of chromosomes as the parental cell.* The parental cell has the 2n number of chromosomes, while the daughter cells have the n number of chromosomes. Therefore, meiosis is often called reduction division.

The daughter cells that result from meiosis go on to become the gametes. In humans, meiosis occurs in the gonads—that is, in the testes of males and the ovaries of females. Whereas mitosis concerns the passage of chromosomes between generations of somatic cells in the body, meiosis concerns the passage of chromosomes from one generation to the next.

Overview of Meiosis: 2n → n

Meiosis results in four daughter cells because it consists of two divisions, called meiosis I and meiosis II. Before meiosis I begins, each chromosome has duplicated and is composed of two sister chromatids. The parental cell is 2n. When a cell is 2n, the chromosomes occur in pairs. For example, the 46 chromosomes of humans occur in 23 pairs. These pairs are called **homologous chromosomes.**

Meiosis I

During meiosis I, the homologous chromosomes of each pair come together and line up side-by-side due to a means of attraction still unknown. This so-called **synapsis** results in a **tetrad,** an association of four chromatids that stay in close proximity until they separate. During synapsis, nonsister chromatids may exchange genetic material. The exchange of genetic material between chromatids is called **crossing-over** (Fig. 1.8). Crossing-over is significant because it recombines the genes of the parental cell and increases the variability of the gametes and therefore the offspring.

Following synapsis during meiosis I, the homologous chromosomes of each pair separate. This separation means that one chromosome from each homologous pair will be found in each daughter cell. There are no restrictions as to which chromosome goes to each daughter cell, and therefore, all possible combinations of chromosomes may occur within the gametes.

Following meiosis I, the daughter cells have half the number of chromosomes, because they received one of each pair of chromosomes. Thus, the daughter cells are not genetically identical. The chromosomes are still duplicated.

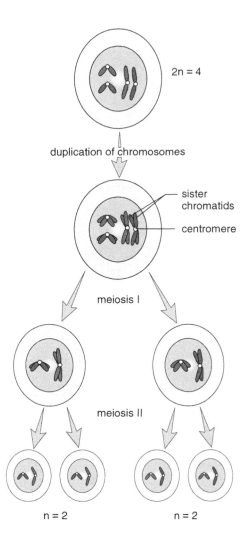

Figure 1.9   Overview of meiosis.
Following duplication of chromosomes, the parental cell undergoes two divisions, meiosis I and meiosis II. During meiosis I, homologous chromosomes separate, and during meiosis II, chromatids separate. The final daughter cells are haploid. (The blue chromosomes were originally inherited from one parent, and the red chromosomes were originally inherited from the other parent.)

Meiosis II

When meiosis II begins, the chromosomes are still duplicated. Therefore, no duplication of chromosomes is needed between meiosis I and meiosis II. The chromosomes are **dyads** because each one is composed of two sister chromatids. During meiosis II, the sister chromatids separate in each of the cells from meiosis I. Each of the resulting four daughter cells has the haploid number of chromosomes.

Following meiosis, the daughter cells are not genetically identical to the parental cell. Also, notice in Figure 1.9 that the daughter cells on the right do not have the same chromosomes as the daughter cells on the left. Why not? Because the homologous chromosomes of each pair separated during meiosis I. What other chromosome combinations are possible in the daughter cells in addition to those depicted? It's possible that the gametes could contain chromosomes from only one parent (either the father or the mother) instead of both parents as shown here.

The Importance of Meiosis

Because of meiosis, the chromosomal number stays constant in each generation. In humans, meiosis occurs in the testes and ovaries during the production of the gametes. When a haploid sperm fertilizes a haploid egg, the new individual has the diploid number of chromosomes. There are three ways the new individual is assured a different combination of genes than either parent has:

1. Crossing-over recombines the genes on the sister chromatids of homologous pairs of chromosomes.
2. Following meiosis, gametes have all possible combinations of chromosomes.
3. At fertilization, recombination of chromosomes occurs because the sperm and egg carry varied combinations of chromosomes.

Stages of Meiosis

The same four stages of mitosis—prophase, metaphase, anaphase, and telophase—occur during both meiosis I and meiosis II.

The First Division

The stages of meiosis I are diagrammed in Figure 1.10. During prophase I, the spindle appears while the nuclear envelope fragments and the nucleolus disappears. The homologous chromosomes, each having two sister chromatids, undergo synapsis, forming tetrads. Crossing-over occurs now, but for simplicity, this event has been omitted from Figure 1.10. In metaphase I, tetrads line up at the equator of the spindle. During anaphase I, homologous chromosomes of each pair separate and move to opposite poles of the spindle. During telophase I, nucleoli appear, and nuclear envelopes form as the spindle disappears.

During cytokinesis, the plasma membrane furrows to produce two cells. Each daughter cell contains only one chromosome from each homologous pair. The chromosomes are dyads, and each has two sister chromatids. No replication of DNA occurs during a period of time called interkinesis.

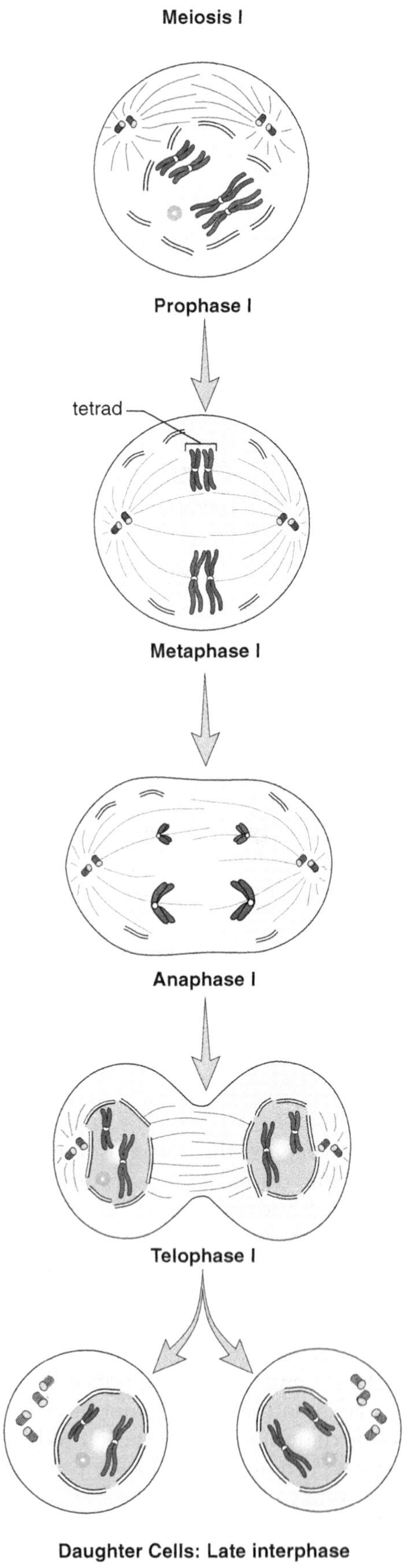

Meiosis I

Prophase I

tetrad

Metaphase I

Anaphase I

Telophase I

Daughter Cells: Late interphase

Figure 1.10   Meiosis I.
During meiosis I, homologous chromosomes undergo synapsis and then separate so that each daughter cell has only one chromosome from each original homologous pair. For simplicity's sake, the results of crossing-over have not been depicted. Notice that each daughter cell is haploid and each chromosome still has two chromatids.

The Second Division

The stages of meiosis II are diagrammed in Figure 1.11. At the beginning of prophase II, a spindle appears while the nuclear envelope disassembles and the nucleolus disappears. Dyads (one dyad from each pair of homologous chromosomes) are present, and each attaches to the spindle independently. During metaphase II, the dyads are lined up at the equator. At the start of anaphase II, the centromeres split. The sister chromatids of each dyad separate and move toward the poles. Each pole receives the same number of chromosomes. In telophase II, the spindle disappears as nuclear envelopes form.

During cytokinesis, the plasma membrane furrows to produce two complete cells, each of which has the haploid, or n, number of chromosomes. Because each cell from meiosis I undergoes meiosis II, there are four daughter cells altogether.

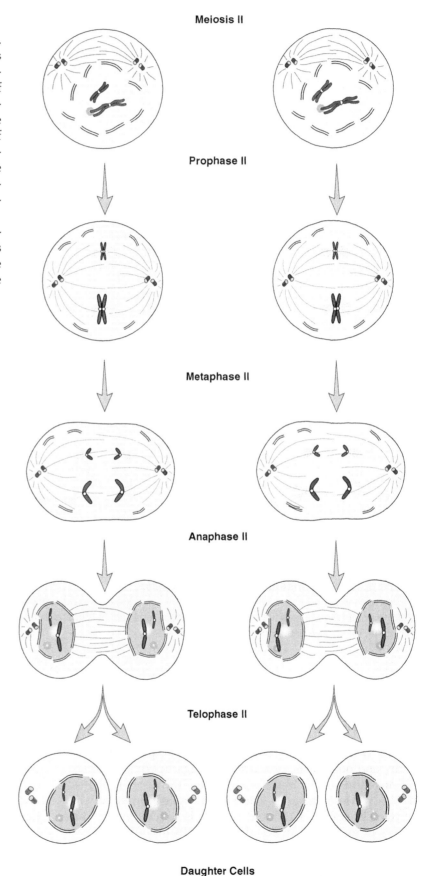

Meiosis II

Prophase II

Metaphase II

Anaphase II

Telophase II

Daughter Cells

Figure 1.11   Meiosis II.

During meiosis II, sister chromatids separate. Each daughter cell is haploid, and each chromosome consists of one chromatid. (The blue chromosomes were inherited from one parent, and the red chromosomes were inherited from the other parent.)

Spermatogenesis

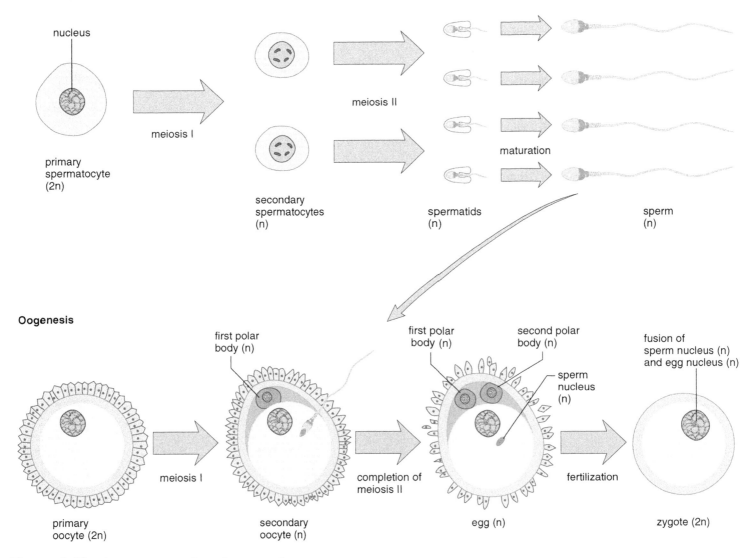

Oogenesis

Figure 1.12   Spermatogenesis and oogenesis.

Spermatogenesis produces four viable sperm, whereas oogenesis produces one egg and at least two polar bodies. Notice that oogenesis does not go to completion unless the secondary oocyte is fertilized. In humans, both sperm and egg have 23 chromosomes each; therefore, following fertilization, the zygote has 46 chromosomes.

Spermatogenesis and Oogenesis

Meiosis is a part of both **spermatogenesis,** production of sperm, and **oogenesis,** production of eggs. Spermatogenesis and oogenesis occur in the sex organs—the testes in males and the ovaries in females. The gametes appear differently in the two sexes (Fig. 1.12), and meiosis is different, too. The process of meiosis in males always results in four cells that become sperm. Meiosis in females produces only one egg. Meiosis I results in one large cell called a secondary oocyte and one polar body. After meiosis II, there is one egg and two (or possibly three) polar bodies, which later degenerate.

Polar bodies are products of oogenesis that contain chromosomes but little cytoplasm. The cytoplasm of the egg is a source of nutrients and organelles for the embryo.

Spermatogenesis, once started, continues to completion, and mature sperm result. In contrast, oogenesis does not necessarily go to completion. Only if a sperm fertilizes the secondary oocyte does it undergo meiosis II and become an egg. Regardless of this complication, however, both the sperm and the egg contribute the haploid number of chromosomes to the zygote (fertilized egg). In humans, each gamete contributes 23 chromosomes.

Reproductive Cloning

Asexual reproduction requires only one parent and does not involve gametes. Humans have no normal means of asexual reproduction; however, it is conceivable that they could be cloned. Reproductive cloning—that is, the production of a copy of an individual—is a form of asexual reproduction because it requires the genes of only one individual. Each human cell is totipotent, meaning that the cell contains a copy of all the genes. But during development, certain genes are turned off as the cells become specialized. Muscle cells, for example, are specialized to contract; nerve cells to conduct nerve impulses; and glandular cells to secrete. Cloning of an adult human would require that all the genes of the chosen nucleus be turned on again. This has long been thought to be impossible.

Despite formidable obstacles, however, investigators never gave up. Up until 1997, a few animals had been cloned, though only under certain circumstances. For frogs, it was possible to take the nucleus from an intestinal cell of a tadpole and transplant it into a frog's egg whose own nucleus had been destroyed, and occasionally, normal development produced an adult frog. For monkeys, the nucleus had to be taken from an even earlier stage—an embryo consisting of several cells. Only if minimal differentiation of cells had occurred was it possible to have the nucleus "start over" to direct the development of a complete monkey. But it would be preferable to use the nuclei of adults for cloning, because only then is it possible to know what phenotypic characteristics might result.

In March 1997, a scientific breakthrough occurred. Ian Wilmut of the Roslin Institute in Edinburgh, Scotland, announced that he and his colleagues had cloned a sheep using a cell taken from an adult sheep. They used the procedure depicted in Figure 1A to achieve their remarkable success. Donor cells were taken from an udder (mammary gland) of a Finn Dorset ewe (female sheep), and egg cells were taken from a Blackface ewe. Although 29 clones were attempted, only one—named Dolly—resulted. How was this procedure different from all the others that had been attempted? Starving the donor cells caused them to stop dividing and go into a resting stage that made the nuclei amenable to cytoplasmic signals for initiation of development.

As soon as Dolly was born, the public and many scientists were taken with the belief that it might be possible to clone human beings. In fact, it took no time at all for then President Clinton to issue an executive order that no federal funds were to be spent on experiments to clone human beings. And this has been the law ever since. Biologists especially want the public to understand that a human can never be an exact copy of the person cloned. The clone would start life as an infant in a different family situation and in a different social environment from its predecessor. Humans, especially, are the product not only of their genes, but also of their environment.

Scientists had always been concerned that Dolly would age more rapidly than normal sheep—after all, she was the product of a 2n nucleus that was already six years old. It was also possible that she would be more susceptible to diseases that would shorten her life. Indeed, Dolly was put down by lethal injection in February of 2003 because she had been suffering from lung cancer and crippling arthritis. She had lived only half the normal life span of a Dorset sheep, but she was a mother to six lambs, bred the normal way.

The cloning of Dolly showed that genetic material from a specialized adult cell could be reprogrammed to generate an entire new organism. Some scientists attribute the low rate of success and the deformities observed among animal clones today to our inability to properly reprogram the genes in the donated nucleus.

The cloning of animals has potential benefits. For example, work goes forward today to couple cloning with genetic engineering to produce improved animal strains. Also, cloning may be used to save endangered animals from extinction. The first clone of an endangered animal—a baby bull gaur (a wild ox) called Noah—was born in 2003.

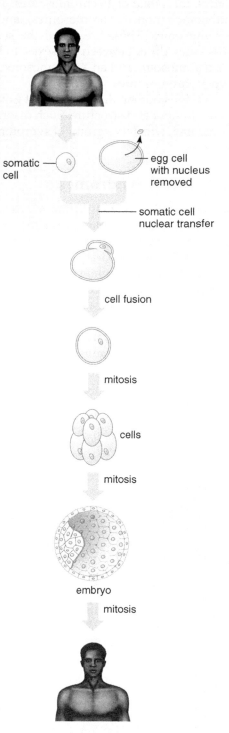

Figure 1A **Proposed methodology for cloning a human being.**

1.5 Chromosomal Inheritance

In humans, males and females have 23 pairs of chromosomes, for a total of 46 chromosomes. Twenty-two pairs are **autosomes** (nonsex chromosomes), and one pair is the sex chromosomes. These are called the **sex chromosomes** because they differ between the sexes. In humans, males have a Y chromosome and an X chromosome, while females have two X chromosomes.

Various human disorders result from abnormal chromosome number and structure. Such disorders often result in a **syndrome,** which is a group of symptoms that always occur together.

Autosomal Syndromes

Nondisjunction occurs during meiosis I, when both members of a homologous pair go into the same daughter cell (Fig. 1.13a). When nondisjunction occurs during meiosis II, sister chromatids fail to separate, and both daughter chromosomes go into the same daughter cell (Fig. 1.13b). If an egg with 24 chromosomes is fertilized with a normal sperm, the result is a *trisomy*, so called because one type of chromosome is present in three copies. If an egg with 22 chromosomes is fertilized with a normal sperm, the result is a *monosomy*, so called because one type of chromosome is present in a single copy.

Down Syndrome

Down syndrome is also called trisomy 21 because the individual usually has three copies of chromosome 21. In most instances, the egg had two copies of this chromosome instead of one. In 23% of the cases studied, however, the sperm had the extra chromosome 21.

Down syndrome (Fig. 1.14) is easily recognized by these characteristics: short stature, an eyelid fold, stubby fingers, a wide gap between the first and second toes, a large, fissured tongue, a round head, a palm crease (the so-called simian line), and unfortunately, mental retardation, which can sometimes be severe.

The chance of a woman having a Down syndrome child increases rapidly with age, starting at about age 40. The frequency of Down syndrome is 1 in 800 births for mothers under 40 years of age and 1 in 80 for mothers over 40 years of age. However, most Down syndrome babies are born to women younger than age 40, because this is the age group having the most babies.

We know that the genes that cause Down syndrome are located on the bottom third of chromosome 21, and extensive investigative work has been directed toward discovering the specific genes responsible for the characteristics of the syndrome. One day it might be possible to control the expression of these genes even before birth, so that the symptoms of Down syndrome do not appear.

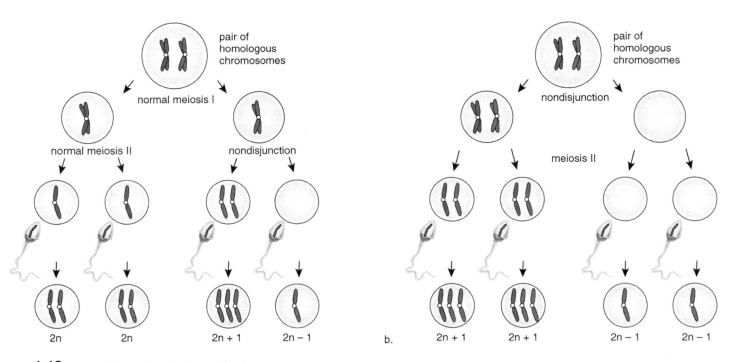

Figure 1.13   Nondisjunction during meiosis.
a. If homologous chromosomes fail to separate during meiosis I, or **(b)** if chromatids fail to separate during meiosis II, abnormal gametes have an extra chromosome or lack a chromosome. Fertilization of these abnormal eggs with normal sperm results in a zygote with abnormal chromosome numbers. (2n = diploid number of chromosomes.)

Figure 1.14 **Down syndrome.**
Down syndrome occurs when the egg or the sperm has an extra chromosome 21 due to nondisjunction in either meiosis I or meiosis II. Characteristics include a wide, rounded face and narrow, slanting eyelids. Mental retardation to varying degrees is usually present.

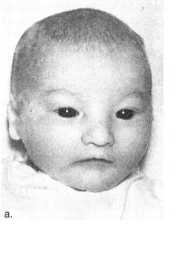
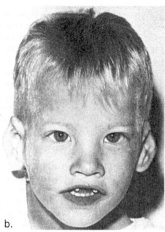

a.

b.

Figure 1.15 **Cri du chat syndrome.**
Cri du chat syndrome occurs when a portion of chromosome 5 is missing. Characteristics include a cry that sounds like the meow of a cat as an infant and misshapen ears. **a.** An infant and **(b)** an older child with this syndrome.

Cri du Chat Syndrome

A chromosomal deletion is responsible for cri du chat (cat's cry) syndrome, which has a frequency of one in 50,000 live births. An infant with this syndrome has a moon face, a small head, and a cry that sounds like the meow of a cat because of a malformed larynx; an older child has an eyelid fold and misshapen ears placed low on the head (Fig. 1.15). Severe mental retardation becomes evident as the child matures because a portion of one chromosome 5 is missing (deleted). The other chromosome 5 is normal, as are all the other chromosomes.

Sex Chromosomal Syndromes

Because females are XX, an egg always bears an X, but because males are XY, a sperm can bear an X or a Y. Therefore, the sex of the newborn child is determined by the father. If a Y-bearing sperm fertilizes the egg, then the XY combination results in a male. On the other hand, if an X-bearing sperm fertilizes the egg, the XX combination results in a female:

	X	Y
X	XX	XY

All factors being equal, there is a 50% chance of each pregnancy resulting in a girl or a boy. However, for reasons that are not clear, more males than females are conceived, though from then on, the death rate among males is higher than for females. By age 85, there are twice as many females as males.

Abnormal Sex Chromosome Number

An abnormal sex chromosome number is the result of inheriting too many or too few X or Y chromosomes. Figure 1.13 can be used to illustrate nondisjunction of the sex chromosomes during oogenesis if you assume that the chromosomes shown represent X chromosomes. Nondisjunction during oogenesis or spermatogenesis can result in gametes that have too few or too many X or Y chromosomes. After fertilization, various syndromes result, the most common being Turner syndrome, Klinefelter syndrome, poly-X female, and Jacobs syndrome.

A person with Turner syndrome (XO) is a female, and a person with Klinefelter syndrome (XXY) is a male. This shows that in humans the presence of a Y chromosome, not the number of X chromosomes, determines maleness. The *SRY* (sex-determining region of the Y chromosome) occurs on the short arm of the Y chromosome and produces a protein called testis-determining factor, which plays a critical role in the development of male genitals.

Why are newborns with an abnormal number of X chromosomes more likely to survive than those with an abnormal autosome number? All individuals, whether males or females, have only one functioning X chromosome. Any others become an inactive mass called a **Barr body** (after the person who discovered it). Because of the formation of Barr bodies, it is normal for cells to function with only a single X chromosome.

Turner Syndrome

An individual with Turner syndrome (XO) has only one sex chromosome, an X; the O signifies the absence of a second sex chromosome. Turner females are short, with a broad chest and folds of skin on the back of the neck. The ovaries, uterine tubes, and uterus are very small and underdeveloped. Turner females do not undergo puberty or menstruate, and their breasts do not develop (Fig. 1.16a). However, some have given birth following in vitro fertilization using donor eggs. They usually are of normal intelligence and can lead fairly normal lives if they receive hormone supplements.

Klinefelter Syndrome

A male with Klinefelter syndrome has two or more X chromosomes in addition to a Y chromosome. The extra X chromosomes become Barr bodies.

In Klinefelter males, the testes and prostate gland are underdeveloped and there is no facial hair, but some breast development may occur (Fig. 1.16b). Affected individuals have large hands and feet and very long arms and legs. They are usually slow to learn but not mentally retarded unless they inherit more than two X chromosomes. No matter how many X chromosomes are involved, an individual with a Y chromosome is a male.

The reading on page 19 tells the experiences of a person with Klinefelter syndrome. He suggests that it is best for parents to know right away that their child has this disorder because much can be done to help the child lead a normal life.

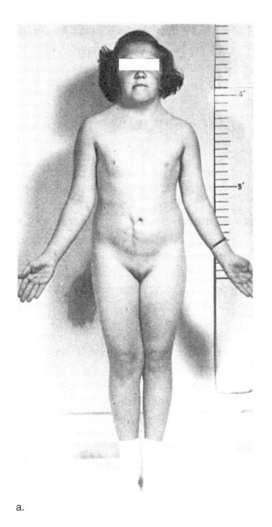
a.

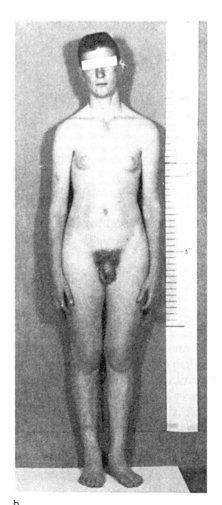
b.

Figure 1.16   Abnormal sex chromosome number.
a. A female with Turner (XO) syndrome has a short thick neck, short stature, and lack of breast development. **b.** A male with Klinefelter (XXY) syndrome has immature sex organs and some development of the breasts.

Poly-X Females

Poly-X females inherit more than two X chromosomes and therefore they have extra Barr bodies in the nucleus. Females with three X chromosomes have no distinctive phenotype aside from a tendency to be tall and thin. Although some have delayed motor and language development, most poly-X females are not mentally retarded. Some may have menstrual difficulties, but many menstruate regularly and are fertile. Their children usually have a normal karyotype.

Females with more than three X chromosomes occur rarely. XXXX females are usually severely retarded and exhibit various physical abnormalities, but they may menstruate normally.

Jacobs Syndrome

Males with Jacobs syndrome (XYY) can only result from nondisjunction during spermatogenesis. Affected males are usually taller than average, suffer from persistent acne, and tend to have speech and reading problems. At one time, it was suggested that these men were likely to be criminally aggressive, but the incidence of such behavior among them has since been shown to be no greater than that among XY males.

Of Special Interest

Living with Klinefelter Syndrome

In 1996, at the age of 25, I was diagnosed with Klinefelter syndrome (KS). Being diagnosed has changed my life for the better.

I was a happy baby, but when I was still very young, my parents began to believe that there was something wrong with me. I knew something was different about me, too, as early on as five years old. I was very shy and had trouble making friends. One minute I'd be well behaved, and the next I'd be picking fights and flying into a rage. Many psychologists, therapists, and doctors tested me because of school and social problems and severe mood changes. Their only diagnosis was "learning disabilities" in such areas as reading comprehension, abstract thinking, word retrieval, and auditory processing. In the seventh grade, a psychologist told me that I was stupid and lazy, I would probably live at home for the rest of my life, and I would never amount to anything. For the next five years, he was basically right, and I barely graduated from high school.

I believe, though, that I have succeeded because I was told that I would fail. When I enrolled at a community college; I decided I could figure things out on my own and did not need tutoring. I received an associate degree there, then transferred to a small liberal arts college. However, I never had a semester below a 3.0, and I graduated with two B.S. degrees. I was accepted into a graduate program but decided instead to accept a job as a software engineer even though I did not have an educational background in this field. As I later learned, many KS'ers excel in computer skills. I had been using a computer for many years and had learned everything I needed to know on my own, through trial and error.

Around the time I started the computer job, I went to my physician for a physical. He sent me for blood tests because he noticed that my testes were smaller than usual. The results were conclusive: Klinefelter syndrome with sex chromosomes XXY. I initially felt denial, depression, and anger, even though I now had an explanation for many of the problems I had experienced all my life. But then I decided to learn as much as I could about the condition and treatments available. I now give myself a testosterone injection once every two weeks, and it has made me a different person, with improved learning abilities and stronger thought processes in addition to a more outgoing personality.

I found, though, that the best possible path I could take was to help others live with the condition. I attended my first support group meeting four months after I was diagnosed. I had decided to work diligently to help people with KS forever. I have been very involved in KS conferences and have helped to start support groups in the U.S., Spain, and Australia.

Since my diagnosis, it has been my dream to have a son with KS, although when I was diagnosed, I found out it was unlikely that I could have biological children. Through my work with KS, I had the opportunity to meet my fiancee, Chris. She has two wonderful children: a daughter, and a son who has the same condition that I do. There are a lot of similarities between my stepson and me, and I am happy I will be able to help him get the head start in coping with KS that I never had. I also look forward to many more years of helping other people seek diagnosis and live a good life with Klinefelter syndrome.

Stefan Schwarz

stefan13@mail.ptd.net

Bioethical Focus

Choosing Gender

Do you approve of choosing a baby's gender even before it is conceived? As you know, the sex of a child is dependent upon whether an X-bearing sperm or a Y-bearing sperm enters the egg. A new technique has been developed that can separate X-bearing sperm from Y-bearing sperm. First, the sperm are dosed with a DNA-staining chemical. Because the X chromosome has slightly more DNA than the Y chromosome, it takes up more dye. When a laser beam shines on the sperm, the X-bearing sperm shine a little more brightly than the Y-bearing sperm. A machine sorts the sperm into two groups on this basis. The results are not perfect. Following artificial insemination, success rates are about 85% for a girl and 65% for a boy.

Some might argue that, while it is acceptable to use vaccines to prevent illnesses or to give someone a heart transplant, it goes against nature to choose gender. But what if doing so would prevent the birth of a child having a genetic disorder?

Some authorities do not find gender selection acceptable for any reason. Even if it doesn't lead to a society with far more members of one sex than another, there could be a problem. Once you separate reproduction from the sex act, they say, it opens the door to children that have been genetically designed in every way.

Decide Your Opinion

1. Do you think it is acceptable to choose the gender of a baby? Why or why not?

Figure 1B   Parents and children.
Some parents prefer a particular sex.

2. Do you see any difference between choosing gender and choosing embryos free of a genetic disease for reproduction purposes ? Explain.
3. Do you think it is acceptable one day to genetically design children before they are born?

Summary

1.1 The Human Cell
A cell is bounded by a plasma membrane and otherwise consists of a nucleus and cytoplasm. The nucleus houses the chromosomes, and the cytoplasm contains organelles, many of which are involved in protein synthesis. The genes on the chromosomes specify protein synthesis.

1.2 Human Life Cycle
The life cycle of higher organisms involves two types of cell divisions: mitosis and meiosis. Mitosis is responsible for growth and repair, while meiosis is required for gamete production.

1.3 Mitosis
Mitosis ensures that all the cells in the body have the diploid number and the same kinds of chromosomes. The cell cycle includes interphase, mitosis, and cytokinesis. During interphase, DNA replication causes each chromosome to have sister chromatids.

Mitosis has the following phases: During prophase, at first the chromosomes have no particular arrangement, but later they are attached to spindle fibers; in metaphase, the chromosomes are aligned at the equator; in anaphase, the sister chromatids separate, becoming daughter chromosomes that move toward the poles; and in telophase, new nuclear envelopes form around the daughter chromosomes. Cytokinesis occurs by furrowing.

1.4 Meiosis
Meiosis involves two cell divisions. During meiosis I, the homologous chromosomes (following crossing-over between nonsister chromatids) separate, and during meiosis II, the sister chromatids separate. The result is four cells with the haploid number of chromosomes, each consisting of one chromatid. Meiosis is a part of gamete formation in humans. Spermatogenesis in males usually produces four viable sperm, while oogenesis in females produces

one egg and at least two polar bodies. Oogenesis does not go on to completion unless a sperm fertilizes the developing egg.

Among sexually reproducing organisms, including humans, each individual is genetically different because (1) crossing-over recombines the genes on the sister chromatids of homologous pairs of chromosomes; (2) following meiosis, gametes have all possible combinations of chromosomes; and (3) upon fertilization, recombination of chromosomes occurs.

1.5 Chromosomal Inheritance

Nondisjunction during meiosis leads to gametes with an abnormal number of chromosomes and several possible syndromes. The major inherited autosomal abnormality is Down syndrome, in which the individual inherits three copies of chromosome 21.

Syndromes caused by inheritance of abnormal numbers of sex chromosomes include Turner syndrome (XO), Klinefelter syndrome (XXY), poly-X females (XXX and higher), and Jacobs syndrome (XYY).

Abnormalities in chromosome structure also sometimes occur. For example, in cri du chat (cat's cry) syndrome, part of chromosome 5 is deleted.

Reviewing the Chapter

1. Where are chromosomes located in a cell? How do organelles function to produce and modify proteins? What is the relationship between genes and protein synthesis? 4–5
2. Draw a diagram to describe the human life cycle. Include mitosis and meiosis and either spermatogenesis or oogenesis. Denote the appropriate chromosome numbers of all structures. 6–14
3. Draw a generalized diagram for mitosis. **a.** In each cell, put the notation 2n or n as appropriate. **b.** Sketch an autosomal pair of chromosomes in the parental cell, and show what happens to the chromosomes during the process of cell division. 7–9
4. Draw a generalized diagram for meiosis. **a.** In each cell, put the notation 2n or n as appropriate. **b.** Place an autosomal pair of chromosomes in the parental cell, and show what happens to the chromosomes during the process of meiosis. 10–13
5. List several differences between mitosis and meiosis, considering the following: the purpose, the number of divisions, the number of daughter cells, the changes in the chromosome number, and the resulting number of chromosomes in the daughter cells. 7, 10–11
6. Diagram spermatogenesis and oogenesis. Note four differences between the two processes. 14
7. What is nondisjunction? Draw diagrams for nondisjunction during meiosis I and meiosis II. 16
8. Name two inherited syndromes caused by autosomal chromosome abnormalities. State the abnormality in each, and describe the appearance of the affected individual. 17
9. Name two syndromes involving sex chromosome abnormalities in females. What are the sex chromosomes for each? Describe the appearance of the individual for each. 18–19
10. Name two syndromes involving sex chromosome abnormalities in males. What are the sex chromosomes for each? Describe the appearance of the individual for each. 18–19

Critical Thinking Questions

1. Assume a mother cell with four chromosomes. Which of the following two cells represents metaphase I? Metaphase II? How do you know? In what two ways do the chromosomes of the cells differ?

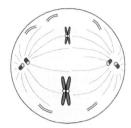 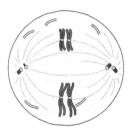

2. Chromosomes contain the genes that occur as alleles. For example, *A* is the allele of *a*, and vice versa. Suppose that one member of a pair of chromosomes contains allele *A* and the other member contains allele *a*. Can both alleles be in the same daughter cell following meiosis, or can only one allele, either *A* or *a*, be in the same daughter cell? How do you know?
3. Assume that one chromosome contains two different alleles, *A* and *B*. Will both *A* and *B* be in one daughter cell following meiosis? How do you know?

Understanding Key Terms

anaphase 9	interphase 6
apoptosis 7	lysosome 5
aster 8	meiosis 6, 10
autosome 16	metaphase 9
Barr body 18	mitochondrion 5
cell 4	mitosis 6, 7
cell cycle 6	nondisjunction 16
centriole 5	nucleolus 5
centromere 7	nucleus 4
chromatid 7	oogenesis 14
chromosome 4	polar body 14
cleavage furrow 9	prophase 8
crossing-over 10	protein 5
cytokinesis 6, 9	ribosome 5
cytoplasm 5	sex chromosome 16
diploid (2n) 6	somatic cell 3
DNA 3	spermatogenesis 14
dyad 11	spindle 8
endoplasmic reticulum (ER) 5	synapsis 10
gamete 6	syndrome 16
gene 5	telophase 9
Golgi apparatus 5	tetrad 10
gonad 6	vesicle 5
haploid (n) 6	zygote 6
homologous chromosome 10	

Chapter 2

Genes and Medical Genetics

2.1 Genotype and Phenotype

Genotype refers to the genes of the individual. Alternate forms of a gene having the same position (locus) on a pair of chromosomes and affecting the same trait are called **alleles.** It is customary to designate an allele by a letter, which represents the specific characteristic it controls; a **dominant allele** is assigned an uppercase (capital) letter, while a **recessive allele** is given the same letter but in lowercase. In humans, for example, unattached (free) earlobes are dominant over attached earlobes, so a suitable key would be *E* for unattached earlobes and *e* for attached earlobes.

Because autosomal alleles occur in pairs, an individual normally has two alleles for a trait. Just as one of each pair of chromosomes is inherited from each parent, so too is one of each pair of alleles inherited from each parent. Figure 2.1 shows three possible fertilizations and the resulting genetic makeup of the zygote and, therefore, the individual. In the first instance, the chromosomes of both the sperm and the egg carry an *E.* Consequently, the zygote and subsequent individual have the alleles *EE*, which is called a **homozygous dominant** genotype. A person with genotype *EE* has unattached earlobes. The physical appearance of the individual— in this case, unattached earlobes—is called the **phenotype.**

In the second fertilization, the zygote has received two recessive alleles (*ee*), and the genotype is called **homozygous recessive.** An individual with this genotype has the recessive phenotype, which is attached earlobes. In the third fertilization, the resulting individual has the alleles *Ee*, which is called a **heterozygous** genotype. A heterozygote shows the dominant characteristic; therefore, the phenotype of this individual is unattached earlobes.

These examples show that a dominant allele contributed from only one parent can bring about a particular dominant phenotype. A recessive allele must be received from both parents to bring about the recessive phenotype (Table 2.1).

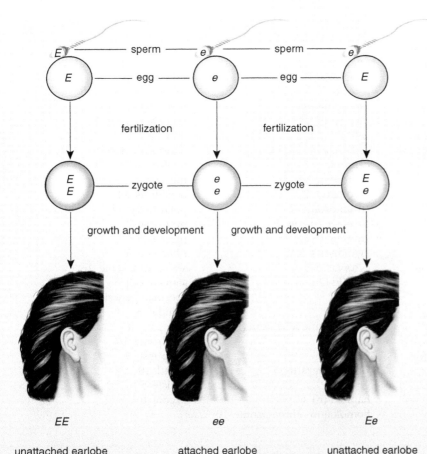

EE	ee	Ee
unattached earlobe	attached earlobe	unattached earlobe

Table 2.1	Genotype and Phenotype	
Genotype (in letters)	**Genotype (in words)**	**Phenotype**
EE	Homozygous (pure) dominant	Unattached earlobes
ee	Homozygous (pure) recessive	Attached earlobes
Ee	Heterozygous (hybrid)	Unattached earlobes

Figure 2.1   Genetic inheritance.
Individuals inherit a minimum of two alleles for every characteristic of their anatomy and physiology. The inheritance of a single dominant allele (*E*) causes an individual to have unattached earlobes; two recessive alleles (ee) cause an individual to have attached earlobes. Notice that each individual receives one allele from the father (by way of a sperm) and one allele from the mother (by way of an egg).

2.2 Dominant and Recessive Traits

The alleles designated by *E* and *e* are on a certain part of the autosomal chromosomes. An individual has two alleles for each trait because a chromosome pair carries alleles for the same traits. How many alleles for each trait will be in the gametes? One, because chromosome pairs separate during meiosis I.

Forming the Gametes

During gametogenesis, the chromosome number is reduced. Whereas the individual has 46 chromosomes, a gamete has only 23 chromosomes. (If this did not happen, each new generation of individuals would have twice as many chromosomes as their parents.) Reduction of the chromosome number occurs when the pairs of chromosomes separate as meiosis occurs. Since the alleles are on the chromosomes, they also separate during meiosis, and therefore, the gametes carry only one allele for each trait. If an individual carried the alleles *EE*, all the gametes would carry an *E* since that is the only choice. Similarly, if an individual carried the alleles *ee*, all the gametes would carry an *e*. What if an individual were *Ee*? Figure 2.2 shows that half of the gametes would carry an *E* and half would carry an *e*. Figure 2.3 shows the genotypes and phenotypes for certain other traits in humans. What alleles would the gametes carry in order to produce these genotypes?

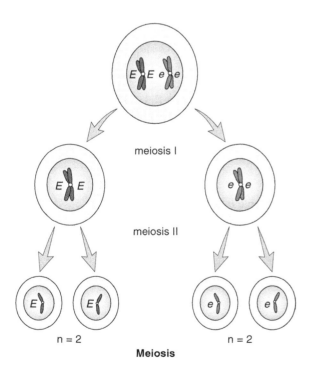

Figure 2.2   Gametogenesis.
Because the pairs of chromosomes separate during meiosis, which occurs during gametogenesis, the gametes have only one allele for each trait.

a.   Widow's peak: *WW* or *Ww*   b.   Straight hairline: *ww*

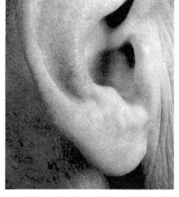 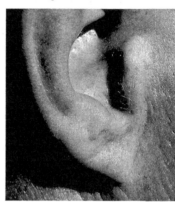

c.   Unattached earlobes: *EE* or *Ee*   d.   Attached earlobes: *ee*

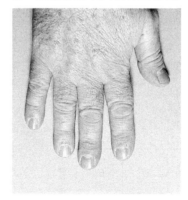 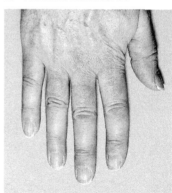

e.   Short fingers: *SS* or *Ss*   f.   Long fingers: *ss*

g.   Freckles: *FF* or *Ff*   h.   No freckles: *ff*

Figure 2.3   Common inherited characteristics in human beings.
The notations indicate which characteristics are dominant and which are recessive.

One-Trait Crosses

Many times, parents would like to know the chances of having a child with a certain genotype and, therefore, a certain phenotype. If one of the parents is homozygous dominant (*EE*), the chance of their having a child with unattached earlobes is 100% because this parent has only a dominant allele (*E*) to pass on to the offspring. On the other hand, if both parents are homozygous recessive (*ee*), there is a 100% chance that each of their children will have attached earlobes. However, if both parents are heterozygous, what are the chances that their child will have unattached or attached earlobes? To solve a problem of this type, it is customary first to indicate the genotypes of the parents and their possible gametes.

Genotypes:	*Ee*	*Ee*
Gametes:	*E* or *e*	*E* or *e*

Second, a **Punnett square** is constructed to determine the phenotypic ratio among the offspring when all possible sperm are given an equal chance to fertilize all possible eggs (Fig. 2.4). The possible sperm are lined up along the side of the square, and the possible eggs are lined up along the top

of the square. The ratio among the offspring in this case is 3:1 (three children with unattached earlobes to one with attached earlobes). This means that there is a 3/4 chance (75%) for each child to have unattached earlobes and a 1/4 chance (25%) for each child to have attached earlobes.

Another cross of particular interest is that between a heterozygous individual (*Ee*) and a homozygous recessive (*ee*). In this case, the Punnett square shows that the ratio among the offspring is 1:1, and the chance of having the dominant or recessive phenotype is 1/2, or 50% (Fig. 2.5).

Comparing the two crosses (Fig. 2.4 and Fig. 2.5), each child has a 75% chance of having the dominant phenotype if the two parents are heterozygous and a 50% chance if one parent is heterozygous and the other is homozygous recessive. Each child has a 25% chance of having the recessive phenotype if the parents are heterozygous and a 50% chance if one parent is heterozygous and the other is homozygous recessive.

One-trait crosses such as these are particularly pertinent when determining the chances of a child having a genetic disorder because usually only one genetic disorder is considered at a time.

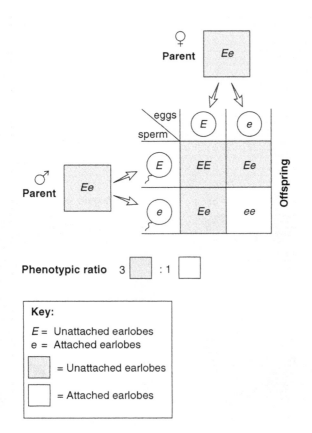

Phenotypic ratio   3 ▨ : 1 ☐

Key:

E = Unattached earlobes
e = Attached earlobes

▨ = Unattached earlobes

☐ = Attached earlobes

Figure 2.4   Heterozygous-by-heterozygous cross.
When the parents are heterozygous, each child has a 75% chance of having the dominant phenotype and a 25% chance of having the recessive phenotype.

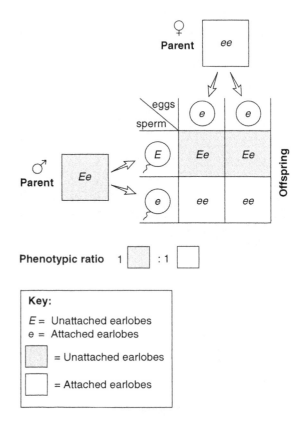

Phenotypic ratio   1 ▨ : 1 ☐

Key:

E = Unattached earlobes
e = Attached earlobes

▨ = Unattached earlobes

☐ = Attached earlobes

Figure 2.5   Heterozygous-by-homozygous recessive cross.
When one parent is heterozygous and the other homozygous recessive, each child has a 50% chance of having the dominant phenotype and a 50% chance of having the recessive phenotype.

Two-Trait Crosses

In two-trait crosses, parents have an allelic pair for each trait. In Figure 2.6, widow's peak is dominant to straight hairline, and short fingers is dominant to long fingers. We begin with one grandparent who is homozygous for widow's peak and short fingers (*WWSS*) and the other who is homozygous for straight hairline and long fingers (*wwss*). Because each grandparent has only one type of gamete, their children will all have the genotype *WwSs* and the same phenotype (widow's peak with short fingers). This genotype is called a **dihybrid** because the individual is heterozygous in two regards: hairline and fingers.

When a dihybrid reproduces with a dihybrid, each parent has four types of gametes because the gametes have only one allele for each trait in all possible combinations. Figure 2.6 shows that the expected phenotypic ratio among the grandchildren is:

9 widow's peak and short fingers:

3 widow's peak and long fingers:

3 straight hairline and short fingers:

1 straight hairline and long fingers.

This 9:3:3:1 phenotypic ratio is always expected for a dihybrid cross when one allele is dominant to the other in each allelic pair.

We can use this expected ratio for a dihybrid cross to predict the chances of each child receiving a certain phenotype. For example, the chance of getting the two dominant phenotypes together is 9 out of 16, and the chance of getting the two recessive phenotypes together is 1 out of 16.

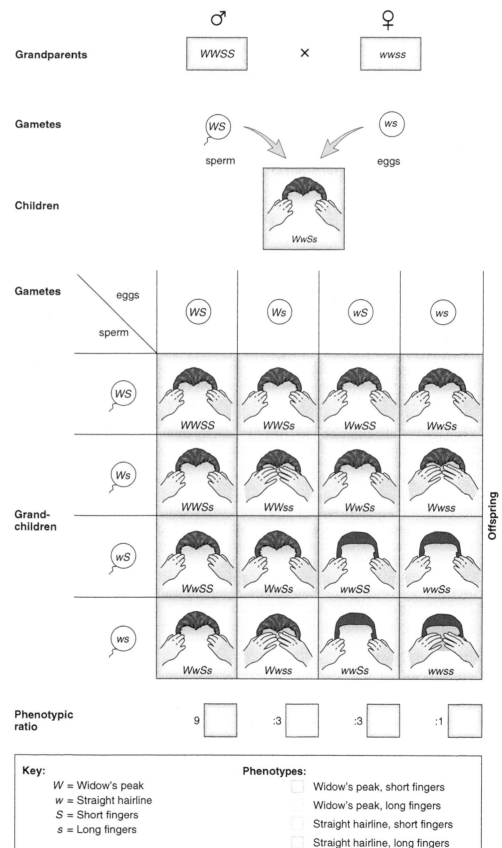

Figure 2.6   Dihybrid cross.
Since each child, when mature, can form four possible types of gametes, four different phenotypes occur among the grandchildren in the proportions shown.

Key:
W = Widow's peak
w = Straight hairline
S = Short fingers
s = Long fingers

Phenotypes:
Widow's peak, short fingers
Widow's peak, long fingers
Straight hairline, short fingers
Straight hairline, long fingers

Autosomal Dominant Disorders

Genetic disorders are caused by **mutations**, permanent changes in the genetic material. If the disorder is autosomal dominant, the mutation pertains to a single allele, and heterozygotes have the disorder. Table 2.2 shows the chances of passing on a dominant genetic disorder. To gain practice in determining these chances, disregard the last column and assume that E = an allele for the disorder.

Of the many autosomal dominant disorders, we will discuss only neurofibromatosis and Huntington disease.

Neurofibromatosis

Neurofibromatosis, sometimes called von Recklinghausen disease, is one of the most common genetic disorders. It affects roughly one in 3,500 newborns and occurs equally in every racial and ethnic group throughout the world.

At birth or later, the affected individual may have six or more large, tan spots on the skin. Such spots tend to increase in size and number and get darker. Small, benign tumors (lumps) called neurofibromas may arise from the fibrous coverings of nerves. This genetic disorder shows variable expressivity. In most cases, symptoms are mild, and patients live a normal life. In some cases, however, the effects are severe. Some patients have skeletal deformities, including a large head; others develop eye and ear tumors that can lead to blindness and hearing loss. Many children with neurofibromatosis have learning disabilities and are hyperactive.

In 1990, researchers isolated the gene for neurofibromatosis, which was known to be on chromosome 17. The gene controls the production of a protein called neurofibromin that normally blocks growth signals leading to cell division. Any number of mutations can result in a type of neurofibromin that fails to block cell growth, and as a result, tumors form. Some mutations are caused by inserted genes that don't belong there. The fact that genes can move between the chromosomes was first discovered in other organisms and only recently in humans.

Huntington Disease

Huntington disease is a neurological disorder that leads to progressive degeneration of brain cells, which in turn causes severe muscle spasms and personality disorders (Fig. 2.7). Most patients appear normal until they are of middle age and have already had children, who may then also be stricken. Occasionally, the first sign of the disease in the next generation appears in teenagers or even younger children. There is no effective treatment, and death comes 10 to 15 years after the onset of symptoms.

Several years ago, researchers found that the gene for Huntington disease is located on chromosome 4. A test was developed for the presence of the gene, but few people want to know if they have inherited the gene because there is no cure. At least now we know the disease stems from a single

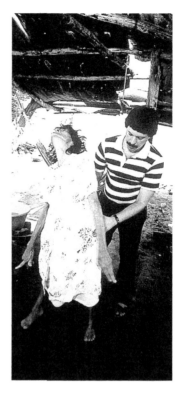

Figure 2.7   **Huntington disease.**
Persons with this condition gradually lose psychomotor control of the body. At first, the disturbances are minor, but the symptoms become worse over time.

mutation that causes the individual to produce an abnormal protein called huntingtin. The protein is the wrong shape, and it forms large clumps inside neurons. Even worse, it attracts and causes other proteins to clump with it. One of these proteins, called CBP, helps nerve cells survive. Researchers hope they may be able to combat the disease by boosting CBP levels.

Table 2.2	Possible Matings		
Genotype of Parents	Chance of Dominant Phenotype	Chance of Recessive Phenotype
$EE \times EE$	100%	0%
$EE \times Ee$	100%	0%
$EE \times ee$	100%	0%
$Ee \times Ee$	75%	25%
$Ee \times ee$	50%	50%
$ee \times ee$	0%	100%

Autosomal Recessive Disorders

Table 2.2 also lets you determine the chances of passing on an autosomal recessive disorder if you disregard the second column and assume that *e* = an allele for the disorder. In addition, you may review Figures 2.4 and 2.5 and make the same assumption. Of the many autosomal (non-sex-linked) recessive disorders, we will discuss only four.

Cystic Fibrosis

Cystic fibrosis (CF) is the most common lethal genetic disease among Caucasians in the United States. About one in 20 Caucasians is a carrier, and about one in 2,500 newborns has the disorder. The *CF* gene, which is located on chromosome 7, has been isolated, and genetic testing for the allele in adult carriers and in fetuses is possible. Attempts to insert a normal *CF* gene into the nasal epithelium of affected individuals has so far met with little success.

In CF patients, the mucus in the bronchial tubes and pancreatic ducts is particularly thick and viscous. Research shows that chloride ions (Cl⁻) fail to pass through plasma membrane channel proteins in affected individuals. Ordinarily, after chloride ions have passed through the membrane, water follows. The lack of water is thought to cause the thick mucus. The clogged pancreatic ducts prevent digestive enzymes from reaching the small intestine, and patients usually take digestive enzymes before every meal. To ease breathing, the mucus in the lungs has to be manually loosened periodically, but still the lungs become infected frequently. New treatments, such as the one shown in Figure 2.8, have raised the average life expectancy to as much as 35 years of age.

Phenylketonuria (PKU)

Phenylketonuria (PKU) occurs once in 5,000 newborns, so it is not as common as cystic fibrosis. However, it is the most commonly inherited metabolic disorder that affects nervous system development.

Affected individuals lack an enzyme that is needed for the normal metabolism of the amino acid phenylalanine, and thus an abnormal breakdown product, phenylketone, accumulates in the urine. The PKU allele is located on chromosome 12, and a prenatal DNA test can determine the presence of this allele. Newborns are routinely tested in the hospital for elevated levels of phenylalanine in the blood. If elevated levels are detected, newborns are placed on a diet low in phenylalanine, which must be continued until around age seven, or else severe mental retardation develops. Some doctors recommend that the diet be followed for life, but in any case, a pregnant woman with phenylketonuria must be on the diet in order to protect her unborn child from harm.

Tay-Sachs Disease

Tay-Sachs disease is a well-known genetic disease that usually occurs among Jewish people in the United States, most of whom are of central and eastern European descent. At

Figure 2.8   Cystic fibrosis therapy.
Antibiotic therapy is used to control lung infections in cystic fibrosis patients. The antibiotic tobramycin can be aerosolized and administered using a nebulizer. It is inhaled twice daily for about 15 minutes.

first, it is not apparent that a baby has Tay-Sachs disease. However, development begins to slow down between four months and eight months of age, and neurological impairment and psychomotor difficulties then become apparent. The child gradually becomes blind and helpless, develops uncontrollable seizures, and eventually becomes paralyzed. There is no treatment or cure for Tay-Sachs disease, and most affected individuals die by the age of three or four.

The gene for Tay-Sachs disease is located on chromosome 15. The disease results from a lack of the enzyme hexosaminidase A (hex A) and the subsequent storage of its substrate, a fatty substance known as glycosphingolipid, in lysosomes. Although more and more nonfunctional lysosomes build up in many body cells, the primary sites of storage are the cells of the brain, which accounts for the onset and the progressive deterioration of psychomotor functions.

Persons heterozygous for Tay-Sachs have about half the level of hex A activity found in normal individuals, but no problems result because enzymes are reusable. Prenatal diagnosis of the disease is possible.

Albinism

When albinism is present, the individual is unable to produce the pigment melanin, which is responsible for coloration of skin, hair, and/or eyes. Therefore, these parts of the body lack color entirely. Sometimes only the eyes are affected, but in any case, albinos do not see well, and their eyes are subject to involuntary rapid eye movements. Albinism is an example of an **epistasis,** in which a gene affects the expression of other genes. In an albino, any genes received for coloring cannot be expressed because of the mutated gene that prevents them from producing melanin.

2.3 Beyond Simple Inheritance Patterns

Certain traits, such as those just studied, follow the rules of simple dominant or recessive inheritance. But there are other, more complicated patterns of inheritance.

Polygenic Inheritance

Polygenic inheritance occurs when one trait is governed by two or more sets of alleles, and the individual has a copy of all allelic pairs, possibly located on many different pairs of chromosomes. Each dominant allele has a quantitative effect on the phenotype, and these effects are additive. The result is a continuous variation of phenotypes, with a dis-

a.

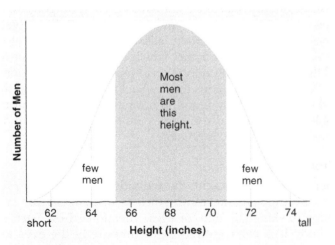

b.

Figure 2.9 Polygenic inheritance.
When you record the heights of a large group of young men **(a),** the values follow a bell-shaped curve **(b).** Such a continuous distribution is due to control of a trait by several sets of alleles. Environmental effects are also involved.

tribution that resembles a bell-shaped curve. The more genes involved, the more continuous are the variation and the distribution of the phenotypes. Also, environmental effects cause many intervening phenotypes; in the case of height, differences in nutrition ensure a bell-shaped curve (Fig. 2.9).

Skin Color

Just how many pairs of alleles control skin color is not known, but a range in colors can be explained on the basis of two pairs. When a very dark person reproduces with a very light person, the children have medium-brown skin; when two people with medium-brown skin reproduce with one another, the children may range in skin color from very dark to very light. This can be explained by assuming that skin color is controlled by two pairs of alleles and that *each dominant allele contributes pigment to the skin:*

Genotypes	Phenotypes
AABB	Very dark
AABb or *AaBB*	Dark
AaBb or *AAbb* or *aaBB*	Medium brown
Aabb or *aaBb*	Light
aabb	Very light

Notice again that there is a range in phenotypes and that several possible phenotypes fall between the two extremes. Therefore, the distribution of these phenotypes is expected to follow a bell-shaped curve—that is, few people have the extreme phenotypes, and most people have the phenotype that lies in the middle.

Multifactorial Disorders

Height and skin color inheritance are **multifactorial traits** because they are determined not only by inheritance but also by the environment. Many human disorders, such as cleft lip and/or palate, clubfoot, congenital dislocation of the hip, hypertension, diabetes, and even allergies and cancers, are controlled by the inheritance of various genes and are subject to environmental influences.

In recent years, reports have surfaced proposing that all sorts of behavioral traits, including mental illness, alcoholism, phobias, and even suicide, have a genetic component. Therefore, many investigators are considering the nature-versus-nurture question; that is, what percentage of the trait mentioned is controlled by genes, and what percentage is controlled by environmental stresses? Thus far, it has not been possible to calculate precise, generally accepted percentages for any particular trait.

As discussed in the reading on page 29, although behavioral traits, including the propensity for violent acts, may be influenced by inheritance, they are not predetermined by our genes. Rather, most biologists believe that our nervous system provides us with the ability to be responsible for our actions.

My Genes Made Me Do It

In 2002, Derek King and his brother Alex bludgeoned their father to death with a baseball bat. Did their genes make them do it? Whether nature (genes) or environment (nurture) control behavior is a question that has been asked for a very long time. A 25-year study involving 400 boys, under the auspices of the University of Wisconsin, concluded that both genetic propensity (determined by a comparative analysis of DNA) and early childhood abuse are required to bring out violent behavior. As genetic propensity increases, less abuse is needed, and vice versa. The investigators also said that other kinds of life stresses may contribute to violence.

Before the mid-1900s, it was generally believed that the mind of a newborn is a blank slate and that environment alone controls behavior. But since that time, various twin studies have shown otherwise. The supposition for early studies is that if a behavior occurs more frequently in identical twins (100% of genes are the same) than in fraternal twins (50% of genes are the same), the behavior most likely has a genetic component. Figure 2A shows the percentages (concordance) for various behaviors that were studied. When one such study concluded that tuberculosis was inherited because it occurs more often in identical twins than in fraternal twins, investigators decided they needed to review their procedure. Twin studies today use twins separated from birth because then it's known that the twins have a

Figure 2B   Do genes determine our behavior?

different environment. The supposition is that, if twins in different environments share the same trait, that trait is most likely inherited. These studies have found that identical twins separated from birth do indeed have behavioral characteristics in common. Identical twins are more similar in their intellectual talents, personality traits, and levels of lifelong happiness than are fraternal twins. The personality traits include whether they are introverts, antagonistic, or conscientious. Similarities in personal quirks, such as giggling incessantly or flushing the toilet both before and after using it, were particularly striking.

Based on twin and other studies, biologists have concluded that all behavioral traits are partly heritable. Even so, no one has found a single gene for a particular behavior. Biologists believe that genes exert their effects by acting together in complex combinations. Just as a computer has no single component that when removed makes the computer perform badly, so no single gene controls a particular behavior. One biologist expresses the situation like this, "There's tremendous plasticity and potential built into the genes of each individual." Therefore, it is not surprising that even twins growing up in the same family are not entirely the same. One twin may be gay and the other heterosexual; one may be more anxious than the other; and so forth.

The effects of genes on behavior are underestimated by some and overestimated by others. During development, genes affect the size, shape, and neural pathways of the brain. After we are born, the pathways used in learning and memory appear to play a significant role in modifying gene expression. Usually, socialization gives us the data our brain uses to reflect on our behavior so that in the end we become responsible for our behavior.

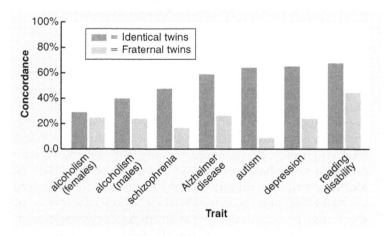

Figure 2A   **Twin traits.**

A trait more often present in both members of identical twin pairs than in both members of fraternal twin pairs is presumed to have a significant inherited component.

Source: Reprinted with permission from "The Genetic Basis of Complex Human Behaviors," by Robert Plomin, 6/17/94. *American Association for the Advancement of Science.*

Multiple Allelic Traits

When a trait is controlled by **multiple alleles,** the gene exists in several allelic forms. But each person usually has only two of the possible alleles. For example, a person's blood type is determined by multiple alleles because three alleles for the same gene control the inheritance of ABO blood types. These alleles determine the presence or absence of antigenic glycoproteins on the red blood cells:

A = A antigen on red blood cells

B = B antigen on red blood cells

O = Neither A nor B antigen on red blood cells

Alleles A and B are dominant over O, and are fully expressed in the presence of the other. This is called codominance, as mentioned on page 31.

Figure 2.10 shows that matings between certain genotypes can have surprising results in terms of blood type because the possible genotypes and phenotypes for blood type are as follows:

Genotypes	Phenotypes
AA, AO	Type A
BB, BO	Type B
AB	Type AB
OO	Type O

Blood typing can sometimes aid in paternity suits. However, a blood test of a supposed father can only suggest that he might be the father, not confirm that he is the father. For example, it is possible, but not definite, that a man with type A blood (having genotype *AO*) is the father of a child with type O blood. On the other hand, a blood test can sometimes definitely prove that a man is not the father. For example, a man with type AB blood cannot possibly be the father of a child with type O blood. Therefore, blood tests can be used in legal cases only to exclude a man from possible paternity.

As a point of interest, the Rh factor is inherited separately from A, B, AB, or O blood types. When you are Rh-positive, a particular antigen is present on the red blood cells, and when you are Rh-negative, it is absent. It can be assumed that the inheritance of this antigen is controlled by a single allelic pair in which simple dominance prevails: The Rh-positive allele is dominant over the Rh-negative allele.

Pleiotropy

Pleiotropy occurs when a single gene has more than one effect. For example, persons with **Marfan syndrome** have disproportionately long arms, legs, hands, and feet; poor eyesight; and a weakened aorta. All of these characteristics are due to the production of abnormal connective tissue. Marfan syndrome has been linked to a mutated gene on chromosome 15 that ordinarily specifies a functional protein called fibrillin. Fibrillin is essential for the formation of elastic

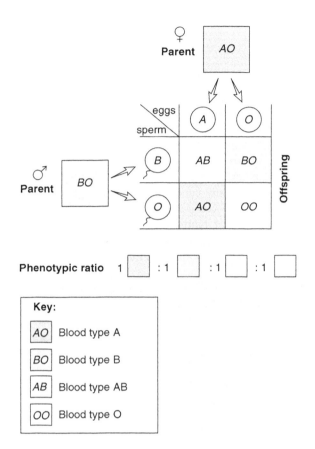

Figure 2.10   Inheritance of blood type.
A mating between blood type A and blood type B can result in any one of the four blood types. Why? Because the parents are *AO* and *BO*. If both parents are blood type AB, the children can have what blood type?

fibers in connective tissue. Without the structural support of normal connective tissue, the aorta can burst, particularly if the person is engaged in a strenuous sport such as volleyball or basketball. Flo Hyman may have been the best American woman volleyball player ever, but she fell to the floor and died when only 31 years old because her aorta gave way during a volleyball game. Now that coaches are aware of Marfan syndrome, they are on the lookout for it among very tall basketball players. Chris Weisheit, whose career was cut short after he was diagnosed with Marfan syndrome, said, "I don't want to die playing basketball."

Many other disorders, including sickle-cell disease discussed in the next section and porphyria, are examples of pleiotropic traits. **Porphyria** is caused by a chemical insufficiency in the production of hemoglobin, the pigment that makes red blood cells red. The symptoms of porphyria are photosensitivity, strong abdominal pain, port-wine-colored urine, and paralysis in the arms and legs. Many members of the British royal family in the late 1700s and early 1800s suffered from this disorder, which can lead to epileptic convulsions, bizarre behavior, and coma.

Incompletely Dominant Traits

The field of human genetics also has documented examples of codominance and incomplete dominance. **Codominance** occurs when alleles are equally expressed in a heterozygote. We have already mentioned that the multiple alleles controlling blood type are codominant. An individual with the genotype *AB* has type AB blood. Also, skin color is controlled by polygenes in which all dominants (capital letters) add equally to the phenotype. For this reason, it is possible to observe a range of skin colors from very dark to very light.

Incomplete dominance is exhibited when the heterozygote has a phenotype intermediate between that of either homozygote. For example, incomplete dominance pertains to the inheritance of curly versus straight hair in Caucasians. When a curly-haired Caucasian reproduces with a straight-haired Caucasian, their children have wavy hair. When two wavy-haired persons reproduce, the expected phenotypic ratio among the offspring is 1:2:1—that is, one curly-haired child to two with wavy hair to one with straight hair (Fig. 2.11).

a. Normal red blood cells

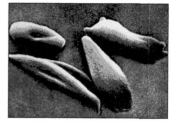
b. Sickled red blood cells

Figure 2.12   Normal versus sickled red blood cells.
In persons with sickle-cell disease, the red blood cells aren't biconcave disks like normal red blood cells (a); they are sickle-shaped (b).

Sickle-Cell Disease

Sickle-cell disease is an example of a human disorder that is controlled by incompletely dominant alleles. The defect in the shape of the red blood cell (Fig. 2.12) is caused by an abnormal hemoglobin. The homozygous dominant individual is normal; the heterozygote has sickle-cell trait; and the homozygous recessive has sickle-cell disease. Two individuals with sickle-cell trait can produce children with all three phenotypes in the same manner as shown in Figure 2.11 for an incompletely dominant trait.

Because sickle-shaped cells can't pass through narrow capillary passageways as disk-shaped cells do, they clog the vessels and break down. This is why persons with sickle-cell disease suffer from poor circulation, anemia, and poor resistance to infection. Internal hemorrhaging leads to further complications, such as jaundice, episodic pain in the abdomen and joints, and damage to internal organs. Persons with sickle-cell trait do not usually have any sickle-shaped cells unless they experience dehydration or mild oxygen deprivation.

Among regions of malaria-infested Africa, infants with sickle-cell disease die, but infants with sickle-cell trait have a better chance of survival than the normal homozygote. When the malaria parasite invades the red blood cells of a person with sickle-cell trait, the cells become sickle-shaped, and the parasite dies. The protective nature of the sickle-cell allele explains why as many as 60% of the population in malaria-infested regions of Africa have the allele. In the United States, where malaria is not prevalent, about 10% of the African American population carries the allele.

Both standard and innovative therapies for sickle-cell disease are being explored. For example, a bone marrow transplant can sometimes be successful in curing the disease. On the other hand, persons with sickle-cell disease produce normal fetal hemoglobin during development, and researchers are developing drugs that turn on the genes for fetal hemoglobin in adults. Mice have been genetically engineered to produce sickled red blood cells in order to test new anti-sickling drugs and various genetic therapies.

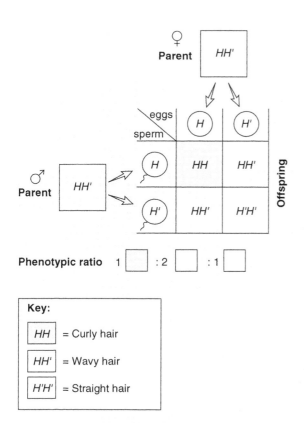

Figure 2.11   Incomplete dominance.
Among Caucasians, neither straight nor curly hair is dominant. When two wavy-haired individuals reproduce, each offspring has a 25% chance of having either straight or curly hair and a 50% chance of having wavy hair, the intermediate phenotype.

Of Special Interest

Barr Bodies

You know that mammalian males have one X and one Y chromosome while females have two X chromosomes. You might wonder how males manage to develop normally with only one X chromosome. After all, they would be producing only half of the needed amount of a particular gene product.

The answer to this question surprised biologists. In females but not in males, a small, darkly staining mass of condensed chromatin adheres to the inner edge of the nuclear envelope. This structure, called a **Barr body** after its discoverer, is an inactive X chromosome. One of the X chromosomes undergoes inactivation in the cells of female embryos. In other words, this X chromosome is not producing gene products, and therefore it is normal in females too for cells to have a reduced amount of product from genes on the X chromosome.

How do we know that Barr bodies are inactive X chromosomes that are not producing gene product? Suppose 50% of the cells have one X chromosome active and 50% have the other X

chromosome active. Wouldn't the body of a heterozygous female be a mosaic, with "patches" of genetically different cells? This is exactly what investigators have discovered. For example, human females who are heterozygous for an X-linked recessive form of ocular albinism have patches of pigmented and nonpigmented cells at the back of the eye. Women heterozygous for Duchenne muscular dystrophy have patches of both normal muscle tissue and degenerative muscle tissue (the normal tissue increases in size and strength to make up for the defective tissue). And women who are heterozygous for hereditary absence of sweat glands have patches of skin lacking sweat glands (Fig. 2C). The female calico cat also provides dramatic support for a difference in X-inactivation in its cells. In these cats, an allele for black coat color is on one X chromosome, and a corresponding allele for orange coat color is on the other X chromosome. The patches of black and orange in the coat can be related to which X chromosome is in the Barr bodies of the cells found in the patches.

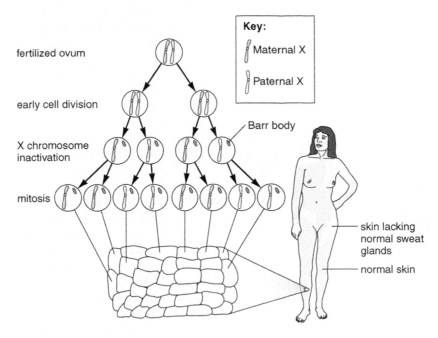

Figure 2C   Barr bodies.
A Barr body is an inactivated X chromosome. It's a matter of chance which X chromosome (the one inherited from the mother or the one from the father) condenses into a dark-staining spot called a Barr body. If a woman is heterozygous for an X-linked recessive disorder, her body becomes a mosaic of some cells that have the mutation and others that do not.

2.4 Sex-Linked Traits

The sex chromosomes contain genes just as the autosomal chromosomes do. Some of these genes determine whether the individual is a male or a female. Investigators have now discovered a series of genes on the Y chromosome that determine the development of male genitals, and at least one on the X chromosome that seems to be necessary for the development of female genitals.

Traits controlled by alleles on the **sex chromosomes** are said to be **sex-linked;** an allele that is only on the X chromosome is **X-linked,** and an allele that is only on the Y chromosome is Y-linked. Most sex-linked alleles are on the X chromosome, and the Y chromosome is blank for these. Very few alleles have been found on the Y chromosome, as you might predict, since it is much smaller than the X chromosome.

The X chromosomes carry many genes unrelated to the sex of the individual, and we will look at a few of these in depth. It would be logical to suppose that a sex-linked trait is passed from father to son or from mother to daughter, but this is not the case. A male always receives a sex-linked condition from his mother, from whom he inherited an X chromosome. *The Y chromosome from the father does not carry an allele for the trait.* Usually, the trait is recessive; therefore, a female must receive two alleles, one from each parent, before she has the condition.

X-Linked Alleles

When considering X-linked traits, the allele on the X chromosome is shown as a letter attached to the X chromosome. For example, this is the key for red-green color blindness:

X^B = normal vision

X^b = color blindness

The possible genotypes and phenotypes in both males and females are:

Genotypes	Phenotypes
$X^B X^B$	Female who has normal color vision
$X^B X^b$	Carrier female who has normal color vision
$X^b X^b$	Female who is color blind
$X^B Y$	Male who has normal vision
$X^b Y$	Male who is color blind

Recall that carriers are individuals who appear normal but can pass on an allele for a genetic disorder. Note here that the heterozygous female is a carrier because although she appears to be normal, she is capable of passing on an allele for color blindness. (The reading on page 32 explains why the recessive mutation shows up in some but not all cells of a heterozygous female.) Color-blind females are rare be-

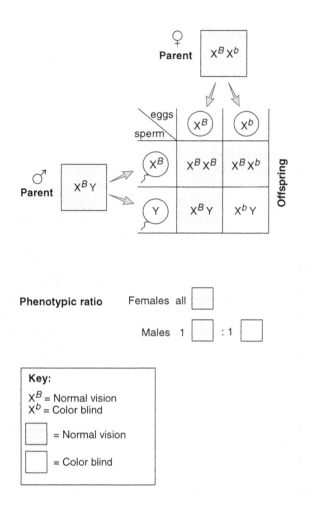

Figure 2.13   Cross involving an X-linked allele.
The male parent is normal, but the female parent is a carrier; an allele for color blindness is located on one of her X chromosomes. Therefore, each son stands a 50% chance of being color blind. The daughters will appear normal, but each one stands a 50% chance of being a carrier.

cause they must receive the allele from both parents; color-blind males are more common since they need only one recessive allele to be color blind. The allele for color blindness has to be inherited from their mother because it is on the X chromosome; males only inherit the Y chromosome from their father.

Now, let us consider a mating between a man with normal vision and a heterozygous woman (Fig. 2.13). What are the chances of this couple having a color-blind daughter? A color-blind son? All daughters will have normal color vision because they all receive an X^B from their father. The sons, however, have a 50% chance of being color blind, depending on whether they receive an X^B or an X^b from their mother. The inheritance of a Y chromosome from their father cannot offset the inheritance of an X^b from their mother. Notice in Figure 2.13 that the phenotypic results for sex-linked traits are given separately for males and females.

X-Linked Disorders

X-linked conditions can be dominant or recessive, but most of the X-linked conditions we know about are recessive. More males than females have the trait because recessive alleles on the X chromosome are always expressed in males, whose Y chromosome does not have a corresponding allele. If a male has an X-linked recessive condition, his daughters are carriers; therefore, the condition passes from grandfather to grandson. Females who have the condition inherited the allele from both their mother and their father, and all the sons of such a female will have the condition. Three well-known X-linked recessive disorders are color blindness, muscular dystrophy, and hemophilia.

Color Blindness

The retina of the human eye has three different classes of cone cells, the receptors for color vision. Only one pigment protein is present in each type of cone cell; there are blue-sensitive, red-sensitive, and green-sensitive cone cells. The allele for the blue-sensitive protein is autosomal, but the alleles for the red- and green-sensitive proteins are on the X chromosome. About 8% of Caucasian men have red-green color blindness. Most of these see brighter greens as tans, olive greens as browns, and reds as reddish-browns. A few cannot tell reds from greens at all. They see only yellows, blues, blacks, whites, and grays. Opticians use special charts to diagnose people who are color blind.

Muscular Dystrophy

Muscular dystrophy, as the name implies, is characterized by a wasting away of the muscles (Fig. 2.14). The most common form, Duchenne muscular dystrophy, is X-linked and occurs in about one out of every 3,600 male births. Symptoms, such as waddling gait, toe walking, frequent falls, and difficulty in rising, may appear as soon as the child starts to walk. Muscle weakness intensifies until the individual is confined to a wheelchair. Death usually occurs by age 20; therefore, affected males are rarely fathers. The recessive allele remains in the population through passage from carrier mother to carrier daughter.

Recently, scientists isolated the gene for Duchenne muscular dystrophy, and discovered that the absence of a protein now called dystrophin is the cause of the disorder. Much investigative work determined that dystrophin is involved in the release of calcium from the endoplasmic reticulum in muscle fibers. The lack of dystrophin causes calcium to leak into the cell, which promotes the action of an enzyme that leads to the destruction of muscle fibers. When the body attempts to repair the tissue, fibrous tissue forms, and this cuts off the blood supply so that more and more cells die.

A test is now available to detect carriers of Duchenne muscular dystrophy. Also, various treatments are being

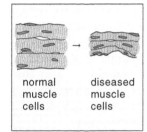

normal muscle cells → diseased muscle cells

Figure 2.14   Muscular dystrophy.
This child has the oversized calves typical of muscular dystrophy. The oversized calves are due to fibrous, rather than muscle tissue.

attempted. Normal muscle cells can be injected into muscles, and for every 100,000 cells injected, dystrophin production occurs in 30–40% of muscle fibers. When the allele for dystrophin was inserted into the thigh muscle cells of mice, about 1% of these cells then produced dystrophin.

Hemophilia

About one in 10,000 males is a hemophiliac; the reading on page 35 tells about the experiences of one of these. There are two common types of hemophilia: Hemophilia A is due to the absence or minimal presence of a clotting factor known as factor VIII, and hemophilia B is due to the absence of clotting factor IX. Hemophilia is called the bleeder's disease because the affected person's blood either does not clot or clots very slowly. Although hemophiliacs bleed externally after an injury, they also bleed internally, particularly around joints. Hemorrhages can be stopped with transfusions of fresh blood (or plasma) or concentrates of the clotting protein. Also, factor VIII is now available as a biotechnology product.

At the turn of the century, hemophilia was prevalent among the royal families of Europe, and all of the affected males could trace their ancestry to Queen Victoria of England. Among Queen Victoria's 26 grandchildren, her carrier daughters Alice and Beatrice introduced the allele into the ruling houses of Russia and Spain, respectively. Alexis, the last heir to the Russian throne before the Russian Revolution, was a hemophiliac. There are no hemophiliacs in the present British royal family because Victoria's eldest son, King Edward VII, did not receive the allele and therefore could not pass it on to any of his descendants.

Living with Hemophilia

Don Miller was born in 1949 and is semiretired from running the math library at the University of Pittsburgh. Today, he has a sheep farm. On June 1, 1999, he was the first hemophilia patient to receive a disabled virus that delivered a functional gene for clotting factor VIII to his bloodstream. Within weeks, he began to experience results. Miller is one of the first of a new breed of patients—people helped by gene therapy. Here he describes his life with hemophilia.

The hemophilia was discovered when I was circumcised, and I almost bled to death, but the doctors weren't really sure until I was about 18 months old. No one where I was born was familiar with it.

When I was three, I fell out of my crib and was black and blue from my waist to the top of my head. The only treatment then was whole-blood replacement. So, I learned not to play sports. A minor sprain would take a week or two to heal. One time I fell at my grandmother's house and had a 1-inch-long cut on the back of my leg. It took five weeks to stop bleeding, just leaking real slowly. I didn't need whole-blood replacement, but if I moved a little the wrong way, it would open and bleed again.

I had transfusions as seldom as I could. The doctors always tried not to infuse me until it was necessary. Of course, there was no AIDS then, but there were problems with transmitting hepatitis through blood transfusions, and other blood-borne diseases. All that whole blood can kill you from kidney failure. When I was nine or ten, I went to the hospital for intestinal polyps. I was operated on and they told me I'd have a 10% chance of pulling through. I met other kids there with hemophilia who died from kidney failure due to the amount of fluid from all the transfusions. Once a year, I went to the hospital for blood tests. Some years, I went more often than that. Most of the time, I would just lay there and bleed. My joints don't work from all the bleeding.

By the time I got married at age 20, treatment had progressed to gamma globulin from plasma. By then, I was receiving gamma globulin from donated plasma and small volumes of cryoprecipitate, which is the factor VIII clotting protein that my body cannot produce, pooled from many donors. We decided not to have children because that would end the hemophilia in the family.

I'm one of the oldest patients at the Pittsburgh Hemophilia Center. I was HIV negative and over age 25, which is what they want. By that age, a lot of people with hemophilia are HIV positive, because they lived through the time period when we had no choice but to use pooled cryoprecipitate. I took so little cryoprecipitate that I wasn't exposed to very much. And, I had the time. The gene therapy protocol involves showing up three times a week.

The treatment is three infusions, one a day for three days, on an outpatient basis. So far, there have been no side effects. Once the gene therapy is perfected, it will be a three-day treatment. A dosage study will follow this one, which is just for safety. Animal studies showed it's best given over three days. I go in once a week to be sure there is no adverse reaction. They hope it will be a one-time treatment. The virus will lodge in the liver and keep replicating.

In the eight weeks before the infusion, I used eight doses of factor. In the 14 weeks since then, I've used three. Incidents that used to require treatment no longer do. As long as I don't let myself feel stressed, I don't have spontaneous bleeding. I've had two nosebleeds that stopped within minutes without treatment, with only a trace of blood on the handkerchief, as opposed to hours of dripping.

I'm somewhat more active, but 50 years of wear and tear won't be healed by this gene therapy. Two of the treatments I required started from overdoing activity, so now I'm trying to find the middle ground.

Sex-Influenced Traits

Sex-influenced traits are traits that occur in either sex but at different frequencies because they are specified by an autosomal gene whose expression is influenced by sex hormones. Pattern baldness is thought to be influenced by the male sex hormone testosterone because males who take the hormone to increase masculinity begin to lose their hair. A more detailed explanation has been suggested by some investigators. They reason that, due to the effect of hormones, men require only one allele for baldness in order for the condition to appear, whereas women require two alleles. In other words, the allele for baldness acts as a dominant in men but as a recessive in women. This means that men who have a bald father and a mother with a normal hairline have a 50% chance at best and a 100% chance at worst of going bald. Women who have a bald father and a mother with a normal hairline have no chance at best and a 50% chance at worst of going bald (Fig. 2.15).

Another sex-influenced trait of interest is the length of the index finger. In females, an index finger longer than the fourth finger (ring finger) seems to be dominant. In males, an index finger longer than the fourth finger seems to be recessive.

Sex-Limited Traits

Sex-limited traits may be autosomal or sex-linked, but they occur in only one gender because of anatomical or hormonal differences. For example, ovaries only develop in females, and sperm only develop in males. To take another example, prostate cancer only occurs in men, and uterine cancer only occurs in women.

Precocious puberty is due to the inheritance of a dominant allele that is only expressed in males. Therefore, heterozygous females do not experience it, while heterozygous males undergo puberty as early as four years of age. Preeclampsia is high blood pressure that occurs in some women, usually toward the end of their first and/or second pregnancy. Because high blood pressure constricts the vessels in the uterus that supply the fetus with oxygen and nutrients, the baby's growth may be slowed. Preeclampsia also increases the risk of placental separation from the uterine wall before delivery. Preeclampsia is more apt to occur if the woman's mother also experienced it; therefore, it seems to have a genetic component. Strangely enough, if the woman's mother-in-law had preeclampsia, she is also more likely to develop it. In some undetermined way, a woman's partner may influence development of the condition, perhaps by way of the fetus.

Mitochondrial Inheritance

Leber's hereditary optic neuropathy (LHON) is a maternally inherited disease of the optic nerve that can occur in males and females. The difficulty can be traced to a gene that occurs in mitochondria and not in the nucleus.

Mitochondria, which are the organelles involved in energy conversions, contain several genes, most of which have to do with the work of mitochondria. Organs particularly sensitive to disturbances in energy supply, such as muscles and nerves, are most often affected by a mutation that occurs in mitochondrial genes.

When a sperm fertilizes an egg, only its nucleus enters and fuses with the egg's nucleus. Therefore, essentially all of our mitochondria come from our mothers. If a father has a mitochondrial disorder, none of his children inherit it. If a mother has a mitochondrial disorder, all of her children inherit it.

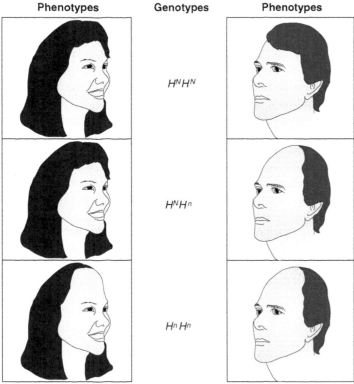

Phenotypes	Genotypes	Phenotypes
	$H^N H^N$	
	$H^N H^n$	
	$H^n H^n$	

H^N = Normal hair growth
H^n = Pattern baldness

Figure 2.15   **Pattern baldness, a sex-influenced characteristic.**
Due to hormonal influences, the presence of only one allele for baldness causes the condition in men, whereas the condition does not occur in women unless they possess both alleles for baldness.

Bioethical Focus

Environmentally Induced Birth Defects

Our increased knowledge of genetics has led to concern for protecting the fetus from environmental influences that can cause mutations and/or alter the expression of genes in a way that results in birth defects. The question that arises is, Who is responsible for protecting the fetus from possible genetic harm? To protect themselves, Johnson Controls, a U.S. battery manufacturer, developed a fetal protection policy. No woman capable of bearing a child was offered a job that might expose her to toxins that could negatively affect the development of her baby. To get such a job, a woman had to show that she had been sterilized or was otherwise incapable of having children. In 1991, the U.S. Supreme Court declared this policy unconstitutional on the basis of sexual discrimination. The decision was hailed as a victory for women, but was it? The decision was written in such a way that women alone, not an employer, are responsible for any harm done to the fetus by workplace toxins.

To what degree should a couple be responsible for providing a healthy environment for their unborn child? Should the couple be responsible for investigating their environment and making sure it is free of any possible harmful chemicals and/or radiation, or should the government and industry be required to make sure the environment is free of harmful influences? Even so, can we expect the government and industry to bear all the responsibility? Young women are being informed that such substances as drugs, alcohol, and tobacco, for example, can cause harm to their unborn child. Should they refrain from such indulgences as long as they are of childbearing age? After all, harm can occur even before a woman knows she is pregnant. What if her child is born with a defect that could have been prevented had she acted more responsibly? Should she be subject to prosecution, as many suggest? What if a doctor prescribed a medication that led to a birth defect? Should he or she be subject to prosecution?

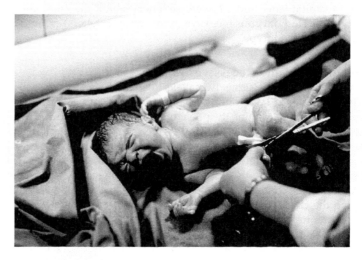

Figure 2D　**Birth of a child.**
Who is responsible for protecting newborns from a birth defect caused by environmental influences—the government, industry, the medical profession, or the mother herself?

Decide Your Opinion

1. Are the government and industry responsible for providing a safe environment for unborn children? If so, what should they do—merely be informants, or take active steps to clean up and prevent the occurrence of harmful environments?
2. How much responsibility should a couple bear for protecting their child against detrimental environmental influences before it is born?
3. What should be done if a woman obviously failed to protect her unborn child from harmful environmental influences? Should she be subject to prosecution?

Summary

2.1 Genotype and Phenotype
It is customary to use letters to represent the genotypes of individuals. Homozygous dominant (two capital letters) and heterozygous (a capital letter and a lowercase letter) exhibit the dominant phenotype. Homozygous recessive (two lowercase letters) exhibits the recessive phenotype.

2.2 Dominant and Recessive Traits
Whereas the individual has two alleles (copies of a gene) for each trait, the gametes have only one allele for each trait. A Punnett square can help determine the phenotypic ratio among offspring by showing what could happen if all possible sperm types of a particular male were given an equal chance to fertilize all possible egg types of a particular female. In one-trait crosses, when a heterozygous individual reproduces with another heterozygote, there is a 75% chance the child will have the dominant phenotype and a 25% chance the child will have the recessive phenotype. When a heterozygous individual reproduces with a pure recessive, the offspring has a 50% chance of having either phenotype.

In two-trait crosses, parents have an allelic pair for each trait. When two dihybrids reproduce, the results are 9:3:3:1, in which 9 out of 16 have the two dominant characteristics; the 3s are mixed; and one has both recessive characteristics.

Several autosomal dominant disorders, such as neurofibromatosis and Huntington disease, are known. Autosomal recessive disorders include cystic fibrosis, phenylketonuria, Tay-Sachs disease, and albinism. Albinism is also an example of epistasis, in which one gene affects the expression of another gene.

2.3 Beyond Simple Inheritance Patterns
Polygenic traits are controlled by more than one gene, and the individual inherits an allelic pair for each gene. As with skin color, the phenotype is also subject to environmental effects. Therefore, skin color is an example of a multifactorial disorder, as are many other disorders, such as clubfoot and cleft palate. It's possible that behavioral disorders are also multifactorial.

When a trait is controlled by multiple alleles, each person has one pair of all possible alleles. ABO blood types illustrate inheritance by multiple alleles.

Pleiotropy occurs when a single gene has more than one effect. Examples are Marfan syndrome, caused by a defect in the production of connective tissue; porphyria, caused by a chemical insufficiency in the production of hemoglobin; and sickle-cell disease, in which the red blood cells are sickle-shaped. Determination of inheritance is sometimes complicated by codominance (e.g., blood type) and by incomplete dominance (e.g., hair curl among Caucasians and sickle-cell disease).

2.4 Sex-Linked Traits
Sex-linked genes are located on the sex chromosomes, and most of these alleles are X-linked because they are on the X chromosome. Since the Y chromosome is blank for X-linked alleles, males are more apt to exhibit the recessive phenotype, which they inherited from their mother. If a female does have the phenotype, her father must also have it, and her mother must be a carrier or have the trait. Usually, X-linked traits skip a generation and go from maternal grandfather to grandson by way of a carrier daughter. Several disorders are X-linked, including color blindness, muscular dystrophy, and hemophilia.

Sex-influenced traits are controlled by an allele that acts as if it were dominant in one sex but recessive in the other. Most likely, the activity of such genes is influenced by the sex hormones. Sex-limited traits may be autosomal or sex-linked, but they occur in only one gender because of anatomical or hormonal differences. Mitochondrial inheritance is purely maternal in males and females because the egg passes on mitochondria and not a sperm.

Reviewing the Chapter

1. What is the difference between the genotype and the phenotype of an individual? For which phenotype—dominant or recessive—are there two possible genotypes? 22
2. Why do the gametes have only one allele for each trait? 23
3. What is the chance of producing a child with the dominant phenotype from each of the following crosses? 24

    $AA \times AA$

    $Aa \times AA$

    $Aa \times Aa$

    $aa \times aa$

4. Which of the crosses in question 3 can result in an offspring with the recessive phenotype? Explain. 24
5. Give examples of genetic disorders caused by inheritance of a single dominant allele and disorders caused by inheritance of two recessive alleles. 26–27
6. Give examples of polygenic inheritance. Why are these traits multifactorial? What disorders are believed to be multifactorial traits? 28
7. Explain why there are four phenotypes for ABO blood type. 30
8. Explain pleiotropy and give some examples. 30
9. How do the phenotypic results of an incomplete dominance cross differ from those of a cross involving simple dominance? 31
10. If a trait is on an autosome, how would you designate a homozygous dominant female? If a trait is on an X chromosome, how would you designate a homozygous dominant female? 33
11. Give examples of genetic disorders caused by X-linked recessive alleles. 34
12. Why do more men have pattern baldness than women? 36
13. What is meant by the term sex-limited trait? 36
14. Why are mitochondrial genetic disorders inherited only from the mother? 36

Additional Genetics Questions

In questions 1–5, the trait is dominant.

1. Black hair is dominant over blond hair. A woman with black hair whose father had blond hair reproduces with a blond-haired man. What are the chances of this couple having a blond-haired child? 26

2. A woman heterozygous for polydactyly, a condition characterized by extra fingers and toes, is married to a man without this condition. What are the chances that their children will have extra fingers and toes? 26

3. Could a person who can curl her tongue have parents who cannot curl their tongues? Explain your answer. 26

4. A young man's father has just been diagnosed as having Huntington disease. What are the chances that the son will inherit this condition? 26

5. Your maternal Grandmother Smith had Huntington disease. Aunt Jane, your mother's sister, also had the disease. Your mother dies at age 75 with no signs of Huntington disease. What are your chances of getting the disease? 26

In questions 6–8, the trait is recessive.

6. Parents who do not have Tay-Sachs disease produce a child who has Tay-Sachs disease. What is the genotype of each parent? What are the chances that each child will have Tay-Sachs disease? 26–27

7. A child has cystic fibrosis. His parents are normal. What is the genotype of all persons mentioned? 26–27

8. One parent has lactose intolerance, the inability to digest lactose, the sugar found in milk, and the other is heterozygous. What are the chances that their child will have lactose intolerance? 26

Questions 9–11 are two-trait problems.

9. A man with widow's peak (dominant) who cannot curl his tongue (recessive) reproduces with a woman who has a straight hairline and can curl her tongue. They have a child who has a straight hairline and cannot curl the tongue. Give the genotypes of all the persons involved. 25

10. Both Mr. and Mrs. Smith have freckles (dominant) and attached earlobes (recessive). Some of their children do not have freckles. What is the chance that their next child will have freckles and attached earlobes? 25

11. What is the genotype of a male who is color blind and can curl the tongue (dominant) but whose mother has normal vision and cannot curl the tongue? 33–34

In questions 12–14, the trait is controlled by multiple alleles.

12. The genotype of a woman with type B blood is *BO*. The genotype of her husband is *AO*. What could be the genotypes and phenotypes of the children? 30

13. A man has type AB blood. What is his genotype? Could this man be the father of a child with type B blood? If not, why not? If so, what blood types could the child's mother have? 30

14. Baby Susan has type B blood. Her mother has type O blood. What type blood could her father have? 30

In questions 15–18, the trait is incompletely dominant.

15. What are the chances that a person homozygous for straight hair who reproduces with a person homozygous for curly hair will have children with wavy hair? 31

16. One parent has sickle-cell disease, and the other is perfectly normal. What are the phenotypes of their children? 31

17. A child has sickle-cell disease, but her parents do not. What is the genotype of each parent? 31

18. Both parents have the sickle-cell trait. What are their chances of having a perfectly normal child? 31

Questions 19 and 20 are otherwise controlled.

19. Skin color is a polygenic trait. A woman with very light skin has medium-brown parents. If this woman reproduces with a light-skinned man, what is the darkest skin color possible for their children? The lightest? 28

20. Pattern baldness is a sex-influenced trait. When two individuals heterozygous for pattern baldness have children, what proportion of males will lose their hair? What proportion of females will lose their hair? 36

Critical Thinking Questions

1. In fruit flies, long wings are dominant over short wings. A student observing the results of a cross counts 300 long-winged flies and 98 short-winged flies. What was the genotype of the parent flies? How do you know? Of the long-winged flies, how many do you predict are homozygous dominant and how many are heterozygous? Why do you say so?

2. Persons with sickle-cell disease tend to die at a young age and leave no offspring. Why doesn't sickle-cell disease cease to be a threat in future generations?

3. If a woman with genotype *BODd* reproduces with a person having genotype *AOdd* ($D = Rh^+, d = Rh^-$), what blood types might their children have? What is your reasoning?

4. A male is color blind and has a straight hairline. What is his genotype?

Understanding Key Terms

allele 22	multiple alleles 30
Barr body 32	mutations 26
codominance 31	phenotype 22
dihybrid 25	polygenic inheritance 28
dominant allele 22	porphyria 30
epistasis 27	Punnett square 24
genotype 22	recessive allele 22
heterozygous 22	sex chromosome 33
homozygous dominant 22	sex-influenced trait 36
homozygous recessive 22	sex-limited trait 36
incomplete dominance 31	sex-linked 33
Marfan syndrome 30	X-linked 33
multifactorial trait 28	

Chapter 3

DNA and Molecular Genetics

Our approach to genetics thus far has been to consider the genes as particulate units of a chromosome. In contrast, biochemical genetics considers the chemical nature of the gene and the biochemical function of genes in the cell.

Genes are made up of a chemical called **DNA (deoxyribonucleic acid).**

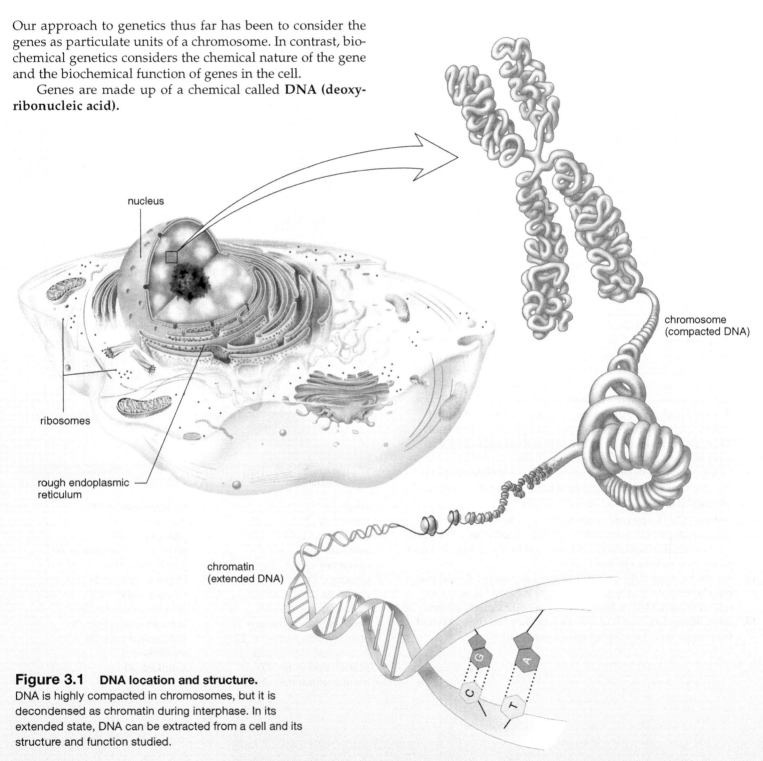

nucleus

chromosome
(compacted DNA)

ribosomes

rough endoplasmic
reticulum

chromatin
(extended DNA)

Figure 3.1 **DNA location and structure.**
DNA is highly compacted in chromosomes, but it is
decondensed as chromatin during interphase. In its
extended state, DNA can be extracted from a cell and its
structure and function studied.

3.1 DNA and RNA Structure and Function

DNA is found principally in the chromosomes, which are located in the nucleus of a cell. (Small amounts of DNA are also found in mitochondria.)

When a cell is about to divide, the chromosomes are very compact structures. In between cell divisions, chromosomes uncoil and decondense. At that time, the chromosomes exist as a mass of very long, fine threads known as chromatin. Chromosomes, but not chromatin, can be seen with the light microscope. Within chromatin, the DNA molecule is an extended double-stranded helix, and as we shall see, the two-stranded structure of DNA permits replication of the molecule. Figure 3.1 shows the levels of organization, from chromosome to chromatin to DNA.

DNA Structure and Replication

DNA is a type of nucleic acid, and like all nucleic acids, it is formed by the sequential joining of molecules called nucleotides. Nucleotides, in turn, are composed of three smaller molecules—a phosphate, a sugar, and a nitrogen-containing base. The sugar in DNA is deoxyribose, which accounts for the name deoxyribonucleic acid. The four nucleotides that make up the DNA molecule have the following bases: **adenine (A), thymine (T), cytosine (C),** and **guanine (G)** (Fig. 3.2).

Nucleotides are joined together in a specific order, with the sugar and phosphate molecules forming the backbone of a strand, and the bases projecting to the side. In DNA, there are two strands of nucleotides; consequently, DNA is double stranded. Weak hydrogen bonds between the bases hold the strands together. Each base is bonded to another particular base, an arrangement called **complementary base pairing.** Adenine (A) is always paired with thymine (T), and cytosine (C) is always paired with guanine (G), and vice versa. The dotted lines in Figure 3.3*a* represent the hydrogen bonds between the bases. The structure of DNA is said to resemble a ladder; the sugar-phosphate backbone makes up the sides of the ladder, and the paired bases are the rungs. The ladder structure of DNA twists to form a spiral staircase called a double helix (Fig. 3.3*b*).

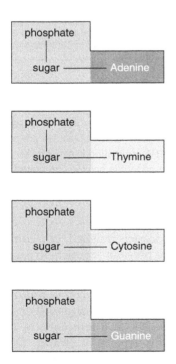

Figure 3.2   DNA nucleotides.
DNA contains four different kinds of nucleotides, molecules that in turn contain a phosphate, a sugar, and a base. The base of a DNA nucleotide can be adenine (A), thymine (T), cytosine (C), or guanine (G).

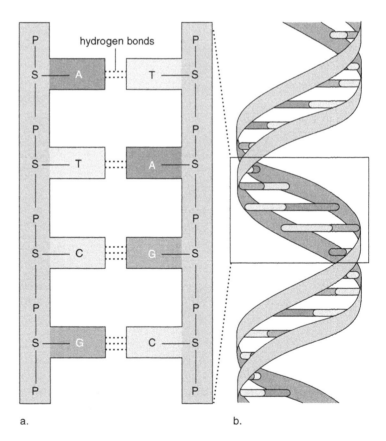

a.   b.

Figure 3.3   DNA is double stranded.
a. When the DNA nucleotides join, they form two strands so that the structure of DNA resembles a ladder. The phosphate (P) and sugar (S) molecules make up the sides of the ladder, and the bases make up the rungs of the ladder. Each base is weakly bonded (dotted lines) to its complementary base (T is bonded to A, and vice versa; G is bonded to C, and vice versa). **b.** The DNA ladder twists to form a double helix. Each chromatid of a duplicated chromosome contains one double helix.

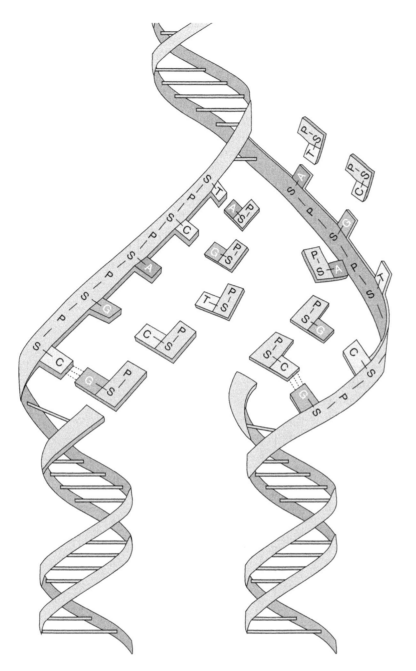

Region of parental DNA helix. (Both backbones are shown in purple.)

Region of replication (simplified). Parental DNA helix is unwound and unzipped. New nucleotides are pairing with those in parental strands.

Region of completed replication. Each double helix is composed of an old parental strand (purple) and a new daughter strand (red).

Figure 3.4   DNA replication.
When replication is finished, two complete DNA double-helical molecules are present. Note that DNA replication is semiconservative because each new double helix is composed of an old parental strand and a new daughter strand.

Replication of DNA

Replication of DNA occurs as a part of chromosome duplication. Replication is facilitated by the structure of DNA. Replication requires these steps:

1. The hydrogen bonds between the two strands of DNA break as enzymes unwind and "unzip" the molecule.
2. New nucleotides, always present in the nucleus, fit into place beside each old (parental) strand by the process of complementary base pairing.
3. These new nucleotides become joined by an enzyme that is called **DNA polymerase** because it forms a DNA polymer (molecule).
4. When the process is finished, two complete DNA molecules are present, identical to each other and to the original molecule.

Each new double helix is composed of an old (parental) strand and a new (daughter) strand (Fig. 3.4). Because each strand of DNA serves as a **template,** or mold, for the production of a complementary strand, DNA replication is called semiconservative. Rarely, a replication error occurs—that is, the sequence of the complementary bases is not correct. But if an error does occur, the cell has repair enzymes that usually fix it. A replication error that persists is a **mutation,** a permanent change in a gene that can cause a change in the phenotype.

The Structure and Function of RNA

RNA (ribonucleic acid) is made up of nucleotides containing the sugar ribose. This sugar accounts for the scientific name of this polynucleotide. The four nucleotides that make up the RNA molecule have the following bases: adenine (A), **uracil (U),** cytosine (C), and guanine (G) (Fig. 3.5a). Notice that in RNA, the base uracil replaces the base thymine.

RNA, unlike DNA, is single stranded (Fig. 3.5b), but the single RNA strand sometimes doubles back on itself and complementary base pairing still occurs. Similarities and differences between these two nucleic acid molecules are listed in Table 3.1.

In general, RNA is a helper to DNA, allowing protein synthesis to occur according to the genetic information that DNA provides. There are three types of RNA, each with a specific function in protein synthesis.

Ribosomal RNA

Ribosomal RNA (rRNA) is produced in the nucleolus of a nucleus, where a portion of DNA serves as a template for its formation. Ribosomal RNA joins with proteins made in the cytoplasm to form the subunits of ribosomes. The subunits leave the nucleus and come together in the cytoplasm when protein synthesis is about to begin. Proteins are synthesized at the ribosomes, which in low-power electron micrographs look like granules arranged along the endoplasmic reticulum, a system of tubules and saccules within the cytoplasm. Some ribosomes appear freely in the cytoplasm or in clusters called polyribosomes.

Messenger RNA

Messenger RNA (mRNA) is produced in the nucleus, where DNA serves as a template for its formation. Therefore, the bases in messenger RNA are complementary to a portion of DNA. This type of RNA carries genetic information from DNA to the ribosomes in the cytoplasm where protein synthesis occurs. Messenger RNA is a linear molecule.

Transfer RNA

Transfer RNA (tRNA) is produced in the nucleus, and a portion of DNA also serves as a template for its production. Appropriate to its name, tRNA transfers amino acids to the ribosomes, where the amino acids are joined, forming a protein. Twenty different types of amino acids make up proteins; therefore, at least 20 tRNAs must be functioning in the cell. Each type of tRNA carries only one type of amino acid.

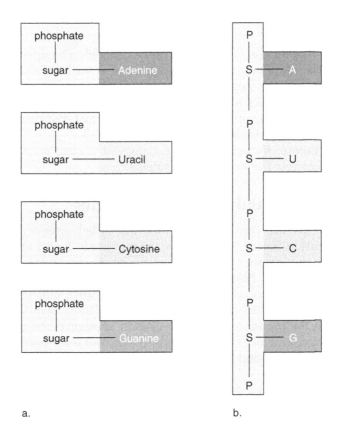

a.   b.

Figure 3.5   **RNA structure.**
a. The four nucleotides in RNA each have a phosphate (P) molecule; the sugar (S) is ribose; and the base may be either adenine (A), uracil (U), cytosine (C), or guanine (G). **b.** RNA is single stranded. The sugar and phosphate molecules join to form a single backbone, and the bases project to the side.

Table 3.1	DNA-RNA Similarities and Differences

DNA-RNA Similarities

Both are nucleic acids

Both are composed of nucleotides

Both have a sugar-phosphate backbone

Both have four different types of bases

DNA-RNA Differences

DNA	RNA
Found in nucleus	Found in nucleus and cytoplasm
The genetic material	Helper to DNA
Sugar is deoxyribose	Sugar is ribose
Bases are A, T, C, G	Bases are A, U, C, G
Double stranded	Single stranded
Is transcribed (to produce mRNA)	Is translated (to produce proteins)

3.2 Gene Expression

As we shall see, DNA provides the cell with a blueprint for synthesizing proteins. DNA resides in the nucleus, and protein synthesis occurs in the cytoplasm. Messenger RNA (mRNA) carries a copy of DNA's blueprint into the cytoplasm, and the other RNA molecules we just discussed are involved in bringing about protein synthesis.

Before discussing the mechanics of protein synthesis, let's review the structure of proteins.

Structure and Function of Proteins

Proteins are composed of subunits called amino acids. Twenty different amino acids are commonly found in proteins, which are synthesized at the ribosomes in the cytoplasm of cells. Proteins differ because the number and order of their amino acids differ. Figure 3.6 shows that the sequence of amino acids in one protein differs completely from the sequence of amino acids in another protein. The unique sequence of amino acids in a protein leads to its particular shape, and the shape of a protein helps determine its function.

Proteins are found in all parts of the body; some are structural proteins, and others are enzymes. The protein hemoglobin is responsible for the red color of red blood cells. Albumins and globulins (antibodies) are well-known plasma proteins. Muscle cells contain the proteins actin and myosin, which give muscles substance and the ability to contract.

Enzymes are organic catalysts that speed reactions in cells. The reactions in cells form metabolic or chemical pathways. A pathway can be depicted as follows:

$$E_A \quad E_B \quad E_C \quad E_D$$
$$A \rightarrow B \rightarrow C \rightarrow D \rightarrow E$$

In this pathway, the letters represent molecules, and the notations over the arrows are enzymes: Molecule A becomes molecule B, and enzyme E_A speeds the reaction; molecule B becomes molecule C, and enzyme E_B speeds the reaction; and so forth. Enzymes are *specific*: Enzyme E_A can only convert A to B, enzyme E_B can only convert B to C, and so forth.

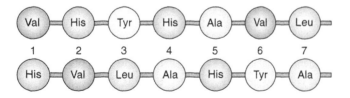

Figure 3.6   **Structure of proteins.**
Proteins differ by the sequence of their amino acids; the top row shows one possible sequence, and the bottom row shows another possible sequence in a portion of a protein. Each amino acid is represented by the first three letters of its name—for example, val = valine and ala = alanine.

The DNA Code

The discovery that metabolic disorders run in certain families suggested to early investigators that genes control the metabolism of a cell. The mental retardation seen in persons with phenylketonuria (PKU) is caused by an inability to convert phenylalanine to tyrosine. The lack of pigment in albinos is caused by an inability to convert tyrosine to melanin. These and other human conditions are caused by the deficiency of particular enzymes.

Laboratory experiments performed over many years finally showed that a gene is a segment of DNA that codes for a protein. If a person inherits a faulty gene, the sequence of bases in DNA is abnormal, and a particular protein is not constructed normally. We now know that DNA contains a triplet code—every three bases (a *triplet*) represents (*codes for*) one amino acid (Table 3.2).

The genetic code is essentially universal. The same mRNA **codons** stand for the same amino acids in most organisms, from bacteria to humans. This illustrates the remarkable biochemical unity of living things and suggests that all living things have a common evolutionary ancestor.

Transcription

Gene expression requires two steps, called transcription and translation. It is helpful to remember that in other applications the word *transcription* means making an exact copy of written information, while *translation* means putting this information into another language.

Table 3.2	Some DNA Codes and RNA Codons		
DNA Triplet	**mRNA Codon**	**tRNA Anticodon**	**Amino Acid**
TTT	AAA	UUU	Lysine
TGG	ACC	UGG	Threonine
CCG	GGC	CCG	Glycine
CAT	GUA	CAU	Valine
CTC	GAG	CUC	Glutamate
GAG	CUC	GAG	Leucine
AGA	UCU	AGA	Serine
ACT	UGA	ACU	Stop
GCT	CGA	GCU	Arginine
TAA	AUU	UAA	Isoleucine
GGA	CCU	GGA	Proline
CGA	GCU	CGA	Alanine
TTG	AAC	UUG	Asparagine

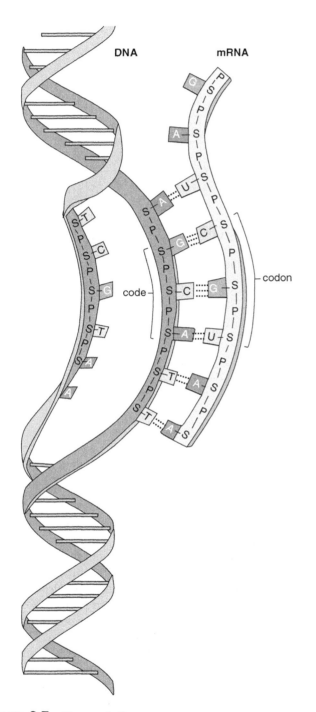

Figure 3.7   Transcription.
During transcription, mRNA is formed when nucleotides complementary to the sequence of bases in a portion of DNA (i.e., a gene) join. Note that DNA contains a triplet code (sequences of three bases) and that mRNA contains codons (sequences of three complementary bases). *Top:* The mRNA transcript is ready to move into the cytoplasm. *Middle:* Transcription has occurred, and mRNA nucleotides have joined together. *Bottom:* The rest of the DNA molecule may yet be transcribed.

During **transcription** of DNA, a strand of mRNA forms that is complementary to a portion of DNA. Preparatory to transcription, a segment of the DNA helix unwinds and

unzips. Then mRNA is produced as complementary RNA nucleotides pair with the nucleotides of one DNA strand: G (in RNA) pairs with C (in DNA), U pairs with A, and A pairs with T. An enzyme called **RNA polymerase** joins the nucleotides together, and the RNA that results has a sequence of bases complementary to those of a gene. While DNA contains a **triplet code** in which every three bases stand for one amino acid, mRNA contains codons, each of which is made up of three bases that also stand for the same amino acid (see Table 3.2).

In Figure 3.7, mRNA has formed and is ready to be processed, as discussed next.

Processing of mRNA

Most genes in humans are interrupted by segments of DNA that are not part of the gene. These portions are called *introns* because they are intragene segments. The other portions of the gene are called *exons* because they are ultimately expressed. Only exons result in a protein product.

When DNA is transcribed, the mRNA contains bases that are complementary to both exons and introns, but before the mRNA exits the nucleus, it is *processed.* During processing, the introns are removed, and the exons are joined to form an mRNA molecule consisting of continuous exons. There has been much speculation about the role of introns. It is possible that they allow crossing-over within a gene during meiosis. It is also possible that introns divide a gene into domains, which can then be joined in different combinations to yield mRNAs that result in different protein products (Fig. 3.8).

In human cells, processing occurs in the nucleus. After the mRNA strand is processed, it passes from the cell nucleus into the cytoplasm. There it becomes associated with the ribosomes.

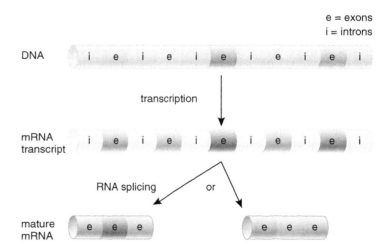

Figure 3.8   Function of introns.
Introns allow alternative splicing and therefore the production of different versions of mature mRNA from the same gene.

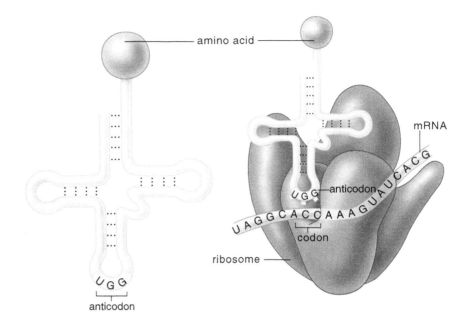

Figure 3.9   **Anticodon-codon base pairing.**
a. A tRNA, which is single stranded but folded this way, has an amino acid attached to one end and an anticodon at the other end. **b.** The anticodon is complementary to a codon. The pairing between codon and anticodon at a ribosome ensures that the sequence of amino acids in a polypeptide is the same sequence directed originally by DNA. For example, if the codon is ACC, the anticodon is UGG, and the amino acid is threonine.

a. tRNA–amino acid

b. tRNA–amino acid at ribosome

Translation

Translation is the synthesis of a polypeptide (many amino acids) under the direction of an mRNA molecule. (Some proteins, such as insulin, consist of one polypeptide, and others, such as hemoglobin, require more than one polypeptide.) During translation, transfer RNA (tRNA) molecules bring amino acids to the ribosomes. Usually, there is more than one tRNA molecule for each of the 20 amino acids found in proteins. The amino acid binds to one end of the molecule. Therefore, the entire complex is designated as a tRNA–amino acid (Fig. 3.9a).

At the other end of each tRNA is a specific **anticodon,** a group of three bases complementary to an mRNA codon. The tRNA molecules come to the ribosome (Fig. 3.9b), where each anticodon pairs with a codon in the order directed by the sequence of the mRNA codons. In this way, the order of codons in mRNA brings about a particular order of amino acids in a protein.

If the codon sequence is ACC, GUA, and AAA, what will be the sequence of amino acids in a portion of the polypeptide? Inspection of Table 3.2 (see page 44) allows us to determine this:

Codon	Anticodon	Amino Acid
ACC	UGG	Threonine
GUA	CAU	Valine
AAA	UUU	Lysine

Polypeptide synthesis requires three steps: initiation, elongation, and termination.

1. During *initiation,* mRNA binds to the smaller of the two ribosomal subunits; then the larger subunit associates with the smaller one.
2. During *elongation,* the polypeptide lengthens one amino acid at a time (Fig. 3.10). A ribosome is large enough to accommodate two tRNA molecules: the incoming tRNA molecule and the outgoing tRNA molecule. The incoming tRNA–amino acid complex receives the peptide from the outgoing tRNA. The ribosome then moves laterally so that the next mRNA codon is available to receive an incoming tRNA–amino acid complex. In this manner, the peptide grows, and the linear structure of a polypeptide comes about. (The particular shape of a polypeptide is formed later.)
3. Finally, *termination* of synthesis occurs at a codon that means "stop" and does not code for an amino acid. The ribosome dissociates into its two subunits and falls off the mRNA molecule.

As soon as the initial portion of mRNA has been translated by one ribosome, and the ribosome has begun to move down the mRNA, another ribosome attaches to the mRNA. Therefore, several ribosomes, collectively called a **polyribosome,** can move along one mRNA at a time. And several polypeptides of the same type can be synthesized using one mRNA molecule (Fig. 3.11).

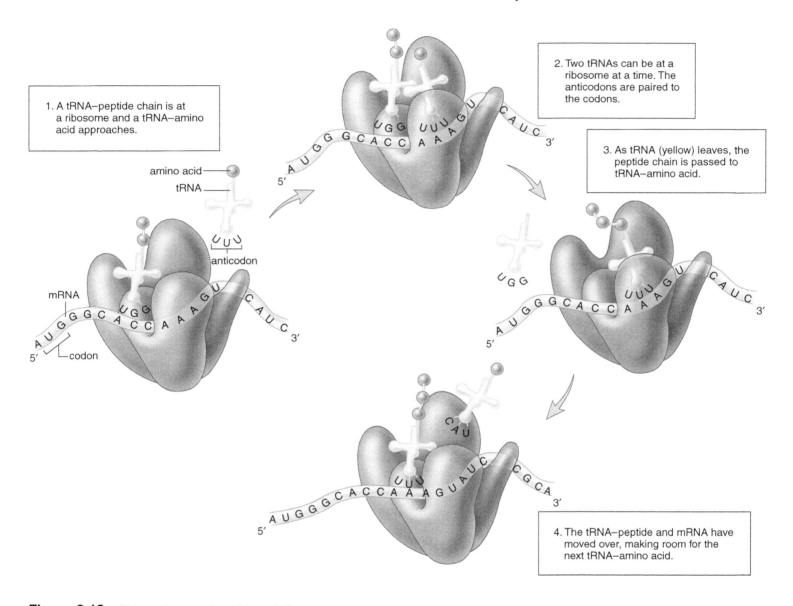

1. A tRNA–peptide chain is at a ribosome and a tRNA–amino acid approaches.

amino acid
tRNA
mRNA
anticodon
codon

2. Two tRNAs can be at a ribosome at a time. The anticodons are paired to the codons.

3. As tRNA (yellow) leaves, the peptide chain is passed to tRNA–amino acid.

4. The tRNA–peptide and mRNA have moved over, making room for the next tRNA–amino acid.

Figure 3.10   Elongation portion of translation.
Transfer RNA (tRNA)–amino acid molecules arrive at the ribosome, and the sequence of messenger RNA (mRNA) codons dictates the order in which amino acids become incorporated into a polypeptide.

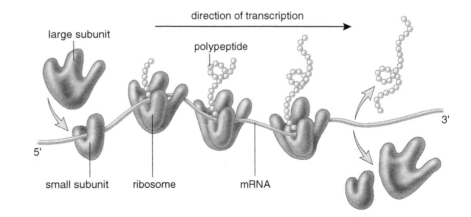

direction of transcription
large subunit
polypeptide
small subunit   ribosome   mRNA

Figure 3.11   Polyribosome structure.
Several ribosomes, collectively called a polyribosome, move along a messenger RNA (mRNA) molecule at one time. They function independently of one another; therefore, several polypeptides can be made at the same time.

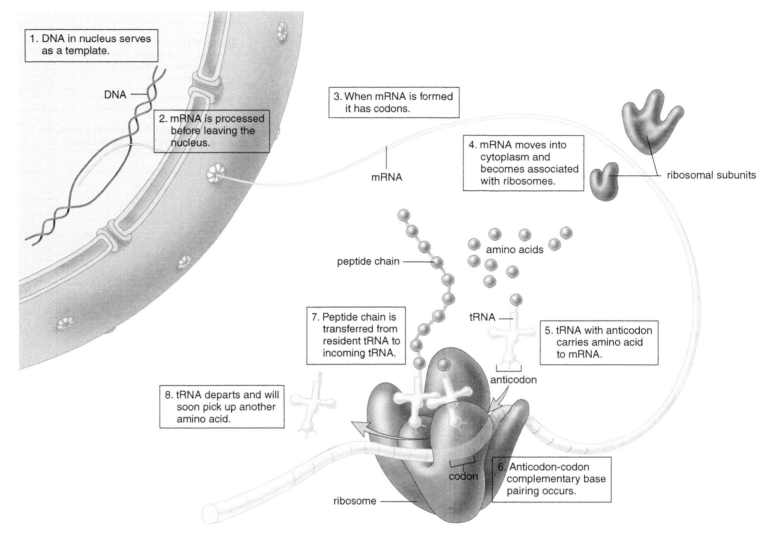

Figure 3.12   **Summary of gene expression.**

Review of Gene Expression

The following list, along with Table 3.3 and Figure 3.12, provides a summary of the events involved in gene expression that results in a protein product.

1. DNA in the nucleus contains a triplet code. Each group of three bases stands for a specific amino acid.
2. During transcription, a segment of a DNA strand serves as a template for the formation of messenger RNA (mRNA). The bases in mRNA are complementary to those in DNA; every three bases is a codon for a certain amino acid.
3. mRNA is processed before it leaves the nucleus, during which time the introns are removed.
4. mRNA carries a sequence of codons to the ribosomes, which are composed of ribosomal RNA (rRNA) and proteins.
5. Transfer RNA (tRNA) molecules, each of which is bonded to a particular amino acid, have anticodons that pair complementarily to the codons in mRNA.

Table 3.3	Participants in Gene Expression	
Molecule	**Special Significance**	**Definition**
DNA	Triplet code	Sequence of bases in threes
mRNA	Codon	Complementary sequence of bases in threes
tRNA	Anticodon	Sequence of three bases complementary to codon
Amino acids	Building blocks	Transported to ribosomes by tRNAs
Protein	Enzymes and structural proteins	Amino acids joined in a predetermined order

6. During translation, tRNA molecules and their attached amino acids arrive at the ribosomes, and the linear sequence of codons of the mRNA determines the order in which the amino acids become incorporated into a protein.

Genetic Mutations

Early geneticists understood that genes undergo mutations, but they didn't know what causes mutations. It is apparent today that a **genetic mutation** is a permanent change in the sequence of bases in DNA. The effect of a DNA base sequence change on protein activity can range from no effect to complete inactivity. To substantiate this statement, we will consider two types of mutations—point mutations and frameshift mutations.

Point and Frameshift Mutations

Point mutations involve a change in a single DNA nucleotide, and therefore a change in a specific codon. Figure 3.13 gives an example in which a single base change could have no effect or a drastic effect, depending on the particular base change that occurs. For example, you already know that sickle-cell disease is due to a single base change in DNA. Because the β chain of hemoglobin now contains valine instead of glutamate at one location, hemoglobin molecules form semirigid rods. The resulting sickle-shaped cells clog blood vessels and die off more quickly than normal-shaped cells.

Frameshift mutations occur most often because one or more nucleotides are either inserted or deleted from DNA. The result of a frameshift mutation can be a completely new sequence of codons and nonfunctional proteins. Here is how this occurs: The sequence of codons is read from a specific starting point, as in the sentence THE CAT ATE THE RAT. If the letter C is deleted from this sentence and the reading frame is shifted, we read THE ATA TET HER AT—something that doesn't make sense.

Effect of Mutations

Genetic disorders are often inborn errors of metabolism because the inheritance of a faulty genetic code leads to a defective enzyme. For example, one particular metabolic pathway in cells is as follows:

$$\underset{\text{(phenylalanine)}}{\text{A}} \xrightarrow{\text{E}_\text{A}} \underset{\text{(tyrosine)}}{\text{B}} \xrightarrow{\text{E}_\text{B}} \underset{\text{(melanin)}}{\text{C}}$$

If a faulty code for enzyme E_A is inherited, a person is unable to convert molecule A to molecule B. Phenylalanine builds up in the system, and the excess causes mental retardation and the other symptoms of the genetic disorder phenylketonuria. In the same pathway, if a person inherits a faulty code for enzyme E_B, then B cannot be converted to C, and the individual is an albino.

Mutated genes for structural proteins also can have dramatic effects. In people who have hemophilia B, the gene for clotting factor IX contains a premature stop codon. Cystic fibrosis is due to the inheritance of a faulty code for a chloride channel protein in the plasma membrane. A rare condition called androgen (e.g., testosterone) sensitivity is due to a faulty cellular receptor for testosterone, the primary male sex hormone. Although there is plenty of testosterone in the blood, the cells are unable to respond to it. The individual, who appears to be a normal female (Fig. 3.14), may be prompted to seek medical advice when menstruation never occurs. At that time, both an X and a Y chromosome are discovered in the cells, and the individual is found to lack the internal sexual organs of a female.

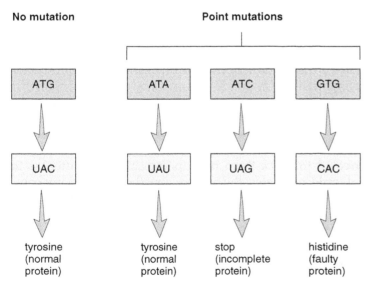

Figure 3.13 Point mutation.
The effect of a DNA base alteration can vary. Starting at the left, if the DNA codes for the same amino acid after the base change, there is no noticeable effect; if it now codes for a stop codon, the resulting protein will be incomplete; and if it now codes for a different amino acid, a faulty protein is possible.

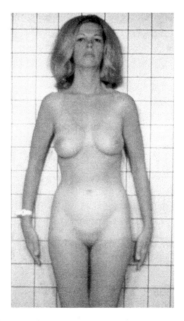

Figure 3.14 Androgen insensitivity.
This individual has a female appearance but the chromosomes of a male. Her abdominal cavity contains testes instead of ovaries and a uterus. Her cells are unable to respond to the male sex hormones because of a mutation that makes the androgen receptor ineffective.

3.3 Biotechnology

Genetic engineering is the use of technology to alter the genotypes of unicellular organisms as well as the genotypes of plants and animals, including ourselves. **Biotechnology** includes genetic engineering and other techniques that make use of natural biological systems to mass-produce a product that is sold commercially or to achieve an end desired by human beings. Biotechnology products tend to be proteins produced as a result of recombinant DNA technology.

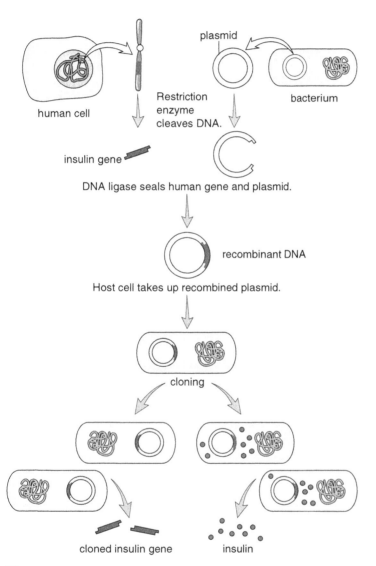

Figure 3.15   Cloning of a human gene.
Human DNA and plasmid DNA are cleaved by a specific type of restriction enzyme and spliced together by the enzyme DNA ligase. Gene cloning is achieved when a host cell takes up the recombinant plasmid, and as the cell reproduces, the plasmid is replicated. Genetically engineered bacteria can be grown in large vats, and the protein product—in this case, insulin—can be collected, packaged, and sold as a commercial product.

Recombinant DNA Technology

Recombinant DNA (rDNA) contains DNA from two or more different sources, such as a human cell and a bacterial cell. To make rDNA, a researcher needs a **vector,** such as a plasmid, by which rDNA will be introduced into a host cell. **Plasmids** are small accessory rings of DNA from bacteria that can be genetically altered and returned to a host cell, and cloning can occur (Fig. 3.15).

Two enzymes are needed to introduce foreign DNA into vector DNA: (1) a **restriction enzyme,** which cleaves DNA, and (2) an enzyme called **DNA ligase,** which seals DNA into an opening created by the restriction enzyme. Hundreds of restriction enzymes occur naturally in bacteria, where they cut up any viral DNA that enters the cell. For example, the restriction enzyme called *Eco*RI always cuts double-stranded DNA in the following manner when it has this sequence of bases:

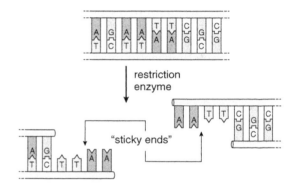

Notice that a gap now exists in the DNA molecule. The single-stranded ends of the two DNA molecules are called "sticky ends" because they can bind a piece of foreign DNA by complementary base pairing. To ensure that a piece of foreign DNA can be placed in the gap, it is only necessary to cleave the foreign DNA with the same type of restriction enzyme.

Next, genetic engineers use DNA ligase to seal the foreign piece of DNA into the vector. DNA splicing is now complete; an rDNA molecule has been prepared. Bacterial cells take up recombinant plasmids, especially if they are treated to make them more permeable. Thereafter, as the plasmid replicates, the gene is cloned, and the many copies of the gene actively specify a protein that can be extracted and sold as a biotechnology product, such as the insulin shown in Figure 3.15.

Biotechnology Products

Today, bacteria, plants, and animals are genetically engineered using recombinant technology to mass produce a product sold commercially. Such proteins as insulin, human growth hormone, clotting factor VIII, hepatitis B vaccine, and many more are now on the market. Since these proteins are specified by human genes (albeit in another type of organism), they do not cause untoward effects.

The Polymerase Chain Reaction

The **polymerase chain reaction (PCR)** is a technique used in genetic research and analysis. PCR can create millions of copies of a segment of DNA very quickly in a test tube. It is very specific—PCR amplifies (makes copies of) a targeted DNA sequence. The targeted sequence can be less than one part in a million of the total DNA sample!

PCR takes its name from the use of DNA polymerase, the enzyme that carries out DNA replication. PCR is a chain reaction because the targeted DNA is repeatedly replicated as long as the process continues. Almost every laboratory has automated PCR machines because an enzyme was discovered that can withstand the high temperature used to separate double-stranded DNA.

Analyzing DNA Segments   DNA amplified by PCR is often analyzed for various purposes. For example, it has been possible to amplify and sequence a very small amount of DNA taken from a 76,000-year-old mummified human brain. In addition, mitochondrial DNA has been amplified and sequenced to decipher the evolutionary history of ethnic groups even back to the so-called "original Eve." (The original Eve is actually the ethnic group from which the others are descended.)

DNA amplified by PCR can be subjected to **DNA fingerprinting.** First, the DNA is treated with restriction enzymes, resulting in a unique collection of different-sized fragments. Then, gel electrophoresis separates the fragments. During gel electrophoresis, the fragments are applied to a gel, and they migrate in an electrical field according to their charge/size ratios. Finally, probes that bind to just certain segments of DNA are applied, and the result is a pattern of distinctive bands. If two DNA patterns match, it is highly probable that the DNA came from the same person.

DNA fingerprinting has many uses. For example, when a sample of DNA from an embryo matches that of a mutated gene, we know the embryo will develop into an individual with a certain genetic disorder. In forensic science, the DNA from a single sperm can be amplified to supply enough DNA to identify a suspected rapist (Fig. 3.16).

As was the case with the World Trade Center victims, human remains can be identified by comparing a sample of DNA to that of a cell left on a personal item (e.g., a toothbrush or cigarette butt). The sample of DNA could have been provided before death, or if necessary the DNA of parents can be used because each parent contributes one-half of a child's chromosomes. DNA fingerprinting also makes it possible to decide when a person is or is not the parent of a child.

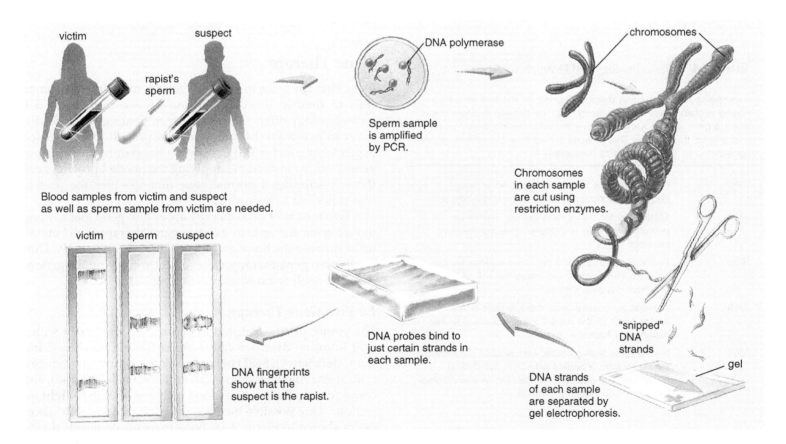

Figure 3.16   DNA fingerprinting.
To confirm that a suspect is the rapist, blood samples are taken from the victim and the suspect, and sperm is taken from the vagina of the victim. The DNA from a single sperm or more can be amplified using the polymerase chain reaction (PCR). The DNA in the three samples is cut using restriction enzymes, and then the fragments are separated using gel electrophoresis. Probes that seek particular sequences of DNA are applied, and the result reveals black bands where the probes stuck. The pattern of bands is unique to the person, so it constitutes a DNA fingerprint.

Donovan Decker

Cindy Cutshall

Salsabil Abu Sa'ad

Wilco Conradi

Figure 3.17   **Human beings who have undergone either ex vivo or in vivo gene therapy.**

Table 3.4	Biotechnology and Hemophilia A

Hemophilia A is a bleeding disorder caused by the lack of a functioning protein called clotting factor VIII. The genetic disorder arises when a gene on the X chromosome mutates and no longer codes properly for this protein. This timeline shows how biotechnology has contributed to the treatment of hemophilia A.

1980	Hemophilia A is treated with pooled plasma. Recipients contract hepatitis and/or HIV infections.
1984	Clotting factor VIII gene is cloned. Thereafter, prenatal diagnosis and carrier detection become possible.
1990	Recombinant factor VIII becomes a biotechnology product. The product eliminates the risk of infection from donated plasma.
1999	The first successful gene therapy uses a viral vector given to the patient intravenously. See the reading in Chapter 2, page 35.
2001	In new gene therapy trials, culture cells (fibroblasts) are taken from a patient with DNA for clotting factor VIII. The cells are reimplanted into abdominal fat; four of six patients improve.

Gene Therapy

Gene therapy is the insertion of genetic material into human cells to treat a disorder. As you can see from Table 3.4, biotechnology offers the possibility of treating a genetic disorder in two ways: by supplying the protein that is needed (e.g., clotting factor VIII in hemophiliacs) or by carrying out gene therapy. Instead of supplying the needed protein, gene therapy supplies a normal gene that specifies the protein that is needed to be healthy.

Two means of gene therapy are *ex vivo* gene therapy and *in vivo* gene therapy. In **ex vivo gene therapy,** cells are altered outside the body and then returned to the body. During **in vivo gene therapy,** either a vector carrying the gene or the gene itself is introduced directly into the body.

Ex Vivo Gene Therapy

The young people featured in Figure 3.17 were born with a rare immune disorder called SCID (severe combined immunodeficiency). SCID patients lack the ability to produce a critical enzyme known as ADA (adenosine deaminase), and consequently their white blood cells are unable to fight infections. One possible method of treating this genetic disorder is shown in Figure 3.18. Bone marrow stem cells divide to produce many cells, some of which go on to become white blood cells. When bone marrow stem cells are genetically engineered, they give rise to white blood cells that also carry the effective gene and therefore are able to fight infections.

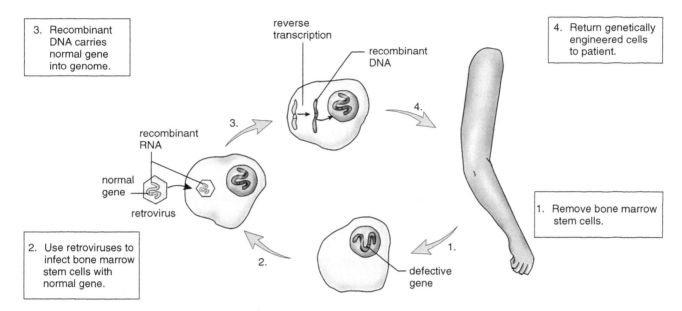

3. Recombinant DNA carries normal gene into genome.

reverse transcription

recombinant DNA

4. Return genetically engineered cells to patient.

recombinant RNA

normal gene

retrovirus

2. Use retroviruses to infect bone marrow stem cells with normal gene.

1. Remove bone marrow stem cells.

defective gene

Figure 3.18   **Ex vivo gene therapy in humans.**
Bone marrow stem cells are withdrawn from the body, a virus is used to insert a normal gene into them, and then they are returned to the body.

Bone marrow stem cells are removed from the blood and infected with a virus that carries a normal gene for the enzyme. Then the cells are returned to the patient. Bone marrow stem cells are preferred for this procedure because they divide to produce more cells with the same genes. Patients who have undergone this procedure show significantly improved immune function associated with a sustained rise in the level of ADA enzyme activity in the blood.

Among the many gene therapy trials, one is for the treatment of familial hypercholesterolemia, a condition that develops when liver cells lack a receptor protein for removing cholesterol from the blood. The high levels of blood cholesterol make the patient subject to fatal heart attacks at a young age. A small portion of the liver is surgically excised and then infected with a virus containing a normal gene for the receptor before being returned to the patient. Several patients have experienced lowered serum cholesterol levels following this procedure.

In Vivo Gene Therapy

Because of a genetic defect, children with Canavan disease accumulate a chemical in the brain that destroys the normal coating of nerve cells. Symptoms, including rapidly increasing head circumference, lack of head control, and abnormal muscle tone, begin to appear at about 3 to 9 months of age. In vivo gene therapy has been tried and appears to be successful in these patients. A virus has been used to introduce the required gene directly into the brain.

Cystic fibrosis patients lack a gene that codes for the transmembrane carrier of the chloride ion. They often die due to numerous infections of the respiratory tract. In gene therapy trials, the gene needed to cure cystic fibrosis is sprayed into the nose or delivered to the lower respiratory tract by adenoviruses or by the use of liposomes, microscopic vesicles that spontaneously form when lipoproteins are put into a solution. Investigators are trying to improve uptake, and are also hypothesizing that a combination of all three vectors might be more successful.

Genes are being used to treat medical conditions such as poor coronary circulation. It has been known for some time that VEGF (vascular endothelial growth factor) can cause the growth of new blood vessels. The gene that codes for this growth factor can be injected alone or within a virus into the heart to stimulate branching of coronary blood vessels. The adult in Figure 3.17 reports that he has less chest pain and can run longer on a treadmill as a result of this type of gene therapy.

Gene therapy is increasingly used as a part of cancer therapy. In one study, a virus carrying a gene that is normally not present in cancer cells was injected directly into the tumors of lung cancer patients. This gene, which helps regulate the cell cycle and brings about the death of cells with damaged DNA, is often mutated in tumor cells. No cures were reported, but the tumors shrank in three patients and stopped growing in three others. Genes are also being used to make healthy cells more tolerant of chemotherapy, and to make tumors more vulnerable to chemotherapy.

The Human Genome

A **genome** is all the genetic information in all the chromosomes of an individual. For several years now, scientists have been engaged in an analysis of the human genome called the Human Genome Project. The goals of this project were to map the human chromosomes in two ways. First, researchers wanted to construct a map that shows the sequence of base pairs along our chromosomes. (Recall that in DNA, base A is always paired with base T, and base G is always paired with base C.) Second, they wanted to construct a map that shows the sequence of genes along the human chromosomes. As you know, each gene has a particular location on a particular chromosome.

The Base Sequence Map

Researchers have now reached their first goal. They know the sequence of the three billion base pairs, one after the other, along the length of the human chromosomes. It took some 15 years to complete this monumental task. Two rival groups have been at work on the project. The International Human Genome Sequencing Consortium, which consists of laboratories in many different countries, depends on the support of public funds, including substantial contributions from the United States government. Celera Genomics, a private company that is supported by a pharmaceutical firm, has been sequencing the genome for only a few years. These competing groups used slightly different techniques, but their data match.

Even though we now know the sequence of bases in the human genome, much work still needs to be done to make sense out of what we have discovered. Thus far, we know that there is little difference between the sequence of our bases and that of other organisms whose DNA sequences are also known. From this we can conclude that we share a large number of genes with much simpler organisms, including bacteria! It's possible that eventually we will discover that human uniqueness is due to the regulation of these genes.

The Genetic Map

A genetic map depicts the locations of genes along each chromosome. The map in Figure 3.19 shows our current knowledge of the loci of significant mutant genes on human chromosome 17. Many genes have had their loci determined. Still, today we do not know the sequence of all the genes on any particular chromosome.

Completing the chromosomal genetic map should accelerate now that the base sequence map is done. Researchers need only know a short sequence of bases in a gene of interest in order for the computer to search the genome for a match. Then, the computer can tell the researcher where this gene is located.

A question still being hotly debated concerns the total number of human genes. Much of our DNA consists of nucleotide repeats that do not code for a protein. So far, researchers have found only 30,000 genes that code for proteins. This number seems terribly low; that is, a roundworm has 20,000 genes, so a human, which is certainly more complex than a roundworm, should have many more genes. Some researchers think more genes are yet to be identified. Others, believing they have found most of our genes, speculate that each of these genes could code for about three proteins, simply by using different combinations of exons.

As discussed in the reading on page 55, researchers hope that mapping the human chromosomes will help them not only discover mutant genes for many more human disorders but also develop medicines to treat these disorders. In addition, it may be possible to locate genes suitable for gene therapy to cure human illnesses or to enhance a phenotype. Such genes might be inserted into the egg before it is fertilized.

Many ethical questions arise regarding how our knowledge of the human genome should be used. Therefore, it is imperative that everyone be educated about the human genome, because in the end everyone in our society should help decide these issues.

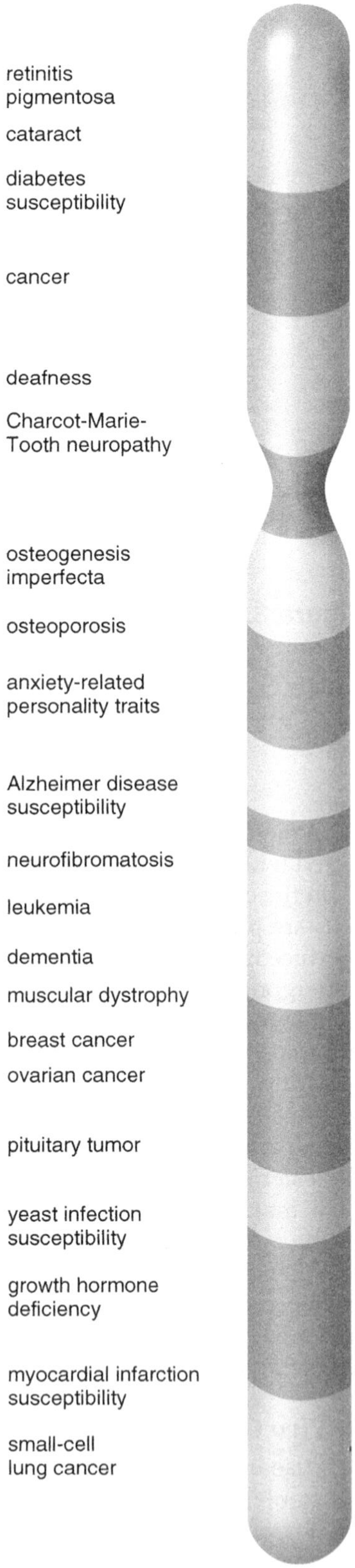

retinitis pigmentosa

cataract

diabetes susceptibility

cancer

deafness

Charcot-Marie-Tooth neuropathy

osteogenesis imperfecta

osteoporosis

anxiety-related personality traits

Alzheimer disease susceptibility

neurofibromatosis

leukemia

dementia

muscular dystrophy

breast cancer

ovarian cancer

pituitary tumor

yeast infection susceptibility

growth hormone deficiency

myocardial infarction susceptibility

small-cell lung cancer

Figure 3.19 **Genetic map of chromosome 17.**
This map shows the sequence of mutant genes that cause the diseases noted.

New Cures on the Horizon

Now that we know the sequence of the bases in the DNA of all the human chromosomes, biologists all over the world believe this knowledge will result in rapid medical advances for ourselves and our children.

First prediction: Many new medicines will be available.

Most drugs are either proteins or small chemicals that are able to interact with proteins. In the past, drugs were often discovered in a hit-or-miss fashion, but now researchers will be able to take a more systematic approach to finding effective medicines. In a recent search for a medicine that makes wounds heal, researchers cultured skin cells with 14 proteins (found by chance) that can cause skin cells to grow. Only one of these proteins made skin cells grow and did nothing else. They expect this protein to become an effective drug for conditions such as venous ulcers, which are skin lesions that affect many thousands of people in the United States. Tests leading to effective medicines can be carried out with many more proteins, which scientists will discover by scanning the human genome.

Second prediction: Medicines will be safer due to genome scans.

Genome scans are expected to make drugs safer to take. As you know, many drugs potentially have unwanted side effects. Why do some people and not others experience one or more of the side effects? Most likely, because people have different genotypes. In the future, it is expected that physicians will be able to match patients to drugs that are safe for them on the basis of their genotypes.

The use of a gene chip will quickly and efficiently provide knowledge of your genotype. A gene chip is an array of thousands of genes on one or several glass slides packaged together. After a gene chip contains an individual's DNA, a technician can note any mutant sequences present in the individual's genes.

One study found that various combinations of mutations can lead to the development of asthma. A particular drug, called albuterol, is effective and safe for asthmatic patients with a certain combination of mutations and not others. This example and others show that many diseases are polygenic, and that only a genome scan is able to detect which mutations are causing an individual to have a disease, and how it should be properly treated.

Third prediction: A longer and healthier life will be yours.

Stem cell gene therapy, described in Figure 3.18, may become routine once we discover the genes that contribute to a longer and healthier life. We know that the presence of free radicals causes cellular molecules to become unstable and cells to die. Certain genes are believed to code for antioxidant enzymes that detoxify free radicals. It is possible that human beings with particular forms of these genes have more efficient antioxidant enzymes, and therefore live longer. If so, researchers will no doubt be able to locate these genes as well as others that promote a longer, healthier life.

Perhaps certain genotypes allow some people to live far beyond the normal life span. Researchers may be able to find which genes allow individuals to live a long time and make them available to the general public. Then many more people would live longer and healthier lives.

Fourth prediction: You will be able to design your children.

Genome sequence data will be used to identify many more mutant genes that cause genetic disorders than are presently known. In the future, it may be possible to cure genetic disorders before the child is born by adding a normal gene to any egg that carries a mutant gene. Or, an artificial chromosome, constructed to carry a large number of corrective genes, could automatically be placed into eggs. In vitro fertilization would have to be utilized to take advantage of such measures for curing genetic disorders before conception.

Genome sequence data can also be used to identify polygenic genes for traits such as height, intelligence, and behavioral characteristics. A couple could decide on their own which genes they wish to use to enhance a child's phenotype. In other words, the sequencing of the human genome may bring about a genetically just society, in which all types of genes would be accessible to all parents.

Figure 3A
Benefits of the Human Genome Project.
A more carefree life is predicted for us because of the Human Genome Project.

Bioethical Focus

Genetic Profiling

In the future, your genetic profile is expected to tell physicians which diseases you are likely to develop. For example, knowledge of your genes might indicate your susceptibility to various types of cancer. This information could be used to develop a prevention program, including the avoidance of environmental influences associated with the disease. No doubt, you would be less inclined to smoke if you knew your genes make it almost inevitable that smoking will give you lung cancer.

People worry, however, that their genetic profile could be used against them. Perhaps employers will not hire, or insurance companies will not insure, those who have a propensity for particular diseases. About 25 states have passed laws prohibiting genetic discrimination by health insurers, and 11 states have passed laws prohibiting genetic discrimination by employers. Is such legislation enough to allay our fears of discrimination?

On the other hand, employers may fear that one day they will be required to provide an environment specific to every employee's need for preventing future illness. Would you approve of this, or should individuals be required to leave an area or job that exposes them to an environmental factor that could be detrimental to their health?

People's medical records are usually considered private. But if scientists could match genetic profiles to environmental conditions that bring on illnesses, they would come up with better prevention guidelines for the next generation. Should genetic profiles and health records become public information under these circumstances? It would particularly help in the study of complex diseases such as cardiovascular disorders, non-insulin-dependent diabetes mellitus, and juvenile rheumatoid arthritis.

Figure 3B   Genetic profiling.
Will genetic profiling become a standard part of routine medical examinations in the future?

Decide Your Opinion

1. Should people be encouraged—or even required—to have their genes analyzed so that they can develop programs to possibly prevent future illness?
2. Should employers be encouraged or required to provide an environment suitable to a person's genetic profile? Or should the individual avoid a work environment that could bring on an illness?
3. How can we balance individual rights with the public health benefit of matching genetic profiles to appropriate environments?

Summary

3.1 DNA and RNA Structure and Function
DNA is a double helix composed of two nucleic acid strands that are held together by weak hydrogen bonds between the bases: A is bonded to T, and C is bonded to G. During replication, the DNA strands unzip, and then a new complementary strand forms opposite each old strand. This results in two identical DNA molecules.

RNA is a single-stranded nucleic acid in which U (uracil) occurs instead of T (thymine). Both DNA and RNA are involved in gene expression.

3.2 Gene Expression
Proteins differ from one another by the sequence of their amino acids. DNA has a code that specifies this sequence. Gene expression requires transcription and translation. During transcription, the DNA code (triplet of three bases) is passed to an mRNA that then contains codons. Introns are removed from mRNA during

mRNA processing. During translation, tRNA molecules bind to their amino acids, and then their anticodons pair with mRNA codons. In the end, each protein has a sequence of amino acids according to the blueprint provided by the sequence of nucleotides in DNA.

Today, we know that genetic mutations are a change in the sequence of bases in DNA. Two well-exemplified types of mutations that can affect the phenotype are point mutations and frameshift mutations. In point mutations, a single nucleotide (and consequently, a base) has changed. In frameshift mutations, an insertion or deletion of a single base has changed the genetic message entirely. Genetic diseases are often inborn errors of metabolism because the inheritance of a faulty genetic code leads to a defective enzyme, as in PKU and albinism. Mutated genes for structural proteins can also have a dramatic effect, as in androgen (e.g., testosterone) insensitivity.

3.3 Biotechnology

Biotechnology includes genetic engineering and other techniques that make use of natural biological systems to produce a product or to achieve an end desired by human beings.

Recombinant DNA contains DNA from two different sources. A restriction enzyme is used to cleave both plasmid DNA and foreign DNA. The "sticky ends" produced facilitate the insertion of foreign DNA into vector DNA. The foreign gene is sealed into the vector DNA by DNA ligase. Both bacterial plasmids and viruses can be used as vectors to carry foreign genes into host cells. This technology has permitted the mass production of human proteins that are sold as commercial products.

PCR uses the enzyme DNA polymerase to quickly make multiple copies of a specific piece (target) of DNA. Because of PCR only a small amount of DNA is needed to determine DNA base sequences or to carry out DNA fingerprinting.

Gene therapy is the insertion of genetic material into human cells to treat a disorder. Successful gene therapy has been carried out for SCID (severe combined immunodeficiency) utilizing an ex vivo methodology and for Canavan disease utilizing an in vivo method.

Due to the Human Genome Project, researchers now know the sequence of the base pairs along the length of the human chromosomes. So far, researchers have found only 30,000 genes that code for proteins; the rest of our DNA consists of nucleotide repeats that do not code for a protein. Little difference seems to exist between the DNA sequence of our bases and those of other organisms that have also been studied. It's possible we will discover that humans' uniqueness is due to the regulation of their genes.

Researchers hope knowing the sequence of the human genome will help them discover the root causes of many illnesses. Also, it may lead to the development of specific drugs based on DNA differences between individuals.

Reviewing the Chapter

1. Describe the structure of DNA. What does the term *complementary base pairing* mean? 41
2. Explain how DNA replicates itself. 42
3. How does DNA structure differ from RNA structure? 43

4. What are the different types of RNA, and how do they function? 43
5. Describe the structure of proteins. How many different types of amino acids make up proteins? 44
6. Explain gene expression, starting with DNA and finishing with the protein. Be sure to mention the terms code, codon, anticodon, mRNA, tRNA, amino acids, and ribosomes in your answer. 44–48
7. If ATCGTACCG were in DNA, what would the triplet code be? The codons? The anticodons? 44
8. What is a genetic mutation? A point mutation? A frameshift mutation? 49
9. Explain how bacteria can be genetically engineered using recombinant DNA technology. 50
10. What is the polymerase chain reaction? DNA fingerprinting? 51
11. Give examples of both ex vivo and in vivo gene therapy in children. 52–53
12. What are two possible types of maps of our chromosomes? Which one has been completed? What benefits are expected for human beings? 54–55

Critical Thinking Questions

1. A card file stores information and so does DNA. Comparing these two, the piece of furniture that holds the card file, the cards, and the letters on the cards are each equivalent to what in the organism? DNA stores information for what?
2. Considering that there are many different types of living things, why is it beneficial that DNA can mutate?
3. It is possible to produce a transgenic plant that contains a functioning animal gene. What does this tell you about plant cells?

Understanding Key Terms

adenine (A) 41
anticodon 46
biotechnology 50
codon 44
complementary base pairing 41
cytosine (C) 41
DNA (deoxyribonucleic acid) 40
DNA fingerprinting 51
DNA ligase 50
DNA polymerase 42
ex vivo gene therapy 52
frameshift mutation 49
gene therapy 52
genetic engineering 50
genetic mutation 49
genome 54
guanine (G) 41
in vivo gene therapy 52
messenger RNA (mRNA) 43
mutation 42
plasmid 50
point mutation 49
polymerase chain reaction (PCR) 51
polyribosome 46
recombinant DNA (rDNA) 50
replication 42
restriction enzyme 50
ribosomal RNA (rRNA) 43
RNA (ribonucleic acid) 43
RNA polymerase 45
template 42
thymine (T) 41
transcription 45
transfer RNA (tRNA) 43
translation 46
triplet code 45
uracil (U) 43
vector 50

Chapter 4

Genetic Counseling

4.1 Viewing the Chromosomes for Genetic Counseling

Now that potential parents are becoming aware that many illnesses are caused by abnormal chromosomal inheritance or by faulty genes, more couples are seeking genetic counseling. For example, they might be prompted to seek counseling if several relatives have a particular medical condition, if the woman has experienced several miscarriages, or if they already have a child with a genetic defect.

During **genetic counseling**, the counselor helps determine the genotype of prospective parents and whether an unborn child will have a genetic disorder. The counselor usually begins by asking questions about the family's medical history. Then s(he) recommends a suitable course of action regarding chromosomal and genetic testing. For example, it is well known that the chance of having a child with a trisomy (three chromosomes of one type) increases as a mother ages, particularly beyond 35. The chances of an offspring having Down syndrome (trisomy 21, see Chapter 1, page 16) are one in 1,200 for women in their 20s, one in 400 by age 35, and one in 100 at age 40. Therefore, if a woman older than 35 is pregnant, the genetic counselor routinely recommends amniocentesis or chorionic villi sampling in order to view the chromosomes of the fetus.

Amniocentesis

Amniocentesis is a procedure for obtaining a sample of amniotic fluid from the uterus of a pregnant woman. Amniocentesis is usually not performed until about the twelfth week of pregnancy. Guided by ultrasound, a long, thin needle is passed through the abdominal and uterine walls to withdraw a small amount of fluid, which contains fetal cells (Fig. 4.1a).

Analyzing the chromosomes may be delayed as long as four weeks so that the cells can be cultured to increase their number. Aside from analyzing the chromosomes for abnormalities, biochemical tests can be done on the amniotic fluid. For example, if a chemical called alpha fetoprotein (AFP) is present in excess, the fetus many have a neural tube defect (malformation of the spinal cord or brain).

Because the risk of spontaneous abortion increases by about 0.5% due to amniocentesis, doctors only use the procedure if it is medically warranted.

Chorionic Villi Sampling

Chorionic villi sampling (CVS) is a procedure for obtaining a sample of chorionic villi, a fetal tissue that forms part of the placenta. This procedure can be done as early as the fifth week of pregnancy. A long, thin suction tube is inserted through the vagina into the uterus (Fig. 4.1b). Ultrasound, which gives a picture of the uterine contents, is used to place the tube between the uterine lining and the chorionic villi. Then a sampling of chorionic villi is obtained by suction. Because tissue, rather than individual cells, is obtained, an analysis can be done immediately. This sampling procedure does not include any amniotic fluid, so the biochemical tests done on the amniotic fluid following amniocentesis are not possible. Also, CVS carries a greater risk of spontaneous abortion than amniocentesis—0.8% compared to 0.5%. The advantage of CVS is in getting the results of chromosome analysis sooner—at about 10 days for CVS compared to about 20 days for amniocentesis.

Karyotyping

A **karyotype** is a visual display of the chromosomes arranged by size, shape, and banding pattern. Normally, as you know, males and females have 23 pairs of chromosomes; 22 pairs are autosomes, and one pair is the sex chromosomes. The sex chromosomes of females are XX, and those of males are XY.

After a cell sample has been obtained, the cells are stimulated to divide in a culture medium. A chemical is used to stop mitosis during metaphase when chromosomes are the most highly compacted and condensed. The cells are then killed, spread on a microscope slide, and dried. Stains are applied to the slides, and the cells are photographed. Staining produces dark and light cross-bands of varying widths, which can be used in addition to size and shape to help pair up the chromosomes. Today, a computer is used to arrange the chromosomes in pairs (Fig. 4.1c). A television camera and a computer are linked to a microscope. As the microscope views the chromosomes, their images are recorded by the camera, digitized, and transmitted to the computer, which arranges them into a karyotype.

Figure 4.1d,e compares a normal karyotype with that of a fetus who has Down syndrome. Many other types of chromosomal abnormalities can also be detected by doing a karyotype.

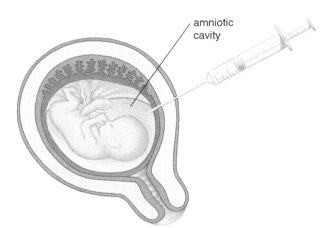

amniotic cavity

a. During amniocentesis, a long needle is used to withdraw amniotic fluid containing fetal cells.

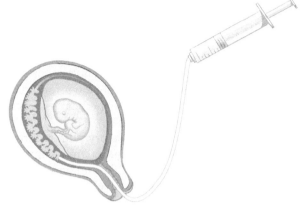

b. During chorionic villi sampling, a suction tube is used to remove cells from the chorion, where the placenta will develop.

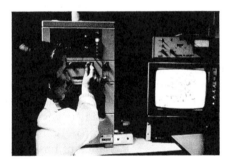

c. Cells are microscopically examined and photographed. Computer arranges the chromosomes into pairs.

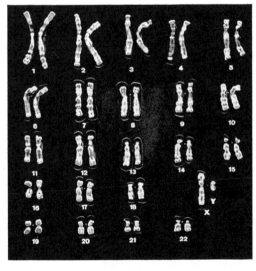

d. Normal male karyotype with 46 chromosomes

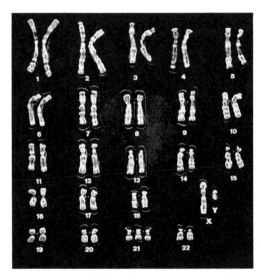

e. Down syndrome karyotype with an extra chromosome 21

Figure 4.1   Human karyotype preparation.

A karyotype is an arrangement of an individual's chromosomes into numbered pairs according to their size, shape, and banding pattern. **a.** Amniocentesis and **(b)** chorionic villi sampling provide cells for karyotyping to determine if the unborn child has a chromosomal abnormality. **c.** After cells are treated as described in the text, a computer constructs the karyotype. **d.** Karyotype of a normal male. **e.** Karyotype of a male with Down syndrome. A Down syndrome karyotype has three number 21 chromosomes.

4.2 Analyzing the Family History

Even if no chromosomal abnormality is likely, amniocentesis still might be done because it is now possible to perform chromosomal and biochemical tests to detect over 400 different genetic disorders in the fetus. The genetic counselor determines ahead of time what tests might be warranted. To do this, the counselor needs to know the medical history of the family in order to construct a pedigree.

A **pedigree** is a chart of a family's history with regard to a particular genetic trait. In the chart, males are designated by squares and females by circles. Shaded circles and squares are affected individuals; they have a genetic disorder. A line between a square and a circle represents a union. A vertical line going downward leads directly to a single child; if there are more children, they are placed off a horizontal line.

Autosomal Dominant and Recessive Disorders

From the counselor's knowledge of genetic disorders, s(he) might already know if an inherited trait is autosomal dominant, autosomal recessive, or X-linked recessive. If not, the pedigree might help the counselor decide the pattern of inheritance.

Could the following pattern of inheritance represent an autosomal dominant or an autosomal recessive characteristic?

In this pattern, the child is affected, but neither parent is; this can only happen if the disorder is recessive and the parents are *Aa*. Notice that the parents are **carriers** because they are unaffected but are capable of having a child with the genetic disorder. If the family pedigree suggests that the parents are carriers for an autosomal recessive disorder, the counselor might suggest confirming this by doing the appropriate genetic test. Then, if the parents so desire, prenatal (before birth) testing for the genetic disorder might also be done.

See Figure 4.2 for other ways that a counselor may recognize an autosomal recessive pattern of inheritance. After studying these carefully, construct a pedigree that illustrates the example. Notice that in the pedigree shown in Figure 4.2, cousins are the parents of three children, two of whom have the disorder. Aside from illustrating that reproduction between cousins is more likely to bring out recessive traits, this pedigree also illustrates that "chance has no memory"; therefore, each child born to heterozygous parents has a 25% chance of having the disorder. In other words, it is possible that if a heterozygous couple has four children, each child might have the condition.

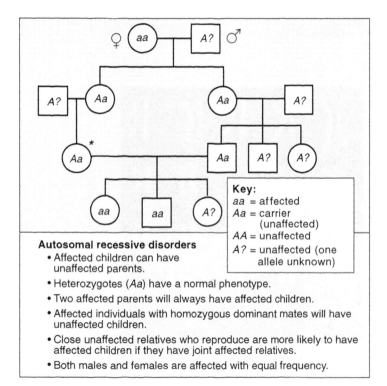

Figure 4.2   Autosomal recessive pedigree chart.
The list gives ways to recognize an autosomal recessive disorder.
How would you know that the individual at the * is heterozygous?[1]

[1]See Appendix B for answers.

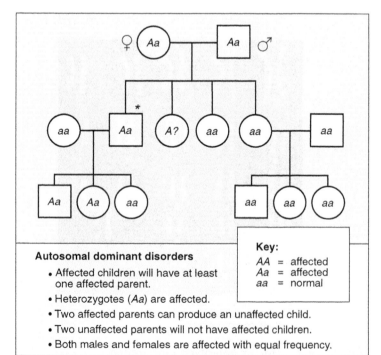

Figure 4.3   Autosomal dominant pedigree chart.
The list gives ways to recognize an autosomal dominant disorder.
How would you know that the individual at the * is heterozygous?[1]

Now consider this pattern of inheritance:

In this pattern, the child is unaffected, but the parents are both affected. This can happen if the condition is autosomal dominant and the parents are *Aa*. Figure 4.3 illustrates other ways to recognize an autosomal dominant pattern of inheritance. This pedigree illustrates that when both parents are unaffected, all their children are unaffected. Why? Because neither parent has a dominant gene that causes the condition to pass on.

Sex-Linked Disorders

Sex-linked disorders can be carried on the X or Y chromosome.

X-Linked Disorders

Figure 4.4 gives a pedigree chart for an *X-linked recessive disorder*. Recall that sons inherit an X-linked recessive allele from their mothers because their fathers gave them a Y chromosome. More males than females have the trait because recessive alleles on the X chromosome are always expressed in males—the Y chromosome lacks an allele for the disorder. Females who have the condition inherited the allele from both their mother and their father, and all the sons of such a female will have the condition.

If a male has an X-linked recessive condition, his daughters are carriers; therefore, the condition often passes from grandfather to grandson. Figure 4.4 lists other ways to recognize a recessive X-linked disorder.

Only a few known traits are *X-linked dominant traits*. If a condition is X-linked dominant, affected males pass the trait *only* to daughters, who have a 100% chance of having the condition. If the condition is autosomal dominant, affected males pass the trait to both sons and daughters. Heterozygous females pass an X-linked dominant trait to *both* sons and daughters, but each has a 50% chance of escaping the condition. After all, they could inherit a recessive allele from both the father and the mother.

Y-Linked Disorders

A few known genetic disorders are carried on the Y chromosome. One that is well known is involved in determining gender during development. Others code for membrane proteins, including an enzyme that regulates the movement of ADP into and ATP out of mitochondria!

How would a counselor recognize a Y-linked pattern of inheritance? Y-linked conditions are present only in males and are passed directly from father to *all* sons because males inherit a Y chromosome from their fathers.

Unusual Inheritance Patterns

No doubt a genetic counselor will occasionally come across some rather unusual inheritance patterns. As an example, the reading on page 62 discusses the inheritance pattern for fragile X syndrome. Also, recall that the mother passes mutated mitochondrial genes to all her offspring because only the egg donates cytoplasm to an offspring (see Chapter 1, page 14).

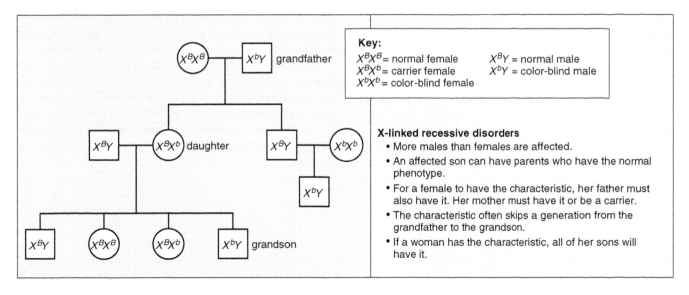

Figure 4.4   X-linked recessive pedigree chart.
The list gives ways of recognizing an X-linked recessive disorder—in this case, color blindness.

Of Special Interest

Pedigree for Fragile X Syndrome

Fragile X syndrome is one of the most common genetic causes of mental retardation, second only to Down syndrome. It affects about one in 1,500 males and one in 2,500 females and is seen in all ethnic groups. It is called fragile X syndrome because its diagnosis used to be dependent upon observing an X chromosome whose tip is attached to the rest of the chromosome by a thin thread (Fig. 4A*a*).

The inheritance pattern of fragile X syndrome is not like any other pattern we have studied (Fig. 4A*b*). The chance of being affected increases in successive generations almost as if the pattern of inheritance switches from being recessive to dominant. Then, too, an unaffected grandfather can have grandchildren with the disorder; in other words, he is a carrier for an X-linked disease. This is contrary to normality—we have learned that males with mutant alleles on the X chromosome always show the disorder!

In 1991, the DNA sequence at the fragile site was isolated and found to have base triplet repeats: CGG was repeated over and over again. An unaffected person has only 6 to 50 repeats, while a person with fragile X syndrome has 230 to 2,000 repeats. This mutation affects a gene located at the site, and the result is mental retardation. Carrier males have an intermediate number of repeats—from 50 to 230 copies. A female who inherits this number of repeats from her father may have mild symptoms of retardation, and her sons may have fragile X syndrome. Therefore, anyone with an intermediate number of repeats is said to have a premutation. And premutations can lead to full-blown mutations in future generations (Fig. 4A*b*).

Why do females with a premutation pass on a full-blown mutation while males with a premutation do not? According to the genomic imprinting hypothesis, the sperm and egg carry chromosomes that have been "imprinted" differently. Imprinting is believed to occur during gamete formation, and thereafter the genes are expressed one way if donated by the father and another way if donated by the mother. Perhaps when we discover why more repeats are passed on by one parent than the other, we will discover the cause of so-called genomic imprinting.

This type of mutation—called by some a dynamic mutation because it changes, and by others an expanded trinucleotide repeat because the number of triplet copies increases—is now known to characterize other conditions. Huntington disease is

a. Fragile X chromosome

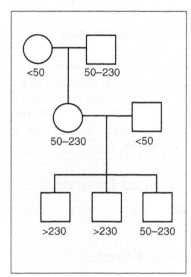

b. Inheritance pattern for fragile X syndrome

Figure 4A   Pedigree for fragile X syndrome.
a. An arrow points out the fragile site of this X chromosome.
b. The numbers indicate the number of base triplet repeats at the fragile site. A grandfather who has a premutation with 50–230 repeats has no symptoms but transmits the condition to his grandsons through his daughter. Two grandsons have full-blown mutations with more than 230 base repeats.

caused by a base triplet repeat of CAG that is more likely to be inherited from the paternal parent.

What might cause repeats to occur in the first place, and why does this cause a syndrome? Repeats might arise during DNA replication prior to cell division, and their presence undoubtedly leads to nonfunctioning or malfunctioning proteins.

Scientists have developed a new technique that can identify repeats in DNA, and testing for repeats should help genetic counselors know when to expect an unusual type of inheritance pattern for a disorder. If the woman has family members with fragile X, she will be more concerned than if the man has family members with fragile X. The opposite is the case for Huntington disease.

4.3 Testing for Genetic Disorders

Prospective parents often want to know if they are carriers for one of the recessive disorders that runs in their family. Following genetic testing, if warranted, a genetic counselor can explain to them the chances that a child of theirs will have the disorder (see Figs. 2.4 and 2.5). If a woman is already pregnant, the parents may want to know if the unborn child has the disorder. If the woman is not pregnant, the parents may opt for testing of the egg or embryo before it is introduced into the uterus for further development.

Types of Genetic Testing

Today, genetic testing is often done on an egg, on an embryo, on an unborn fetus, on newborns, and on adults. There are two types of genetic testing: biochemical testing and DNA testing.

Testing for a Protein

Biochemical testing is done for genetic diseases that are caused by a missing enzyme or by an abnormal end product of metabolism due to a missing enzyme. For example, babies with Tay-Sachs disease, which is described in Chapter 2 and in Table 4.1, lack an enzyme called hexosaminidase A (hex A). The laboratory is able to test for the quantity of hex A in a sample of cells and from that determine whether the individual is likely homozygous normal, is a carrier, or has Tay-Sachs disease. Biochemical tests are not as definitive as DNA testing, however.

Testing DNA

Two types of DNA testing are possible. One type uses a genetic marker, and the other uses a DNA probe.

Genetic Markers As an example, consider that individuals with sickle-cell trait or Huntington disease have an abnormality in the sequence of their bases at a particular location on a chromosome. This difference is a **genetic marker.** Recall that restriction enzymes (see Chapter 3, page 50) cleave DNA at particular base sequences. Therefore, the fragments that result after the use of a restriction enzyme may be different in people who have a gene mutation compared to those who do not have the mutation (Fig. 4.5).

DNA Probes A **DNA probe** is a piece of single-stranded DNA that will bind to a complementary piece of DNA. In this instance, the DNA probe will bind to the genetic mutation of interest. The newest technology utilizes a DNA chip that can test for many genetic diseases at a time. A DNA chip is a very small glass square that contains several rows of DNA probes. To do the testing, the DNA sample is cut into smaller pieces using restriction enzymes, and the fragments are tagged with a fluorescent dye and converted to single strands before being applied to the chip (Fig. 4.6). Fragments that bear a mutation will bind to the probes and can be detected by a laser scanner.

Testing the Fetus

If a woman is already pregnant and the couple wants to test fetal cells for a genetic disorder, fetal cells may be acquired through amniocentesis or chorionic villi sampling, or fetal cells that have leaked into the mother's bloodstream may be tested. We have already discussed amniocentesis and chorionic villi sampling on page 58. Testing fetal cells in the mother's blood is a new and rarely used procedure that is described in the reading on page 64.

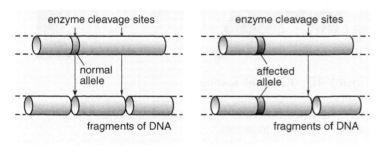

a. Normal fragmentation pattern   b. Genetic disorder fragmentation pattern

Figure 4.5 **Use of a genetic marker to test for a genetic mutation.**
a. In this example, DNA from a normal individual has certain restriction enzyme cleavage sites. **b.** DNA from another individual lacks one of the cleavage sites, and this loss indicates that the person has a mutated gene. In heterozygotes, half of their DNA would have the cleavage site and half would not have it. (In other instances, the gain in a cleavage site could be an indication of a mutation.)

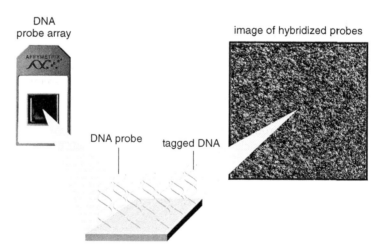

Figure 4.6 **Use of a DNA chip to test for mutated genes.**
This DNA chip contains rows of DNA probes for mutations that indicate the presence of a particular genetic disorder. If single-stranded DNA fragments derived from an individual's DNA bind to a probe, the individual has the mutation. Heterozygotes would not have as much binding as homozygotes.

Prenatal Genetic Test Analyzes DNA from Fetal Cells

Researchers at Howard Hughes Medical Institute (HHMI) have designed a prenatal blood test to diagnose a fetus at risk for developing sickle-cell anemia or β-thalassemia.

To test a fetus for a genetic disorder, doctors collect fetal cells that may contain DNA with telltale disease-causing mutations. Getting these fetal cells is tricky. Today's techniques—amniocentesis and chorionic villi sampling—require physicians to use a needle to gather fetal cells on or in the amniotic sac surrounding the fetus. These invasive procedures carry a small risk for the fetus.

For years, researchers have studied ways to isolate fetal cells that leak into a mother's bloodstream during pregnancy. Until now, technical hurdles—such as finding the right kind of fetal cell and gathering enough to study—hampered these efforts. But Yuet Wai Kan (Fig. 4B), a Hughes investigator at the University of California in San Francisco, and his colleagues have now overcome the hurdles.

Kan's team zeroes in on the fetal erythroblast, a short-lived nucleated red blood cell that migrates into a mother's bloodstream. Using blood drawn from two pregnant women whose fetuses were at risk for β-thalassemia and sickle-cell anemia, the researchers separated maternal and fetal erythroblasts from other cells based on certain physical properties of the cell. Next, they applied an antibody (a chemical) that recognizes fetal or embryonic hemoglobin and turns the fetal cell red. HHMI research associate Mei-Chi Cheung then pooled the red cells and amplified their DNA for analysis. According to Kan's test, neither fetus was affected by disease—a diagnosis independently confirmed by CVS. The results were reported in the November 1996 issue of *Nature Genetics*.

Kan has been a pioneer in the field of hematology (the study of blood). In 1975, he discovered that a single missing gene causes α-thalassemia, a heritable blood disorder. Months later, his team developed the first prenatal DNA test for α-thalassemia.

In both types of thalassemia, a defective gene produces too little hemoglobin, resulting in anemia. People with thalassemia often descend from the Mediterranean region or from Asia. In the United States, sickle-cell disease is more common, affecting about 80,000 people, most of African American descent. In this disease, a defective gene produces abnormal rodlike hemoglobin molecules that cause the cells to become sickle-shaped and to plug blood vessels, restricting blood and oxygen supplies. As a result, patients suffer bouts of severe pain, organ damage, or stroke.

Like most geneticists, Kan isn't content merely to diagnose disease. He wants to treat it. "Genetic therapy is the real challenge," he says. "That's the next area of research." Kan and colleagues have designed a retroviral vector, or carrier, to shuttle healthy globin genes into a patient's cells. His vector strictly targets cells in which the gene is mutated—an improvement over most gene therapy vectors, which enter many cells, including healthy ones.

Figure 4B **Fetal cell testing.**
A research team led by Hughes investigator Yuet Wai Kan has developed a new technique to isolate and test fetal cells for the presence of genetic mutations.

Comparison of Methods for Obtaining Fetal Cells

Amniocentesis. Amniocentesis is not performed until a woman is at least twelve weeks (three months) pregnant. The major risk—loss of the fetus—is slightly less than for CVS. The wait for genetic testing of cells (about 20 days) is longer than for CVS. Amniotic fluid can be tested for alpha fetoprotein (AFP) to determine if the fetus has a neural tube defect.

Chorionic villi sampling (CVS). This procedure is done earlier than amniocentesis—as early as seven weeks. There is a slightly higher risk of a miscarriage, and the occurrence of induced fetal facial and limb abnormalities has been reported but not confirmed. Because no amniotic fluid is collected, the AFP test cannot be done. The wait for genetic test results (about 10 days) is less than that for amniocentesis.

Fetal cells in mother's blood. As early as nine weeks into the pregnancy, a small number of fetal cells can be isolated from the mother's blood using a cell sorter. The laboratory procedure is more complicated than for amniocentesis and CVS because only about 1/70,000 blood cells in a mother's blood are fetal cells. PCR (see Chapter 3, page 51) has to be used to amplify the DNA from the few cells collected. Only DNA tests can be done, but the procedure poses no risk to the fetus whatsoever.

If genetic testing indicates that the fetus has a serious genetic disorder, such as Tay-Sachs disease for which there is no cure, the parents may wish to consider an abortion. The Bioethical Focus at the end of this chapter considers whether an abortion is ever ethical or not.

Testing the Egg and Embryo

In vitro fertilization (IVF) is fertilization in laboratory glassware. The physician obtains eggs from the prospective mother (Fig. 4.7) and sperm from the prospective father and places them in the same receptacle, where fertilization occurs. Because IVF is now routinely performed, it is possible to test the egg before fertilization or the embryo after fertilization for any genetic disorder.

Testing the Egg

Recall that meiosis in females results in a single egg and at least two polar bodies (see Chapter 1). Polar bodies, which later disintegrate, receive very little cytoplasm, but they do receive a haploid number of chromosomes. When a woman is heterozygous for a recessive genetic disorder, about half the polar bodies will have received the mutated allele, and in these instances the egg received the normal allele. Therefore, if a polar body tests positive for a mutated allele, the egg received the normal allele. Only normal eggs will be used for IVF, and even if the sperm should happen to carry the mutation, the zygote (fertilized egg) will at worst be heterozygous. The phenotype will appear normal.

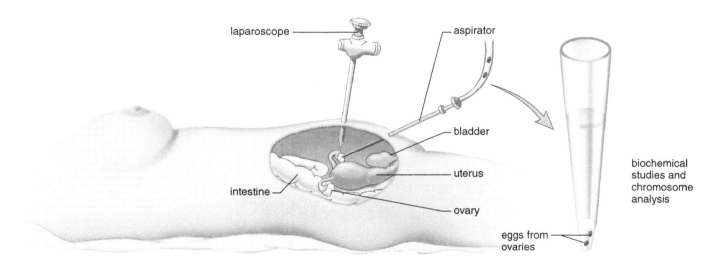

Figure 4.7 **Obtaining eggs for screening.**
Screening eggs for genetic defects is a new technique. Preovulatory eggs are removed by aspiration after a laparoscope (optical telescope) is inserted into the abdominal cavity through a small incision in the region of the navel. The first polar body is tested. If the woman is heterozygous (*Aa*) and the defective gene (*a*) is found in the polar body, then the egg must have received the normal gene (*A*). Normal eggs then undergo in vitro fertilization and are placed in the prepared uterus.

Testing the Embryo

A human is an embryo for the first two months of development and a fetus from the second through the ninth month of development. Suppose potential parents had or were carriers for one of the genetic disorders listed in Table 4.1. If so, wouldn't they want the assurance that their offspring would be free of this disorder? To provide this assurance, researchers have developed a way to test the embryo.

Following fertilization, the zygote begins to divide. Testing of the embryo occurs when the embryo has six to eight cells (Fig. 4.8). The removal of one of these cells for testing purposes has no effect on normal development. Only embryos that test negative for the genetic disorders of interest would then be placed in the uterus of the woman to continue developing to term.

So far, about 500 children free of alleles for genetic disorders that run in their families have been born worldwide following embryo testing. In the future, it's possible that embryo testing might be followed by gene therapy (see Chapter 3, page 52) so that any embryo could be allowed to continue to term. Furthermore, genes that control desirable traits such as musical or athletic ability might eventually be available for enhancement gene therapy.

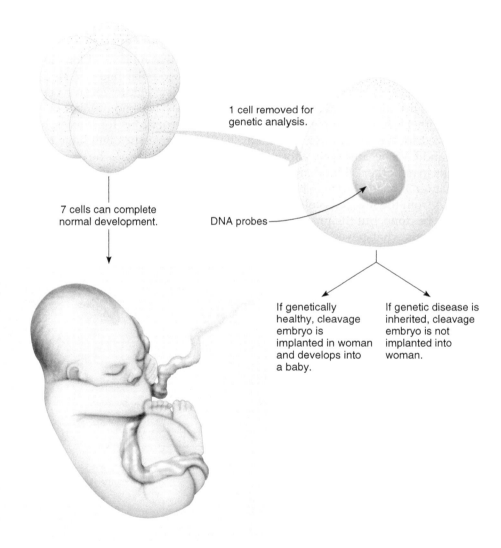

1 cell removed for genetic analysis.

7 cells can complete normal development.

DNA probes

If genetically healthy, cleavage embryo is implanted in woman and develops into a baby.

If genetic disease is inherited, cleavage embryo is not implanted into woman.

Figure 4.8   **Pre-pregnancy testing of embryo.**
Only if a cell removed from the 8-celled embryo is free of genetic mutations, such as those listed in Table 4.1, is the embryo introduced into the uterus to continue development.

Table 4.1 Tests and Treatments for Some Human Genetic Disorders

Name	Description	Chromosome	Incidence Among Newborns in the U.S.	Status
Autosomal Recessive Disorders				
Cystic fibrosis	Mucus in the lungs and digestive tract is thick and viscous, making breathing and digestion difficult	7	One in 2,500 Caucasians	DNA test available;* treatment being investigated
Tay-Sachs disease	Neurological impairment and psychomotor difficulties develop early, followed by blindness and uncontrollable seizures; death usually occurs before age 5	15	One in 3,600 Jews of eastern European descent	Biochemical test available*
Phenylketonuria	Inability to metabolize phenylalanine; if a special diet is not begun, mental retardation develops	12	One in 5,000 Caucasians	Biochemical test available; treatment available
Autosomal Dominant Disorders				
Neurofibromatosis	Benign tumors occur under the skin or deeper	17	One in 3,000	DNA test available*
Huntington disease	Minor disturbances in balance and coordination develop in middle age and progress toward severe neurological disturbances leading to death	4	One in 20,000	DNA test available*
Incomplete Dominance				
Sickle-cell disease	Poor circulation, anemia, internal hemorrhaging due to sickle-shaped red blood cells	11	One in 100 African Americans	DNA test available*
X-Linked Recessive				
Hemophilia A, B	Propensity for bleeding, often internally, due to the lack of a blood-clotting factor	X	One in 15,000 male births	DNA test available
Duchenne muscular dystrophy	Muscle weakness develops early and progressively intensifies until death occurs, usually before age 20	X	One in 5,000 male births	DNA test available; treatment being investigated

*Prenatal testing is done.

Bioethical Focus

Abortions

Whereas a miscarriage is the unexpected loss of an embryo or fetus, an abortion is the purposeful removal of an embryo or fetus from the uterus. Sometimes parents who are told their unborn child has a serious syndrome, such as Down syndrome, or an incurable genetic disorder, such as Tay-Sachs disease, decide to abort the pregnancy. Do you feel that an abortion is justified under these circumstances, or do you feel that abortions under these circumstances may lead to abortions for other reasons?

Whether to have an early abortion is at present a very personal decision. Should the decision remain personal, or do you think others should decide the matter? For example, a panel of physicians might decide whether it is medically appropriate for a woman to have an abortion. If a woman is forced to bear a child that has a serious disorder, should it then be institutionalized so that the government will care for it?

If abortions become tightly restricted or banned in a particular state, what should women who are pro-choice do? Should they bear unwanted children, go to another state where abortions are still legal, or have an illegal abortion in their own state? Poor women may not have the funds to travel to another state or to have an illegal abortion. Some pro-choice advocates suggest that pro-choice women form self-help groups in which all are trained in abortion techniques. What are the pros and cons of seeking such a dramatic recourse?

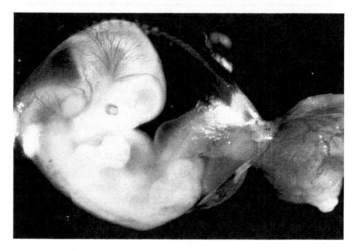

Figure 4C   Human embryo.
A human embryo after about six weeks of development.

Decide Your Opinion

1. When is an abortion justified—when the embryo is tested and found to have an incurable genetic disorder, or when the fetus is tested and found to have an incurable genetic disorder?
2. Who should decide whether a woman can have an abortion—the woman, a panel of medical experts, or the government?
3. If abortions should become illegal, how should women who have an illegal abortion be punished? Should they go to jail or suffer some other penalty?

Summary

4.1 Viewing the Chromosomes for Genetic Counseling
Genetic counseling helps prospective parents determine if genetic testing of themselves before pregnancy or of the fetus after pregnancy is warranted. If the counselor is concerned that a fetus could possibly have a chromosomal abnormality, s(he) will recommend viewing the chromosomes. Amniocentesis (collection of amniotic fluid from the uterus) and chorionic villi sampling (CVS; obtaining a tissue sample from the chorionic villi) are ways to acquire fetal cells for testing. Karyotyping is done to see if the fetus has a normal chromosomal inheritance.

4.2 Analyzing the Family History
A pedigree is a visual representation of the history of a genetic disorder in a family. Constructing pedigrees helps a counselor decide whether a genetic disorder that runs in a family is autosomal recessive (see Fig. 4.2) or dominant (see Fig 4.3); X-linked (see Fig. 4.4); or some other pattern of inheritance (see Fig. 4A). After deciding the pattern of inheritance, a counselor will be able to tell prospective parents the chances that any child born to them will have the genetic disorder.

4.3 Testing for Genetic Disorders
Genetic testing is routinely done today on unborn fetuses, newborns, and adults.

There are two types of genetic testing: biochemical testing and DNA testing. A biochemical test determines the amount of a particular enzyme or an abnormal end-product of metabolism. If the enzyme is missing or an abnormal end-product of metabolism is present, the individual has the genetic disorder. DNA testing is also possible today. Genetic mutations alter the base sequence in DNA and, therefore, alter the sites for cleavage by restriction enzymes. One type of test for a genetic disorder is to compare the pattern of DNA fragments to the normal pattern after the use of restriction enzymes. DNA probes are available for a number of genetic mutations. If the probe binds to the individual's DNA, the genetic mutation is present.

Testing the fetus requires a sample of fetal cells. Each of the three methods available for obtaining fetal cells—amniocentesis, chorionic villi sampling, and fetal cells in the mother's blood—has advantages and disadvantages. It is also possible today to test the egg before in vitro fertilization (IVF) or to test the embryo following IVF.

Reviewing the Chapter

1. What is genetic counseling? 58
2. What is a karyotype, and when and how is karyotyping of fetal cells done? 58–59
3. How is a pedigree constructed? 60
4. List the ways to recognize an autosomal dominant genetic disorder and an autosomal recessive genetic disorder when examining a pedigree chart. 60–61
5. List the ways to recognize an X-linked recessive disorder when examining a pedigree chart. Why do males exhibit such disorders more often than females? 61
6. Why can certain genetic disorders be detected by testing for a protein? 63
7. What are the two types of DNA testing for a genetic disorder? In general, describe each method. 63
8. Contrast and compare the three methods of obtaining fetal cells for genetic testing. 65
9. How is it possible to test an egg before in vitro fertilization and an embryo after in vitro fertilization? Why isn't the egg destroyed and the embryo harmed during the process? 65–66
10. Does the following pedigree represent an autosomal dominant trait, an autosomal recessive trait, or an X-linked recessive trait? What is the genotype of the starred individual? 60–61

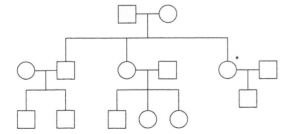

11. Does the following pedigree represent an autosomal dominant trait, an autosomal recessive trait, or an X-linked recessive trait? What is the genotype of the starred individual? 60–61

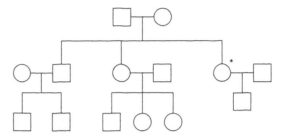

12. Does the following pedigree represent an autosomal dominant trait, an autosomal recessive trait, or an X-linked recessive trait? What is the genotype of the starred individual? 60–61

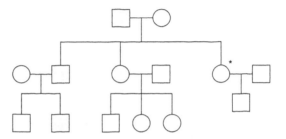

Critical Thinking Questions

1. Frequently, general information for the public refers to blood tests for genetic diseases. This is somewhat misleading, because what is actually removed from blood to do genetic testing?

2. Why would you expect genetic testing of DNA to be more accurate than biochemical testing?

3. Considering the accuracy of DNA testing, why does a genetic counselor bother to do family pedigrees?

Understanding Key Terms

amniocentesis 58
carrier 60
chorionic villi sampling
   (CVS) 58
DNA probe 63

genetic counseling 58
genetic marker 63
in vitro fertilization (IVF) 65
karyotype 58
pedigree 60

Reproduction produces offspring that require parental care.

II

Human Reproduction

Human beings have two sexes, male and female. The anatomy of each sex functions to produce sex cells, which join prior to the development of a new individual. Humans develop in the uterus of the female. The steps of human development can be traced from the fertilized egg to the birth of a child.

We are in the midst of a sexual revolution, and we have the freedom to experience varied lifestyles. With freedom comes a responsibility to be familiar with the biology of reproduction and the potential health hazards, not only for ourselves, but also for future children.

Chapter 5

Reproductive Hormones and Sexual Maturation

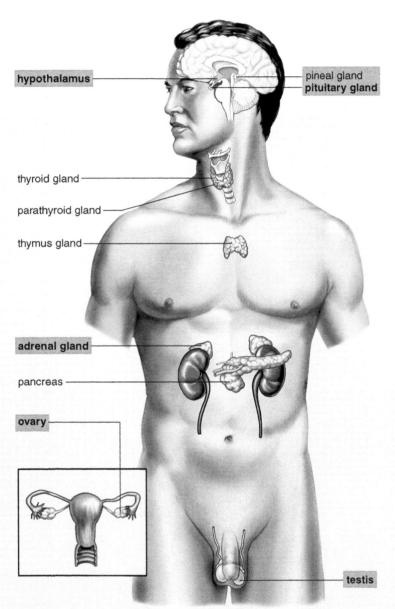

Figure 5.1   The endocrine system.
The anatomical locations of the major endocrine glands in the body are shown. The hypothalamus, pituitary gland, and pineal gland are in the brain. The adrenal glands are in the abdominal cavity. The gonads include the ovaries in females and the testes in males. The testes are located in the scrotum.

5.1 The Endocrine System

Two major systems, the nervous system and the endocrine system, coordinate the various activities of body parts. As discussed in the reading on page 75, both systems utilize chemical signals (messengers) to fulfill their functions. The nervous and endocrine systems evolved together, and they communicate not only with other systems but with each other as well.

The **endocrine system** utilizes hormones, chemical signals that are produced in one body region but affect a different body region. The glands that produce hormones are called **endocrine glands.** Endocrine glands should not be confused with *exocrine glands,* which secrete their products into ducts for transport into body cavities; for example, the salivary glands send saliva into the mouth by way of the salivary ducts. Endocrine glands are ductless; they secrete their hormones into the bloodstream for distribution throughout the body. The cells of these glands border on capillaries whose thin walls allow easy entrance of hormones. Figure 5.1 depicts the locations of the endocrine glands in the body and highlights the ones of interest to us. Table 5.1 lists the hormones secreted by these glands and highlights the *reproductive hormones*—hormones that affect the reproductive organs and bring about the secondary sex characteristics.

Target Organs

The nervous system reacts quickly to external and internal stimuli; for example, it allows you to rapidly pull your hand away from a hot stove. The endocrine system is slower than the nervous system because it takes time for a hormone to travel through the cardiovascular system to its target organ. It may sound as though the hormone is seeking out a particular organ, but quite the contrary is true. The organ is awaiting the arrival of the hormone. The cells able to react to a hormone have specific receptor proteins that combine with the hormone in a lock-and-key manner. To use an analogy, consider that a mailman (the bloodstream) travels all over town (the body) and only certain mailboxes (receptors of particular cells) receive certain letters (particular hormones). In the same way, only certain cells respond to one hormone and not another, depending on their receptors.

Table 5.1	Principal Endocrine Glands and Hormones			
Endocrine Gland	**Hormone Released**	**Chemical Class**	**Target Tissues/Organs**	**Chief Function(s) of Hormone**
Hypothalamus	Hypothalamic-releasing and -inhibiting hormones	Peptide	Anterior pituitary	Regulate anterior pituitary hormones
Pituitary gland				
Posterior pituitary	Oxytocin	Peptide	Uterus, mammary glands	Stimulates uterine muscle contraction, release of milk by mammary glands
	Antidiuretic (ADH)	Peptide	Kidneys	Stimulates water reabsorption by kidneys
Anterior pituitary	Gonadotropic	Protein	Gonads	Egg and sperm production; sex hormone production
	Prolactin (PRL)	Protein	Mammary glands	Milk production
	Growth (GH)	Protein	Soft tissues, bones	Cell division, protein synthesis, and bone growth
	Thyroid-stimulating (TSH)	Protein	Thyroid	Stimulates thyroid
	Adrenocorticotropic (ACH)	Peptide	Adrenal cortex	Stimulates adrenal cortex
Thyroid	Thyroxine (T_4) and triiodothyronine (T_3)	Iodinated amino acid	All tissues	Increases metabolic rate; regulates growth and development
	Calcitonin	Peptide	Bones, kidneys, intestines	Lowers blood calcium level
Parathyroids	Parathyroid (PTH)	Peptide	Bones, kidneys, intestines	Raises blood calcium level
Adrenal gland				
Adrenal cortex	Sex hormones	Steroid	Gonads, skin, muscles, bones	Stimulate reproductive organs and bring about sex characteristics
	Glucocorticoids (cortisol)	Steroid	All tissues	Raise blood glucose level; stimulate breakdown of protein
	Mineralocorticoids (aldosterone)	Steroid	Kidneys	Reabsorb sodium and excrete potassium
Adrenal medulla	Epinephrine and norepinephrine	Modified amino acid	Cardiac and other muscles	Emergency situations; raise blood glucose level
Pancreas	Insulin	Protein	Liver, muscles, adipose tissue	Lowers blood glucose level; promotes formation of glycogen
	Glucagon	Protein	Liver, muscles, adipose tissue	Raises blood glucose level
Gonads				
Testes	Androgens (testosterone)	Steroid	Gonads, skin, muscles, bones	Stimulate male sex characteristics
Ovaries	Estrogens and progesterone	Steroid	Gonads, skin, muscles, bones	Stimulate female sex characteristics
Thymus	Thymosins	Peptide	T lymphocytes	Stimulate production and maturation of T lymphocytes
Pineal gland	Melatonin	Modified amino acid	Brain	Circadian and circannual rhythms; possibly involved in maturation of sex organs

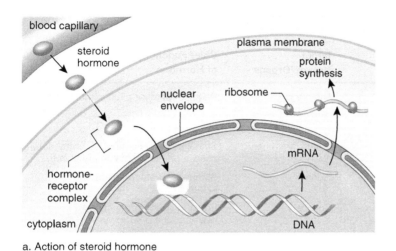

a. Action of steroid hormone

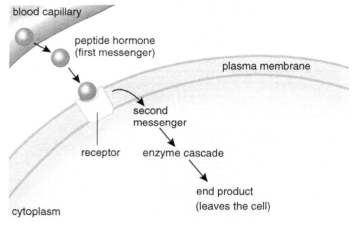

b. Action of peptide hormone

Figure 5.2   **Cellular activity of hormones.**
a. After passing through the plasma membrane, and possibly not until also passing through the nuclear envelope, a steroid hormone binds to a receptor protein. The hormone-receptor complex then binds to DNA, and this leads to activation of certain genes and protein synthesis.
b. Peptide hormones, called first messengers, bind to a specific receptor protein in the plasma membrane. A protein relay in the plasma membrane ends with a second messenger, which activates an enzyme cascade.

How Hormones Work

Hormones, including the reproductive hormones, are chemical signals that have powerful effects on other glands and tissues because they stimulate their metabolism in a particular way. Hormones produced by endocrine glands are either (1) *steroid hormones* or (2) *peptide and related hormones*, which include hormones composed of a single amino acid, several amino acids (peptides), or proteins (many amino acids). Protein hormones, such as insulin, must be administered by injection. If these hormones were taken orally, they would be acted on by digestive enzymes. Steroid hormones, such as those in birth control pills, can be taken orally. Steroids have an entirely different chemical makeup compared to that of proteins. They are constructed of four fused rings to which are attached side chains. The differences in the side chains have a remarkable effect on the body. Consider the chemical difference between testosterone, the main male sex hormone, and estrogen, a female sex hormone:

a. Testosterone

b. Estrogen

Steroid Hormones

Steroid hormones are soluble in plasma membranes, and therefore they can cross plasma membranes and enter a cell (Fig. 5.2a). Only after a steroid is inside the cytoplasm, or in some cases inside the nucleus, do steroid hormones bind to receptor proteins. The hormone-receptor complex then binds to DNA, activating a particular gene. Activation leads to production of a protein, such as a cellular enzyme. Gene activation can lead to the production of more than one copy of the protein. In the end, the protein can be present in multiple quantities. Therefore, reception of the hormone can lead to a marked change in cell metabolism.

Peptide Hormones

Most peptide hormones are not soluble in the plasma membrane, and therefore they cannot pass through plasma membranes. Instead, a peptide hormone binds to a receptor in the plasma membrane (Fig. 5.2b). The peptide hormone, called the **first messenger,** activates a relay system in the plasma membrane, which leads to the formation of a molecule called the **second messenger.** Both the cyclic ATP molecule and calcium are common second messengers. This helps explain why calcium regulation in the body is so important.

The second messenger sets in motion an enzyme cascade, so called because each enzyme in turn activates the next enzyme in the series. Because enzymes work over and over, every step in an enzyme cascade leads to more reactions—for example, the binding of a single peptide hormone molecule can result in as much as a thousandfold response. In this way, peptide hormones also profoundly affect cell metabolism.

Of Special Interest

Chemical Signals

At least three categories of chemical signals are known. Chemical signals that act at a distance between individuals, particularly members of the opposite sex, are called **pheromones** (Fig. 5A*a*). Pheromones are well exemplified in animals other than humans. For example, female moths release a sex attractant that can be received by male moth antennae as much as several miles away. The receptors on the antennae of the male silkworm moth are so sensitive that only 40 out of 40,000 receptor proteins need to be activated in order for the male to respond and find the female.

Some chemical signals, such as hormones released by endocrine glands, act at a distance between organs (Fig. 5A*b*). Other chemical signals act locally between adjacent cells (Fig. 5A*c*). For example, after prostaglandins are produced, they are not carried in the bloodstream; instead, they affect neighboring cells, sometimes promoting pain and inflammation. Also, neurotransmitters released by one nerve cell affect the excitability of only adjacent neurons.

Do humans release and receive pheromones? This question has kept researchers busy for many years. Humans produce a rich supply of airborne chemicals from a variety of areas, including the scalp, oral cavity, armpits, genital areas, and feet. A recent study found that a chemical in male sweat can stimulate the flow of blood to the brain of a female.

Several studies indicate that armpit secretions can affect the menstrual cycle. The cycle length becomes more normal when women with irregular cycles are exposed to secretions collected from male armpits. Women who live in the same household often have menstrual cycles in synchrony. A new finding shows that a woman's armpit secretions collected during one part of the menstrual cycle will shorten another female's cycle by an average of 1.7 days. Armpit secretions from another part of the cycle will lengthen another female's cycle by an average of 1.4 days. The hope is that identifying pheromones could lead to the development of new ways to help couples conceive or to block a pregnancy through cycle manipulation.

Animals seem to have a vomeronasal organ (VNO) located in the nose that is linked to pheromone perception. Some animal studies show that pheromones have no effect if this organ is removed or if its link to the brain is severed. Researchers know that humans have two small pits in the nasal cavity that might represent an opening to a VNO.

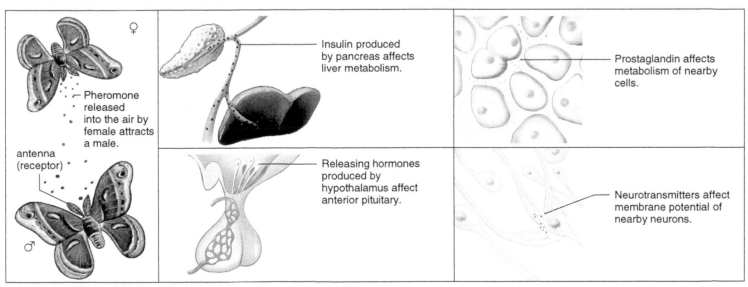

a. Signal acts at a distance between individuals.

b. Signal acts at a distance between body parts.

c. Signal acts locally between adjacent cells.

Figure 5A   Chemical signals.
a. Pheromones are chemical signals that act at a distance between individuals. **b.** Endocrine hormones and neurosecretions typically are carried in the bloodstream and act at a distance within the body of a single organism. **c.** Some chemical signals have local effects only; they pass between cells that are adjacent to one another. Prostaglandins act locally, as do neurotransmitters.

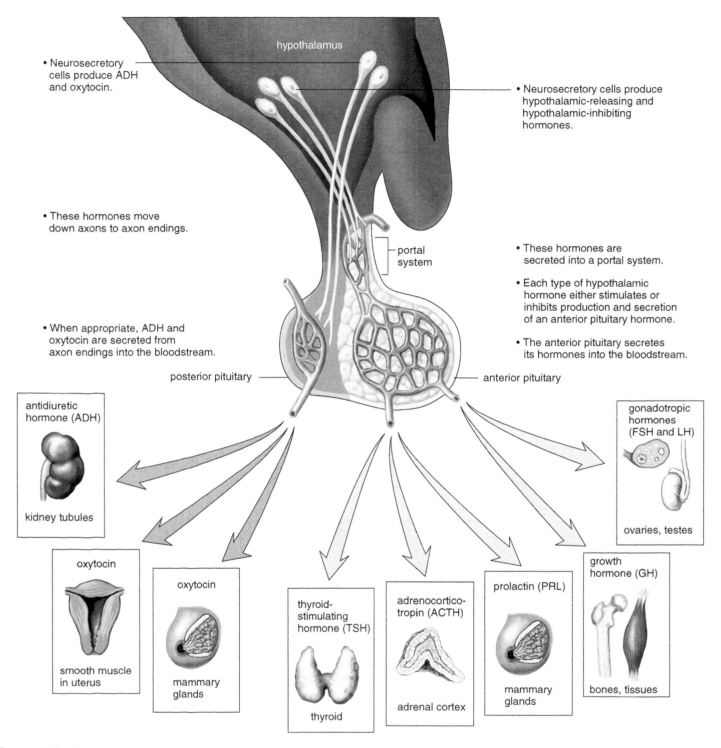

- Neurosecretory cells produce ADH and oxytocin.

- These hormones move down axons to axon endings.

- When appropriate, ADH and oxytocin are secreted from axon endings into the bloodstream.

hypothalamus

- Neurosecretory cells produce hypothalamic-releasing and hypothalamic-inhibiting hormones.

portal system

- These hormones are secreted into a portal system.

- Each type of hypothalamic hormone either stimulates or inhibits production and secretion of an anterior pituitary hormone.

- The anterior pituitary secretes its hormones into the bloodstream.

posterior pituitary

anterior pituitary

antidiuretic hormone (ADH)

kidney tubules

oxytocin

smooth muscle in uterus

oxytocin

mammary glands

thyroid-stimulating hormone (TSH)

thyroid

adrenocortico-tropin (ACTH)

adrenal cortex

prolactin (PRL)

mammary glands

growth hormone (GH)

bones, tissues

gonadotropic hormones (FSH and LH)

ovaries, testes

Figure 5.3 Hypothalamus and the pituitary.
Left: The hypothalamus produces two hormones, ADH and oxytocin, which are stored and secreted by the posterior pituitary. *Right:* The hypothalamus controls the secretions of the anterior pituitary, and the anterior pituitary controls the secretions of the thyroid, adrenal cortex, and gonads, which are also endocrine glands.

5.2 Reproductive Hormones

The **hypothalamus** is a region of the brain that has many effects on the body. One of its functions is to control the glandular secretions of the **pituitary gland.** The pituitary, a small gland about 1 cm in diameter, is connected to the hypothalamus by a stalklike structure. The pituitary has two portions: the **posterior pituitary** and the **anterior pituitary.**

Posterior Pituitary

Nerve cells in the hypothalamus called neurosecretory cells produce the hormones antidiuretic hormone (ADH) and oxytocin (Fig. 5.3, *left*). These hormones pass through extensions of the nerve cells (axons) into the posterior pituitary, where they are stored. ADH causes the kidneys to excrete less urine. **Oxytocin** is of interest to us because it causes uterine contraction during childbirth and milk letdown when a baby is nursing. The more the uterus contracts during labor, the more nerve impulses reach the hypothalamus, causing oxytocin to be released. Similarly, the more a baby suckles, the more oxytocin is released. In both instances, the release of oxytocin from the posterior pituitary is controlled by a **positive feedback mechanism** in which a result (e.g., uterine contraction) ever increases in intensity.

Anterior Pituitary

Blood vessels run between the hypothalamus and the anterior pituitary (Fig. 5.3, *right*). The hypothalamus stimulates the anterior pituitary to secrete hormones by producing hypothalamic-releasing hormones (Table 5.2). Two of the anterior pituitary hormones have a direct effect on the body. **Growth hormone (GH)** promotes cell division, protein synthesis, and bone growth. GH dramatically affects physical appearance because it determines the height of the individual. **Prolactin (PRL),** produced in quantity only after childbirth, causes the mammary glands in the breasts to develop and to produce milk.

The other hormones produced by the anterior pituitary stimulate other endocrine glands to secrete hormones. This results in a three-tier system for controlling these hormones: (1) the hypothalamus, (2) the anterior pituitary, and (3) the specific glands, which will be discussed next.

The Thyroid Gland

The thyroid gland is located in the neck (see Fig 5.1). The hypothalamus produces thyrotropin-releasing hormone (TRH), which stimulates the anterior pituitary to release thyroid-stimulating hormone (TSH). Thereafter, the thyroid secretes thyroxine and triiodothyronine. These hormones do not have a specific target organ; instead, they stimulate most of the cells of the body to metabolize at a faster rate.

The Adrenal Glands

Each **adrenal gland** sits atop a kidney (see Fig. 5.1). Each adrenal gland consists of an inner portion called the **adrenal medulla** and an outer portion called the **adrenal cortex.** These portions, like the anterior pituitary and the posterior pituitary, have no physiological connection with one another.

The hypothalamus, by means of the releasing hormone CRH, controls the anterior pituitary's secretion of ACTH, which in turn stimulates the adrenal cortex. Stress of all types, including both emotional and physical trauma, prompts the anterior pituitary to release CRH. The adrenal cortex secretes a small amount of male sex hormone and a small amount of female sex hormone in both sexes—that is, in the male, both male and female sex hormones are produced by the adrenal cortex, and in the female, both male and female sex hormones are also produced by the adrenal cortex.

The Gonads

One of the hypothalamic-releasing hormones, called **gonadotropin-releasing hormone (GnRH),** stimulates the anterior pituitary to secrete **follicle-stimulating hormone (FSH)** and **luteinizing hormone (LH).** Collectively, FSH and LH are called the **gonadotropic hormones** because they stimulate the gonads—the testes in males and the ovaries in females—to produce gametes and sex hormones.

FSH and LH are named for their action in the female, but they exist in both sexes, stimulating the appropriate gonads in each. In males, LH is sometimes called interstitial-cell-stimulating hormone (ICSH). The testes produce the male sex hormones, called **androgens,** of which the best known is **testosterone.** The ovaries produce the female sex hormones, called **estrogen** and **progesterone.** These sex hormones maintain the structure and function of the gonads and also the secondary sex characteristics, which are discussed in section 5.4, page 82.

Table 5.2	Hypothalamic-Releasing Hormones and Pituitary Hormones
Hypothalamic-Releasing Hormone	**Pituitary Hormone**
Gonadotropin-releasing hormone (GnRH)	Luteinizing hormone (LH), follicle-stimulating hormone (FSH)
Prolactin-releasing hormone (PRH)	Prolactin (PRL)
Growth hormone-releasing hormone (GHRH)	Growth hormone (GH)
Corticotropin-releasing hormone (CRH)	Adrenocorticotropic hormone (ACTH)
Thyrotropin-releasing hormone (TRH)	Thyroid-stimulating hormone (TSH)

Regulatory Control of Sex Hormones

The level of sex hormones is maintained by a negative feedback system. A **negative feedback system** is self-regulating because a physiological result acts to keep that same result under control. For example, Figure 5.4 illustrates how the levels of sex hormones are controlled. Testosterone is hormone 3 in the diagram because it is released after the hypothalamus has stimulated the anterior pituitary and after LH from the anterior pituitary has in turn stimulated the testes to produce testosterone.

When the blood level of testosterone rises, it "feeds back," causing the hypothalamus to stop producing GnRH and the anterior pituitary to stop producing LH. Now the level of testosterone falls, and the hypothalamus and anterior pituitary are no longer inhibited. Then the system starts again with secretion of GnRH by the hypothalamus.

As indicated in Figure 5.4, the hypothalamus can also be controlled by the level of a gonadotropic hormone secreted by the anterior pituitary. In other words, both the blood level of testosterone and the blood level of LH serve to stimulate or depress the production of GnRH by the hypothalamus.

A negative feedback system always results in fluctuation above and below a certain value. For example, a high level of testosterone leads to a low level of testosterone, and vice versa. In the end, the testosterone level is maintained within a normal range.

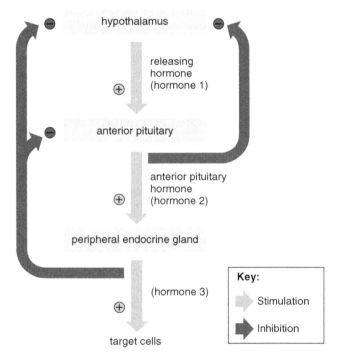

Figure 5.4   Feedback control.
Regulation of the level of a sex hormone in the blood involves negative feedback control of the hypothalamus and the anterior pituitary by the hormone. (+ = stimulation; − = inhibition.)

5.3 Development of Male and Female Sex Organs

The sex of an individual is determined at the moment of fertilization. Both males and females have 23 pairs of chromosomes; in males, one of these pairs (the sex chromosomes) is an X and Y, while females have two X chromosomes. During the first several weeks of development, it is impossible to tell by inspection whether the unborn child is a boy or girl. The tissue that gives rise to the gonads is called *indifferent* because it can become either testes or ovaries, depending on whether a Y chromosome is present.

In Figure 5.5a, notice that at six weeks both males and females have the same types of ducts. During this indifferent stage, an embryo has the potential to develop into a male or a female. If a Y chromosome is present, testosterone appears, and the feedback system described in Figure 5.4 begins. Testosterone stimulates the gonads to become testes and the wolffian ducts to become male genital ducts. The wolffian ducts enter the urethra, which belongs to both the urinary and reproductive systems in males. The testes secrete an anti-müllerian hormone that causes the müllerian ducts to regress.

In the absence of a Y chromosome, ovaries instead of testes develop from the same indifferent tissue. Now the wolffian ducts regress, and the müllerian ducts develop into the uterus and uterine tubes. A developing vagina also extends from the uterus. There is no connection between the urinary and genital systems in females.

At fourteen weeks, the primitive testes and ovaries are located deep inside the pelvic cavity. An inspection of the interior of the testes would show that sperm are even now starting to develop, and similarly, the ovaries already contain large numbers of tiny follicles, each having an ovum. Toward the end of development, the testes descend into the scrotal sac; the ovaries remain in the abdominal cavity.

Figure 5.5b shows the development of the external genitals. These tissues are also indifferent at first, meaning that they can develop into either male or female genitals. At six weeks, a small bud appears between the legs; this can develop into the male penis or the female clitoris, depending on the presence or absence of the Y chromosome and testosterone. At nine weeks, a urogenital groove bordered by two swellings appears. By fourteen weeks, this groove has disappeared in males, and the scrotum has formed from the original swellings. In females, the groove persists and becomes the vaginal opening. Labia majora and labia minora are present instead of a scrotum.

The role of the pineal gland in sexual maturation is discussed in the reading on page 81.

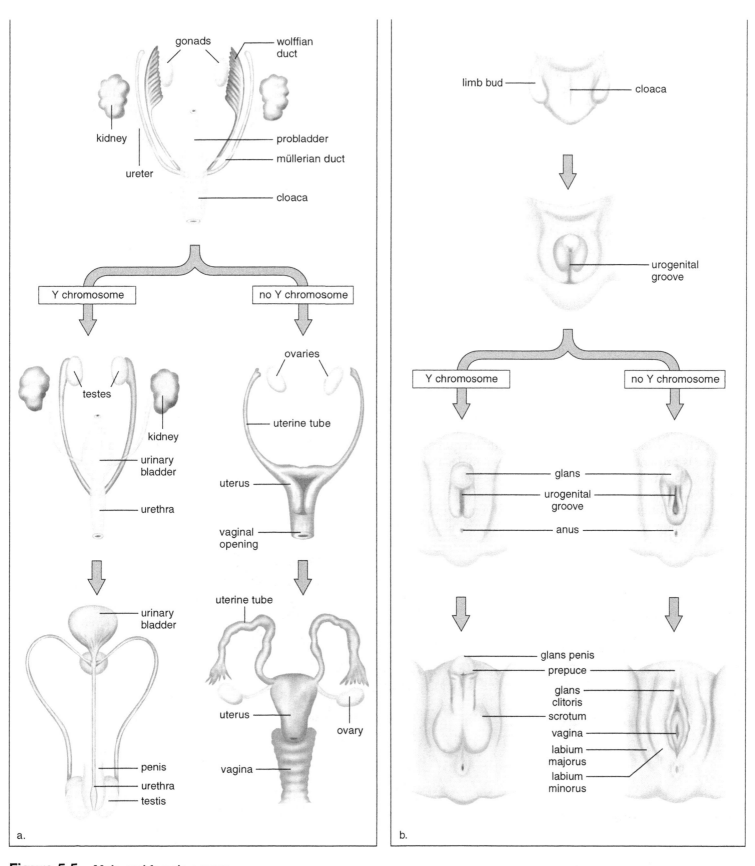

Figure 5.5   Male and female organs.

a. Development of gonads and ducts. **b.** Development of external genitals.

The X and Y Chromosomes

The X chromosome has about 1,400 genes, and most of them have nothing to do with the sexual differences between men and women. The Y chromosome is quite small compared to the X chromosome (Fig. 5.6*a*), and consequently it has far fewer genes. The Y chromosome has only about 26 genes, far fewer than the number on the X chromosome, but most of these genes are concerned with sex differences between men and women. This was an unexpected discovery, because the Y chromosome is a degraded copy of the X chromosome. That is, most of the genes on the Y do have copies on the X chromosome. One of the genes on the Y chromosome, **SRY (sex-determining region of the Y)**, does not have a copy on the X chromosome.

SRY Gene

The reason some people are males and other people are females is due to the presence or absence of the *SRY* gene, which is usually found on the Y chromosome. The powerful effect of the *SRY* gene can be realized by examining the chromosomes of two sets of people: males who have two X chromosomes (XX male syndrome) and females who have one X and one Y chromosome (XY female syndrome). The XX males have a small piece of a Y chromosome attached to one of the X chromosomes, and the XY females lack a small piece of the Y chromosome. The *SRY* gene is in this region. If an *SRY* gene is present, the individual becomes a male, and if it is absent, the individual becomes a female—*there are no genes that determine femaleness.*

Of all the differences between people, the most obvious is whether they are male or female. It is surprising to find that all of the differences in anatomy, physiology, and behavior that separate men and women are due at least indirectly to this one gene. However, the *SRY* gene codes for a type of protein called a transcription factor. Like other transcription factors, the *SRY* gene turns on other genes, and in the end, various proteins—not just one—bring about male features. For example, some of these activated genes lead to the secretion of testosterone and the development of the testes and the male accessory organs, while others lead to the regression of the müllerian ducts. Because a number of different genes (not all of them on the Y chromosome) are involved in male sexual development, several different types of mutations lead to phenotypic abnormalities. In androgen insensitivity (see Fig. 3.14), an XY individual is a female because of a mutation in a gene on the X chromosome that codes for the testosterone receptor. In another disorder, the müllerian tubes degenerate, but the synthesis of testosterone is blocked; therefore, the male structures do not develop until the adrenal glands begin to produce sufficient androgens at about age 12.

Sexual Orientation

Heterosexuals are attracted to members of the opposite sex, while homosexual men and lesbian women are attracted to members of the same sex. It would be interesting to know if sexual orientation is inherited and possibly linked to differences in brain structure and function. Studies have compared the sexual orientation of identical twins reared separately to the sexual orientation of fraternal twins reared together. If one identical twin is homosexual, the chances are better that his twin is also homosexual than if his twin is fraternal. Can such studies be biologically substantiated? We shall see that the male pattern of gonadotropic hormone release is different in males compared to females. And researchers have shown that this difference is due to the effect of testosterone on the development of the hypothalamus rather than on the anterior pituitary. Further, consistent with animal studies, studies of human brain development suggest that structural differences in the hypothalamus may influence sexual behavior. A great deal more remains to be learned about the differences between the male and female brains, but it is possible that a strong relationship exists between brain structure and function and sexual orientation.

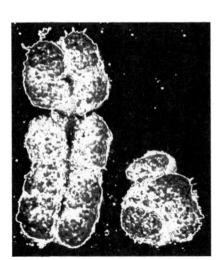

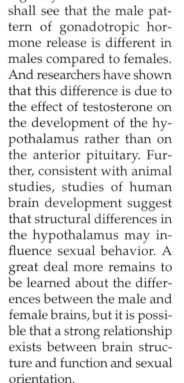

a. X chromosome (left) and Y chromosome   b. Sexual orientation

Figure 5.6   Gender determination and sexual orientation.
a. The much smaller Y chromosome usually contains the *SRY* gene, which turns on other genes coding for proteins that bring about the male sex organs. **b.** It's possible that, among other characteristics, testosterone affects the structure of the hypothalamus and that in turn results in sexual orientation—whether we are attracted to members of the same or the opposite sex.

Of Special Interest

Pineal Gland

Most people have heard of the hormone **melatonin** because the popular press promotes its use in pill form for sleep, aging, cancer treatment, sexuality, and more. At best, melatonin may have some benefits in certain sleep disorders, but physicians are usually reluctant to recommend it because so little is known about its dosage requirements and possible side effects.

Melatonin is a hormone produced by the **pineal gland,** which is located in the brain (see Fig. 5.1). The pineal gland secretes melatonin in greatest quantity at night and in smallest quantity during the day. Notice in Figure 5B that melatonin's production cycle accompanies our natural sleep-wake cycle. Rhythms with a period of about 24 hours are called circadian ("about a day") rhythms. All circadian rhythms seem to be controlled by an internal biological clock because they are free-running—that is, they have a regular cycle even in the absence of environmental cues. For example, in scientific experiments, humans have lived in underground bunkers where they never see the light of day. In a few people, the sleep-wake cycle drifts badly, but in most, the daily activity schedule is just about 25 hours. How do we normally manage to stay on a 24-hour schedule? An individual's internal biological clock is reset each day by the environmental day-night cycle. Characteristically, biological clocks that control circadian rhythms are reset by environmental cues, or else they drift out of phase with the environment.

Research is still going forward to see if melatonin will be effective for circadian rhythm disorders, such as seasonal affective disorder (SAD), jet lag, sleep phase problems, recurrent insomnia in the totally blind, and some other less common conditions. People with SAD become depressed, sometimes severely, as the days get darker and darker during fall and winter. Jet lag occurs when you travel across several time zones and your biological clock is out of phase with local time; you feel wide awake when it is time to sleep and sleepy when it is time to be awake. In clinical trials, it was found that melatonin could shift circadian rhythms and reset our biological clock. The experimenters found that melatonin given in the afternoon shifts rhythms earlier, while melatonin given in the morning shifts rhythms later. For most people, the process was gradual; the average rate of change was about an hour a day.

Before you try melatonin, however, you might want to consider that it is known to affect reproductive behavior in mammals. For example, children whose pineal gland has been destroyed due to a brain tumor experience early puberty. Therefore, you might want to consider whether taking melatonin is worth any potential reproductive side effects.

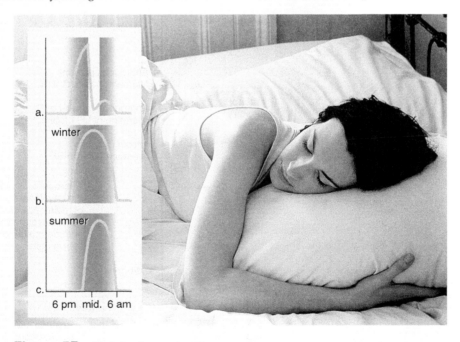

Figure 5B Melatonin production.
Melatonin production is greatest at night when we are sleeping. Light suppresses melatonin production (a), so melatonin's duration is longer in the winter (b) than in the summer (c). It's possible that this is the way melatonin is tied to sexual maturation in animals that reproduce according to the season. If young are born in summer, more food is available for them.

5.4 Secondary Sex Characteristics

At the time of puberty (ages 9–14), the sex organs mature, and the secondary sex characteristics begin to appear. The **secondary sex characteristics** are those differences between the sexes that usually allow us to tell males from females. The cause of puberty is related to the level of sex hormones in the body. It is now recognized that the hypothalamic-pituitary-gonad system functions long before puberty, but the level of hormones is low because the hypothalamus is supersensitive to feedback control. At the start of puberty, the hypothalamus becomes less sensitive to feedback control and begins to increase its production of GnRH, causing the pituitary and the gonads to increase their production of hormones. The sensitivity of the hypothalamus continues to decrease until the gonadotropic and sex hormones reach the adult level.

The secondary sex characteristics include differences in muscular and skeletal development, skin and hair growth, depth of voice, and breast development. Testosterone is partially responsible for the muscular strength of males, and this is why some athletes take supplemental amounts of anabolic steroids, which are either testosterone or a related chemical. The contraindications of taking anabolic steroids are discussed in the reading on pages 84–85.

Male Secondary Sex Characteristics

During puberty in males, the gonadotropic hormones stimulate the testes to produce sperm and the androgens. Androgens (e.g., testosterone) stimulate development of the male secondary sex characteristics, which consist of:

Changes in body hair. Increased growth of body hair, particularly on the face, chest, axillary (armpit) region, and pubic region. (Pubic refers to the front of the pelvic [hip] girdle.) In males, pubic hair tapers toward the navel.

Changes in skin. In males, the skin thickens. Sweat and oil-producing glands become active, so that body odor is present and acne occurs.

Change in voice. The larynx (voice box) enlarges, and the vocal cords thicken. The result is a deepening of the voice.

Change in muscle strength. Males experience increased muscular strength and a broadening of the shoulders.

Change in the skeleton. In males, the bones thicken and become stronger. Males experience a growth spurt later than females, but they grow for a longer length of time. Therefore, they become taller than females.

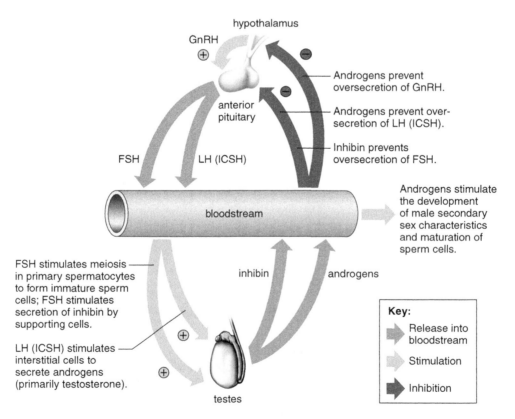

Figure 5.7   **Regulation of testosterone blood level in males.**
Androgens (e.g., testosterone), which bring about male secondary sex characteristics, inhibit gonadotropic hormone secretion by the anterior pituitary, and in this way the blood level of testosterone is regulated.

Regulation of Male Sex Hormones

In males, negative feedback regulates the amount of androgens secreted (Fig. 5.7). The GnRH from the hypothalamus stimulates the anterior pituitary to release FSH and LH, called interstitial-cell-stimulating hormone (ICSH) in males. FSH stimulates the testes to produce sperm along with a hormone called inhibin. Inhibin suppresses the release of FSH by the anterior pituitary. As the amount of inhibin declines, the cycle begins again.

ICSH stimulates the interstitial cells of the testes to produce androgens (e.g., testosterone). Androgens suppress the release of GnRH from the hypothalamus and LH by the anterior pituitary. As the amount of testosterone declines, the cycle begins again.

Female Secondary Sex Characteristics

At puberty, the gonadotropic hormones stimulate the ovaries to begin producing eggs and estrogen. Estrogen maintains the sexual organs and is necessary to the menstrual cycle, as discussed in Chapter 6. Estrogen is also responsible for the secondary sex characteristics, which include:

Development of breasts. This includes development of the ductile system of the mammary glands within the breasts.

Change in fat deposition. Increased deposition of adipose tissue, particularly in the breasts, thighs, and buttocks. Females have a more rounded appearance than males.

Change in body hair. Increased growth in body hair, particularly in the axillary (armpit) region and pubic region. In females, pubic hair is usually horizontal.

Change in pelvic girdle. In females, the pelvic girdle is wider than that of males; therefore, females tend to have wider hips.

Change in skeletal growth. Skeletal growth decreases; therefore, females are shorter than males.

Change in skin. Sweat and oil-producing glands become active, so that body odor is present and acne occurs.

Regulation of Female Sex Hormones

As we shall see in Chapter 6, hormonal control in females is cyclical, but in general GnRH stimulates the anterior pituitary to release the gonadotropins FSH and LH, which stimulate the ovaries to produce estrogens. Estrogens suppress the release of gonadotropic hormones by the anterior pituitary. When the blood level of estrogens declines, the cycle begins again (Fig. 5.8).

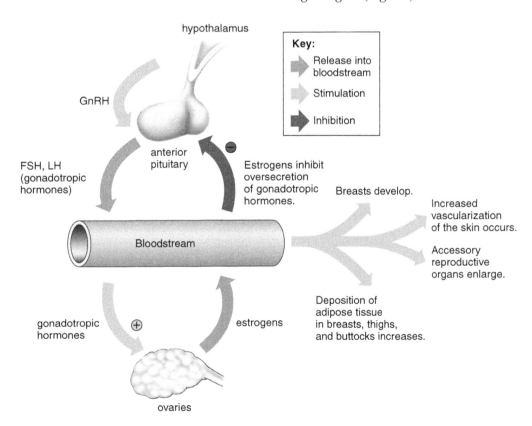

Figure 5.8   Regulation of estrogen levels in females.
Estrogens, which bring about female secondary sex characteristics, inhibit gonadotropic hormone secretion by the anterior pituitary, and in this way the blood level of estrogen is regulated.

Of Special Interest

Dangers of Anabolic Steroids

Anabolic steroids are synthetic forms of the male sex hormone testosterone. These drugs were developed in the 1930s for medical reasons. They prevent muscular atrophy in patients with debilitating illness, speed recovery in surgery and burn patients, and are helpful in treating rare forms of anemia and breast cancer.

However, when taken in large doses (10 to 100 times the amount prescribed by doctors for illnesses), anabolic steroids promote larger muscles when the person also exercises. The result in muscle cells is increased amounts of the proteins actin and myosin. Trainers may have been the first to acquire anabolic steroids for weight lifters, bodybuilders, and other athletes, such as professional football players. Unfortunately, taking such large amounts of these steroids has been found to affect the body in many harmful ways.

The Federal Food and Drug Administration now bans most steroids, but they are brought into the United States and sold through the mail or in gyms and health clubs. Steroid use has also been banned by the National Collegiate Athletic Association (NCAA), the National Football League (NFL), and the International Olympic Committee (IOC). Occasionally, however, steroid abuse makes the news—for example, when an Olympic winner tests positive for the drug and must relinquish a medal. According to federal officials, 1–3 million Americans now take anabolic steroids. Of great concern is increased use of steroids by teenagers wishing to build bulk quickly, possibly due to society's emphasis on physical appearance and adolescents' need to feel better about how they look. The National Institute on Drug Abuse and the American Academy of Pediatrics report that 3% of all U.S. high school students are users/abusers, and there is great concern for our middle school students as well.

The taking of anabolic steroids upsets the body's normal hormonal balance, which is based on negative feedback. The presence of the anabolic steroid in the blood causes the hypothalamus to signal the anterior pituitary gland to stop the production of testosterone by the testes. You would expect, then, that when males stop taking the anabolic steroid, the hypothalamus would signal the anterior pituitary to start the production of testosterone again. However, the hypothalamus fails to do so. Analogous hormonal imbalances are also seen in females.

Hormonal imbalance in steroid users causes detrimental effects in both males and females. Men often experience decreased sperm counts and decreased sexual desire due to atrophy of the testes. Some develop an enlarged prostate gland or grow breasts. On the other hand, women can develop male sexual characteristics. They grow hair on their chests and faces, and lose hair from their heads; many experience abnormal enlargement of the clitoris. Some cease ovulating or menstruating, sometimes permanently.

Several other health risks are associated with steroid use. Steroids have even been linked to heart disease in both sexes and implicated in the deaths of young athletes from liver cancer and a certain type of kidney tumor. Steroids can cause the body to retain fluid, which results in increased blood pressure. Users then try to get rid of "steroid bloat" by taking large doses of diuretics. A young California weight lifter had a fatal heart attack after using steroids, and the postmortem showed a lack of electrolytes, the chemicals that help regulate the heart, due to taking diuretics. In addition, the risk of contracting HIV or hepatitis B increases for people who inject steroids using needles. Finally, steroid abuse has psychological effects, including depression, hostility, aggression, and eating disorders.

The many and varied harmful effects of anabolic steroids are listed in Figure 5C. Some researchers predict that two or three months of high-dosage use of anabolic steroids as a teen can cause death by age 30 or 40. Unfortunately, these drugs also increase aggression, and they can make a person feel invincible. One abuser had his friend videotape him as he drove his car at 40 miles an hour into a tree!

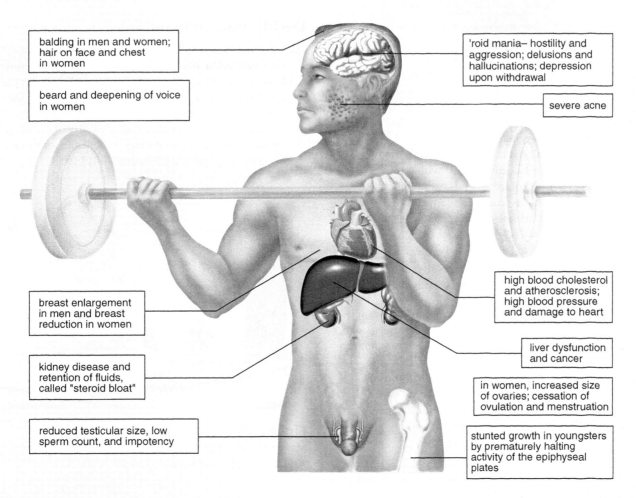

balding in men and women; hair on face and chest in women

beard and deepening of voice in women

'roid mania– hostility and aggression; delusions and hallucinations; depression upon withdrawal

severe acne

breast enlargement in men and breast reduction in women

kidney disease and retention of fluids, called "steroid bloat"

reduced testicular size, low sperm count, and impotency

high blood cholesterol and atherosclerosis; high blood pressure and damage to heart

liver dysfunction and cancer

in women, increased size of ovaries; cessation of ovulation and menstruation

stunted growth in youngsters by prematurely halting activity of the epiphyseal plates

Figure 5C   **The effects of anabolic steroid use.**
The numerous effects of anabolic steroids are injurious to the body.

Bioethical Focus

Hormone Replacement Therapy

Menopause occurs in women at about age 50 when their ovaries no longer produce estrogen and progesterone. The most noticeable outward indication of menopause is cessation of menstruation. For years, hormone replacement therapy (HRT) was commonly used to combat menopausal symptoms, such as hot flashes and sleeplessness. Also, it was thought that HRT would help combat heart disease and osteoporosis, which is bone loss particularly seen in postmenopausal women.

In recent years, the National Institutes of Health conducted a study that followed 16,608 healthy women with a uterus (ages 50 to 79), who took HRT or a placebo. The goal of this eight-year study was to determine the relationship between HRT and its possible benefits for heart disease and hip fracture, as well as its possible risks for breast cancer, endometrial cancer, and blood clots. In July 2002, the NIH halted this study after 5.2 years, because physicians had concluded that the risks for the group on combined HRT outweighed the benefits. (The published report is in the July 17, 2002, issue of the *Journal of the American Medical Association*.) The women on HRT had a small but significant increased risk for breast cancer, coronary heart disease, stroke, and blood clots. Benefits of HRT use included lower risks for hip fractures and colon cancer.

Women are now advised to discuss the pros and cons of HRT with their physician and decide for themselves if they wish to be on HRT. In other words, the patient has to be aware of the risks and accept the responsibility for taking replacement hormones.

Decide Your Opinion

1. Should physicians wait to recommend medications until they are certain about their benefits? Or are they duty-bound to make recommendations based on incomplete information if there is a possibility of improving the health of millions of people?
2. Should patients accept the responsibility of deciding for themselves if they should take a medicine, or should physicians assume this responsibility?

Figure 5D Thinking it through.
Menopausal women are now told to decide for themselves if they wish to be on hormone replacement therapy.

Summary

5.1 The Endocrine System
The endocrine system consists of a number of different glands that secrete hormones. Hormones enter the bloodstream and travel to target organs. Hormones circulate about the body and enter those cells that have receptor proteins to receive them. Only certain glands produce reproductive hormones (i.e., hormones that affect the reproductive system and bring about the secondary sex characteristics).

Hormones are of two types: steroid hormones or peptide and related hormones. Steroid hormones enter cells, and the hormone-receptor complex turns on genes that code for particular proteins. Peptide hormones bind to a receptor in the plasma membrane. The peptide hormone is the first messenger, and a relay system in the plasma membrane leads to the formation of a second messenger that sets in motion an enzyme cascade. In both cases, the hormone affects the metabolism of the cell.

5.2 Reproductive Hormones
The hypothalamus controls the pituitary gland. The hypothalamus produces oxytocin, a hormone secreted by the posterior pituitary. Oxytocin causes the uterus to contract during childbirth. Oxytocin is under positive feedback control—the more the uterus contracts, the greater the amount of oxytocin produced until childbirth occurs. Oxytocin also causes milk letdown when a baby is nursing.

The hypothalamus produces hypothalamic-releasing hormones that stimulate the anterior pituitary to secrete its hormones. Prolactin, which is produced in quantity only after childbirth, causes the mammary glands to produce milk. The other hormones produced by the anterior pituitary affect other glands. ACTH from the anterior pituitary stimulates the adrenal glands that, among other hormones, also produce both male and female sex hormones. The anterior pituitary gonadotropic hormones—follicle-stimulating hormone (FSH) and luteinizing hormone (LH)—stimulate the gonads, which produce male and female sex hormones. Male hormones are called androgens, of which the best known is testosterone. The female hormones are estrogen and progesterone.

A three-tier negative feedback mechanism controls the level of sex hormones in the body. For example, a high blood level of testosterone inhibits the secretion of GnRH by the hypothalamus and the secretion of LH by the anterior pituitary; thereafter, the blood level of testosterone falls. Then the system reverses, and stimulation occurs again. The blood level of testosterone rises and falls but remains within a certain range.

5.3 Development of Male and Female Sex Organs

The presence of a Y chromosome causes testosterone to be produced in the indifferent gonad. Thereafter, testes develop, and wolffian ducts persist and enter the urethra. The müllerian ducts regress. In the absence of a Y chromosome, the indifferent gonad becomes ovaries, and the müllerian ducts persist while the wolffian ducts regress.

The Y chromosome contains an *SRY* gene that leads to production of the hormones and organs of a male. Further, it appears that the hypothalamus has structural differences that may correlate with sexual orientation.

5.4 Secondary Sex Characteristics

Increasing desensitivity at puberty causes the hypothalamus to increase its production of gonadotropin-releasing hormone (GnRH), which causes the anterior pituitary to increase its production of gonadotropic hormones. The gonadotropic hormones stimulate the gonads to produce the sex hormones, with subsequent development of the secondary sex characteristics. In males, these characteristics include changes in hair distribution, activity of oil and sweat glands, voice depth, and muscle and bone strength. In females, there is breast development, increased pelvic width, increased fat deposition, growth of the pelvic girdle, change in body and pubic hair, cessation of skeletal growth, and increased activity of oil and sweat glands. Regulation of the male and female sex hormone blood levels follows the three-tier feedback mechanism discussed previously.

Reviewing the Chapter

1. How do endocrine glands differ from exocrine glands? Name the endocrine glands involved in sex hormone production and regulation. Define a hormone. 72–74
2. Explain the expression "target organ." How does the action of steroid hormones differ from that of peptide hormones at the cellular level? 72, 74
3. How does the hypothalamus control the anterior pituitary, and how does the anterior pituitary gland control other glands? Name these glands and the hormones they produce. 76–77
4. How does a negative feedback mechanism operate in relation to the hypothalamic-pituitary-gonad system? 78

5. Describe the development of male and female sex organs, and explain the role of the Y chromosome in bringing about the features of a male. 78–79
6. Describe the male and female secondary sex characteristics and the specific hypothalamic-pituitary-gonad system in males and in females. 82–83

Critical Thinking Questions

1. Muscles contain two proteins, actin and myosin. Using the information provided in Chapters 4 and 6, outline the precise steps by which you would expect testosterone to increase muscle size.
2. An XX individual has inherited a genetic defect so that cellular receptors for estrogen are lacking.
   a. Would you expect this individual to have testes or ovaries? Why?
   b. Can this individual respond to estrogen? Why or why not? What effect will this have on the body?
   c. Taking into account that the adrenal cortex produces some testosterone, might this individual have the secondary sex characteristics of a male?
   d. Would you expect this individual to be fertile? Why or why not?

Understanding Key Terms

adrenal cortex 77
adrenal gland 77
adrenal medulla 77
androgen 77
anterior pituitary 77
endocrine gland 72
endocrine system 72
estrogen 77
first messenger 74
follicle-stimulating hormone
   (FSH) 77
gonadotropic hormone 77
gonadotropin-releasing
   hormone (GnRH) 77
growth hormone (GH) 77
hormone 74
hypothalamus 77
luteinizing hormone (LH) 77

melatonin 81
negative feedback system 78
oxytocin 77
pheromone 75
pineal gland 81
pituitary gland 77
positive feedback mechanism
   77
posterior pituitary 77
progesterone 77
prolactin (PRL) 77
secondary sex characteristics
   82
second messenger 74
SRY (sex-determining region of
   the Y) 80
testosterone 77

Chapter 6

Human Reproductive Systems

6.1 Male Reproductive System

The male reproductive system includes the organs depicted in Figure 6.1. The *primary sex organs* of a male are the paired testes (sing., **testis**), which are suspended within the sacs of the **scrotum**. The testes are the primary sex organs because they produce sperm and the male sex hormones **(androgens).**

The other organs depicted in Figure 6.1 are the *accessory* (or secondary) *sex organs* of a male. Sperm produced by the testes are stored within the **epididymis** (pl., epididymides). Then they enter a **vas deferens** (pl., vasa deferentia), which transports them to an **ejaculatory duct.** The ejaculatory ducts enter the **urethra.** (The urethra in males is a part of both the urinary system and the reproductive system.) The urethra passes through the penis and transports sperm to outside the body.

At the time of **ejaculation**, sperm leave the penis in a fluid called **semen** (which is also called seminal fluid). The seminal vesicles, the prostate gland, and the bulbourethral glands (Cowper glands) add secretions to semen. The **seminal vesicles** are lateral to the vas deferens, and their ducts join to form an ejaculatory duct. The **prostate gland** is a single, donut-shaped gland that surrounds the upper portion of the urethra just inferior to the bladder. **Bulbourethral glands** are pea-sized organs that lie inferior to the prostate on either side of the urethra.

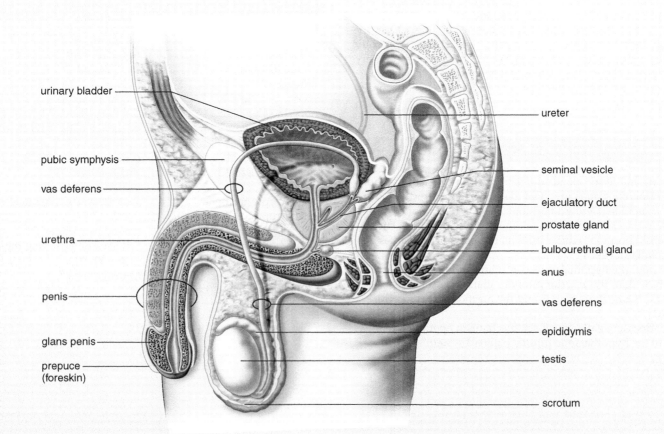

Figure 6.1   The male reproductive system.
The testes produce sperm. The seminal vesicles, the prostate gland, and the bulbourethral glands provide a fluid medium for the sperm, which move from the vas deferens through the ejaculatory duct to the urethra in the penis. The foreskin (prepuce) is removed when a penis is circumcised.

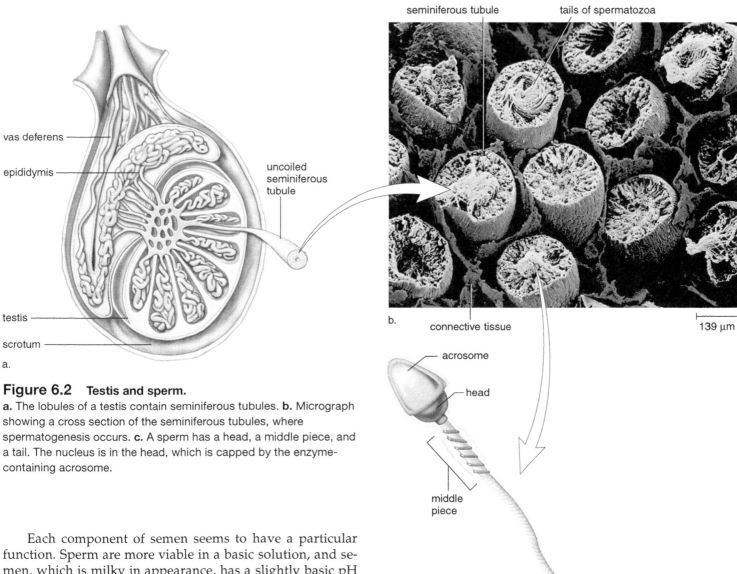

Figure 6.2 **Testis and sperm.**
a. The lobules of a testis contain seminiferous tubules. **b.** Micrograph showing a cross section of the seminiferous tubules, where spermatogenesis occurs. **c.** A sperm has a head, a middle piece, and a tail. The nucleus is in the head, which is capped by the enzyme-containing acrosome.

Each component of semen seems to have a particular function. Sperm are more viable in a basic solution, and semen, which is milky in appearance, has a slightly basic pH (about 7.5). Swimming sperm require energy, and semen contains the sugar fructose, which presumably serves as an energy source. Semen also contains prostaglandins, chemicals that cause the uterus to contract. Uterine contractions help propel the sperm toward the egg.

The Testes

The testes, which produce sperm and also the male sex hormones, are outside the pelvic cavity of the male within the scrotum. The testes begin their development inside the pelvic cavity but descend into the scrotal sacs during the last two months of fetal development. If, by chance, the testes do not descend and the male is not treated or operated on to place the testes in the scrotum, sterility—the inability to produce offspring—usually follows. This is because the internal temperature of the body is too high to produce viable sperm. A subcutaneous muscle and an adjoining muscle raise the scrotum during sexual excitement and when a higher temperature is need to warm the testes.

Anatomy of a Testis

A sagittal section of a testis shows that it is enclosed by a tough, fibrous capsule. The connective tissue of the capsule extends into the testis, forming septa that divide the testis into compartments called lobules. Each lobule contains one to three tightly coiled **seminiferous tubules** (Fig. 6.2a). Altogether, these tubules have a combined length of approximately 250 m. A microscopic cross section of a seminiferous tubule reveals that it is packed with cells undergoing spermatogenesis (Fig. 6.2b), the production of sperm.

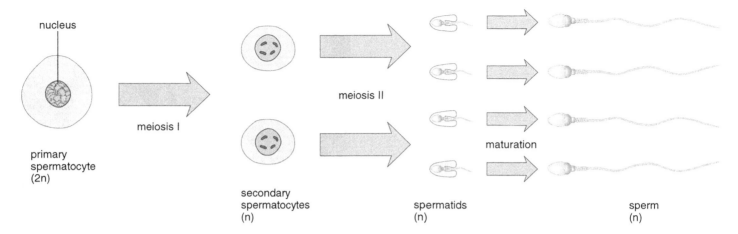

Figure 6.3   **Spermatogenesis.**
Spermatogenesis produces four viable sperm per each meiotic division (see Chapter 1, page 14).

Delicate connective tissue surrounds the seminiferous tubules. Cells that secrete the male sex hormones, the androgens, are located here between the seminiferous tubules. Therefore, these endocrine cells are called **interstitial cells.** The most important of the androgens is **testosterone,** whose functions are discussed in the next section.

Testicular cancer, or cancer of the testes, is one type of cancer that can be detected by self-examination, as explained in the reading on page 94.

Spermatogenesis

Spermatogenesis, the production of sperm, includes the process of meiosis as the sperm form. Before puberty, the testes, including the seminiferous tubules, are small and nonfunctioning. At the time of puberty, the interstitial cells get larger and start producing androgens. Then, the seminiferous tubules also enlarge, and they start producing sperm.

The seminiferous tubules contain two types of cells: germ cells, which are involved in spermatogenesis, and sustentacular (Sertoli) cells. Sustentacular cells are large; they extend from the capsule to the lumen of the seminiferous tubule. The sustentacular cells support, nourish, and regulate the development of cells undergoing spermatogenesis.

The germ cells near the capsule are called spermatogonia. The spermatogonia divide, producing more cells by mitosis. Some of these cells remain as spermatogonia, and some are **primary spermatocytes** (Fig. 6.3). The spermatocytes start the process of meiosis, which requires two divisions. Following meiosis I, cells called **secondary spermatocytes** have the reduced (or n) number of chromosomes—that is, 23 chromosomes. Following meiosis II, there are four spermatids. **Spermatids** then differentiate into sperm.

Mature **sperm,** or spermatozoa, have three distinct parts: a head, a middle piece, and a tail (see Fig. 6.2c). Mitochondria

in the middle piece provide energy for the movement of the tail, which has the structure of a flagellum. The head contains a nucleus covered by a cap called the **acrosome,** which stores enzymes needed to penetrate the egg. Notice in Figure 6.2b that the sperm are situated so that their tails project into the lumen of the seminiferous tubules.

When formed, the sperm are transported to the epididymis because the seminiferous tubules unite to form a complex network of channels that join, forming ducts. When the ducts join, an epididymis is formed.

The ejaculated semen of a normal human male contains several hundred million sperm, but only one sperm normally enters an egg. Sperm usually do not live more than 48 hours in the female genital tract.

Male Internal Accessory Organs

Table 6.1 lists and Figure 6.4 depicts the internal accessory reproductive organs in the male—that is, those located inside the body. Sperm are transported to the urethra by a series of ducts. Along the way, various glands add secretions to semen.

Table 6.1	**Male Internal Accessory Organs**
Organ	**Function**
Epididymides	Ducts where sperm mature and some sperm are stored
Vasa deferentia	Conduct and store sperm
Seminal vesicles	Contribute nutrients and fluid to semen
Prostate gland	Contributes basic fluid to semen
Urethra	Conducts sperm
Bulbourethral glands	Contribute mucosal fluid to semen

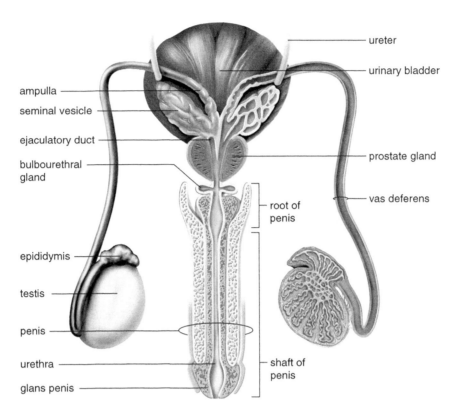

Figure 6.4   **Male reproductive system, posterior view.**
This posterior view shows the testes, the penis, and the internal accessory organs of the male reproductive system.

Epididymides

Each epididymis is a tightly coiled, threadlike tube that would stretch about 6 m if uncoiled. An epididymis runs posteriorly down along a testis and becomes a vas deferens that ascends the testis medially.

The lining of an epididymis consists of pseudostratified columnar epithelium with long cilia. Sperm are stored in the epididymides, and the lining secretes a fluid that supports them. The wall of an epididymis contains a thin layer of smooth muscle. Peristaltic contractions move the sperm along as they mature. By the time the sperm leave the epididymis, they are capable of fertilizing an egg even though they do not "swim" until they enter the vagina.

Vas Deferens

Each vas deferens is a continuation of an epididymis. As the vas deferens ascends into the abdomen, it passes through an inguinal canal. This is the passageway by which a testis descended from the abdomen into the scrotum. The canal contains the *spermatic cords*, which consist of connective tissue and muscle fibers that enclose a vas deferens, blood vessels, and nerves. The inguinal canal remains a weak point in the abdominal wall. As such, it is frequently a site of hernias. A **hernia** is an opening or separation of some part of the abdominal wall through which a portion of an internal organ, usually the intestine, protrudes.

After the vas deferens enters the abdomen, it loops as it crosses over to reach the posterior side of the urinary bladder.

The vas deferens is lined with pseudostratified columnar epithelium that is ciliated at the testicular end. A vas deferens has an expanded portion called the ampulla, but it is slender again when it joins with the duct of a seminal vesicle to form an ejaculatory duct. The ejaculatory ducts pass through the prostate gland to join the urethra.

Seminal Vesicles

The seminal vesicles lie lateral to the vas deferens on the posterior side of the bladder. They are coiled, membranous pouches about 5 cm long. The glandular lining of the seminal vesicles secretes an alkaline fluid containing fructose and prostaglandins into an ejaculatory duct. The pH of the fluid helps modify the pH of semen; the fructose provides energy for sperm; and the prostaglandins promote muscular contractions of the female genital tract that help move sperm along.

Prostate

The prostate gland encircles the urethra just inferior to the bladder. The donut-shaped gland is about 4 cm across, 2 cm thick, and 3 cm in length. The fibrous connective tissue of its capsule extends inward to divide the gland into lobes, each of which contains about 40 to 50 tubules. The epithelium lining

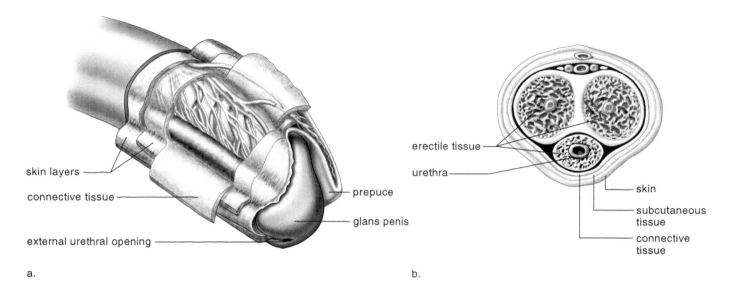

Figure 6.5   Penis anatomy.
a. Beneath the skin and the connective tissue lies the urethra, surrounded by erectile tissue. This tissue expands to form the glans penis, which in uncircumcised males is partially covered by the foreskin (prepuce). **b.** Two other columns of erectile tissue in the penis are located dorsally.

the tubules secretes a fluid that is thin, milky, and alkaline. In addition to adjusting the pH of semen, prostatic fluid enhances the motility of sperm. The secretion of the prostate gland enters the urethra when the smooth muscle in its capsular wall contracts.

As discussed in the reading on page 93, prostate enlargement frequently occurs in men.

Bulbourethral Glands

The bulbourethral glands (Cowper glands) are two small glands about the size of peas. They are located inferior to the prostate gland and enclosed by fibers of the external urethral sphincter. These glands also contain many tubules that secrete a mucuslike fluid. This fluid lubricates the end of the penis preparatory to sexual intercourse.

External Genitals

The **external genitals** are the sex organs that can be easily observed because they are located outside the body. The penis and the scrotum are the external genitals of the male. The **penis** is the male organ of sexual intercourse by which sperm are introduced into the female reproductive tract.

The penis has an internal root and an external shaft. Internally, it contains three cylindrical bodies of erectile tissue—the urethra passes though one of them (Fig. 6.5). These are supported by fibrous connective tissue, and the whole is covered with a thin, loose skin. At the glans penis, the skin

folds back on itself to form the foreskin, or prepuce. This is the structure that is removed in the surgical procedure called **circumcision.**

The erectile tissues contain distensible blood spaces. During sexual arousal, autonomic nerve impulses lead to the production of a chemical that causes the smooth muscle walls of incoming arteries to relax and the erectile tissue to fill with blood. The veins that take blood away from the penis are compressed, and the penis becomes erect. **Erectile dysfunction** (formerly called impotency) exists when the erectile tissue doesn't expand enough to compress the veins. The drug *Viagra* alters male chemistry in a way that ensures a full erection. However, the same chemical effects cause vision problems in some males taking Viagra.

Ejaculation has two phases: emission and expulsion of semen. During emission, sperm enter the urethra from each ejaculatory duct, and the prostate, seminal vesicles, and bulbourethral glands contribute secretions to the semen. Once semen is in the urethra, rhythmic muscle contractions cause semen to be expelled from the penis in spurts. During ejaculation, a sphincter closes off the bladder so that no urine enters the urethra. (Notice that the urethra carries either urine or semen at different times.)

There may be in excess of 400 million sperm in the 3.5 ml of semen expelled during ejaculation. However, the sperm count can be much lower than this, and fertilization of the egg by a sperm can still take place.

Of Special Interest

Prostate Enlargement and Cancer

The prostate gland, which is part of the male reproductive system, surrounds the urethra at the point where the urethra leaves the urinary bladder (Fig. 6A). The prostate gland produces and adds a fluid to semen as semen passes through the urethra within the penis. At about age 50, the prostate gland often begins to enlarge, growing from the size of a walnut to that of a lime or even a lemon. This condition is called **benign prostatic hyperplasia (BPH).** As it enlarges, the prostate squeezes the urethra, causing urine to back up—first into the bladder, then into the ureters, and finally, perhaps, into the kidneys.

Treatment for BPH can involve (1) taking a drug that is expected to shrink the prostate and/or improve urine flow, or (2) a more invasive procedure to reduce the size of the prostate. Prostate tissue can be destroyed by applying microwaves to a specific portion of the prostate. In many cases, however, a physician may decide that prostate tissue should be removed surgically. Sometimes, rather than performing abdominal surgery, which requires an incision of the abdomen, the physician gains access to the prostate via the urethra. This operation, called transurethral resection of the prostate (TURP), requires careful consideration because one study found that the death rate during the 5 years following TURP is much higher than that following abdominal surgery.

Prostate enlargement is due to a prostate enzyme (5a-reductase) that acts on the male sex hormone testosterone, converting it into a substance that promotes prostate growth. That growth is fine during puberty, but continued growth in an adult is undesirable. Two substances, one a nutrient supplement and the other a prescription drug for BPH, interfere with the action of this enzyme. Saw palmetto, which is sold in tablet form as an over-the-counter nutrient supplement, is derived from a plant of the same name. This drug should not be taken unless the need for it is confirmed by a physician, but it is particularly effective during the early stages of prostate enlargement. Finasteride, a prescription drug, is a more powerful inhibitor of the enzyme, but patients complain of erectile dysfunction and loss of libido while on the drug.

Two other medications have a different mode of action. Nafarelin prevents the release of LH, thus suppressing testosterone production. When it is administered, approximately half of the patients report relief of urinary symptoms even after drug treatment is halted. However, again the patients experience erectile dysfunction and other side effects, such as hot flashes. The drug terazosin, which is on the market for hypertension because it relaxes arterial walls, also relaxes muscle tissue in the prostate. Improved urine flow was experienced by 70% of the patients taking this drug. However, the drug has no effect on the prostate's overall size.

Many men are concerned that BPH may be associated with prostate cancer, but the two conditions are not necessarily related. BPH occurs in the inner zone of the prostate, while cancer tends to develop in the outer area. If prostate cancer is suspected, blood tests and a biopsy, in which a tiny sample of prostate tissue is surgically removed, can confirm the diagnosis.

Although prostate cancer is the second most common cancer in men, it is not a major killer. Typically, prostate cancer is so slow growing that the survival rate is about 98% if the condition is detected early.

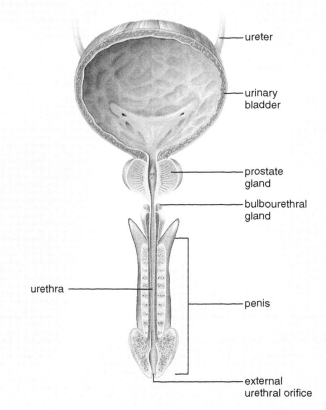

Figure 6A **Longitudinal section of a male urethra leaving the bladder.**
Note the position of the prostate gland, which can enlarge to obstruct urine flow.

Of Special Interest

Shower Check for Cancer

The American Cancer Society urges women to do a breast self-exam and men to do a testicle self-exam every month. Breast cancer and testicular cancer are far more curable if found early, and we must all take on the responsibility of checking for one or the other.

Breast Self-Exam for Women

1. Check your breasts for any lumps, knots, or changes about one week after your period.
2. Place your right hand behind your head. Move your *left* hand over your *right* breast in a circle. Press firmly with the pads of your fingers (Fig. 6B). Also check the armpit.
3. Now place your left hand behind your head and check your *left* breast with your *right* hand in the same manner as before. Also check the armpit.
4. Check your breasts while standing in front of a mirror right after you do your shower check. First, put your hands on your hips and then raise your arms above your head (Fig. 6C). Look for any changes in the way your breasts look: dimpling of the skin, changes in the nipple, or redness or swelling.

5. If you find any changes during your shower or mirror check, see your doctor right away.

You should know that the best check for breast cancer is a mammogram. When your doctor checks your breasts, ask about getting a mammogram.

Testicle Self-Exam for Men

1. Check your testicles once a month.
2. Roll each testicle between your thumb and finger as shown in Figure 6D. Feel for hard lumps or bumps.
3. If you notice a change or have aches or lumps, tell your doctor right away so he or she can recommend proper treatment.

Cancer of the testicles can be cured if you find it early. You should also know that prostate cancer is the most common cancer in men. Men over age 50 should have an annual health checkup that includes a prostate examination.

Information provided by the American Cancer Society. Used by permission.

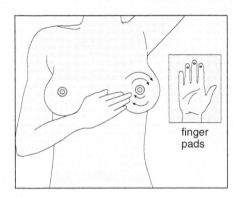

Figure 6B Shower check for breast cancer.

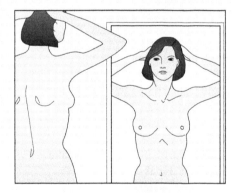

Figure 6C Mirror check for breast cancer.

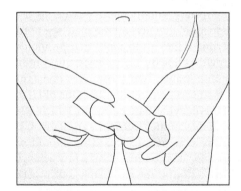

Figure 6D Shower check for testicular cancer.

6.2 Female Reproductive System

The female reproductive system includes the organs depicted in Figure 6.6. The primary sex organs of a female are the paired **ovaries** that occur in shallow depressions, one on each side of the upper pelvic cavity. The ovaries are the primary sex organs because they produce eggs and the female sex hormones, estrogen and progesterone.

The other organs depicted in Figure 6.6 are the accessory (or secondary) sex organs of a female. When an egg leaves an ovary, it is usually swept into a **uterine** (fallopian) **tube** by the combined action of the fimbriae (fingerlike projections of a uterine tube) and the beating of cilia that line the uterine tube.

Once in a tube, the egg is transported toward the uterus. Fertilization, and therefore zygote formation, usually takes place in the uterine tube. The developing embryo normally arrives at the **uterus** several days later, and then **implantation** occurs—the embryo embeds in the uterine lining, which has been prepared to receive it.

Development of the embryo and fetus normally takes place in the uterus. The lining of the uterus, called the **endometrium,** participates in the formation of the placenta (see Chapter 8, page 132), which supplies nutrients needed for embryonic and fetal development.

The uterine tubes join the uterus at its upper end, while at its lower end, the **cervix** enters the vagina nearly at a right angle. A small opening in the cervix leads from the uterus to the vagina.

The **vagina** is the birth canal and organ of sexual intercourse in females. The vagina also acts as an exit for menstrual flow. If fertilization and implantation do not occur, the endometrium is sloughed off during menstruation.

The external genital organs of the female are known collectively as the **vulva.** The vulva is recognized by two folds of skin, the labia majora and the labia minora. The cleft between the labia minora contains the openings of the urethra and the vagina.

Notice that the urinary and reproductive systems in the female are entirely separate. For example, the urethra carries only urine, and the vagina has functions that pertain only to reproduction.

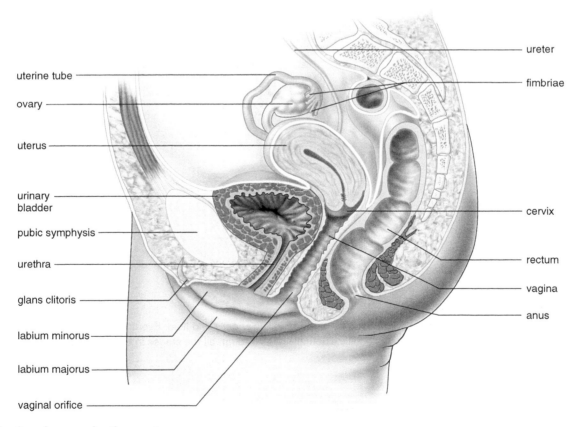

Figure 6.6   The female reproductive system.
The ovaries release one egg a month; fertilization occurs in the uterine tube, and development occurs in the uterus. The vagina is the birth canal as well as the organ of sexual intercourse.

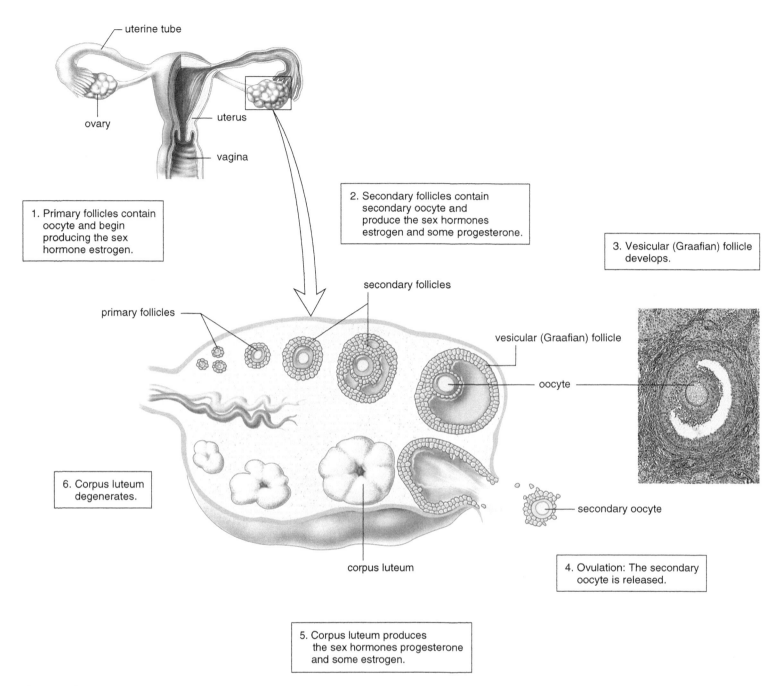

1. Primary follicles contain oocyte and begin producing the sex hormone estrogen.

2. Secondary follicles contain secondary oocyte and produce the sex hormones estrogen and some progesterone.

3. Vesicular (Graafian) follicle develops.

6. Corpus luteum degenerates.

5. Corpus luteum produces the sex hormones progesterone and some estrogen.

4. Ovulation: The secondary oocyte is released.

uterine tube

ovary

uterus

vagina

primary follicles

secondary follicles

vesicular (Graafian) follicle

oocyte

secondary oocyte

corpus luteum

Figure 6.7   Anatomy of ovary and follicle.
As a follicle matures, the oocyte enlarges and is surrounded by layers of follicular cells and fluid. Eventually, ovulation occurs, the vesicular follicle ruptures, and the secondary oocyte is released. A single follicle actually goes through all the stages in one place within the ovary.

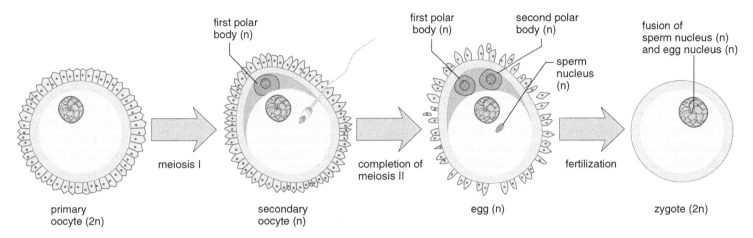

Figure 6.8   **Oogenesis in an ovary.**
Oogenesis involves meiosis I, during which the chromosome number is reduced, and meiosis II, which results in a single egg. At the end of oogenesis, there are also at least two polar bodies, nonfunctional cells that later disintegrate.

The Ovary

The ovaries are paired, oval bodies about 3 to 4 cm in length by 2 cm in width and less than 1 cm thick. They lie to either side of the uterus on the lateral walls of the pelvic cavity.

Several ligaments hold the ovaries in place (see Fig. 6.9). The largest of these, the broad ligament, is also attached to the uterine tubes and the uterus. The suspensory ligament holds the upper end of the ovary to the pelvic wall, and the ovarian ligament attaches the lower end of the ovary to the uterus.

A sagittal section through an ovary shows that it is made up of an outer cortex and an inner medulla. In the cortex are many **follicles,** each containing an immature egg, called an **oocyte** (Fig. 6.7). A female is born with as many as 2 million follicles, but the number is reduced to 300,000–400,000 by the time of puberty. Only a small number of follicles (about 400) ever mature because a female usually produces only one egg per month during her reproductive years. Because oocytes are present at birth, they age as the woman ages. This may be one reason older women are more likely to produce children with genetic defects.

Cancer of an ovary, or ovarian cancer, causes more deaths than cervical and uterine cancer.

Oogenesis

Oogenesis, the production of an egg, includes the process of meiosis (Fig. 6.8). Similar to spermatogenesis, oogenesis begins with a primary oocyte that undergoes meiosis I to become a secondary oocyte that has 23 chromosomes. The secondary oocyte undergoes meiosis II to produce an egg.

Oogenesis begins within a follicle. As the follicle matures, it develops from a primary follicle to a secondary follicle to a **vesicular (Graafian) follicle.** The epithelium of a primary follicle surrounds a primary oocyte. Pools of follicular fluid surround the oocyte in a secondary follicle. In a vesicular follicle, a fluid-filled cavity increases to the point that the follicle wall balloons out on the surface of the ovary.

As a follicle matures, the primary oocyte divides, producing two cells. One cell is a secondary oocyte, and the other is a polar body. A **polar body** is a nonfunctioning cell that occurs only during oogenesis. The vesicular follicle bursts, releasing the secondary oocyte surrounded by a clear membrane and attached follicular cells. This process is referred to as **ovulation.**

The secondary oocyte, often called an egg for convenience, enters a uterine tube. If fertilization occurs, a sperm enters the secondary oocyte, and it completes meiosis II. An egg with 23 chromosomes and a second polar body result. When the sperm nucleus unites with the egg nucleus, a zygote with 46 chromosomes is present.

A follicle that has lost its egg develops into a **corpus luteum,** a glandlike structure. If implantation does not occur, the corpus luteum begins to degenerate after about 10 days. The remains of a corpus luteum are a white scar called the **corpus albicans.** If implantation does occur, the corpus luteum continues for about six months and produces hormones that help keep the uterine lining intact.

Although a number of follicles start growing each month, only one becomes fully mature and ruptures to release a secondary oocyte. Presumably the ovaries alternate in producing functional ova. The number of secondary oocytes produced by a female during her lifetime is minuscule compared to the number of sperm produced by a male.

Female Internal Accessory Organs

Table 6.2 lists and Figure 6.9 depicts the internal accessory reproductive organs in a female—namely, the uterine tubes, the uterus including the cervix, and the vagina. The vagina serves as an organ of sexual intercourse, and sperm have to swim through the uterus to reach a secondary oocyte (egg) in a uterine tube. Development begins in the uterine tube but is completed in the uterus. If pregnancy does not take place, the lining of the uterus is shed as menstruation occurs.

Table 6.2	Female Internal Accessory Organs
Organ	**Function**
Uterine tubes (fallopian tubes)	Conduct egg; location of fertilization
Uterus (womb)	Houses developing fetus
Cervix	Contains opening to uterus
Vagina	Receives penis during sexual intercourse; serves as birth canal and as an exit for menstrual flow

Uterine Tubes

The uterine tubes, also called fallopian tubes, extend from the uterus to the ovaries. Simple columnar epithelial cells line the tubes, and some of these are ciliated. A secondary oocyte leaving an ovary usually enters a uterine tube because the **fimbriae** sweep over the ovary at the time of ovulation and the beating of the cilia creates a suction effect.

If fertilization occurs, it normally takes place in the upper one-third of a uterine tube. Once fertilization occurs, oogenesis finishes, and a zygote is present. The developing embryo is propelled slowly toward the uterus by the action of the cilia and by muscular contractions in the wall of the uterine tubes. The developing embryo usually does not arrive at the uterus for several days, and when it does, it embeds itself in the uterine lining, which has been prepared to receive it.

If fertilization does not occur, the secondary oocyte enters the uterus where it either disintegrates or is swept out with the menstrual flow.

Ectopic Pregnancy   Occasionally, the embryo becomes embedded in the wall of a uterine tube, where it begins to develop. Such tubular pregnancies cannot succeed because the tubes are not anatomically capable of allowing full development to occur. Any pregnancy that occurs outside the uterus is called an **ectopic pregnancy.**

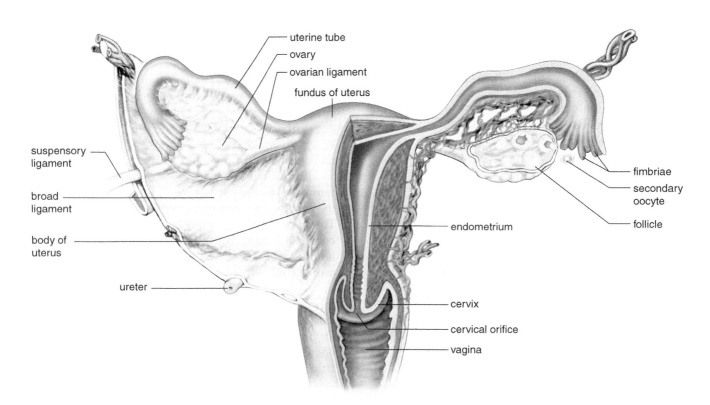

Figure 6.9   Female reproductive system, posterior view.
This posterior view shows the ovaries and the internal accessory organs of the female reproductive system. Also shown are the ligaments that support these organs.

Uterus

The *uterus* lies above and is tipped over the urinary bladder. It is a thick-walled, muscular organ about the size and shape of an inverted pear. Its wall has three layers: The outer layer is a part of the covering for the pelvic cavity. The middle layer is muscular and contracts during childbirth in response to the hormone oxytocin. The inner layer of the uterine wall, the *endometrium,* has two parts: One lines the uterus and is shed during menstruation, but the other part is permanent and gives rise to a new lining after each menstruation. Otherwise, the endometrium participates in the formation of the placenta, which supplies nutrients needed for development.

The uterus has three sections. The *fundus* is the region superior to the entrance of the uterine tubes. The *body* of the uterus is the major region. The *cervix* is the narrow end of the uterus that projects into the vagina. A cervical orifice leads to the lumen of the vagina.

The uterus has one primary function: Development of the embryo and fetus takes place in the uterus. The ordinary size of this organ, sometimes called the womb, is only a few inches, but it is capable of stretching to accommodate the growing baby.

The Cervix As mentioned, the cervix is the inferior portion of the uterus that contains an opening to the vagina. Cancer of the cervix is a common form of cancer in women. Early detection is possible by means of a **Pap smear,** which entails the removal of a few cells from the region of the cervix for microscopic examination. If the cells are cancerous, a hysterectomy (the removal of the uterus) may be recommended. Removal of the ovaries in addition to the uterus is termed an **ovariohysterectomy.** Because the vagina remains intact, the woman still can engage in sexual intercourse.

Vagina

The *vagina* is a fibromuscular tube about 9 cm long that makes a 45° angle with the small of the back. The vagina is anterior to the rectum but posterior to the bladder (see Fig. 6.6).

The mucosal lining of the vagina lies in folds that extend when the fibromuscular wall stretches. This capacity to extend is especially important when the vagina serves as the birth canal, and it can also facilitate intercourse, when the vagina receives the penis. In addition to these two functions, the vagina conveys menstrual flow to the exterior through its opening, called the vaginal orifice.

The vaginal orifice is at first enclosed by a ring of tissue called the *hymen.* The hymen ordinarily is ruptured by initial sexual intercourse; however, it can also be disrupted by other types of physical activity. If the hymen persists after sexual intercourse, it can be surgically ruptured.

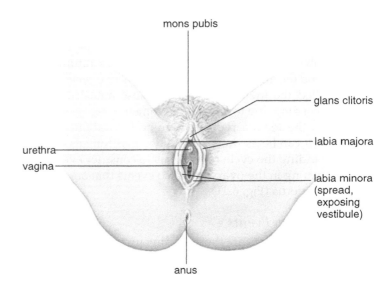

Figure 6.10 **External genitals of the female.**
At birth, the opening of the vagina is partially blocked by a membrane called the hymen. Physical activities and sexual intercourse disrupt the hymen.

External Genitals

The labia majora, labia minora, glans clitoris, and vestibular glands are the external genitals of the female (Fig. 6.10). The female external genitals are known collectively as the *vulva.*

Vulva

The **labia majora** (sing., labium majus) are two large, hair-covered folds of skin that extend posteriorly from the **mons pubis,** a fatty prominence underlying the pubic hair.

The **labia minora** (sing., labium minus) are two small folds of skin lying just inside the labia majora. They extend forward from the vaginal opening to encircle and form a foreskin for the **clitoris** (also called the glans clitoris), an organ that is homologous to the penis. Although quite small, the clitoris has a shaft of erectile tissue and is capped by a pea-shaped glans. The clitoris also has sensory receptors that allow it to function as a sexually sensitive organ.

The **vestibule,** a cleft between the labia minora, contains the orifices of the urethra and the vagina. The urinary and reproductive systems in the female are entirely separate: The urethra carries only urine, and the vagina serves as the birth canal and as the organ for sexual intercourse. The vestibular glands, which lie on either side of the vaginal opening, correspond to the bulbourethral glands in males.

Female Reproductive Cycle

The female reproductive cycle is a monthly series of events that involves the hypothalamus, the anterior pituitary, the ovaries, and the uterus. The female reproductive cycle is sometimes called the **menstrual cycle** because menstruation—a time of bleeding due to a loss of endometrial tissue—occurs. Typically, the female reproductive cycle is about 28 days long, but it can be as short as 18 days or as long as 40 days. Understanding the cycle requires us to consider events that are happening in the ovary and also events that are happening in the uterus (Fig. 6.11).

Pre-Ovulation Events

Pre-ovulation events are those leading up to ovulation. Ovulation usually occurs on day 14 of a 28-day cycle, but this is the part of the cycle that varies the most. The day of ovulation can vary from month to month, and it can be earlier or later than day 14.

The Ovary   Under the influence of follicle-stimulating hormone (FSH) from the anterior pituitary, several follicles begin developing in the ovary. Therefore, this period of time (days 1–14) is called the *follicular phase* of the ovary (Fig. 6.11). Although several follicles begin growing, only one follicle continues developing, and it secretes increasing amounts of estrogen. This particular follicle becomes more and more sensitive to FSH and then to LH. Eventually, the very high level of estrogen exerts *positive feedback* control over the hypothalamus so that it secretes ever greater amounts of GnRH. GnRH induces a surge in FSH and LH secretion by the pituitary. The LH level rises to a greater extent than does the FSH level. Under the influence of so much stimulation, ovulation occurs.

The Uterus   While the ovary is experiencing its follicular phase, *menstruation* and proliferation are occurring in the uterus. During menstruation (days 1–5), a low level of female sex hormones in the body causes the endometrial tissue to disintegrate and its blood vessels to rupture. A flow of blood and tissues passes out of the vagina during menstruation, also called the menstrual period.

During the proliferative phase (days 6–13), increased production of estrogen by a new ovarian follicle in the ovary causes the endometrium to thicken and become vascular and glandular. Proliferation ends when ovulation occurs.

Post-Ovulation Events

Post-ovulation events lead up to menstruation again if the egg is not fertilized or to implantation of the embryo in the uterine lining if the egg is fertilized. The embryo becomes a fetus that completes development in the uterus.

The Ovary   Under the influence of LH, the ovulated follicle becomes the *corpus luteum*. Therefore, this period of time (days 15–28) is known as the luteal phase of the ovary. The corpus luteum secretes progesterone and some estrogen. As the blood level of progesterone rises, it exerts *negative feedback* control over the anterior pituitary's secretion of LH so that the corpus luteum in the ovary begins to degenerate. As the luteal phase comes to an end, menstruation occurs. If fertilization of the egg does occur, the corpus luteum persists for reasons that will be discussed shortly.

The Uterus   Under the influence of progesterone secreted by the corpus luteum, a secretory phase (days 15–28) begins in the uterus. During the *secretory phase*, the endometrium of the uterus doubles or even triples in thickness (from 1 mm to 2–3 mm), and the uterine glands mature, producing a thick, mucoid secretion. The endometrium is now prepared to receive the developing embryo. If implantation of an embryo does not occur, the corpus luteum disintegrates, and menstruation occurs.

Pregnancy

If fertilization is followed by implantation, the developing placenta produces **human chorionic gonadotropin (HCG)**, which maintains the corpus luteum in the ovary until the placenta begins its own production of progesterone and estrogen. These hormones shut down the anterior pituitary so that no new follicle in the ovaries matures, and they maintain the endometrium so that the corpus luteum in the ovary is no longer needed. Usually, no menstruation occurs during pregnancy.

Menopause

Menopause, the period in a woman's life during which the female reproductive cycle ceases, is likely to occur between ages 45 and 55. The ovaries are no longer responsive to the gonadotropic hormones produced by the anterior pituitary, and the ovaries no longer secrete estrogen or progesterone. At the onset of menopause, the uterine cycle becomes irregular, but as long as menstruation occurs, it is still possible for a woman to conceive. Therefore, a woman is usually not considered to have completed menopause until menstruation has been absent for a year.

The hormonal changes during menopause often produce physical symptoms, such as "hot flashes" (caused by circulatory irregularities), dizziness, headaches, insomnia, sleepiness, and depression. These symptoms may be mild or even absent. If they are severe, women should seek medical attention. Women sometimes report an increased sex drive following menopause. It has been suggested that this may be due to androgen production by the adrenal cortex.

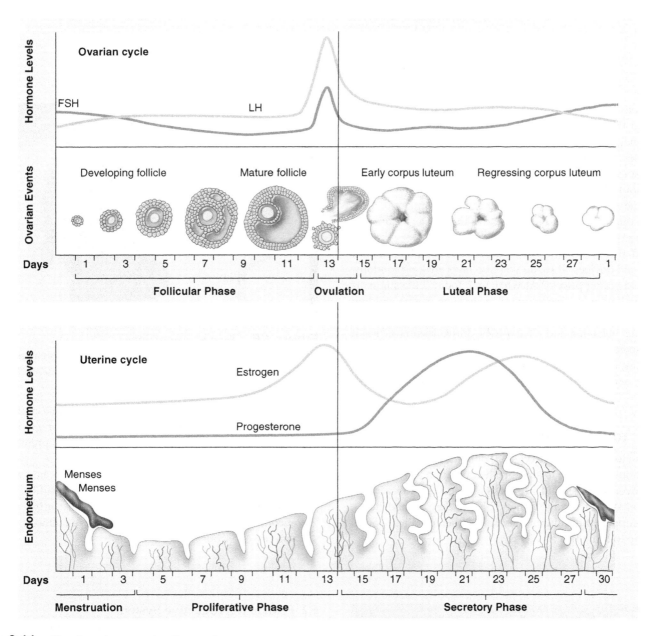

Figure 6.11   The female reproductive cycle.
Before ovulation occurs, FSH released by the anterior pituitary promotes the maturation of a follicle in the ovary. The ovarian follicle produces increasing levels of estrogen, which causes the endometrium to thicken during the proliferative phase within the uterus. After ovulation, LH released by the anterior pituitary promotes the development of the corpus luteum. This structure produces increasing levels of progesterone, which causes the endometrial lining to become secretory. Menstruation due to the breakdown of the endometrium begins when progesterone production declines to a low level.

Bioethical Focus

Sex Education in Schools

Most public schools now have some sort of sex education program, and these are widely accepted because of our concerns about teenage pregnancies, AIDS, and other sexually transmitted diseases. Sex education, however, raises a number of controversial issues, such as when it should begin and how explicit the course should be. Some people argue that the earlier sex is discussed, the earlier young people will engage in sex. Others think the opposite is true. If we remove the mystery from sex, will young people not be so anxious to try it?

Should the course include a description of birth control methods and devices? If so, do you also favor making condoms available to young people? At what age? Today, little stigma is attached to having sex before marriage or even having children out of wedlock. What are the benefits of this new attitude toward sexual behavior, and what are the drawbacks? How has it affected society today? Do you predict that this new attitude is here to stay, or will we eventually change back to a more conservative one? Should a sex education course discuss these issues?

Decide Your Opinion

1. Often, teenage mothers (Fig. 6E) don't have enough education to be able to support their children. Do you feel the government should support single moms and their babies? What about the fathers? Should they be made to help support the children they have fathered? What would you do to bring this about?

Figure 6E   Teenage pregnancy.
A wide range of attitudes is possible with regard to teenage pregnancies. How do you feel about this important societal issue?

2. Do you think sex education in school should be confined to the medical consequences of certain actions, or should it also include discussions about the morality of premarital sexual relationships?
3. If you view teenage pregnancies as a problem, how might they be stemmed—by making birth control readily available with necessary instructions for use or by encouraging abstinence? What persuasive methods would you use to encourage abstinence?

Summary

6.1 Male Reproductive System
In males, spermatogenesis, occurring in the seminiferous tubules of the testes, produces sperm that mature and are stored in the epididymides. Sperm may also be stored in the vasa deferentia before entering the urethra, along with secretions produced by the seminal vesicles, prostate gland, and bulbourethral glands. Sperm and these secretions are called semen, or seminal fluid.

The external genitals of males are the penis, the organ of sexual intercourse, and the scrotum, which contains the testes. Orgasm in males is a physical and emotional climax during sexual intercourse that results in ejaculation of semen from the penis.

6.2 Female Reproductive System
In females, oogenesis occurring within the ovaries typically produces one mature follicle each month. This follicle balloons out of the ovary and bursts, releasing an egg, which enters a uterine tube. The uterine tubes lead to the uterus, where implantation and development occur. The external genital area includes the vaginal opening, the clitoris, the labia minora, and the labia majora.

The female reproductive cycle is under the hormonal control of the hypothalamus and anterior pituitary. The pre-ovulation events include: A follicular phase occurs in the ovary because FSH from the anterior pituitary causes maturation of a follicle, which at first secretes estrogen and then progesterone. Due to positive feedback control, the hypothalamus produces increasing amounts of GnRH, and the anterior pituitary produces increasing amounts of

LH. Due primarily to the LH surge, ovulation usually occurs on day 14 of a 28-day cycle.

In the uterus, menstruation occurs, and then, under the influence of estrogen from the ovarian follicle, the endometrium rebuilds. In other words, the uterus undergoes a proliferative phase.

The post-ovulation events include: During a luteal phase in the ovary, LH from the anterior pituitary converts the ovulated follicle into the corpus luteum, which secretes progesterone and some estrogen. This phase comes to an end because of negative feedback control of the anterior pituitary. During a secretory phase in the uterus, progesterone produced by the corpus luteum causes the endometrium to thicken and become secretory. If fertilization of the oocyte does not occur, a low level of hormones causes the endometrium to break down as menstruation occurs again.

If fertilization takes place, the embryo implants itself in the thickened endometrium. Under these circumstances, the corpus luteum in the ovary is maintained because of HCG production by the placenta, and therefore, progesterone production does not cease. The endometrial lining is maintained; menstruation usually does not occur during pregnancy.

Reviewing the Chapter

1. Name two functions of the testes and the part of the organ associated with each function. 88

2. What organ in males serves to transport both urine and semen? 88

3. Name the glands that contribute to semen. Are these glands endocrine glands? 88

4. State the path of sperm prior to and during ejaculation. 90

5. Give the normal sperm count per ejaculation. Offer reasons why the sperm count is so high. 92

6. Describe the structure of the penis. 92

7. Describe the processes of erection and ejaculation. 92

8. Name the primary and accessory organs in the female reproductive system, and give a function for each. 95–99

9. Describe the anatomy of the uterus and vagina. 99

10. Name the external genitals of the female, and state their anatomical position in relation to each other. 99–100

11. Describe the events of the female reproductive cycle, and name the hormones associated with each event. 100–101

Critical Thinking Questions

1. How could you redesign the male reproductive system so that the path of urine and the path of sperm are separate?

2. Animals that reproduce in water typically do not have a penis. What advantage does a penis serve for humans, who reproduce on land? The penis has what disadvantage?

3. How could you redesign the female reproductive system so that the vagina is not both the organ of copulation and the birth canal?

4. Following menopause, females stop producing eggs and cannot get pregnant. Males produce sperm their entire lives. Relate this discrepancy to differences in the reproductive function and expected behavior of the sexes.

Understanding Key Terms

acrosome 90
androgen 88
benign prostatic hyperplasia (BPH) 93
bulbourethral gland 88
cervix 95
circumcision 92
clitoris 99
corpus albicans 97
corpus luteum 97
ectopic pregnancy 98
ejaculation 88
ejaculatory duct 88
endometrium 95
epididymis 88
erectile dysfunction 92
external genitals 92
fimbria 98
follicle 97
hernia 91
human chorionic gonadotropin (HCG) 100
implantation 95
interstitial cell 90
labia majora 99
labia minora 99
menopause 100
menstrual cycle 100
mons pubis 99
oocyte 97
oogenesis 97
ovariohysterectomy 99
ovary 95
ovulation 97
Pap smear 99
penis 92
polar body 97
primary spermatocyte 90
prostate gland 88
scrotum 88
secondary spermatocyte 90
semen 88
seminal vesicle 88
seminiferous tubule 89
sperm 90
spermatid 90
spermatogenesis 90
testis 88
testosterone 90
urethra 88
uterine tube 95
uterus 95
vagina 95
vas deferens 88
vesicular (Graafian) follicle 97
vestibule 99
vulva 95

Chapter 7

Human Sexual Response

7.1 Models of Human Sexual Response

Over the centuries, the human body's sexual responses have been explained and interpreted in many different ways. They have been assigned religious significance in some cultures and shunned as unclean in others. Sexual arousal and responsiveness, and how they are perceived and expressed, cannot be understood outside the context of the culture in which a person lives. When Margaret Mead studied the Mundugumor of New Guinea, she remarked that lovemaking was conducted "like the first round of a prizefight," with scratching and biting as part of the foreplay. She later found that in Samoa, men preceded sexual activity by singing romantic songs and reciting poetry for their women, first preparing their minds with sensual thoughts and then their bodies with sensual touching.

Sexuality has often become intertwined with the spiritual beliefs within cultures as well. In the Jewish tradition, for example, sexuality is intimately associated with concepts of creativity and unity. In Eastern Tantric traditions of yoga, Buddhism, Hinduism, and Taoism, sexual response is perceived as an expression of spiritual energies. It is believed that the energy of life and the spirit may be focused in different ways in the body and that properly used sexual energy can help convey people to the highest levels of spiritual consciousness. The emphasis is on savoring all of the sensual and spiritual aspects of sex rather than looking toward the goal of immediate gratification or satisfaction.

Western cultural imperatives often place sexual response in a more goal-oriented context, with orgasm and satisfying release being one of the primary objectives. A view of sexual arousal and response as holistic experiences involving mind, body, emotions, and spirit may be neglected in cultures that approach such issues from a more specific perspective. In 1966, in their pioneering book *Human Sexual Response*, William Masters and Virginia Johnson provided

the most thoroughly researched information on how the human body responds to sexual stimulation. Their study concentrated on careful observation and instrumental monitoring of men and women who were engaging in sexual activity. The 694 people who participated in the study were carefully interviewed and screened to obtain as "average" a sample as possible. These individuals were helped to feel comfortable with sexual activity alone in the laboratory setting before they were observed by the research team. Although Masters and Johnson saw their work as an incomplete, preliminary step to understanding human sexual response and some controversies have grown out of their study, the findings quickly gained general acceptance among professionals.

For easier understanding, Masters and Johnson divided the body's sexual responses into separate phases. Also, it is clear that human response to sexual arousal is not confined to reactions of the sex organs but involves marked changes throughout the body, especially in the muscular and cardiovascular systems.

The Masters and Johnson Four-Phase Model

As Masters and Johnson observed the sexual responses of men and women in their laboratory, they noted many similarities in responses between the two sexes. After gathering a great deal of data, they divided the sexual response process into a four-phase cycle (Fig. 7.1) It has been argued that the Masters and Johnson model may not represent a fair view of human sexual responsiveness because they only accepted people into their research who had indicated that they reached orgasm. They built their cyclical view of sexual responsiveness on the assumptions that orgasm is a natural, built-in response, and that the response cycle is programmed to repeat itself over and over during a person's lifetime, given the proper stimuli. Some sexologists believe that this may be a narrow and incomplete perspective on human

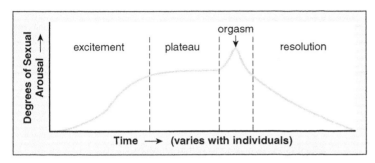

Figure 7.1 **Masters and Johnson's four-phase model.**
Masters and Johnson divided the human physical responses of
sexual arousal into four different phases: excitement, plateau,
orgasm, and resolution.

Adapted from Gary F. Kelly, *Sexuality Today*, © 2001 McGraw-Hill Companies, Inc.

sexual response. It has also been posited that our present models of sexual response are overly male-centered, still tending to create the impression that the male sex organs are more extensive, active, and explosive than those of females. Nevertheless, the phases that Masters and Johnson invented to describe sexual responsiveness constitute one way to understand some fundamental aspects of human sexuality.

Masters and Johnson labeled their first phase **excitement,** during which the body begins to show signs of arousal. Blood is routed to the pelvic region, resulting in the earliest signs of arousal, such as erection of the penis and clitoris and vaginal lubrication. A wide range of physical and psychological stimuli can initiate this excitement phase. The intensity of the body's reactions to sexual arousal gradually builds to a higher level and is maintained at that level for varying lengths of time. Masters and Johnson labeled this phase **plateau** because of its stable, or level, state of arousal.

The plateau phase, if held for sufficient periods of time, can be a major highlight of sexual response. The intensity of plateau may ebb and flow somewhat during sustained sexual activity and thus provide some special "highs" of sensual enjoyment. In any case, the buildup of tension may eventually lead to the triggering of a pleasurable sexual release called **orgasm,** or **climax.** This is a brief phase, lasting from a few seconds to slightly less than a minute, but one during which thought is momentarily suspended, and the mind becomes focused inward on a rush of pleasurable physical sensations. Almost immediately after orgasm, the body relaxes and begins to return to its unexcited state, although some people may experience more than one orgasm relatively soon. Masters and Johnson called the time of relaxation **resolution.**

Although it remains only one model for describing human sexual response, the Masters and Johnson four-phase model is used in this chapter to explain the various components of responsiveness. Other researchers have raised legitimate criticisms and offered alternative models that remain open for consideration and further study. For example, research has not shown a clear demarcation between the excitement and plateau phases in males. Instead, there tends to be a steady and continuous buildup of sexual tension that is not readily divided into phases. Some researchers have maintained that they have been unable to distinguish a measurable plateau phase at all in either men or women. It has been proposed both that the Masters and Johnson approach attempts to impose a model on male sexual response that is far more applicable to women only and, conversely, that it may actually be more applicable to men than to women.

Kaplan's Three-Phase Model

Another sex researcher and therapist, Helen Singer Kaplan, first proposed that it makes more sense, from the standpoint of the body's actual neurophysiological mechanisms, to view sexual response as occurring in two phases. The first phase is characterized by vasocongestion, or buildup of blood in the pelvic area, and an accumulation of muscular tension throughout the body, causing increases in heart rate, breathing, blood pressure, and other involuntary functions. Orgasm acts as the trigger for the second phase, **orgasmic release,** in which the vasocongestion and muscular tension are released through sudden orgasmic bursts, and then more gradually as the body returns to less excited levels of functioning.

As Kaplan worked with people's problems in sexual arousal, often referred to generally as **sexual dysfunctions,** she realized that some people simply did not seem to have much desire to become sexually aroused. This led her to suggest that a **desire phase** precedes the body's physiological responses to arousal. The desire phase represents a psychological component that can lead to physical response. It was a modification of the Masters and Johnson model, focusing on the subjective, emotional aspects of sexual arousal.

Sexual desire has been one of the more elusive and interesting areas of sexuality research, and it has also been closely tied to psychological studies of the human motivations behind behavior. For centuries, the longing for sexual interaction was assumed to be innate, and an inner drive model was used to explain it. This model has been compared to a steam boiler. Internal sexual "steam" would build up until the pressure became so great that the drive to release it

Table 7.1	Female and Male Sexual Response	
Phase	**Female Responses**	**Male Responses**
EXCITEMENT	Clitoris swells in diameter and length.	Penis becomes erect; urethral diameter begins to widen.
	Vagina lubricates; becomes expanded, lengthened, and darker in color.	Scrotal skin tenses and thickens.
	Labia majora and labia minora thicken and may open slightly.	Testes elevate slightly within scrotum.
	Breasts increase in size, and nipples become erect.	Nipples become erect in some males.
	Sex flush appears in some females.	
	Muscular tension increases.	Muscular tension increases.
	Heart rate begins to increase.	Heart rate begins to increase.
	Blood pressure begins to rise.	Blood pressure begins to rise.
PLATEAU	Clitoris retracts under foreskin.	Penis increases in diameter; becomes fully erect.
	Vagina expands and lengthens more; orgasmic platform develops.	Scrotum has no changes.
	Uterus is completely elevated.	Testes enlarge and elevate up toward body.
	Labia swell more; labia minora have deep red coloration.	Bulbourethral (Cowper) glands secrete a few drops of fluid.
	Breasts further increase in size, and nipples become turgid.	Nipples become erect and more turgid.
	Sex flush has appeared in most females, and spreads.	Sex flush appears in some males and may spread.
	Muscular tension increases further.	Muscular tension increases further.
	Respiration and heart rates increase.	Respiration and heart rates increase.
	Blood pressure elevates markedly.	Blood pressure elevates markedly.
ORGASM	Clitoris shows no changes.	Penis and urethra undergo contractions that expel semen.
	Uterus undergoes wavelike contractions.	There are no changes in the scrotum or testes.
	There are no changes in the labia.	
	Breasts and nipples show no changes during orgasm.	Nipples remain erect.
	Sex flush deepens.	Sex flush deepens.
	Loss of voluntary muscle control and spasms of some muscles occur.	Loss of voluntary muscle control and spasms of some muscles occur.
	Respiration and heart rates reach peak intensity.	Respiration and heart rates reach peak intensity.
	Blood pressure reaches its peak.	Blood pressure reaches its peak.
RESOLUTION	Clitoris returns to nonaroused position and loses its erection.	Penis erection is lost, rapidly at first and then more slowly.
	Vaginal walls relax and return to nonaroused coloration.	Scrotal skin relaxes and returns to nonaroused thickness.
	Uterus lowers to usual position, and cervical opening widens for 20–30 minutes.	Testes return to nonaroused size and position in scrotum.
	Labia return to nonaroused size, position, and color.	There is a period (refractory period) during which the male cannot be restimulated to orgasm.
	Breasts and nipples return to nonaroused size, position, and color.	Nipples return to nonaroused size.
	Sex flush disappears.	Sex flush disappears.
	Muscles relax rapidly.	Muscles relax rapidly.
	Respiration, heart rate, and blood pressure return to normal.	Respiration, heart rate, and blood pressure return to normal.
	Film of perspiration may appear on skin.	Film of perspiration may appear on skin, usually confined to soles of feet and palms of hands.

Kaplan's Three-Phase Model		
Desire Phase	**Vasocongestive Phase**	**Orgasmic-Release Phase**
Psychological components of sexual desire	Vasocongestion in pelvic region	Reversal of vasocongestion
	Increased muscular tension in body	Release of muscular tension

Figure 7.2   Kaplan's three-phase model.
Helen Kaplan divided the human physical responses of sexual arousal into these phases.

Adapted from Gary F. Kelly, *Sexuality Today*, © 2001 McGraw-Hill Companies, Inc.

was very strong. This view also assumed that there was some adverse physical consequence of not releasing the pressure, which later was shown not to be the case. Human motivation theory eventually began to focus more on the external incentives behind sexual and other forms of motivation. Although sexual desire is still a very complex phenomenon under study, it appears that the incentive motivation model is a more accurate one. Rather than assuming that sexual desire emanates from the physical sexual response system, this model suggests that a complex interaction of external stimuli triggers certain responses; interpretations of reactions, sensations, and memories; and social rules that regulate sexual activity. The motivation for sexual activity seems to be rooted not only in seeking pleasurable sensations but also in experiencing social and emotional rewards, such as feeling valued by others and oneself.

What has become known as Kaplan's three-phase model (Fig. 7.2) has special validity when considering the various dysfunctions that can interfere with sexual responsiveness. These problems may involve inhibited sexual desire, sexual aversion, erectile dysfunction, or painful intercourse, and are usually centered in either the desire phase, the vasocongestive phase, or the orgasmic-release phase of the sexual response cycle.

Individual Differences in Sexual Response

It is clear that there are more physiological similarities in the sexual responses of males and females than differences. Both males and females experience pelvic vasocongestion and a general buildup of muscular tension. Orgasm is very similar in both sexes, although it may not always be experienced. Table 7.1 summarizes the sexual response cycles of females and males. It is also evident that, within certain bounds, there can be great variation in sexual response among individuals. On the average, males tend to reach orgasm more rapidly than females during intercourse, but this phenomenon may well be influenced by the kind of stimulation and

by the past learning of the individual. Many women respond with orgasm more quickly during masturbation than in intercourse. In fact, it is not unusual for women to respond almost as quickly as men during masturbation. The amount of time for completion of the entire cycle varies with learning, the sexual situation, the kind and intensity of stimulation, and age. An entire cycle from excitement through resolution may take only a few minutes or last for several hours.

There seem to be subjective differences in the orgasms of males and females. Although male orgasms may vary in intensity and degrees of pleasure, the experience is relatively standard among all males. Women often report experiencing different physical and psychological reactions during different orgasms. Some women even appear to have a very pleasurable feeling of sexual satisfaction but do not exhibit the usual physiological responses associated with orgasm.

Women can fake orgasm, and some women feel that faking is necessary to please their sexual partners. Research has shown that with the new emphasis on female sexual pleasure, some women experience guilt feelings if they do not reach orgasm during sexual intercourse. Even though faking orgasms is less easy for men because of ejaculation, some men do fake orgasm from time to time. When such a deception enters a relationship, it can establish conditions for eventual problems. Openness and honesty about sex are a crucial part of a healthy relationship. Individual differences in sexual response patterns make it all the more important for sexual partners to take time to learn about one another's responsiveness. This will also require developing effective lines of communication about emotions, needs, and sex.

7.2 Activating the Response: Models of Sexual Arousal

The early models of an innate human "sex drive" presumed that the body had a preprogrammed sexual mechanism that could be activated by sufficient "sexual stimulation." However, it is now widely accepted within the field of sexology that no such thing as sex drive exists in the sense that some identifiable biological need is generated during times of sexual abstinence or that the body is physiologically harmed by lack of sex. The models never adequately defined what was meant by sexual stimulation. Thus, although the models have clarified how the human body *responds* sexually, they have not really helped us understand how those responses are activated.

Components of Sexual Arousal

Although various theorists have conceptualized the details in different ways, all models of sexual arousal seem to include both stimuli that are *internal,* referring to phenomena of the mind such as fantasizing about or remembering sexual activity, and stimuli that are *external,* such as direct touching of the sex organs or actually seeing someone who is considered sexy. These two aspects of activating sexual response have been divided into distinct categories: the **central arousal system,** referring to internal factors, and the **peripheral arousal system,** referring to external factors. The central arousal system seems to be located largely in the emotional and pleasure centers of the brain, and the stimuli generated there form the central, fundamental template for the person's sexual response. The peripheral arousal system refers more to the aspects of stimulation that stem from the spinal cord and its voluntary and involuntary nervous control mechanisms. This system picks up cues directly from the skin, genitals, and sense organs. Sexual arousal from both the central and peripheral systems can be measured by physiological responses, verbal reports, and behavior, although studies continue to show that there can be very real discordance among various systems and reporting mechanisms.

We do know that some people have a greater propensity toward activation of sexual response than others, a quality that might be described as *sexual arousability.* An individual's degree of arousability seems to be influenced by the sensitivity of the entire sexual response system, including not only the genitals and other body systems but also the ways in which the mind and emotions become involved. All human responses tend to be activated by stimuli, and high arousability probably reflects a high sensitivity to both external and internal stimuli that the individual has learned to interpret as sexual. In the same way, arousability may be inhibited or "turned off" by certain negative stimuli.

Research on sexual arousal has demonstrated that people's perceptions of their own degree of arousal do not always seem to coincide with the ways their sex organs are actually responding, especially for women. Using a probe that is inserted into the vagina to measure the amount of blood flow to that organ, researchers have been able to compare the genital responses to various stimuli with women's subjective reports of their degree of sexual arousal. Similar studies have been done using penile plethysmography. Women are less likely than men to pick up on the physiological cues of their own sexual arousal. When shown sexually explicit films, for example, women seem to have genital responses just as quickly as men do, but they are much less likely to identify themselves as being sexually aroused. This may be partly due to the fact that erection of the penis is anatomically more easily noticed than the internal vaginal changes associated with arousal. What is happening within the body's sexual response system may not always be recognized by the information-processing systems of the person's mind or be interpreted in the same way by different people.

Many contemporary theorists hold that genital response alone does not constitute sexual arousal because the genitals may respond to nonsexual stimuli. In other words, sexual arousal includes both physiological response and some inner, subjective experience that defines the response and perhaps the surrounding situation as sexual. All models of sexual arousal seem to recognize that psychological processes are an essential component. Emotions and the ways in which the brain processes information play a major role in activating—or deactivating—a person's sexual response. The various stimuli that come to the attention of the human mind must be cognitively transformed to result in emotional or sexual responses. This is obviously a very complex process, profoundly influenced by the learning processes and environments experienced by different people. Things that may seem intrinsically sexual to one individual may represent a turnoff to someone else. Then again, a stimulus that is not even perceived by the individual to be pleasurable or sexual can still cause a physical response of the genitals. Emotions that have nothing to do with sex per se—such as depression or anxiety—may still exert a strong influence on sexual arousal mechanisms, both positively and negatively.

Although theories of sexual arousal are still in the earlier stages of development, Figure 7.3 summarizes what is presently believed regarding the activation of sexual response. It is generally agreed that a sequence of events leads to sexual arousal, involving the combination of central and peripheral mechanisms, the mind and body interacting in many different ways. If the mind ascribes sexual meaning to a particular stimulus, sexual arousal can result. In some cases, this processing seems relatively *automatic,* leading to rapid physiological response such as erection or vaginal lubrication. A *controlled* processing of stimuli may result in more complicated reactions, including the inhibition of sexual response. When human sexual response is easily activated, it is probably the result of the automatic arousal mechanisms. When people are sexually dysfunctional for psychological reasons, these automatic mechanisms are disrupted by controlling factors such as emotions and negative interpretations.

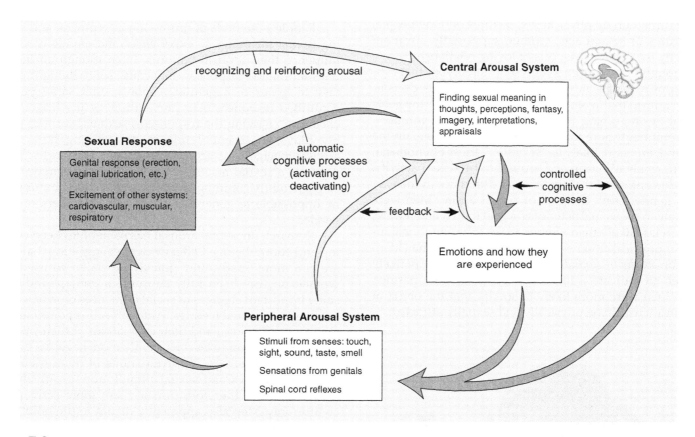

Figure 7.3   Mind-body interactions in sexual arousal.

This diagram summarizes the models that explain how human sexual response is activated. The initiating mechanism is the central arousal system, mediated by the brain and its ways of processing information. The peripheral arousal system is partly influenced by input from the brain, but it also processes cues that come directly from sensory stimulation. The brain continues to participate in activation, or deactivation, of sexual response, depending on complex positive and negative feedback loops influenced by the individual's learned ways of processing potential sex cues.

Sources: Lawerence Erlbaum, and E. Janssen & W. Everaerd, "Determinants of Male Sexual Arousal," in *Annual Review of Sex Research,* Vol. 4 (1993); E. Laan & W. Everaerd, "Determinants of Female Sexual Arousal: Psychological Theory and Data," *Annual Review of Sex Research,* Vol. 4 (1995).

Women, Men, and Sexual Arousal

Of the many purported differences between men and women, the differences in sexual arousability are among the most rigidly believed. From as far back as the nineteenth century, it was believed that males spontaneously get in touch with their potentials for sexual arousal, whereas females become initiated into their sexual potentials within the context of a romantic relationship and the loving touch of a man. These generalizations persist today in the form of assumptions that women become sexually aroused less often and less rapidly than men. Men and women are also said to become sexually aroused by different stimuli—whereas men are turned on by physical sex, pictures of nude people, and pictures of sexual acts, women supposedly are more aroused by the romantic aspects of loving relationships.

Although these concepts represent stereotypes that cannot be applied to all individuals, research studies do continue to confirm that women tend to "romanticize" the goals of sexual desire, seeing them as love, emotional intimacy, and commitment more than do men (Fig. 7.4). Men, on the other hand, are more likely to "sexualize" these phenomena, seeing the goals of desire and arousal to be sexual activity. One study confirmed that there was a difference in the way the two genders saw the goal of sexual desire. Men were more likely to see sexual activity as a goal than women were, and much less likely than women to see love, emotional intimacy, or physical closeness as goals of arousal. When identifying the *objects* of sexual desire, women were more likely than men to indicate a loved one or a romantic partner, whereas men were more likely to specify that the object of sexual desire would be physically and sexually attractive.

Figure 7.4   Sexual arousal.
Women tend to believe that the goals of sexual desire are love, emotional intimacy, and commitment, while men tend to see sexual activity as the goal of sexual desire.

The majority of sexologists now generally agree that people learn to be sexual. The physiological responses of the genitals and other organ systems provide the physical template on which subjective interpretations and experiences are socially constructed. We know that social standards have generally been less permissive toward the sexual activity of females than toward that of males. In many laboratory settings, it has been found that men are more attuned to their bodies' responses and more likely to interpret them accurately. It seems likely, then, that women's genital responses are less involved in the determination of their subjective experience of sexual arousal than are external factors such as a relationship.

People's methods of processing information and attaching sexual meanings to experiences and emotions seem to influence their arousal patterns. Even though an individual's automatic responses may cause some thought or fantasy to generate a genital response, that same person's controlled responses may prevent him or her from experiencing or enjoying the response as sexual. Learning probably plays an essential role in determining how sexual arousal mechanisms actually function in each individual to generate a sexual response. Some of these differences may be particularly common to males or to females, but it would be impossible to generalize them to all members of either gender.

Research on sexual arousal has sometimes been confusing and contradictory. Older evidence suggesting that males are far more easily and quickly sexually aroused than women has not been fully supported, perhaps indicating some important changes in social influences on women concerning their sexual feelings. Women's self-reported feelings about sexual arousal and their evaluations of their own sexual responses tend to be consistently more negative than the self-reported feelings and evaluations of men. Males still seem to value sex and sexual stimuli more positively than do women and therefore pursue them more actively and comfortably. Men also apparently dream to the point of orgasm more frequently than do women.

7.3 Female Sexual Response

Excitement Phase

When the female body begins to respond sexually, changes are often first noticed in the vagina. As blood begins to build up (vasocongestion) in the blood vessels of the genital region, the vaginal walls darken in color, a change that is not visible externally. This vasocongestion causes a slippery, alkaline fluid to seep through the lining of the vagina. This substance functions as a lubricant for sexual activity and may also help to create alkaline conditions in the vagina that are beneficial to sperm. The amount of lubrication in the vagina is not, however, necessarily a sign of how sexually aroused the woman is or how ready she might be for sexual activity. Particularly for females, genital responses must be supported by environmental cues and stimuli in order to create a sexual context.

Another change during the excitement phase is the lengthening and distention of the inner one-third of the vagina. The uterus is also pulled upward from its usual position (Fig. 7.5). The vasocongestion causes changes in the labia majora and minora as they begin to enlarge and sometimes to open slightly. The clitoris begins to swell somewhat, and its shaft may elongate slightly. Some of the vaginal lubrication may flow out onto the labia and clitoris, depending on its copiousness and on whether or not the particular sexual activity is apt to bring internal secretions to the exterior.

Other areas of the body respond to sexual excitement as well. Often the nipples become harder and erect, although this response also may result from nonsexual stimuli. Many women show a darkening of the skin through the neck, breasts, and upper abdomen during sexual excitement; this is termed the "sex flush." General muscular tension begins to build throughout the body as heart rate and blood pressure increase.

Plateau Phase

The second stage of the female sexual response cycle leads to further changes in the vagina. The outer third of the vaginal wall becomes swollen with blood, narrowing the space within the vagina slightly. The inner two-thirds of the vagina show slightly more lengthening and expansion. The labia minora also become engorged with blood, causing thickening and a flaring outward. The swelling of the outer third of the vagina and the minor lips seems to create the tension that is an important precursor of orgasm, so together they are termed the "orgasmic platform" (Fig. 7.6). During the plateau phase, the clitoral glans retracts back under its foreskin so that it no longer receives any direct stimulation.

The breasts have usually become somewhat engorged by this time, and nipple erection may be maintained. Increase in breast size is not as pronounced in women who have breast-fed a baby. The sex flush, if present, sometimes spreads to the shoulders, back, buttocks, and thighs during the plateau phase. Muscular tension continues to increase, along with heart rate, respiration rate, and blood pressure. The heart rate usually increases to between 100 and 175 beats per minute.

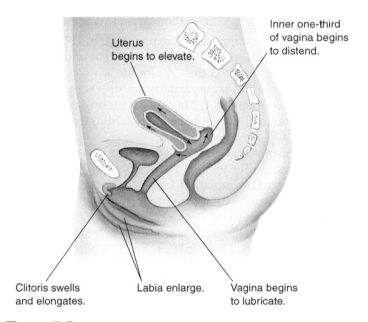

Figure 7.5   Female excitement phase.
In the female, the first sign of sexual arousal is often the lubrication of the vagina. This is accompanied by the enlargement of the vaginal area, including the clitoris and the major and minor labia, and a darkening of the color of the vaginal walls.

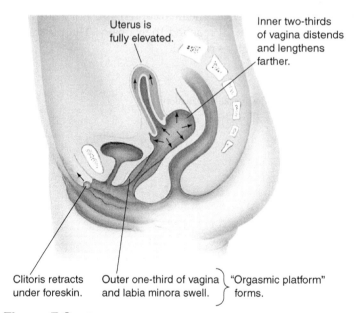

Figure 7.6   Female plateau phase.
In the plateau phase of female sexual response, high levels of arousal are maintained. The orgasmic platform is caused by swelling of tissues in the outer third of the vagina, which causes the entrance to it to narrow. The clitoris retracts under its foreskin.

Orgasm

The pleasurable release of sexual tension occurs during the sexual climax, or orgasm. This is an intense experience, both physically and emotionally, and in females, it is immediately preceded by a sensation of "suspension," at which time the pulse rate reaches its peak. Then there is a feeling of increased sexual awareness in the area of the clitoris, which spreads upward, and a "suffusion" of warmth that spreads from the pelvis throughout the body. Many women also experience a sensation of throbbing in the lower pelvic area.

During the pleasurable feelings of the orgasmic phase, there are muscular contractions in the outer third of the vagina and in the anal area. Following the initial contraction, which may last two to four seconds, there are three or four rhythmic contractions at intervals of about 0.8 second. There may be up to 15 such contractions, the interval between them gradually lengthening, and their intensity gradually decreasing. Two to four seconds after orgasm begins, the uterus has some mild, wavelike contractions that move from its top to the cervix (Fig. 7.7).

During orgasm, muscles throughout the body may contract involuntarily, causing pelvic thrusting and spastic movements of the neck, hands, arms, feet, and legs. The woman may scream, gasp, moan, or shout out words during the orgasmic experience. The heart and respiratory rates and blood pressure have all reached their peaks. The pulse rate may be twice as high as normal.

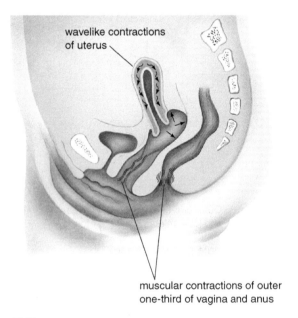

wavelike contractions of uterus

muscular contractions of outer one-third of vagina and anus

Figure 7.7   Female orgasmic phase.
Orgasm is the release of sexual tension involving a total body response. The female physical response is marked by simultaneous rhythmic muscular contractions of the uterus, the outer third of the vagina, and the anal sphincter.

Resolution Phase

Following the release of sexual tension through orgasm, the body gradually returns to its unexcited state. As blood leaves the pelvic region, the vagina returns to its usual size and color, and the labia return to their prearoused state. Within 10 seconds, the glans of the clitoris emerges from the foreskin to its typical position, and within 15 to 30 minutes, it has returned to its usual size. The uterus also lowers to its prearoused position.

During resolution, the other signs of sexual arousal also gradually disappear. The breasts decrease in size, and the nipples lose their erection. The sex flush leaves the body in the reverse order from which it developed, and respiration, pulse, and blood pressure soon return to their normal levels. It is quite common for the body to become wet with perspiration during resolution. As the muscles throughout the body relax, there is often a feeling of drowsiness that may lead to sleep.

Multiple Orgasms in Women

During the resolution phase of sexual response, many females may be restimulated to orgasm. Unlike males, who go through a period when they cannot be restimulated to climax, some females are capable of experiencing numerous orgasms during a single sexual experience. In 1953, Alfred C. Kinsey, preeminent sex researcher and founder of the Kinsey Institute, reported that 14% of the women surveyed regularly experienced sequential (or multiple) orgasms during sexual encounters, and Masters and Johnson proposed that most, if not all, women have the potential for more than one orgasm.

Research since that time has suggested that the multiorgasmic experience for women may depend a great deal on the type of sexual stimulation involved in their sexual responsiveness, and not all women report having been multiorgasmic. In one study of 720 women, about 47% indicated they usually had a single orgasm, and 43% reported that they had experienced multiple orgasms. It would appear that women tend to be multiorgasmic through particular means of stimulation. In this study, for example, 26% of the women had experienced multiple orgasms through masturbation; 18.3% through stimulation by a partner; and 24.7% by sexual intercourse. Only 7% had experienced more than one orgasm by all three types of stimulation. Of those women who tended to have only single orgasms, 27% were interested in being able to experience multiple orgasms. It has been suggested that we should stop assuming that female sexual satisfaction rests solely on whether one or more orgasms is experienced and also that we should stop undervaluing women's capacity for multiple orgasms by giving precedence to a male-centered single orgasm norm.

Controversies About Female Sexual Response

Orgasms

For many years, there has been a controversy over the existence of two types of female orgasm: clitoral and vaginal. Masters and Johnson concluded that, regardless of how it is produced, female orgasm proceeds physiologically in basically the same manner as previously described. They believe that, at least from a biological viewpoint, the clitoral-vaginal dichotomy is unfounded. However, the controversy continues as researchers report distinct differences between how women experience orgasm produced by clitoral or vulval stimulation and that produced by deeper vaginal stimulation. Some women experience orgasm as the result of stimulation of the cervix. This has been called a "uterine orgasm." It has also been suggested that some women experience a "blended orgasm," which is a combination of the clitoral-vulval experience and the uterine orgasm. The difference in orgasmic responses could be due to the two different nerve pathways that serve the sex organs: the *pudendal nerves* and the *pelvic nerves.* In women, the pudendal nerve system connects with the clitoris, and the pelvic system innervates the vagina, cervix, and uterus. It is therefore hypothesized that there may be two different neurological routes to producing orgasm.

This controversy may well represent one of those cases in which it is difficult to reconcile the objective measures of science and the subjective reports of people's experiences. It does seem clear that orgasm has both physiological and psychological components, meaning that each person will have individualized perceptions and interpretations of the experience. Regardless of what sort of orgasm a woman might experience, the most important issue is that she be able to feel that a sexual activity has been fulfilling to her personally.

The G Spot

There is a possibility that an area on the inner front wall of the vagina may become particularly sexually sensitive. The existence of such an area was proposed years ago by a German physician named Gräfenberg. The idea was revived in the 1980s by other researchers who claimed that, indeed, a mass of tissue in the anterior vagina swells during sexual arousal and can lead to intense orgasmic experiences. They named it the **G spot,** after Gräfenberg. Some scientists have objected, feeling that the sensitive "spot" is not found in a large percentage of women and that, when it is present, it is not in a clearly defined location. Evidence does seem to indicate that stimulation of the anterior wall of the vagina usually results in more sexual arousal than stimulation of the back wall. It has been suggested that this be referred to as an "area" rather than a spot because it seems to vary in size.

The confusion here may well result from the fact that the spongy tissue in this area may not become fully engorged with blood and sensitized until the clitoris is fully engorged. This may take up to 25 minutes in some women, and so they may never experience the sensitivity of the G spot. There has also been speculation that this vaginal region may be activated by a different set of nerves (pelvic nerves) than is the clitoris (pudendal nerves), and so it has been difficult to separate the different types of orgasm that may result from their stimulation. As the media created the impression that the G spot was some sort of magic button that could be pushed to enhance female sexual enjoyment, the picture became confusing for both women and their partners. The one thing that this controversy has confirmed is that many women are sensitive to vaginal stimulation, thus laying to rest a traditional view of the vagina as a rather insensitive organ. It also reminds us that there are individual differences in sexual response, emphasizing the need for good patterns of communication between sexual partners.

Ejaculation

Gräfenberg also suggested in his 1950 article that some women might ejaculate a semenlike substance from their urethras at the time of orgasm. This contention has also seen a recent revival, and it has been hypothesized that **Skene glands,** located inside the urethra, might be similar to the prostate of males. During particularly intense orgasms, some women report that a liquid is expelled from their urethras that does not seem to be urine. A survey of 1,230 women in North America found that 40% of them had experienced such ejaculation. Those who had ejaculated were more likely to report their sexual responsiveness as above average in intensity. Some women seem to assume that the fluid is urine and are therefore reluctant to pursue the matter. Some of those women may even try to prevent themselves from experiencing intense orgasms in an effort to reduce the chances of emitting this fluid. Only further research will finally resolve these issues.

Social factors play an important role in how female orgasm, the G spot, and female ejaculation are perceived in our culture. There may well be male power issues involved. If the sexual focus in our society has traditionally been on what pleases men and glorifies their sexual organs, it may be difficult to shift that focus toward those places in women that are associated with intense sexual pleasure.

Sexual Arousal and Response in Your Life

This is a highly personal assessment meant for your individual use only. It can help you evaluate and understand some of your reactions to and feelings about your own sexual arousability and responsiveness. As this chapter has emphasized, different people seem to have different levels of arousability and different cues or sensitivities that can activate or deactivate (turn on or turn off) sexual response. There is no single "right" or "normal" way to be.

Complete the questionnaire first, and then continue reading to understand what you may learn from it. This is not in any way meant to be a scientific test; it is only a simple instrument to help you further clarify some of your own reactions.

Using the following scale, rate statements 1–15 for yourself. (You may not want to write your responses in the book for others to see.)

5 — Strongly agree

4 — Somewhat agree

3 — Neutral/uncertain

2 — Somewhat disagree

1 — Strongly disagree

1. I find myself thinking about sexual things frequently.
2. I think about sex more than the average person.
3. My thoughts about sex often lead to sexual arousal.
4. I experience sexual arousal several times a week.
5. I can reach orgasm during a sexual experience anytime I wish.
6. In general, I have positive feelings about my own sexual responsiveness.
7. I enjoy the sensations of sexual excitement in my sex organs and in the rest of my body.
8. I like experiencing orgasm (or do not mind at all if I do not reach orgasm) during sexual activity.
9. I know very clearly what turns me on sexually.
10. I am very comfortable with the place that sexual arousal and responsiveness have in my life.
11. Sometimes I get sexually aroused at inappropriate or embarrassing times.
12. I wish I could get sexually aroused more easily than I do.
13. I never/rarely reach orgasm, and this concerns me.
14. (If applicable now or in the past) My partner sometimes seems dissatisfied with my sexual responses.
15. (If applicable) My partner wishes I would get sexually aroused more easily/often.

Figure 7A

Evaluating Your Responses

As you examine your responses to the various items, it would be helpful to evaluate them in three different blocks:

Items 1–5: These items relate to the frequency with which you experience sexual thoughts and arousal. The higher your numbers, the more frequently you think about sexuality and experience arousal and response. As you look at the numbers, do you see any trend? What do they say to you about your sexuality?

Items 6–10: These items can help you examine your reactions to your sexual responsiveness. The higher the numbers, the greater degree of relative satisfaction you are indicating for your patterns of sexual arousal and response. The lower the numbers, the greater the likelihood that you are not particularly happy or satisfied with the ways in which you respond to sexual stimuli.

Items 11–15: These items focus on the dissatisfactions you may be experiencing with regard to your sexual responsiveness and—if applicable—with how that responsiveness fits into a relationship. Higher numbers would suggest that you have a fair amount of discomfort and negative reaction to various aspects of your sexual arousal and response.

What Does It All Mean for You?

Keep in mind that this assessment is a very rough measure of some of your own perceptions. It should help you clarify some of your own thoughts and reactions regarding your sexual responses. As you survey your responses, does any picture seem to emerge? Do you seem to be an individual who is quite comfortable and satisfied with his/her patterns of sexual arousal and response? Are you unsure of yourself and unable to get a very clear look at how sexual responsiveness fits into your life? Have your responses to the items suggested that you have a great deal of dissatisfaction about your sexuality?

If you are able to get some general sense of how you react to your own sexual arousal and responses, it may be valuable to you. It may also alert you that you have some issues worth considering, some of which may be positive and some negative.

Figure 7B

Kegel Exercises and Sexual Response

In the early 1950s, a surgeon by the name of Arnold Kegel developed exercises for the pubococcygeal (PC) muscle that surrounds the vagina. He originally intended the exercises for girls and women who had difficulty with urine leaking from their bladders. Eventually, Kegel found that in some of his subjects a well-toned PC muscle increased the ability to experience orgasmic satisfaction. Kegel exercises have also been recommended for pregnant women, and they seem to help the vagina and uterus return to normal shape and tone more quickly after the delivery of a baby. It has been suggested that men keep their PC muscles in good shape to ensure good orgasms as well. Although there is controversy over whether the PC muscle actually affects orgasmic capacity, keeping it in good shape is at least a healthy thing, and it may also enhance general sexual sensitivity.

Kegel exercises are accomplished by first locating the PC muscle. This is best accomplished by stopping and starting the flow of urine during urination because the same muscle is involved. Once the individual is familiar with its location, it is usually suggested that the muscle be contracted firmly for two or three seconds and then released. Although it has been recommended that these contractions be done in sets of 10, building up to several sets each day, some experts now believe it is unnecessary, or even unwise, to exercise the PC muscle too much.

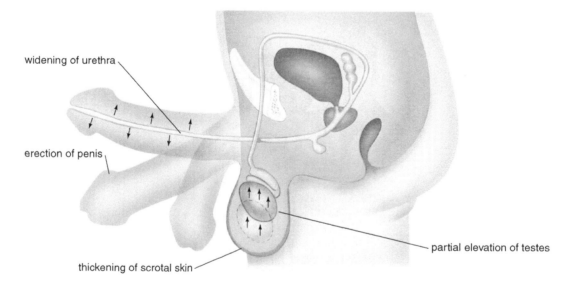

Figure 7.8   Male excitement phase.
Vasocongestion in the male leads to erection of the penis, the first physical sign of sexual arousal. The testes are lifted up into the scrotum as a result of the shortening of the spermatic cords and contraction of the scrotal sacs. The scrotal tissue itself thickens.

7.4 Male Sexual Response

Excitement Phase

Vasocongestion in the pelvic area during early sexual arousal contributes to erection of the penis, the first sign of the excitement phase in males. The degree of erection during this phase depends on the intensity of sexual stimuli. Eventually, the inner diameter of the urethra doubles. Vasocongestion also causes thickening of the scrotal tissue, and the scrotum pulls upward toward the body. The testes become elevated within the scrotum, although if the excitement phase continues for more than 5 or 10 minutes, the testes return to their original position for a time (Fig. 7.8).

Nipple erection and the appearance of the sex flush are less common in males than in females, but both phenomena are usually first observed during the excitement phase if they occur at all. Muscular tension increases throughout the body during the late excitement phase, and heart rate and blood pressure both increase. Sometimes secretion from the bulbourethral (Cowper) glands appears during this stage, or even preceding erection.

Plateau Phase

The penis does not change markedly during the second stage of sexual response, although it is less likely that a man will lose his erection if distracted during the plateau phase than during excitement. As orgasm nears, the corona of the glans of the penis becomes more swollen, and the glans itself may take on a deeper, often reddish-purple color. There are no further changes in the scrotum, but the testes increase in size by 50% or more and become elevated up toward the body. During plateau, the bulbourethral glands often secrete a few drops of fluid, some of which may appear at the tip of the penis. The longer plateau stimulation is maintained, the more fluid is produced (Fig. 7.9).

Muscular tension heightens considerably during the plateau phase, and involuntary body movements increase as orgasm approaches. The nipples may become erect. Males often display clutching or grasping movements of the hands in late plateau. The heart rate increases to between 100 and 175 beats per minute, and the blood pressure also increases. The respiratory rate increases as well, especially in the later plateau phase. If the sex flush is present, it may spread to the neck, back, and buttocks.

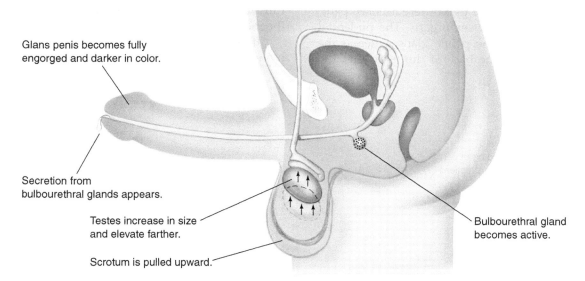

Figure 7.9   Male plateau phase.
A generalized increase in neuromuscular tension is experienced in both males and females in the plateau phase. In the male, the head of the penis increases slightly in size and deepens in color. The testes swell by 50 to 100%. The testes continue to elevate. A secretion from the bulbourethral glands may appear from the male urethra and may carry live sperm.

Orgasm

In males, actual orgasm and ejaculation are preceded by a distinct inner sensation that orgasm is imminent. This has been called **ejaculatory inevitability.** Almost immediately after that feeling is reached, the male senses that ejaculation cannot be stopped. The most noticeable response in the penis during orgasm is the ejaculation of semen. The muscles at the base of the penis and around the anus contract rhythmically, with intervals of about 0.8 second between the first three or four contractions. This varies in different individuals. The intensity of the contractions then diminishes, and the interval between contractions lengthens. It is the first few contractions that expel the largest amount of semen. The testes are held at their maximum elevation throughout orgasm (Fig. 7.10).

Males often experience strong involuntary muscle contractions throughout the body during orgasm and usually exhibit involuntary pelvic thrusting. The hands and feet show spastic contractions, and the entire body may arch backward or contract in a clutching manner. Many men moan or yell during orgasm and have a grimacing facial expression. Breathing, heart rate, and blood pressure all reach a peak during orgasm, and some men begin perspiring during this stage.

Like women, men also have two different nerve pathways to different parts of their sex organs. The pudendal nerve system connects with the penile glans, whereas the pelvic nerve system serves the base of the penis and the prostate gland. This could explain why orgasm is not necessarily always accompanied by ejaculation of semen. Orgasm produced from localized stimulation of the glans is somewhat less likely to be accompanied by ejaculation. It is also known that different sets of nerves are involved, depending on whether erection is generated by direct touching of the genitals or by psychological stimuli such as erotic thoughts and fantasies, although the two systems are somewhat interactive. In any case, male orgasm and ejaculation should be viewed as two essentially separate sexual responses that most often happen at the same time.

Resolution

Immediately following ejaculation, the male body begins to return to its unexcited state. About 50% of the penile erection is lost right away, and the remainder of the erection is lost over a longer period of time, depending on the degree of stimulation and nonsexual activity. Urination, walking, and other distracting activities usually lead to a more rapid return of the penis to its fully flaccid state. The diameter of the urethra returns to its usual width. The scrotum begins to relax as vasocongestion decreases, and the testes return to their prearoused size and position. Resolution in the scrotum and testes takes varying lengths of time, depending on the individual.

If nipple erection and sex flush have appeared, they gradually diminish. Muscular tension usually is fully dissipated

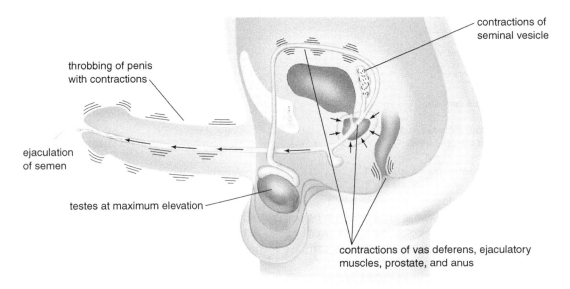

Figure 7.10   **Male orgasmic phase.**
Male orgasm and ejaculation occur in two distinct phases but are perceived as occurring simultaneously. The vas deferens and prostate and seminal vesicles begin a series of contractions that force semen into the urethra. The contractions continue until the semen is ejaculated.

within five minutes after orgasm, and the male feels relaxed and drowsy. Many men fall asleep quickly during the resolution phase. About one-third of men begin a perspiration reaction during this stage. Heart rate, respiration rate, and blood pressure rapidly return to normal. Resolution is a gradual process that may take as long as two hours.

Refractory Period

During resolution, most males experience a period of time during which they cannot be restimulated to ejaculation. This period of time is known as the **refractory period.** The duration of the refractory period depends on a variety of factors, including the amount of available sexual stimulation, the man's mood, and his age. On the average, men in their late 30s cannot be restimulated to orgasm for 30 minutes or more. The period gradually increases with age. Very few men beyond their teenage years are capable of more than one orgasm during sexual encounters, except occasionally. Most men feel sexually satiated with one orgasm.

Multiple Orgasms in Men

There have always been tales of men who are capable of experiencing more than one orgasm during a single sexual experience, presumably without experiencing a refractory period. Some studies have reported on small numbers of men who claim to be able to experience multiple orgasms, and some laboratory measures of their responses have been taken. These studies suggest that some men seem able to delay ejaculation but still experience some internal contractions and pleasurable sensations associated with orgasm. It has been suggested that men can learn to develop the muscle control enabling them to separate orgasm from ejaculation. However, in at least one case study, the man was able to ejaculate each time while reaching six separate orgasms in 36 minutes. Evidence suggests that this is an unusual pattern, although this particular male had experienced multiple ejaculations since the age of 15. Some men, especially at younger ages, may have a brief refractory period and may experience a second ejaculation quite rapidly, sometimes without losing their erections. The best evidence at present indicates that once ejaculation has occurred, a refractory period follows for most men. For a few men (5% or less), there does seem to be the possibility of experiencing pleasurable orgasmic reactions two or more times prior to ejaculation. When ejaculation does not occur, the refractory period tends not to occur, and so further orgasmic response is possible.

7.5 Hormonal Regulation of Sexual Arousal and Response

A popular notion contends that sex hormones control our levels of interest in sexual activity. This assumption would have us believe that the more "hormones" people produce in their bodies, the stronger are their sex drives. The picture of how hormones affect sexual behavior is a complicated one, but we can conclude that the popular assumptions about a direct correlation between hormone levels and sexual activity may not be entirely accurate.

Although it is known that women's levels of sexual activity vary over the menstrual cycle and could therefore be associated with hormonal changes, many other factors could also play a role. Some research studies have tended to find no direct or immediate correlation between sexual arousal and the concentration of sex hormones in the blood of either men or women, although a positive correlation has been demonstrated in adolescent females.

On the other hand, a direct correlation has been found between the salivary testosterone levels in adolescent males and their levels of sexual activity. It may be that testosterone simply has a more direct effect on the sexual interests and activities of young males than on adult men. However, there is also the indirect effect of testosterone creating physical changes in adolescent boys that are signs of sexual maturity, and this may have the psychological outcome of increasing

sexual activity. In certain males, but not all, where low testosterone levels have been associated with difficulty achieving erections, administering testosterone as a treatment is sometimes effective in reestablishing sexual function. All of this adds up to behavior and levels of testosterone in the body, but there may be a chicken-and-egg issue here that is yet unresolved.

One study measured the amounts of testosterone in the saliva of four male-female couples on nights when they had sexual intercourse and nights when they did not. Saliva samples were taken both before and after the sexual activity. In both the men and the women, the amount of testosterone present in the saliva was greater after the couples had intercourse. There was no increase in hormone levels prior to intercourse. This led the researchers to conclude that the sexual activity seemed to affect the testosterone concentration more than the hormone affected sexual activity. This is consistent with another finding that testosterone levels rise in men when they become involved in watching sporting events, especially when their teams are winning, presumably demonstrating a correlation between hormone levels and general bodily and psychological arousal.

Organizing and Activating Effects

The secretions of endocrine glands may have many different effects on an individual. Traditionally, it has been taught that hormones exert their influences in one of two ways. One is called an **organizing effect** and refers to ways in which hormones control patterns of early development in the body, playing a crucial role in the structure and function of particular organs. Chapter 5 explains how certain hormones control the development of sex glands and external genitals in the fetus and how they may lead to some differences in the way the nervous systems of males and females develop. However, growing evidence indicates that once hormones have done their organizing, the same or other hormones may continue to alter processes of development and patterns of behavior later on.

The other effect that hormones have been thought to exert is referred to as an **activating effect.** This describes the potential some hormones can have for affecting an actual behavior, either by activating or deactivating it. In the matter of sexual response, it has been tempting to assume that levels of particular sex hormones in the bloodstream might increase or decrease a person's level of sexual desire or activity, but the evidence in support of such a model has been mixed. Recent studies demonstrate that the central arousal system, in which internal stimuli are processed by the brain, is probably more dependent on the presence of hormones for activation than is the peripheral arousal system,

which is far more susceptible to localized stimuli, such as touch or viewing erotic material. There is also increasing evidence that environmental chemicals and events may disrupt the effects of some sex hormones.

The hormone that has been shown to have the most effect on sexual desire and behavior in humans is testosterone. Although this is an **androgen,** or "male" hormone, it is produced by both males and females in the sex glands (testes or ovaries) and in the adrenal glands. Men's bodies tend to produce 10 to 15 times more testosterone than do women's bodies. However, the hormone also plays a vital role in enabling women to become sexually aroused.

For both men and women, testosterone apparently has an activating effect on sexual interest. It might be viewed as a "switch" for sexual desire, and human beings seem to require some minimal levels of androgen in order to have any potential for sexual desire. What that minimum is seems to vary with different individuals. Increased levels of testosterone beyond this minimal activating level do not seem to result in increased interest in sex or amounts of sexual activity. It would be a mistake to conclude that, because women produce generally lower levels of testosterone, they have a naturally lower interest in sex. It appears instead that women have a greater degree of sensitivity to testosterone, and therefore their bodies respond to smaller quantities of the hormone. The "female" hormones, or estrogens, have little effect on sexual desire or activity in females. If males are given doses of estrogen, their interest in sex tends to decrease.

7.6 Effects of Aging on Sexual Response

There is a prevalent attitude in our culture that aging puts an end to responding sexually. Older people who accept this myth may allow their beliefs to become self-fulfilling prophecy. There is evidence of a gradual decrease in both sexual desire and frequency of sexual activity as people age, but this does not have to signal the loss of sexual responsiveness or pleasure altogether. Attitudes toward one's own sexual functioning can play an important role in maintaining sexual functioning into old age.

In the original Masters and Johnson study, 212 men beyond 50 years of age were interviewed concerning their sexual lives. Thirty-nine of these men, the oldest of whom was 89, agreed to have their sexual responses observed by the research team. Thirty-four women over the age of 50 were also observed, and another 118 interviews were conducted with women between 51 and 80 years of age. The following discussion is partly based on these interviews and observations. A summary of the information is found in Table 7.2.

Aging and Female Sexual Response

Two manifestations of postmenopausal hormonal imbalance can cause unpleasant sensations during sexual activity in some older women. First, because the vaginal lining has thinned and vaginal lubrication has possibly become reduced, intercourse may produce irritation that persists as burning or itching afterward. Water-soluble lubricants can relieve such problems, and estrogen-based creams may also help by increasing natural vaginal secretions. Second, some women also experience uterine cramping during and after orgasm. Masters and Johnson reported that some women beyond the age of 60 were so distressed by these sensations that they began to avoid coitus and orgasm. We know now that these unpleasant symptoms may be relieved by proper medical treatment.

As women age, there seems to be some decrease in orgasmic ability and a general tempering of the usual physiological responses to sexual arousal. This is a very gradual process of change and is somewhat dependent on how sexually active a particular woman remains. For heterosexual women over the age of 70 who have been involved in long-term relationships, their degree of sexual involvement may have a great deal to do with the availability and capability of their male partners. Their partners are generally older and thus more susceptible to medical conditions that interfere with sex. Older people of either gender whose bodies undergo regular sexual stimulation seem to maintain more intense levels of sexual response than do those who seldom participate in sex.

One effect of aging on female sexual response is a lengthening of the time for vaginal lubrication and other early signs of sexual arousal to take place. There is also less enlargement of the clitoris, labia, uterus, and breasts during sexual arousal. Orgasm takes a bit longer to occur in older women, and there are usually fewer orgasmic contractions of the vagina, uterus, and pelvic floor. However, women who have a history of multiple orgasms apparently retain this capability even into very old age. The resolution phase

Table 7.2	Effects of Aging on Female and Male Sexual Response	
Changes in the Aging Female		**Changes in the Aging Male**
Thinning of vaginal lining		Some atrophy of testicular tissue
Reduction in vaginal lubrication		Reduction in secretion of preejaculatory fluid and amount of semen produced
Increase in uterine cramping associated with orgasm		Testes do not elevate as much during sexual arousal
Increase in amount of time needed to experience sexual arousal and vaginal lubrication		Increase in amount of time needed to achieve full penile erection
Increase in time of stimulation required to reach orgasm, and fewer muscular contractions associated with orgasm		Increase in time of stimulation required to reach orgasm, and strength of orgasmic muscular contractions reduced
Resolution to unexcited state remains about the same		Resolution to unexcited state happens more quickly
Women who have been multiorgasmic seem to retain the capability		Refractory period lengthens, so the time before a man may be restimulated to orgasm tends to increase

Source: W. Masters and V.E. Johnson, *Human Sexual Response,* 1966, Little, Brown and Company, Boston, MA. Reprinted by permission of Masters and Johnson Institute, St. Louis, MO.

of female sexual response, during which the body returns to its unexcited state, appears to be relatively unaffected by the aging process.

It is important to emphasize that how much of a decline in sexual response patterns an older woman experiences seems to depend on how sexually involved she remains. This in turn depends on factors such as the woman's health, the availability of a partner, the amount of privacy she is afforded, her attitudes and values about sexuality, and the degree of priority she has always placed on her sexual feelings and behaviors. For these reasons, some women remain sexually vital until the end of their lives, whereas others forgo sexual pleasures long before that time and gradually lose their abilities to respond sexually. Put in simple and direct language, this concept is often summarized by the phrase "Use it or lose it."

Aging and Male Sexual Response

How responsive men remain in their older years seems to depend on a variety of physical, social, and psychological factors. Socially, they may lose their longstanding sexual partner or live in a setting that provides little privacy for sexual expression. Because there is a natural "slowing down" process, some men begin to feel insecure about their sexual capabilities. They may fear sexual "failure," usually meaning erection problems of various sorts, and eventually withdraw from sexual activities. They may assume that aging is rendering them incapable of sexual performance. As a result, the amount of sexual stimulation they seek is drastically reduced, and the priority they assign to sex is lowered. This can eventually lead to at least a temporary loss of the ability to respond. Men who are in good general physical health may eventually restimulate their sexual interests and response patterns, should a change in life situation make this appropriate. This might include the availability of a new sexual partner, a renewed sense of self-worth, or sexuality education that makes the man aware of how his responses can be expected to change.

Three aspects of male sexual response undergo predictable changes as men age. The first is erection. For a man in his 70s, it takes two to three times longer to achieve full penile erection than it did in the man's younger years, and he usually requires direct penile stimulation. Although it is perfectly normal for men of any age to experience waxing and waning of erection during prolonged sexual arousal, it is more difficult for older men to reestablish full rigidity once erection has been partially lost. The angle of the erect penis up from the body also decreases with age.

The second change relates to male orgasm and ejaculation. Older men take longer to reach orgasm than they did earlier in their lives. The strength of the orgasmic contractions is reduced, so that semen is ejaculated with less force, sometimes just seeping out of the urethra. The frequency with which men desire orgasm also seems to decline somewhat as they age. Except in rare instances, men over 60 are completely satisfied by one or, at the most, two orgasms in a week. They may enjoy participating in sexual behavior more frequently than that, experiencing full erection but no orgasm. The urge to achieve orgasm seems to be reduced with age. The third change is a lengthening of the male refractory period, so that by their late 50s or early 60s, most men cannot achieve erections again for 12 to 24 hours after ejaculation.

There are also decreases in other aspects of the aging male's sexual response, including a reduction in the amount of preejaculatory secretion from the bulbourethral glands and in the amount of semen produced. The testes and scrotum do not enlarge as much during sexual arousal, nor do the testes elevate so much within the scrotum. The resolution phase of men tends to occur more rapidly with age, and the penis may lose its erection after ejaculation much more rapidly.

These changes in female and male sexual response are not necessarily negative developments for people's sexual lives. In fact, many men and women find increased enjoyment in the moderating responses brought about by aging (Fig. 7.11).

Figure 7.11   Aging and the sexual response.
Although aging affects the anatomy and physiology of the sexual organs, there is no reason both sexes cannot continue to have an active sex life.

Bioethical Focus

The Study of Human Sexual Response

This chapter describes some of the research that has been done to study male and female sexual response. These studies require that humans allow an investigator to observe behavior patterns that are usually considered private. Do you feel it is proper to encourage people to allow such an invasion of their privacy? If no, for what reasons? If yes, for what reasons?

Masters and Johnson came to the conclusion that human sexual response could be divided into four phases. Do you feel it is proper to be scientific about human sexual response, or do you think it should always remain somewhat of a mystery? Explain your answer.

Following is a quote from page 104 of this chapter:

"Western cultural imperatives often place sexual response in a more goal-oriented context, with orgasm and satisfying release being one of the primary objectives. A view of sexual arousal and response as holistic experiences involving mind, body, emotions, and spirit may be neglected in cultures that approach such issues from a more specific perspective."

The author seems to suggest that people in our culture don't properly appreciate the sexual response because they view it as a goal to an end, namely, orgasm. Does this quote support your views about the scientific study of the human sexual response? Explain your answer.

Decide Your Opinion

1. Do your answers to the questions within this reading stem from how you view human sexual response? How so?
2. Do you believe we should try to determine how we view human sexual response and then use that information to improve our personal lives?

Figure 7C Should our sexual response be analyzed?

3. Do you believe it is morally wrong to consider how we feel about human sexual responses? Explain.

Summary

7.1 Models of Human Sexual Response

Masters and Johnson were among the first researchers to study scientifically the body's physiological changes during sexual response. They developed a four-phase model composed of excitement, plateau, orgasm, and resolution.

A three-phase model proposed by Kaplan views sexual response as beginning with psychological desire, with a subsequent buildup of blood and muscular tension, followed by reversal of these states as triggered by orgasm. The term "desire phase" refers to the level of interest in sexual activity an individual may experience.

There are many individual differences in human sexual response, and good communication is essential to developing mutual understanding in a sexual relationship.

7.2 Activating the Response: Models of Sexual Arousal

Sexual response must be activated by some mechanism of sexual arousal. Several models of arousal have been proposed.

Penile and vaginal plethysmographs have been used in research to measure and compare the degree of sexual arousal in women and men. These studies show that people's perceptions of their own sexual response do not always match physiological measures.

Arousal stimuli may be internal or external, roughly corresponding to a central arousal system located in the brain and to a peripheral arousal system that picks up cues from the genitals, senses, and spinal reflexes.

Emotions and other psychological processes play a significant role in activating or deactivating sexual response. When the mind ascribes sexual meaning to some stimulus, the genital physiological response may be quite automatic.

Studies reveal that there are more similarities than differences between the arousal patterns of males and females.

7.3 Female Sexual Response

In females, the vagina becomes lubricated during sexual excitement, and an orgasmic platform develops with the swelling of the clitoris and labia. The clitoral glans eventually retracts under its foreskin. Resolution refers to the return of the body to its unexcited state.

Some women have the potential for more than one orgasm during a single sexual experience. Women report clitoral, vaginal, uterine, and "blended" orgasms. Some researchers claim that there is a particularly sensitive spot on the inner front part of the vagina that swells during female arousal. This has been called the G spot. It has also been proposed that some women ejaculate a substance from the urethra during intense orgasms.

Kegel exercises can keep the urogenital musculature in good tone and may increase the intensity of pleasure of orgasm.

7.4 Male Sexual Response

In males, penile erection is a major sign of excitement, and there are also increases in the size of the testes and scrotum. The testes move upward in the scrotum.

In both women and men, sexual response involves increases in respiration, heart rate, blood pressure, and general muscular tension. A reddish "sex flush" appears on the skin of the upper body in some individuals, and nipple erection may also occur.

Orgasm is the pleasurable release of sexual tension, involving a series of muscular contractions in both sexes. Ejaculation usually accompanies orgasm in men.

During resolution, at the end of sexual response in men, a refractory period generally occurs, during which there can be no restimulation to orgasm.

7.5 Hormonal Regulation of Sexual Arousal and Response

It is still not completely clear what role hormones may play in regulating sexual response. Testosterone, an androgen present in both men and women, acts as an activator for sexual desire. Androgens may act more directly on the central arousal system than on the peripheral arousal system.

In humans, sexual arousal and responsiveness seem to be controlled by both hormonal and social factors.

7.6 Effects of Aging on Sexual Response

Both men and women may experience slower arousal and somewhat less intensity of response as they age. People who have been more sexually active during their younger years will tend to maintain a higher level of sexual activity.

Reviewing the Chapter

1. The Masters and Johnson model of human sexual response has how many phases? What are they? 104–6
2. Kaplan concluded that what phase precedes physiological responses to sexual arousal? Why? 107
3. Name and explain the two systems of sexual arousal. 108–9
4. How do men and women differ with regard to sexual arousal? 110
5. In females, what events are typical in each of Masters and Johnson's phases? 110–12
6. Discuss three controversies about female sexual response. 113
7. In males, what events are typical in each of Masters and Johnson's phases? 117–19
8. Distinguish between the organizing and activating effects of hormones. 119–20
9. What changes in sexual response occur in females as they age? 121–22
10. What changes in sexual response occur in males as they age? 122

Critical Thinking Questions

1. Various stimuli arouse people sexually. Hypothesize why certain stimuli are effective for some but not for others.

2. Women are more apt to see sexual desire as a means to love, emotional intimacy, or physical closeness. Is this goal consistent with the female's role of bearing children? Why?

3. What have you learned about the human sexual response that you did not know before and/or that changed some of your former ideas?

Understanding Key Terms

activating effect 120
androgen 120
central arousal system 108
climax 105
desire phase 105
ejaculatory inevitability 118
excitement 105
G spot 113
organizing effect 120

orgasm 105
orgasmic release 105
peripheral arousal system 108
plateau 105
refractory period 119
resolution 105
sexual dysfunction 105
Skene glands 113

Chapter 8

Fertilization, Development, and Birth

8.1 Fertilization

Fertilization, which results in a **zygote,** requires that the sperm and egg interact. A sperm has three distinct parts: a head, a middle piece, and a tail. The tail is a flagellum, which allows the sperm to swim toward the egg, and the middle piece contains energy-producing mitochondria. The head contains a nucleus and is capped by a membrane-bounded acrosome. The plasma membrane of the egg is surrounded by an extracellular region termed the zona pellucida. In turn, the zona pellucida is surrounded by a few layers of adhering follicular cells, collectively called the corona radiata. These cells nourished the egg when it was in a follicle of the ovary.

Figure 8.1 shows how fertilization takes place. After a sperm head binds tightly to the zona pellucida, the acrosome releases digestive enzymes that forge a pathway for the sperm through the zona pellucida. When a sperm binds to the egg, their plasma membranes fuse, and this sperm (the head, the middle piece, and usually the tail) enters the egg. Fusion of the sperm nucleus and the egg nucleus follows.

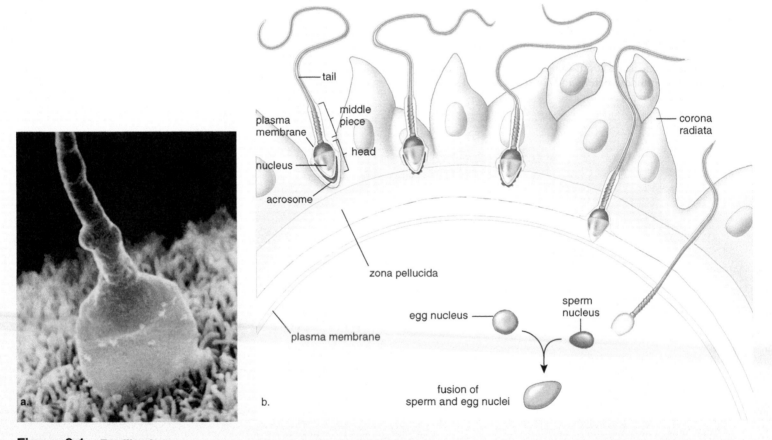

Figure 8.1 Fertilization.
a. During fertilization, a single sperm enters the egg. **b.** The head of a sperm has a membrane-bounded acrosome filled with enzymes. When released, these enzymes digest a pathway for the sperm through the zona pellucida. After it binds to the plasma membrane of the egg, a sperm enters the egg. When the sperm nucleus fuses with the egg nucleus, fertilization is complete.

To ensure proper development, only one sperm should enter an egg. Prevention of polyspermy (entrance of more than one sperm) depends on changes in the egg's plasma membrane and in the zona pellucida. As soon as a sperm touches an egg, chemical changes occur that prevent the binding of any other sperm. Then the egg releases substances that lead to a lifting of the zona pellucida away from the surface of the egg. Now sperm cannot bind to the zona pellucida either.

8.2 Development

Before we discuss the stages of development, you will want to become familiar with the processes of development and the names and functions of the extraembryonic membranes.

Processes of Development

As a human being develops, these processes occur:

Cleavage   Immediately after fertilization, the zygote begins to divide so that there are first 2, then 4, 8, 16, and 32 cells, and so forth. Increase in size does not accompany these divisions (see Fig. 8.3). Cell division during cleavage is mitotic, and each cell receives a full complement of chromosomes and genes.

Growth   During embryonic development, cell division is accompanied by an increase in the size of the daughter cells.

Morphogenesis   Morphogenesis refers to the shaping of the embryo and is first evident when certain cells are seen to move, or migrate, in relation to other cells. By these movements, the embryo begins to assume various shapes.

Differentiation   When cells take on a specific structure and function, differentiation occurs. The first system to become visibly differentiated is the nervous system.

Extraembryonic Membranes

The **extraembryonic membranes** are not part of the embryo and fetus; instead, as implied by their name, they are outside the embryo (Fig. 8.2). The names of the extraembryonic membranes in humans are strange to us because they are named for their function in shelled animals! In shelled animals, the chorion lies next to the shell and carries on gas exchange. The amnion contains the protective amniotic fluid, which bathes the developing embryo. The allantois collects nitrogenous wastes, and the yolk sac surrounds the yolk, which provides nourishment.

The functions of the extraembryonic membranes are different in humans because humans develop inside the uterus. The extraembryonic membranes have these functions in humans:

1. The **chorion** develops into the fetal half of the **placenta,** the organ that provides the embryo/fetus with nourishment and oxygen and takes away its waste.
2. The **yolk sac** has little yolk and is the first site of blood cell formation.
3. The **allantois** blood vessels become the umbilical blood vessels.
4. The **amnion** contains fluid to cushion and protect the embryo, which develops into a fetus.

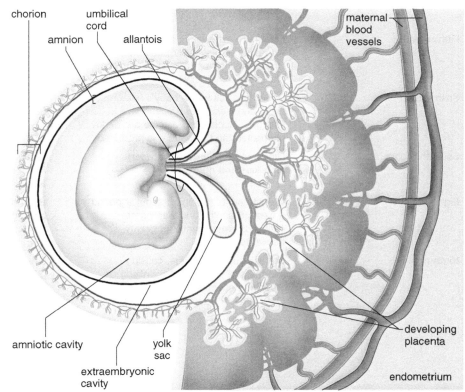

Figure 8.2   The extraembryonic membranes. The chorion and amnion surround the embryo. The two other extraembryonic membranes, the yolk sac and allantois, contribute to the umbilical cord.

Table 8.1   Human Development

Time	Events for Mother	Events for Baby
PRE-EMBRYONIC DEVELOPMENT		
First week	Ovulation occurs.	Fertilization occurs. Cell division begins and continues. Chorion appears.
EMBRYONIC DEVELOPMENT		
Second week	Symptoms of early pregnancy (nausea, breast swelling and tenderness, fatigue) are present. Blood pregnancy test is positive.	Implantation occurs. Amnion and yolk sac appear. Embryo has tissues. Placenta begins to form.
Third week	First menstruation is missed. Urine pregnancy test is positive. Symptoms of early pregnancy continue.	Nervous system begins to develop. Allantois and blood vessels are present. Placenta is well formed.
Fourth week		Limb buds form. Heart is noticeable and beating. Nervous system is prominent. Embryo has tail. Other systems form.
Fifth week	Uterus is the size of a hen's egg. Mother feels frequent need to urinate due to pressure of growing uterus on bladder.	Embryo is curved. Head is large. Limb buds show divisions. Nose, eyes, and ears are noticeable.
Sixth week	Uterus is the size of an orange.	Fingers and toes are present. Skeleton is cartilaginous.
Two months	Uterus can be felt above the pubic bone.	All systems are developing. Bone is replacing cartilage. Facial features are becoming refined. Embryo is about 38 mm (1½ in.) long.
FETAL DEVELOPMENT		
Third month	Uterus is the size of a grapefruit.	Gender can be distinguished by ultrasound. Fingernails appear.
Fourth month	Fetal movement is felt by a mother who has previously been pregnant.	Skeleton is visible. Hair begins to appear. Fetus is about 150 mm (6 in.) long and weighs about 170 g (6 oz).
Fifth month	Fetal movement is felt by a mother who has not previously been pregnant. Uterus reaches up to level of umbilicus, and pregnancy is obvious.	Protective cheesy coating, called vernix caseosa, begins to be deposited. Heartbeat can be heard.
Sixth month	Doctor can tell where baby's head, back, and limbs are. Breasts have enlarged, nipples and areolae are darkly pigmented, and colostrum is produced.	Body is covered with fine hair called lanugo. Skin is wrinkled and reddish.
Seventh month	Uterus reaches halfway between umbilicus and rib cage.	Testes descend into scrotum. Eyes are open. Fetus is about 300 mm (12 in.) long and weighs about 1,350 g (3 lb).
Eighth month	Weight gain is averaging about a pound a week. Standing and walking are difficult because center of gravity is thrown forward.	Body hair begins to disappear. Subcutaneous fat begins to be deposited.
Ninth month	Uterus is up to rib cage, causing shortness of breath and heartburn. Sleeping becomes difficult.	Fetus is ready for birth. It is about 530 mm (20½ in.) long and weighs about 3,400 g (7½ lb).

Stages of Development

Development encompasses the events that occur from fertilization to birth. In humans, this **gestation** period is usually calculated by adding 280 days to the start of the last menstruation, a date that is usually known. However, only about 5% of babies actually arrive on the predicted date.

Pre-Embryonic Development

Table 8.1 shows that we can subdivide development into pre-embryonic, embryonic, and fetal development. **Pre-embryonic development** encompasses the events of the first week.

Immediately after fertilization, the zygote divides repeatedly as it passes down the uterine tube to the uterus (Fig. 8.3). A **morula** is a compact ball of embryonic cells that becomes a **blastocyst.** The many cells of the blastocyst arrange themselves so that there is an **inner cell mass** surrounded by a layer of cells, the **trophoblast.** The trophoblast will become the *chorion*. The early appearance of the chorion emphasizes the complete dependence of the developing embryo on this extraembryonic membrane. The inner cell mass will become the **embryo.**

Each cell within the morula and blastocyst has the genetic capability of becoming any tissue. This recognition has recently led to the ability to genetically analyze pre-embryos (see page 66). Sometimes during development, the cells of the morula separate, or the inner cell mass splits, and two pre-embryos are present rather than one. If all goes well, these two pre-embryos will be *identical twins* because they have inherited exactly the same chromosomes. *Fraternal twins,* who arise when two different eggs are fertilized by two different sperm, do not have identical chromosomes.

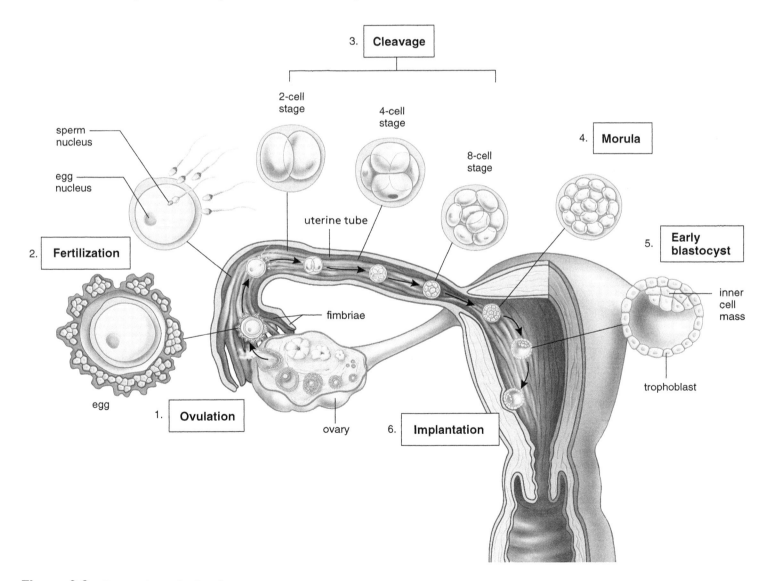

Figure 8.3 **Pre-embryonic development.**
At ovulation, the egg leaves the ovary. Fertilization occurs in the upper one-third of the uterine tube. The zygote is termed a pre-embryo when cell division (cleavage) begins. When the pre-embryo begins implanting itself into the endometrium, it becomes an embryo.

Embryonic Development

Embryonic development begins with the second week and lasts until the end of the second month of development.

Second Week

At the end of the first week, the embryo usually begins the process of implanting itself in the wall of the uterus. If **implantation** is successful, the woman is clinically pregnant. On occasion it happens that the embryo implants itself in a location other than the uterus—most likely, the uterine tube. As mentioned previously, such a so-called ectopic pregnancy cannot succeed because a uterine tube is unable to support it.

During implantation, the trophoblast secretes enzymes to digest away some of the tissue and blood vessels of the endometrium of the uterus. The trophoblast (Fig 8.4a) also

begins to secrete **human chorionic gonadotropin (HCG),** the hormone that is the basis for the pregnancy test. HCG acts like luteinizing hormone in that it serves to maintain the corpus luteum past the time it normally disintegrates. Because it is being stimulated, the corpus luteum secretes progesterone, the endometrium is maintained, and the expected menstruation does not occur.

The embryo is now about the size of the period at the end of this sentence. As the week progresses, the inner cell mass detaches itself from the trophoblast and becomes the **embryonic disk,** and two more extraembryonic membranes form (Fig. 8.4a). The yolk sac is the first site of blood cell formation. The amniotic cavity surrounds the embryo (and then the fetus) as it develops. In humans, amniotic fluid acts as an insulator against cold and heat and also absorbs shock, such as that caused by the mother exercising.

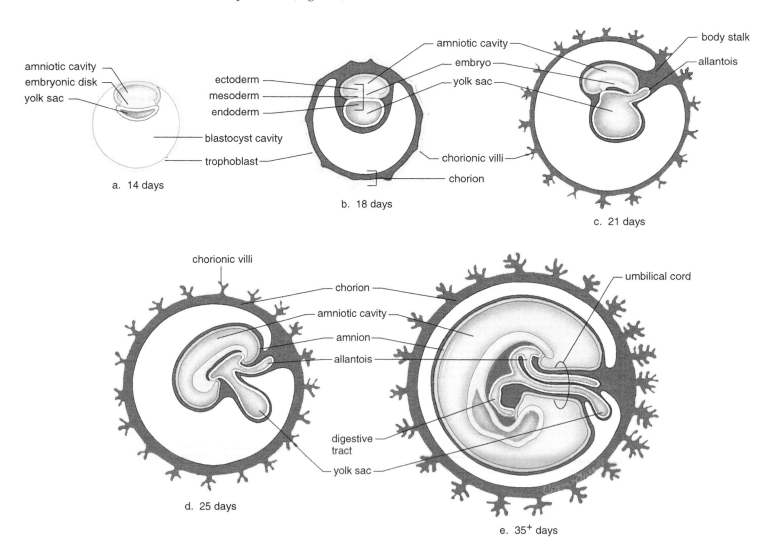

Figure 8.4   Embryonic development.
a. At first, the embryo has no organs, only tissues. The amniotic cavity is above the embryonic disk, and the yolk sac is below. **b.** The chorion develops villi, the structures so important to gas, nutrient, and waste exchange between mother and child. **c, d.** The allantois and yolk sac, two more extraembryonic membranes, are positioned inside the body stalk as it becomes the umbilical cord. **e.** At 35+ days, the embryo has a head region and a tail region. The umbilical cord takes blood vessels between the embryo and the chorion (placenta).

Primary Germ Layers With the start of the major event called **gastrulation,** the inner cell mass becomes the embryonic disk. Gastrulation is an example of morphogenesis (see page 127) during which cells move or migrate, in this case to become tissue layers called the **primary germ layers.** By the time gastrulation is complete, the embryonic disk has become an embryo with three primary germ layers: ectoderm, mesoderm, and endoderm. All the organs of an individual can be traced back to one of the primary germ layers. Notice also that when the trophoblast is reinforced by mesoderm, it becomes the chorion (see Fig. 8.4*b*).

Third Week

Two important organ systems make their appearance during the third week. The nervous system is the first organ system to be visually evident. At first, a thickening appears along the entire dorsal length of the embryo, and then invagination occurs as neural folds appear. When the neural folds meet at the midline, the neural tube, which later develops into the brain and the spinal cord, is formed.

Development of the heart begins in the third week and continues into the fourth week. At first, there are right and left heart tubes; when these fuse, the heart begins pumping blood, even though the chambers of the heart are not fully formed. The veins enter posteriorly, and the arteries exit anteriorly from this largely tubular heart, but later the heart twists so that all major blood vessels are located anteriorly.

Fourth and Fifth Weeks

At four weeks, the embryo is barely larger than the height of this print. A body stalk connects the caudal (tail) end of the embryo with the chorion, which has treelike projections called **chorionic villi** (see Fig. 8.4*c,d*). The fourth extraembryonic membrane, the allantois, lies within the body stalk, and its blood vessels become the umbilical blood vessels. The head and the tail then lift up, and the body stalk moves anteriorly by constriction. Once this process is complete, the **umbilical cord,** which connects the developing embryo to the placenta, is fully formed (see Fig. 8.4*e*).

Little flippers called limb buds appear (Fig. 8.5); later, the arms and the legs develop from the limb buds, and even the hands and the feet become apparent. At the same time—during the fifth week—the head enlarges, and the sense organs become more prominent. It is possible to make out the developing eyes and ears, and even the nose.

Sixth Through Eighth Weeks

During the sixth through the eighth weeks of development, the embryo changes to a form that is easily recognized as a human being. Concurrent with brain development, the head achieves its normal relationship with the body as a neck region develops. The nervous system is developed well enough to permit reflex actions, such as a startle response to touch. At the end of this period, the embryo is about 1.5 in. long and weighs no more than an aspirin tablet, even though all organ systems have been established.

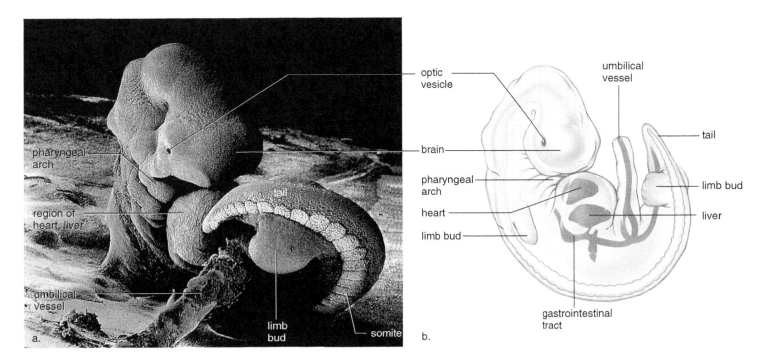

Figure 8.5 **Human embryo at beginning of fifth week.**
a. Scanning electron micrograph. **b.** The embryo is curled so that the head touches the region of the heart and liver. The organs of the gastrointestinal tract are forming, and the arms and the legs develop from the bulges called limb buds. The tail is an evolutionary remnant; its bones regress and become those of the coccyx (tailbone).

Placenta

The placenta is shaped like a pancake, being wider in diameter than it is thick. The placenta is normally fully formed and functional by the end of the embryonic period and before the fetal period begins. The placenta is expelled as the afterbirth following the birth of an infant.

The placenta has two portions, a fetal portion composed of chorionic tissue and a maternal portion composed of uterine tissue. Chorionic villi cover the entire surface of the chorion until about the eighth week when they begin to disappear, except in one area. These villi are surrounded by maternal blood, and it is here that exchanges of materials take place across the placental membrane. The **placental membrane** consists of the epithelial wall of an embryonic capillary and the epithelial wall of a chorionic villus. Maternal blood rarely mingles with fetal blood. Instead, oxygen and nutrient molecules, such as glucose and amino acids, diffuse from the maternal blood across the placental membrane into the fetal blood, and carbon dioxide and other wastes, such as urea, diffuse out of the fetal blood into the maternal blood.

Note that the digestive system, lungs, and kidneys do not function in the fetus. The functions of these organs are not needed because the placenta supplies the fetus with its nutritional and excretory needs.

The umbilical cord transports fetal blood to and from the placenta (Fig. 8.6). The umbilical cord is the fetal lifeline because it contains the umbilical arteries and vein, which transport waste molecules (carbon dioxide and urea) to the placenta for disposal and oxygen and nutrient molecules from the placenta to the rest of the fetal circulatory system.

First the trophoblast, then the chorion, and then the placenta produce HCG. HCG prevents the normal degeneration of the corpus luteum and, instead, stimulates it to secrete even larger quantities of progesterone. Later, the placenta begins to produce progesterone and estrogen, and the corpus luteum degenerates—it is no longer needed. Placental estrogen and progesterone maintain the endometrium and have a negative feedback effect on the anterior pituitary so that it ceases to produce gonadotropic hormones during pregnancy. Menstruation does not occur during the length of pregnancy.

Harmful chemicals in the mother's blood can cross the placenta, and this is of particular concern during the embryonic period, when various structures are first forming. Each organ or part seems to have a sensitive period during which a substance can alter its normal function. The reading on pages 134–35 concerns maternal behaviors that can prevent certain birth defects.

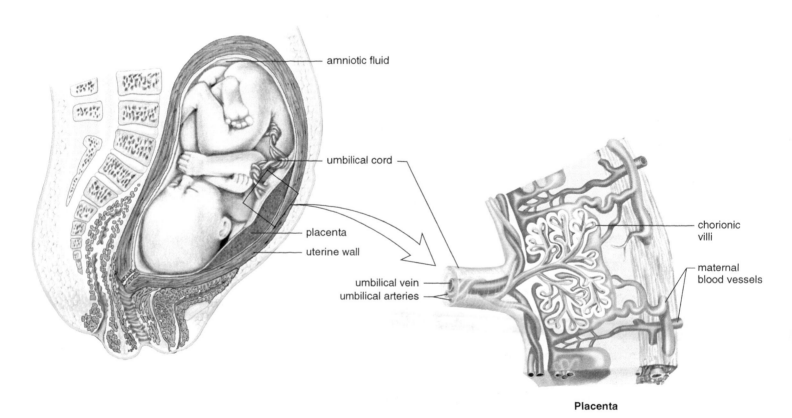

Placenta

Figure 8.6   The placenta.
Blood vessels within the umbilical cord lead to the placenta, where exchange takes place between fetal blood and maternal blood.

Fetal Development and Birth

Fetal development includes the third through the ninth months of development. At this time, the fetus looks human (Fig. 8.7).

Third and Fourth Months

At the beginning of the third month, the fetal head is still very large, the nose is flat, the eyes are far apart, and the ears are well formed. Head growth now begins to slow as the rest of the body increases in length. Epidermal refinements, such as fingernails, nipples, eyelashes, eyebrows, and hair on the head, appear.

Cartilage begins to be replaced by bone as ossification centers appear in most of the bones. Cartilage remains at the ends of the long bones, and ossification is not complete until age 18 to 20 years. The skull has six large membranous areas called **fontanels,** which permit a certain amount of flexibility as the head passes through the birth canal and allow rapid growth of the brain during infancy. Progressive fusion of the skull bones causes the fontanels to close, usually by 2 years of age.

Sometime during the third month, it is possible to distinguish males from females. Researchers have discovered a series of genes on the X and Y chromosomes that cause the differentiation of gonads into testes and ovaries. Once these have differentiated, they produce the sex hormones that influence the differentiation of the genital tract.

At this time, either testes or ovaries are located within the abdominal cavity, but later, in the last trimester of fetal development, the testes descend into the scrotal sacs (scrotum). Sometimes the testes fail to descend, and in that case, an operation may be done later to place them in their proper location.

During the fourth month, the fetal heartbeat is loud enough to be heard when a physician applies a stethoscope to the mother's abdomen, and fetal movement can be felt by women who previously have been pregnant. By the end of this month, the fetus is about 6 in. long and weighs about 6 oz.

Fifth Through Seventh Months

During the fifth through the seventh months (see Fig. 8.7), fetal movement increases. At first, there is only a fluttering sensation, but as the fetal legs grow and develop, kicks and jabs are felt. The fetus, though, is in the fetal position, with the head bent down and in contact with the flexed knees.

The wrinkled, translucent, pink-colored skin is covered by a fine down called **lanugo.** This in turn is coated with a white, greasy, cheeselike substance called **vernix caseosa,** which probably protects the delicate skin from the amniotic fluid. The eyelids are now fully open.

At the end of this period, the fetus's length has increased to about 12 in., and the weight is about 3 lb. It is possible that, if born now, the baby will survive.

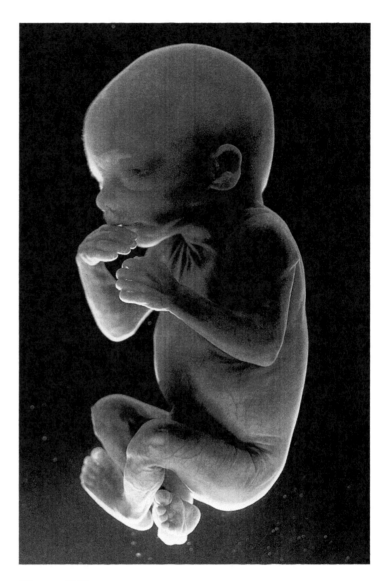

Figure 8.7   Five- to seven-month-old fetus.

Eighth Through Ninth Months

As the end of development approaches, the fetus usually rotates so that the head is pointed toward the cervix. However, if the fetus does not turn, a **breech birth** (rump first) is likely. It is very difficult for the cervix to expand enough to accommodate this form of birth, and asphyxiation of the baby is more likely to occur. Thus, a **cesarean section** (incision through the abdominal and uterine walls) may be prescribed for delivery of the fetus.

At the end of nine months, the fetus is about 20½ in. long and weighs about 7½ lb. Weight gain is due largely to an accumulation of fat beneath the skin. Full-term babies have the best chance of survival.

Preventing Birth Defects

While some **congenital (birth) defects** are not preventable, certain ones are, and therefore all females of childbearing age are advised to take everyday precautions to protect any future and/or presently developing embryos and fetuses from these defects. For example, it is best if a woman has a physical exam even before she becomes pregnant. At that time, it can be determined if she has been immunized against **rubella (German measles).** Depending on exactly when a pregnant woman has the disease, rubella can cause blindness, deafness, mental retardation, heart malformations, and other serious problems in an unborn child. A vaccine to prevent the disease can be given to a woman before she gets pregnant, but cannot be given to a woman who is already pregnant because it contains live viruses. Also, the presence of HIV (the causative agent of AIDS) should be tested for because preventative therapies are available to improve maternal and infant health.

Good health habits are a must during pregnancy, including proper nutrition, adequate rest, and exercise. Moderate exercise can usually continue throughout pregnancy and hopefully will contribute to ease of delivery. Basic nutrients are required in adequate amounts to meet the demands of both fetus and mother. A growing number of studies confirm that small, thin newborns are more likely to develop certain chronic diseases, such as diabetes and high blood pressure, when they become adults than are babies who are born heavier. An increased amount of minerals, such as calcium for bone growth and iron for red blood cell formation, and certain vitamins, such as vitamin B_6 for proper metabolism and folate (folic acid), are required. A pregnant woman needs more folate (folic acid) daily to meet an increased rate of cell division and DNA synthesis in her own body and that of the developing child. A maternal deficiency of folate has been linked to development of neural tube defects in the fetus. These defects include **spina bifida** (spinal cord or spinal fluid bulge through the back) and **anencephaly** (absence of a brain). Perhaps as many as 75% of these defects could be avoided by adequate folate intake even before pregnancy occurs. Consuming fortified breakfast cereals is a good way to meet folate needs, because they contain a more absorbable form of folate.

Good health habits include avoiding substances that can cross the placenta and harm the fetus (Table 8A). Cigarette smoke poses a serious threat to the health of a fetus because it contains not only carbon monoxide but also other fetotoxic chemicals. Children born to smoking mothers have a greater chance of a cleft lip or palate, increased incidence of respiratory diseases, and later on more reading disorders than those born to mothers who did not smoke during their pregnancy.

Alcohol easily crosses the placenta, and even one drink a day appears to increase the chance of a spontaneous abortion. The more alcohol consumed, the greater are the chances of physical abnormalities if the pregnancy continues. Heavy consumption of alcohol puts a fetus at risk of a mental defect because alcohol enters the brain of the fetus. Babies born to heavy drinkers are apt to undergo **delirium tremens** after birth—shaking, vomiting, and extreme irritability—and to have **fetal alcohol syndrome (FAS).** Babies with FAS have decreased weight, height, and head size, with malformation of the head and face (Fig. 8A). Later, mental retardation is common, as are numerous other physical malformations.

Certainly, illegal drugs, such as marijuana, cocaine, and heroin, should be completely avoided during pregnancy. **Cocaine babies** now make up 60% of drug-affected babies. Cocaine causes severe fluctuations in a mother's blood pressure that temporarily deprive the developing fetus's brain of oxygen. Cocaine babies have visual problems, lack coordination, and are mentally retarded.

Children born to women who received X-ray treatment during pregnancy for, say, cancer are apt to have birth defects and/or to develop leukemia later. It takes a lower amount of X rays to cause mutations in a developing embryo or fetus than it does in an adult. Dental and other diagnostic X rays that use only a small amount of radiation are probably safe. Still, a woman should be sure her health-care provider knows that she is or may be pregnant. Similarly, toxic chemicals, such as pesticides, and many organic industrial chemicals, such as vinyl chloride, formaldehyde, asbestos, and benzenes, are mutagenic and can cross the placenta, resulting in abnormalities. Lead circulating in a pregnant woman's blood can cause a child to be mentally retarded. Agents that produce abnormalities during development are called **teratogens.**

Table 8A	Behaviors Harmful to the Unborn

Drinking alcohol

Smoking cigarettes

Taking illegal drugs

Taking any medication not approved by a physician

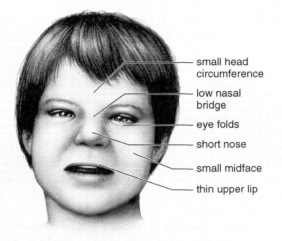

- small head circumference
- low nasal bridge
- eye folds
- short nose
- small midface
- thin upper lip

a.

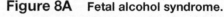

Figure 8A **Fetal alcohol syndrome.**
a. The features of fetal alcohol syndrome include malformations of the head and face.
b–d. Photos of children who have fetal alcohol syndrome.

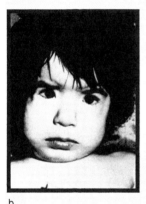

b.

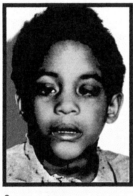

c.

d.

A woman has to be very careful about taking medications while pregnant. Excessive vitamin A, sometimes used to treat acne, may damage an embryo. In the 1950s and 1960s, DES (diethylstilbestrol), a synthetic hormone related to the natural female hormone estrogen, was given to pregnant women to prevent cramps, bleeding, and threatened miscarriage. But in the 1970s and 1980s, some adolescent girls and young women whose mothers had been treated with DES showed various abnormalities of the reproductive organs and an increased tendency toward cervical cancer. Other sex hormones, including birth control pills, can possibly cause abnormal fetal development, including abnormalities of the sex organs. The drug thalidomide was a popular tranquilizer during the 1950s and 1960s in many European countries and to a degree in the United States. The drug, which was taken to prevent nausea in pregnant women, arrested the development of arms and legs in some children and also damaged heart and blood vessels, ears, and the digestive tract. Some mothers of affected children report that they took the drug for only a few days. Because of such experiences, physicians are generally very cautious about prescribing drugs during pregnancy, and no pregnant woman should take any drug—even ordinary cold remedies—without checking first with her physician.

Unfortunately, immunization for sexually transmitted diseases is not possible. The HIV virus can cross the placenta and cause mental retardation. As mentioned, proper medication can greatly reduce the chance of this happening. When a mother has herpes, gonorrhea, or chlamydia, newborns can become infected as they pass through the birth canal. Blindness and other physical and mental defects may develop. Birth by cesarean section could prevent these occurrences.

An Rh-negative woman who has given birth to an Rh-positive child should receive an Rh immunoglobulin injection within 72 hours to prevent her body from producing Rh antibodies. She will start producing these antibodies when some of the child's Rh-positive red blood cells enter her bloodstream, possibly before but particularly at birth. Rh antibodies can cause nervous system and heart defects in a fetus. The first Rh-positive baby is not usually affected. But in subsequent pregnancies, antibodies created at the time of the first birth cross the placenta and begin to destroy the blood cells of the fetus, thereby causing anemia and other complications.

The birth defects we have been discussing are particularly preventable because they are not due to inheritance of an abnormal number of chromosomes or to any other genetic abnormality. More women are having babies after the age of 35, and first births among women older than 40 have increased by 50% since 1980. The chance of an older woman bearing a child with a birth defect unrelated to genetic inheritance is no greater than that of a younger woman. However, there is a greater risk of an older woman having a child with a chromosomal abnormality leading to premature delivery, cesarean section, a low birth weight, or certain syndromes. Some chromosomal and other genetic defects can be detected in utero so that therapy for these disorders can begin as soon as possible.

Now that physicians and laypeople are aware of the various ways birth defects can be prevented, it is hoped that the incidence of birth defects will decrease in the future.

8.3 Birth

The uterus has contractions throughout pregnancy. At first, these are light, lasting about 20–30 seconds and occurring every 15–20 minutes. Near the end of pregnancy, the contractions may become stronger and more frequent so that a woman thinks she is in labor. "False-labor" contractions are called **Braxton Hicks contractions.** However, the onset of true labor is marked by uterine contractions that occur regularly every 15–20 minutes and last for 40 seconds or longer.

A positive feedback mechanism can explain the onset and continuation of labor. Uterine contractions are induced by a stretching of the cervix, which also brings about the release of oxytocin from the posterior pituitary gland. Oxytocin stimulates the uterine muscles, both directly and through the action of prostaglandins. Uterine contractions push the fetus downward, and the cervix stretches even more. This cycle keeps repeating itself until birth occurs.

Prior to or at the first stage of **parturition,** which is the process of giving birth to an offspring, there can be a "bloody show" caused by expulsion of a mucous plug from the cervical canal. This plug prevents bacteria and sperm from entering the uterus during pregnancy.

Stage 1

During the first stage of labor, the uterine contractions occur in such a way that the cervical canal slowly disappears as the lower part of the uterus is pulled upward toward the baby's head. This process is called effacement, or "taking up the cervix." With further contractions, the baby's head acts as a wedge to assist cervical dilation (Fig. 8.8b). If the amniotic membrane has not already ruptured, it is apt to do so during this stage, releasing the amniotic fluid, which leaks out the vagina (an event sometimes referred to as "breaking water"). The first stage of parturition ends once the cervix is dilated completely.

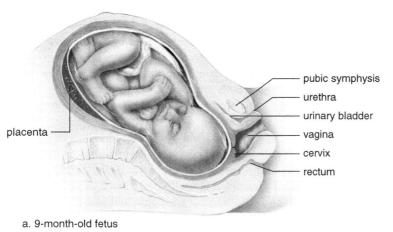

placenta

pubic symphysis
urethra
urinary bladder
vagina
cervix
rectum

a. 9-month-old fetus

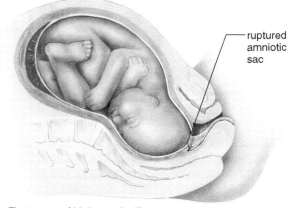

ruptured amniotic sac

b. First stage of birth: cervix dilates

placenta

c. Second stage of birth: baby emerges

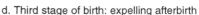

placenta
uterus
umbilical cord

d. Third stage of birth: expelling afterbirth

Figure 8.8   Three stages of parturition (birth).
a. Position of fetus just before birth begins. **b.** Dilation of cervix. **c.** Birth of baby. **d.** Expulsion of afterbirth.

Stage 2

During the second stage of parturition, the uterine contractions occur every 1–2 minutes and last about one minute each. They are accompanied by a desire to push, or bear down.

As the baby's head gradually descends into the vagina, the desire to push becomes greater. When the baby's head reaches the exterior, it turns so that the back of the head is uppermost (Fig. 8.8c). Since the vaginal orifice may not expand enough to allow passage of the head, an **episiotomy** is often performed. This incision, which enlarges the opening, is sewn together later. As soon as the head is delivered, the baby's shoulders rotate so that the baby faces either to the right or the left. At this time, the physician may hold the head and guide it downward, while one shoulder and then the other emerges. The rest of the baby follows easily.

Once the baby is breathing normally, the umbilical cord is cut and tied, severing the child from the placenta. The stump of the cord shrivels and leaves a scar, which is the umbilicus.

Stage 3

The placenta, or **afterbirth,** is delivered during the third stage of parturition (Fig. 8.8d). About 15 minutes after delivery of the baby, uterine muscular contractions shrink the uterus and dislodge the placenta. The placenta then is expelled into the vagina. As soon as the placenta and its membranes are delivered, the third stage of parturition is complete.

Table 8.2	Effect of Placental Hormones on Mother
Hormone	**Chief Effects**
Progesterone	Relaxation of smooth muscle; reduced uterine motility; reduced maternal immune response to fetus
Estrogen	Increased uterine blood flow; increased renin-angiotensin-aldosterone activity; increased protein biosynthesis by the liver
Peptide hormones	Increased insulin resistance

Source: Moore, Thomas R., *Gestation Encyclopedia of Human Biology*, Vol. 7, 7th edition. Copyright © 1997 Academic Press.

8.4 Effects of Pregnancy on the Mother

Major changes take place in the mother's body during pregnancy. When first pregnant, the mother may experience nausea and vomiting, loss of appetite, and fatigue. These symptoms subside, and some mothers report increased energy levels and a general sense of well-being despite an increase in weight. During pregnancy, the mother gains weight due to breast and uterine enlargement, weight of the fetus, amount of amniotic fluid, size of the placenta, her own increase in total body fluid, and an increase in the storage of proteins, fats, and minerals. The increased weight can lead to lordosis (swayback) and lower back pain.

Aside from the increase in weight, many of the physiological changes in the mother are due to the presence of the placental hormones that support fetal development (Table 8.2). Progesterone decreases uterine motility by relaxing smooth muscle, including the smooth muscle in the walls of arteries. The arteries expand, and this leads to a low blood pressure that sets in motion the renin-angiotensin-aldosterone mechanism. Aldosterone activity promotes sodium and water retention, and blood volume increases until it reaches its peak sometime during weeks 28–32 of pregnancy. Altogether, blood volume increases from 5 liters to 7 liters—a 40% rise. An increase in the number of red blood cells follows. With the rise in blood volume, cardiac output increases by 20–30%. Blood flow to the kidneys, placenta, skin, and breasts rises significantly. Smooth muscle relaxation also explains the common gastrointestinal effects of pregnancy. The heartburn experienced by many is due to relaxation of the esophageal sphincter and reflux of stomach contents into the esophagus. Constipation is caused by a decrease in intestinal tract motility.

Of interest is the increase in pulmonary values in a pregnant woman. The bronchial tubes relax, but this alone cannot explain the typical 40% increase in vital capacity and tidal volume. The increasing size of the uterus from a nonpregnant weight of 60–80 g to 900–1,200 g contributes to an improvement in respiratory functions. The uterus comes to occupy most of the abdominal cavity, reaching nearly to the xiphoid process of the sternum. This increase in size not only pushes the intestines, liver, stomach, and diaphragm superiorly, but it also widens the thoracic cavity. Compared to nonpregnant values, the maternal oxygen level changes little, but blood carbon dioxide levels fall by 20%, creating a concentration gradient favorable to the flow of carbon dioxide from fetal blood to maternal blood at the placenta.

The enlargement of the uterus does result in some problems. In the pelvic cavity, compression of the ureters and urinary bladder can result in stress incontinence. Compression of the inferior vena cava, especially when lying down, decreases venous return, and may result in edema and varicose veins.

In addition to the steroid hormones progesterone and estrogen, the placenta also produces some peptide hormones. One of these makes cells resistant to insulin, and the result can be pregnancy-induced diabetes. Some of the skin changes observed during pregnancy are also due to placental hormones. **Striae gravidarum,** commonly called "stretch marks," typically form over the abdomen and lower breasts in response to increased hormone levels rather than stretching of the skin. Darkening of the skin also increases during pregnancy, most commonly in the areolae, the skin in the line from the navel to the pubis, areas of the face and neck, and the vulva.

Female Breast and Lactation

A female breast contains 15 to 25 lobules, each with a milk duct that begins at the nipple and divides into numerous other ducts ending in blind sacs called alveoli (Fig. 8.9).

During pregnancy, the breasts enlarge as the ducts and alveoli increase in number and size. The same hormones that affect the mother's breasts can also affect the child's. Some newborns, including males, even secrete a small amount of milk for a few days.

Usually, no milk is produced during pregnancy. The hormone prolactin is needed for lactation to begin, and the production of this hormone is suppressed because of the feedback control that the increased amount of estrogen and progesterone during pregnancy has on the pituitary. Once the baby is delivered, however, the pituitary begins secreting prolactin. It takes a couple of days for milk production to begin, and in the meantime, the breasts produce **colostrum,** a thin, yellow, milky fluid rich in protein, including antibodies.

The continued production of milk requires a suckling child. When a breast is suckled, the nerve endings in the areolae are stimulated, and a nerve impulse travels along neural pathways from the nipples to the hypothalamus, which directs the pituitary gland to release the hormone oxytocin. When this hormone arrives at the breast, it causes the lobules to contract so that milk flows into the ducts (called milk letdown), where it may be drawn out of the nipple by the suckling child.

Whether to breast-feed or not is a private decision based in part on a woman's particular circumstances. However, it is well known that breast milk contains antibodies produced by the mother that can help a baby survive. Babies have immature immune systems, less stomach acid to destroy foreign antigens, and also unsanitary habits. Breast-fed babies are less likely to develop stomach and intestinal illnesses, including diarrhea, during the first 13 weeks of life. Breast-feeding also has physiological benefits for the mother. Suckling causes uterine contractions that can help the uterus return to its normal size, and breast-feeding uses up calories and can help a woman return to her normal weight.

The reading on page 139 discusses the pros and cons of breast-feeding.

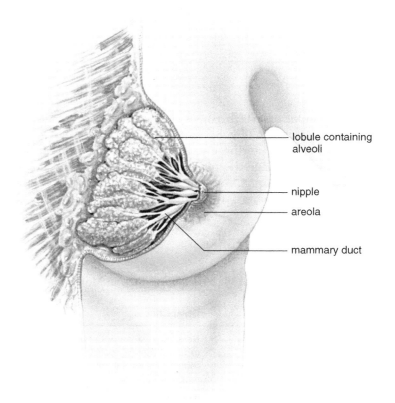

Figure 8.9 **Female breast anatomy.**
The female breast contains lobules consisting of ducts and alveoli. The alveoli are lined by milk-producing cells in the lactating (milk-producing) breast.

Deciding Between Feeding by Breast or by Bottle

Breast-feeding has come back into vogue in a big way. Not 20 years ago, only one mother in five breast-fed her baby. Today, an estimated two out of every three newborns are being given breast milk. The shift has many advantages, not just for the infant but for the mother as well. One is that when the baby is ready to eat, the milk is ready for the drinking. There are no bottles to sterilize or formulas to measure. Breast milk is also less expensive than formula, even taking into account the cost of the extra food a mother needs to ensure that she will produce enough milk and that it will contain enough calories. In addition, hormones released during breast-feeding cause contractions in the uterus that assist it in shrinking closer to its prepregnancy size. And the calories a mother's body spends producing breast milk may help her lose the 7 to 8 pounds—or more—of fat she puts on during pregnancy but does not "deliver" along with the baby, placenta, and amniotic and other fluids.

As for the baby, "human milk is unquestionably the best source of nutrition during the first months of life," says the American Academy of Pediatrics. That's especially true if conditions in the home are unsanitary (breast milk, unlike formula, does not need to be kept "clean," because it goes directly from mother to child), if money is too scarce to ensure that formula will always be affordable, or if the educational level of the parents is too low (or the emotional level of the household too "chaotic") for the family to read, fully understand, and consistently apply the rules of proper formula preparation and storage. But even full-term infants born to reasonably well-educated, financially secure parents who live in clean environments may benefit from breast-feeding.

It isn't that today's formulas are not reliable. Healthy babies can grow well on either breast or bottle milk. But breast milk is an amazingly sophisticated substance; for example, it contains more zinc in the first few weeks than later on to meet the newborn's higher zinc needs. And although scientists have been able to imitate breast milk safely enough in store-bought formula, "there may still be some subtle, not-yet-discovered ways in which breast milk is preferable to bottle milk," says Ronald Kleinman, M.D., head of the Committee on Nutrition at the American Academy of Pediatrics. "There remain differences between the two," he adds, "whose significance isn't understood."

These differences may be behind such findings as a *British Medical Journal* report that breast-fed infants appear better protected against wheezing during the first few months of life. The journal has also published a report suggesting that breast-fed newborns are less prone to stomach and intestinal illness during the first 13 weeks of life and, thus, suffer less than bottle-fed babies from vomiting and diarrhea.

Can the bottle ever be a better choice? Despite the many advantages of breast-feeding, it may not always be the appropriate way for a mother to nourish her child. Some women do not want to breast-feed because they are taking prescription drugs that may get into the milk and harm the baby, or they cannot breast-feed because they will return to work soon after giving birth and would find "pumping" breast milk to be given to the infant while they are away from home too tiring. Others may not wish to breast-feed because they are uncomfortable with the sexuality of the process or with some other emotionally related aspect. All these reasons are considered valid. In other words, mothers who do not want to breast-feed should not be pressured or made to feel guilty about it. As the family therapist and dietitian Ellyn Satter says in her book *Child of Mine: Feeding with Love and Good Sense* (Bull Publishing: Palo Alto, California), "You will have plenty of opportunities to feel guilty as a parent without feeling guilty about that, too." Besides, if a mother breast-feeds but hates doing it, her baby is going to sense that, and it will do greater harm than the breast milk will do good.

Indeed, more important than whether a mother breast-feeds, especially in countries such as the United States, where the standard of living for the average family is such that breast-feeding is not a life-or-death matter, is that she develops a relaxed, loving relationship with her child. "Even the sophisticated components of breast milk can't make up for that," Ms. Satter says. The closeness, warmth, and stimulation provided by an infant's caretakers are as important to his normal growth and development as the source of his food.

Source: *Tufts University Diet and Nutrition Letter* (ISSN 0747-4105) is published monthly by Tufts University Diet and Nutrition Letter, 53 Park Place, New York, NY 10007. This article extracted from a Special Report in the December 1990 issue. Reprinted by permission.

Bioethical Focus

Maternal Health Habits

The fetus is subject to harm if the mother uses medicines and drugs of abuse, including nicotine and alcohol. Also, various sexually transmitted diseases, notably HIV infection, can be passed on to the fetus by way of the placenta. Women need to know how to protect their unborn children from harm. Indeed, if they are sexually active, their behavior should be protective, even if they are using a recognized form of birth control. Harm can occur before a woman even realizes she is pregnant!

Because maternal health habits can affect a child before it is born, there has been a growing acceptance of prosecuting women when a newborn has a condition, such as fetal alcohol syndrome, that could only have been caused by the drinking habits of the mother. Employers have also become aware that they might be subject to prosecution if the workplace exposes pregnant employees to toxins. To protect themselves, Johnson Controls, a U.S. battery manufacturer, developed a fetal protection policy. No woman capable of bearing a child was offered a job that might expose her to toxins that could negatively affect the development of her baby. To get such a job, a woman had to show that she had been sterilized or was otherwise incapable of having children. In 1991, the U.S. Supreme Court declared this policy unconstitutional on the basis of sexual discrimination. The decision was hailed as a victory for women—but was it? The decision was written in such a way that women alone, and not an employer, are responsible for any harm done to the fetus by workplace toxins.

Some have noted that prosecuting women for causing prenatal harm can itself have a detrimental effect. The women may tend to avoid prenatal treatment, thereby increasing the risk to their children. Or they may opt for an abortion in order to avoid the possibility of prosecution. Women feel they are in a no-win situation. If they have a child that has been harmed due to their behavior, they are bad mothers; if they abort, they are also bad mothers.

Figure 8B   Health habits.
Should a pregnant woman be liable for poor health habits that could harm her child?

Decide Your Opinion

1. Do you believe a woman should be prosecuted if her child is born with a preventable condition? Why or why not?
2. Is the woman or the physician responsible when a woman of childbearing age takes a prescribed medication that harms an unborn child? Is the employer or the woman responsible when a workplace toxin harms an unborn child?
3. Should sexually active women who can bear a child be expected to avoid substances or situations that could possibly harm an unborn child, even if they are using birth control? Why or why not?

Summary

8.1 Fertilization
During fertilization, one sperm enters the egg, and then the sperm nucleus fuses with the egg nucleus.

8.2 Development
Development requires the processes of cleavage, growth, morphogenesis, and differentiation. The extraembryonic membranes, placenta, and umbilical cord allow humans to develop internally within the uterus. These structures protect the embryo and allow it to exchange wastes and nutrients with the mother's blood.

Development is divided into pre-embryonic development, embryonic development, and fetal development. During pre-embryonic development, the zygote begins to develop into a mass of cells, which travels down the uterine tube and embeds itself in the endometrium. Embryonic development begins when the embryo implants itself in the endometrium. Cells surrounding the embryo produce HCG, the hormone whose presence indicates that the female is pregnant. At the end of the embryonic period, all organ systems have been established, and there is a mature and functioning placenta. The embryo is only about 1.5 in. long.

Fetal development extends from the third through the ninth months. During the third and fourth months, the skeleton is becoming ossified. The sex of the fetus becomes distinguishable.

During the fifth through the ninth months, the fetus continues to grow and to gain weight. Babies born after six or seven months may survive, but full-term babies have a better chance of survival.

8.3 Birth
During stage 1 of parturition, the cervix dilates. During stage 2, the child is born. During stage 3, the afterbirth is expelled.

8.4 Effects of Pregnancy on the Mother
During pregnancy, the mother's uterus enlarges greatly, resulting in weight gain, standing and walking difficulties, and general discomfort. Aside from these changes, many of the physiological changes in the mother are due to the presence of the placental hormones. Smooth muscle relaxation leads to an increase in blood volume, including the number of red blood cells and various gastrointestinal complaints. So-called "stretch marks" and a darkening of the skin are also due to placental hormones. Lactation requires the hormone prolactin, and the suckling reflex involves the hormone oxytocin.

Reviewing the Chapter

1. Describe the process of fertilization. 126
2. List and describe the processes of development and the extraembryonic membranes. 127
3. What events occur during pre-embryonic development immediately following fertilization? 128–29
4. What events occur during embryonic development? What is the basis of the pregnancy test? 130–31
5. Describe the structure and function of the umbilical cord. 132
6. Describe the structure and function of the placenta. 132
7. What events normally occur during fetal development? 133
8. What are the three stages of birth? Describe the events of each stage. 136–37
9. In general, describe the physical changes in the mother during pregnancy. 137–38
10. Describe the anatomy of the breast and the suckling reflex. 138

Critical Thinking Questions

1. Discuss maternal health habits, both good and bad, and possible results of these habits on the health of the fetus.
2. How can an abdominal pregnancy occur and the fetus come to term and be born?

Understanding Key Terms

afterbirth 137
allantois 127
amnion 127
anencephaly 134
blastocyst 129
Braxton Hicks contractions 136
breech birth 133
cesarean section 133
chorion 127
chorionic villi 131
cleavage 127
cocaine babies 134
colostrum 138
congenital (birth) defects 134
delirium tremens 134
differentiation 127
embryo 129
embryonic development 130
embryonic disk 130
episiotomy 137
extraembryonic membrane 127
fertilization 126
fetal alcohol syndrome (FAS) 134
fetal development 133
fontanel 133

gastrulation 131
gestation 129
growth 127
human chorionic gonadotropin (HCG) 130
implantation 130
inner cell mass 129
lanugo 133
morphogenesis 127
morula 129
parturition 136
placenta 127
placental membrane 132
pre-embryonic development 129
primary germ layer 131
rubella (German measles) 134
spina bifida 134
striae gravidarum 138
teratogen 134
trophoblast 129
umbilical cord 131
vernix caseosa 133
yolk sac 127
zygote 126

Chapter 9

Birth Control and Infertility

9.1 Birth Control Methods

Birth control methods are used to regulate the number of children an individual or couple will have. Birth control is also called *contraception*, because birth control methods are often designed to prevent either fertilization or implantation of an embryo in the uterine lining.

The most reliable method of birth control is **abstinence**—that is, not engaging in sexual intercourse. This form of birth control has the added advantage of preventing transmission of sexually transmitted diseases. Figure 9.1 shows some common birth control methods. Table 9.1 lists several other means of birth control used in the United States, and rates their effectiveness. With the most effective methods, including sterilization, the birth control pill, injectable medications, contraceptive implants, and the intrauterine device (IUD), we expect that 90 out 100, or 90%, of sexually active women will not get pregnant, while 10 women will get pregnant. The second most effective group (85–90% effective) includes the diaphragm, cervical cap, vaginal sponge, and

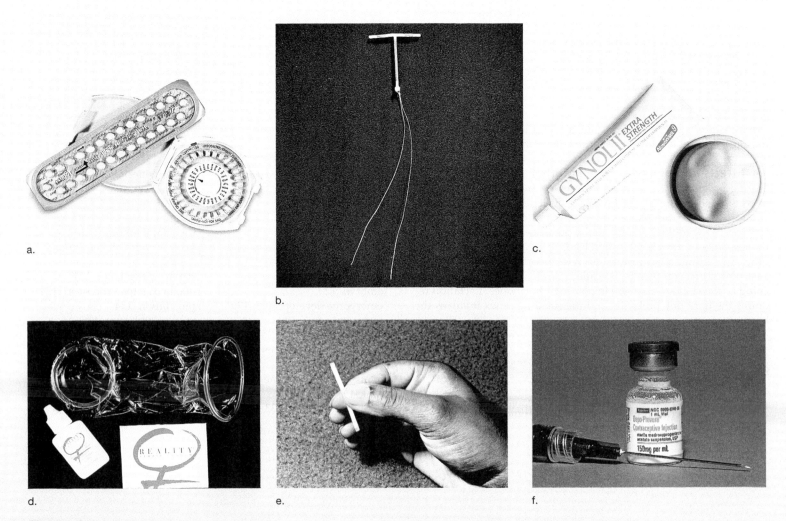

Figure 9.1 Various birth control devices.
a. Oral contraception (birth control pills). **b.** Intrauterine device. **c.** Spermicidal jelly and diaphragm. **d.** Female condom. **e.** Contraceptive implant.
f. Depo-Provera injection.

Table 9.1   Common Birth Control Methods

Name	Procedure	Methodology	Effectiveness	Risk
Abstinence	Refrain from sexual intercourse	No sperm in vagina	100%	None
Sterilization				
Vasectomy	Vasa deferentia cut and tied	No sperm in semen	Almost 100%	Irreversible sterility
Tubal ligation	Uterine tubes cut and tied	No eggs in uterine tube	Almost 100%	Irreversible sterility
Combined estrogen/ progesterone available as a pill, injectable, or vaginal ring and patch	Pill is taken daily, injectable and ring last a month, patch is replaced weekly	Anterior pituitary does not release FSH and LH	About 100%	Thromboembolism, especially in smokers
Progesterone only available as a tube implant and injectable	Injectable lasts three weeks; implant lasts three years	Anterior pituitary does not release FSH and LH	About 95%	Possible link to breast cancer, osteoporosis
Intrauterine device (IUD)	Newest device contains progesterone and lasts up to five years	Prevents implantation	More than 90%	Infection (pelvic inflammatory disease, PID)
Vaginal sponge	Sponge permeated with spermicide is inserted in vagina	Kills sperm on contact	About 90%	Presently none known
Diaphragm	Latex cap inserted into vagina to cover cervix before intercourse	Blocks entrance of sperm to uterus	With jelly, about 90%	Presently none known
Cervical cap	Latex cap held by suction over cervix	Delivers spermicide near cervix	Almost 85%	Cancer of cervix
Male condom	Latex sheath fitted over erect penis	Traps sperm and prevents STDs	About 85%	Presently none known
Female condom	Polyurethane liner fitted inside vagina	Blocks entrance of sperm to uterus and prevents STDs	About 85%	Presently none known
Coitus interruptus	Penis withdrawn before ejaculation	Prevents sperm from entering vagina	About 75%	Presently none known
Jellies, creams, foams	Spermicidal products inserted before intercourse	Kills a large number of sperm	About 75%	Presently none known
Natural family planning	Day of ovulation determined by record keeping; various methods of testing	Intercourse avoided on certain days of the month	About 70%	Presently none known
Douche	Vagina cleansed after intercourse	Washes out sperm	Less than 70%	Presently none known

condoms. The third most effective group (less than 85% effective) includes coitus interruptus and jellies, creams, and foams. Natural family planning is one of the least effective methods given in the table.

Sterilization

Sterilization as a means of birth control is a surgical procedure that renders the individual incapable of reproduction. Successful vasectomy in the male and tubal ligation in the female allow the individual to engage in sexual activities with no fear of pregnancy. The operations do not affect the secondary sex characteristics of the individual, nor do they necessarily affect sexual performance.

Vasectomy

As the name implies, **vasectomy** consists of cutting the vasa deferentia. The operation is very simple (Fig. 9.2*a*). Two small incisions (sometimes one incision) are made on the scrotum to expose the spermatic cords. The vasa deferentia

are carefully separated from the other structures in the spermatic cords, and a small section of each is removed. Each end is then sealed so that sperm are unable to travel to the urethra (Fig. 9.2*b*).

Vasectomies performed on well-adjusted and healthy males do not generally alter sexual motivation, ability to maintain an erection, or ejaculation of semen. However, there is some concern about an unexpected reaction: Antibodies against a man's own sperm have been found in the blood following vasectomy. It has been hypothesized that due to the buildup of sperm in the epididymides, sperm are engulfed by white blood cells that later enter the bloodstream. If remnants of the sperm enter the blood from the white blood cells, antibodies are formed against them. These antibodies will thereafter invade the testes to attack sperm.

A vasectomy does not affect the male sex characteristics because testosterone is still secreted into the bloodstream. A vasectomy should be considered an irreversible operation because resectioning the sperm ducts may be difficult, and fertility is usually reduced, perhaps due to an antibody reaction.

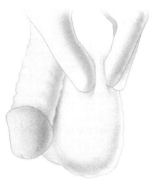

1. The vas deferens is located.

2. A small incision in the scrotum exposes the vas deferens, which is cut.

3. A small section of the vas deferens is removed, and the cut ends are tied and/or cauterized.

4. The incision is stitched closed. Steps 1–4 are repeated on the other side.

a.

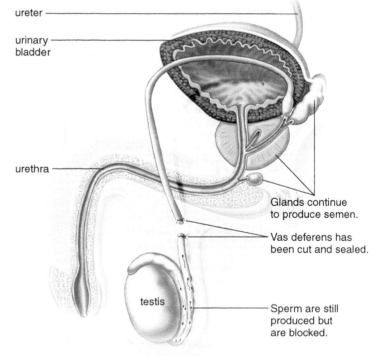

ureter

urinary bladder

urethra

Glands continue to produce semen.

Vas deferens has been cut and sealed.

testis

Sperm are still produced but are blocked.

b.

Figure 9.2   Vasectomy.
Vasectomy involves cutting and sealing the vasa deferentia. **a.** External view of procedure. **b.** Internal view of results.

Tubal Ligation

Tubal ligation refers to an operative procedure in which the uterine tubes are first cut and then either tied or sealed (Fig. 9.3). This prevents sperm from reaching the egg, because the sperm must halt on the far side of the obstruction.

If *laparoscopy* is done, only two incisions (small enough to be covered with adhesive bandages) are needed. A local anesthetic is given, and the abdomen is distended with an inert gas in order to give the physician a clear view of the uterine tubes. The surgeon makes a small incision near the navel and introduces the laparoscope (a small telescope with a "cold" light source) through this cut. A tiny surgical knife inserted through a second incision below the first incision is used to cut and remove a small portion of each tube before the ends are tied or sealed.

If *hysteroscopic sterilization* (hystera means womb) is done, a telescopic device is inserted into the uterus by way of the vagina. This time, the uterine tubes are sealed with an electric current at the point where they enter the uterus. The failure rate, which has been as high as 25%, is reduced if the operation is performed early in the woman's menstrual cycle before the uterine lining has had time to thicken.

As with a vasectomy, the sex characteristics are not affected by tubal ligation because the ovaries still secrete estrogen and progesterone into the bloodstream. But tubal ligation should be considered an irreversible operation. It is possible to resection the tubes, but this requires abdominal surgery, and the resultant fertility is not high.

Birth Control Pill and Alternatives

The **birth control pill** is usually a combination of estrogen and progesterone that is taken for 21 days out of a 28-day cycle. Either no pill or an inactive pill is then taken for the remaining 7 days.

Biological Activity of Pill

The estrogen and progesterone in the pill effectively shut down the pituitary production of both FSH and LH by the feedback mechanism. Theoretically, because the pituitary is not producing FSH, no follicle begins to develop in the ovary, ovulation does not occur, and pregnancy cannot occur. Without the maturation of a follicle, the ovaries do not produce the female sex hormones, but the pill provides these hormones for the patient.

Aside from this primary action of the pill, there are three secondary actions that most likely prevent pregnancy should ovulation happen to occur: (1) The pill prevents the cervical mucus from entering its midcycle phase of being thin and watery. Instead, the mucus remains sticky and fairly impenetrable by sperm. (2) The hormones in the pill are believed to affect the transport of an embryo down the uterine tubes so that it would not arrive in the uterus at the proper time for implantation. (3) The pill also prevents normal buildup of the lining of the uterus, and therefore an embryo is unable to implant itself. This action of the pill accounts for the fact that menstruation lasts fewer days and the flow is lighter when a woman takes the pill.

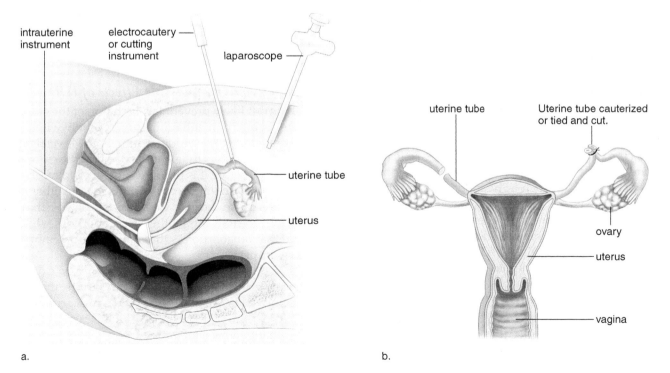

Figure 9.3   Tubal ligation.
Tubal ligation involves cutting and sealing the uterine tubes. **a.** Laparoscopy requires only two small incisions. **b.** Internal view of results.

Since the pill has one primary action and three secondary actions to prevent pregnancy, it is highly effective. It has been calculated that no more than one pregnancy per year should occur per 1,000 women using the pill. However, the pregnancy rate is actually 5 to 7 pregnancies per 1,000 because women do not always follow the directions for use.

Side Effects of Pill

Both beneficial and adverse side effects have been linked to the pill. Women report relief of discomforts associated with menstruation and also relief of acne. They also report several minor adverse side effects, which are not generally considered injurious to health. Many of these are similar to the symptoms associated with early pregnancy and are therefore thought to be related to the estrogen in the pill. They include nausea, vomiting, painful breast swelling, and irregular spotting or bleeding. Less common complaints are weight gain, headache, dizziness, and sometimes *chloasma*, the appearance of areas of darkened skin on the face, particularly over the cheekbones. Most often, these side effects, except for chloasma, either diminish or disappear by the second or third pill cycle.

A well-documented serious side effect of the pill is the increased incidence of blood clots within blood vessels. Blood clotting normally occurs only when a vessel has been cut, but it can occur abnormally within an intact vessel. If the clot remains stationary and obstructs the flow of blood where formed, it is called a *thrombus*. If the clot is carried to a smaller vessel where it prevents blood flow, it is called an *embolus*. If the clogged vessel serves a vital organ such as the lung, brain, or heart, serious illness or death may result.

Thromboembolism in women on the pill has been studied extensively in England and the United States. These studies compare the incidence of thromboembolism in two groups of women—one group taking the pill and the other group not taking the pill. The number of women who are hospitalized or who die due to thromboembolism has been shown to be about five to seven times greater in the group taking the pill than in the group not taking the pill. The higher increased incidence occurs when women taking the pill are 35 to 40 years of age and/or are smokers. If the women both smoke and have another risk factor, such as hypertension, the chance of thromboembolism jumps to 78 times as great for a pill user as for a nonuser. It is therefore recommended that these women consider another form of contraception.

Because of the possible side effects, the pill should only be taken under a physician's continuous care.

Alternate Routes of Administration

Depo Provera is an injectable form of progesterone that is administered every three months. It has been on the market for several years. The administration of progesterone causes changes in the endometrium that make pregnancy less likely to occur. A new product, called *Lunelle*, combines both estrogen and progesterone into a once-a-month injection.

Also newly available are a contraceptive *vaginal ring*, which is worn for 21 days and removed for 7 days, and a contraceptive transdermal patch. Both contain a combination of both estrogen and progesterone. The *hormone patch* (Ortho Evra) is expected to stay in place for a week and deliver both estrogen and progesterone.

Morning-After Pill

The expression "morning-after pill" refers to a medication that will prevent pregnancy after unprotected intercourse. The expression is a misnomer in that medication can begin one to several days after unprotected intercourse.

One type, a kit called Preven, contains four synthetic progesterone pills; two are taken up to 72 hours after unprotected intercourse, and two more are taken 12 hours later. The medication upsets the normal female reproductive cycle, making it difficult for an embryo to implant itself in the endometrium. A recent study estimated that the medication was 85% effective in preventing unintended pregnancies.

Intrauterine Device

An **intrauterine device (IUD)** is a small piece of molded plastic that is inserted into the uterus by a physician (see Fig. 9.1*b*). Two types of IUDs are now available: The copper type has copper wire wrapped around the stem, and the progesterone-releasing type has progesterone embedded in the plastic. A new product, Mirena, is smaller and more flexible than previous models, and it stays in place for five years. The best candidates for an IUD are women who have had at least one child, are of middle to older reproductive age, and have a stable relationship with a partner who does not have a sexually transmitted disease.

Biology Activity and Side Effects of IUD

IUDs most likely prevent implantation of the embryo because there is often an inflammatory reaction where the device presses against the endometrium. Some investigators believe that the IUD alters tubal motility so that the embryo arrives in the uterus before it is properly prepared to receive it. A question arises as to whether an IUD and some other birth control methods cause abortion. Some people believe that preventing an embryo from implanting is an abortion, while others believe that an abortion is the removal of an embryo that is already implanted.

About 1 to 3 pregnancies a year can be expected per 100 women using an IUD. If pregnancy occurs, the device should be removed because the chance of a miscarriage is higher if it is left in place (a 50% chance of a miscarriage compared to a 30% chance after removal).

The minor side effects of the IUD are expulsion, pain, irregular bleeding, or profuse menstruation. The device can be expelled from the uterus, especially in women who have not had any children, usually during menstruation and without the woman realizing it. To guard against this, IUDs have an attached nylon thread that projects into the vagina; the wearer can note the presence of the thread by inserting a finger.

Perforation of the uterus—that is, puncturing of the wall of the uterus—is a rare, but serious, possible side effect of the IUD. Perforation must be corrected by surgery because a general infection of the abdominal cavity can result. IUD users also have a higher risk of a uterine infection because microorganisms may enter the uterus by "climbing" the thread of the IUD. The infection may spread to the uterine tubes, causing *pelvic inflammatory disease (PID)* (see Chapter 10, pages 158–59), with scarring that will increase the chances of infertility. The Dalkon Shield was an IUD that had several strands in its tail, and users of this particular IUD showed a much higher chance of PID than nonusers. A. H. Robbins Company, the manufacturer of the Dalkon Shield, stopped making the device in 1974 and later filed for bankruptcy because of the expense of defending itself in various lawsuits. As a result, other manufacturers were very reluctant to market IUDs in the United States for several years.

Contraceptive Implant

Norplant is a long-lasting hormonal contraceptive that is implanted under a woman's skin. Norplant consists of six, inch-long, silicone rubber tubes containing progestin, a synthetic form of progesterone. Progestin leaks through the tubing at a steady rate that maintains blood hormone levels high enough to prevent the hypothalamus from secreting GnRH and the anterior pituitary from secreting gonadotropic hormones.

A new product called *Implanon* consists of only one tube, which should be easier to insert and remove than Norplant. Clinical studies suggest that implants have no serious side effects. However, progestin does cause irregular menstrual bleeding in 75% of women who use it. Norplant, which lasts up to five years, is said to be 99.7% effective in preventing pregnancy. This would make it the most effective means of reversible contraception available. When the tubes are removed or run out of medicine, fertility is restored in less than 48 hours.

Diaphragm, Cervical Cap, and Vaginal Sponge

The **diaphragm** is a soft rubber or plastic cup with a flexible rim that fits over the cervix (Fig. 9.4; see Fig. 9.1c). A physician determines the proper diaphragm size; therefore, each woman must be individually fitted. The diaphragm must be inserted into the vagina and properly positioned at most two hours before sexual relations. It must be used with a spermicidal jelly or cream and should be left in place for at least six hours after intercourse. An allergic reaction to the diaphragm or spermicide is the only known side effect.

A higher rate of pregnancy occurs with use of the diaphragm (10 to 15 pregnancies per 100 women per year) than with the pill or IUD. This is because insertion may require an interruption to lovemaking, and thus the woman may not bother to use the diaphragm. Also, some women do not like to handle their genital organs and therefore prefer not to use the diaphragm. However, women can learn to use an inserter to put the diaphragm in place.

The *cervical cap*, a widely used and popular contraceptive device in Europe, is currently being introduced in the United States. The cervical cap is thicker and smaller than the diaphragm. The thimble-shaped rubber or plastic cup fits snugly around the cervix. Unlike the diaphragm, the cervical cap is effective even if left in place for several days.

The *vaginal sponge* is shaped to fit the cervix and is permeated with the spermicide nonoxynol-9. Unlike the diaphragm and cervical cap, the sponge need not be fitted by a physician because one size fits everyone. It is effective immediately after placement in the vagina and remains effective for 24 hours.

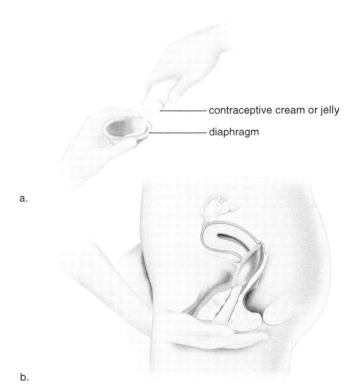

contraceptive cream or jelly

diaphragm

a.

b.

Figure 9.4   Diaphragm.
a. Removal from plastic container and application of spermicide.
b. Insertion and position after insertion.

Condoms

A **male condom** is a thin skin (lambskin) or plastic sheath (latex) that fits over the erect penis. The ejaculate is trapped inside the sheath and therefore does not enter the vagina. When used in conjunction with a spermicidal foam, cream, or jelly, the protection is better than with the condom alone, for which 10 to 15 unplanned pregnancies a year per 100 women are expected.

Condoms cause no side effects, and they may be purchased in a drugstore without a prescription. Condoms are checked during the manufacturing process for any possible defects; therefore, it is believed that their relatively high failure rate is due largely to misuse. The condom must be placed on the penis after it is erect, and a small space should be left at the tip to collect the ejaculate (Fig. 9.5). If added lubrication is desired, a nonpetroleum-base jelly, such as a spermicidal jelly or cream, should be used, since petroleum products—Vaseline, for example—tend to destroy the plastic. Following ejaculation, the upper part of the condom should be held tightly against the penis as it is withdrawn from the vagina.

Some men and women feel that using a condom not only interrupts the sex act, but also dulls sensations; therefore, they prefer one of the other birth control methods. However, there has been a revival of interest in the latex condom as a means of birth control because it offers possible protection against sexually transmitted diseases (STDs), which will be discussed in Chapter 10.

A **female condom,** now available, consists of a large polyurethane tube with a flexible ring that fits onto the cervix (Fig. 9.6; see Fig. 9.1*d*). The open end of the tube has a ring that covers the external genitals. The female condom also protects against STDs.

Coitus Interruptus

Coitus interruptus (withdrawal) is so named because sexual intercourse is abruptly interrupted in order to discharge the semen outside the vagina. Just before orgasm, the male withdraws his penis from the vagina and ejaculates away from the vaginal area. This method of birth control requires careful timing by the male, and he must be sure to direct the penis away from the vagina, since it is possible for sperm deposited near the vagina to work their way into the vagina and up to the uterus and the uterine tubes.

The advantage of coitus interruptus is that it is always available, but it is not considered good protection, especially since the first drop of semen, which is released before orgasm, contains numerous sperm. Also, sexual relations are unsatisfactory for some couples because the male has to concentrate on good timing and the sex act is abruptly discontinued. The rate of unplanned pregnancies is 10 to 20 per 100 women per year with this method of birth control.

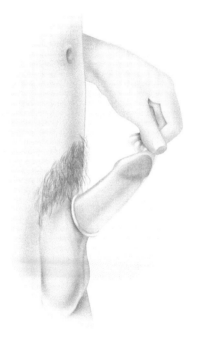

Figure 9.5   **Male condom use.**
Correct method for using a plain-end condom, which has no reservoir for ejaculated semen.

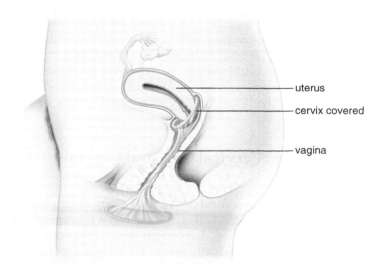

Figure 9.6   **Female condom use.**
Correct method for using a female condom.

Spermicidal Jellies, Creams, and Foams

Jellies, *creams*, and *foams*, which contain sperm-killing ingredients such as nonoxynol-9, are inserted into the vagina with an applicator up to 30 minutes before intercourse. A fresh application is required for each subsequent intercourse. Used alone, they are not a highly effective means of birth control, but the foam is more effective because it reaches all parts of the vagina, whereas the jellies and creams tend to localize centrally. It is estimated that 15 to 25 women out of 100 become pregnant each year while using this method of birth control.

No serious side effects are associated with these products, and they are readily available without a prescription in drugstores. Some women are allergic to certain spermicidal agents and must switch to a new product or discontinue use.

Natural Family Planning

Natural family planning, formerly called the rhythm method of birth control, is based on the fact that a woman ovulates only once a month and that the egg and sperm are viable for a limited number of hours or days. The day of ovulation can vary from month to month, and the fertility of the egg and sperm also varies, perhaps monthly and certainly from person to person. Therefore, the so-called safe period for intercourse without fear of pregnancy cannot be absolutely determined by using a calendar alone. However, the following procedure can be utilized by those who are willing to risk an unexpected pregnancy:

1. Keep a record of the length of the monthly cycle for a year. Note the shortest and the longest cycle. A cycle lasts from the first day of menstruation to its occurrence again.
2. Subtract 18 from the number of days in the shortest cycle. This is the day on which the unsafe period begins.
3. Subtract 11 from the number of days in the longest cycle. This is the day on which the unsafe period ends.

For example, suppose Mary Smith's shortest cycle for the year was 25 days and the longest was 29: $25 - 18 = 7$, and $29 - 11 = 18$. Thus, no intercourse should take place between the seventh and nineteenth days of each cycle (Fig. 9.7). Using this method, 15 to 30 pregnancies per 100 women per year are expected.

A more reliable way to practice the natural family planning method of birth control is to await the day of ovulation each month and then wait three more days before engaging in intercourse. The day of ovulation can possibly be determined by one of the following methods:

1. Body temperature is lower before ovulation than after it. Immediately preceding ovulation, the temperature drops about 0.2°F, but directly following ovulation, the temperature rises about 0.6°F (Fig. 9.8). Special thermometers, called basal thermometers, are calibrated only from 96°F to 100°F so that the tenths-of-degree marks are widely spaced, making it easier to read the small, expected changes in temperature. The temperature should be taken immediately upon waking in the morning and before leaving bed or starting any activity; the rectal basal temperature is more accurate than the oral basal temperature.
2. The level of sugar in the vagina increases near ovulation. Tes-Tape can be purchased at the drugstore and inserted into the vagina every day. When the yellowish tape turns deepest blue, the sugar level is highest and ovulation is near. The level of acidity can also be tested by using pH paper. When the paper shows a change from acid to alkaline, ovulation is near.

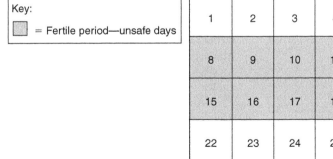

Figure 9.7   Natural family planning calendar.
This calendar shows the fertile days (unsafe for intercourse) for a woman whose shortest uterine cycle of the year is 25 days and longest uterine cycle of the year is 29 days. Each individual woman has to work out her own calendar.

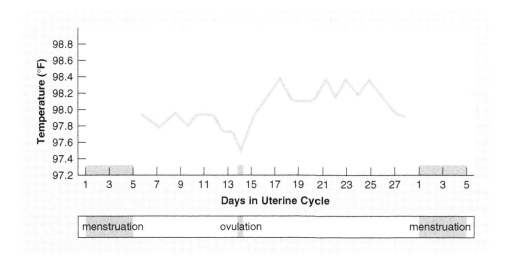

Figure 9.8　**Oral body temperature.**
Typical oral body temperature changes during a 28-day uterine (menstrual) cycle. The body temperature falls slightly before ovulation and then rises immediately after ovulation.

3. It is possible to test the stringiness and/or the weight of the cervical mucus. When testing the stringiness, the mucus threads are stretched out the longest at the time of ovulation. When testing the weight by means of a special weighing device, the weight decreases at the time of ovulation.

The methods of birth control discussed thus far are the only accepted methods available at the present time. Couples should not rely on other methods suggested by friends, nor should they believe that single events of intercourse will not result in pregnancy. It is obvious that as long as the egg is present and the sperm have been ejaculated into the vagina, a pregnancy is possible.

Abortion

Abortion is the termination of a pregnancy before the fetus is capable of survival, which at present is a fetal weight of less than 1 pound. Spontaneous abortions, often called **miscarriages,** are those that occur naturally, and induced abortions are those that are brought about by external procedures.

Surgical Removal

Termination of a pregnancy by surgery is legally available in most states to women who can afford the procedure. Uterine aspiration is used up to three months; dilation and evacuation are required for those who are four or five months pregnant. Legislation against late-term abortions has been passed but is being contested in the courts.

Uterine Aspiration　Induced abortions during the first three months of pregnancy are usually performed by uterine aspiration. After a local anesthetic is given, the cervix is dilated, and the uterine contents are sucked out by means of a small metal or plastic tube attached to an aspirator (suction machine). The uterus contracts spontaneously, reducing blood loss. Uterine aspiration is sometimes performed when menstruation is five to fourteen days overdue without definite proof of pregnancy. Under these circumstances, the procedure is called "menstrual regulation" or "menstrual extraction."

Dilation and Evacuation　During the fourth and fifth months of pregnancy, dilation and evacuation may be used as a means of abortion. A local or general anesthetic is given, and the cervix is dilated by means of a series of cigar-shaped stainless steel dilators of increasing size. Then vacuum suction is used to remove as much as possible of the contents of the uterus. Finally, a long-handled device with a spoon-shaped end, called a curette, is used to scrape the inside of the uterus.

Abortion Pill

A variety of factors—especially the verbal and physical harassment of people entering abortion clinics, and the persecution and killing of doctors who perform abortions—have made it difficult to seek and have a surgical abortion. Now a medical abortion is available that might eventually make it easier for women to end an unwanted pregnancy.

Any family doctor or obstetrician/gynecologist can now prescribe a two-drug regimen, provided he or she has some surgical backup arrangement if it fails to end the pregnancy or if side effects occur. A series of pills are taken over a period of days to induce a miscarriage.

The first medication, *mifepristone,* is an antiprogestin that is taken any time in the first seven weeks of pregnancy. This drug causes the uterus to shed its lining and dislodge the embryo. Then the second drug, *misoprostol,* is taken. Misoprostol induces contractions that expel the embryo in about 95% of cases. Excessive bleeding occurs in about 2% of users.

Endocrine-Disrupting Contaminants

Rachel Carson's book *Silent Spring*, published in 1962, predicted that pesticides would have a deleterious effect on animal life. Soon thereafter, it was found that pesticides caused the thinning of egg shells in bald eagles to the point that their eggs broke and the chicks died. Additionally, populations of terns, gulls, cormorants, and lake trout declined after they ate fish contaminated by high levels of environmental toxins. The concern was so great that the United States Environmental Protection Agency (EPA) came into existence. The efforts of both this agency and civilian environmental groups have brought about a reduction in pollution release and a cleaning up of emissions. Even so, we are now aware of more subtle effects that pollutants can cause.

Hormones influence nearly all aspects of physiology and behavior in animals, including tissue differentiation, growth, and reproduction. Therefore, when wildlife in contaminated areas started to exhibit certain types of abnormalities, researchers began to think that certain pollutants can affect the endocrine system. In England, male fish exposed to sewage developed ovarian tissue and produced a metabolite normally found only in females during egg formation. In California, western gulls displayed abnormalities in gonad structure and nesting behaviors. Hatchling alligators in Florida possessed abnormal gonads and hormone concentrations linked to nesting.

At first, such effects seemed to indicate only the involvement of the female hormone estrogen, and researchers therefore called the contaminants ecoestrogens. However, further study brought more information to light. Many of the contaminants interact with hormone receptors, and in that way cause developmental effects. Others bind directly with sex hormones such as testosterone and estradiol. Still others alter the physiology of the growth hormones and neurotransmitters responsible for brain development and behavior. Therefore, the preferred term today for these pollutants is endocrine-disrupting contaminants (EDCs).

Many EDCs are chemicals used as pesticides and herbicides in agriculture, and some are associated with the manufacture of various other synthetic organic compounds such as PCBs (polychlorinated biphenyls). Some chemicals shown to influence hormones are found in plastics, food additives, and personal hygiene products. In mice, phthalate esters, which are plastic components, affect neonatal development when present in the part-per-trillion range. It is, therefore, of great concern that EDCs have been found at levels one thousand times greater than this—even in amounts comparable to functional hormone levels in the human body. Furthermore, it is not surprising that EDCs are affecting the endocrine systems of a wide range of organisms (Fig. 9A).

Scientists and those representing industrial manufacturers continue to debate whether EDCs pose a health risk to humans. Some suspect that EDCs lower sperm counts, reduce male and female fertility, and increase the rates of certain cancers (breast, ovarian, testicular, and prostate). Additionally, some studies suggest that EDCs contribute to learning deficits and behavioral problems in children. Laboratory and field research continues to identify chemicals that have the ability to influence the endocrine system. Millions of tons of potential EDCs are produced annually in the United States, and the EPA is under pressure to certify these compounds as safe. The European Economic Community has already restricted the use of certain EDCs, and has banned the production of specific plastic components that are found in items intended for use by children, specifically toys. Only through continued scientific research and the cooperation of industry can we identify the risks that EDCs pose to the environment, wildlife, and humans.

Figure 9A **Exposure to endocrine-disrupting contaminants.**
Various types of wildlife, as well as humans, are exposed to endocrine-disrupting contaminants that can seriously affect their health and reproductive abilities.

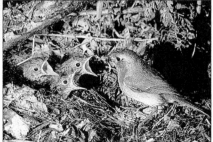

9.2 Infertility

Infertility is the failure of a couple to achieve pregnancy after one year of regular, unprotected intercourse. The American Medical Association estimates that 15% of all couples are infertile. The cause of infertility can be attributed to the male (40%), the female (40%), or both (20%).

Causes of Infertility

The most frequent cause of infertility in males is low sperm count and/or a large proportion of abnormal sperm. Researchers have identified portions of the Y chromosome, called the AZF regions, each of which contains several genes that are necessary to sperm production. If any one of these genes is missing or malfunctions, the man is infertile. Male infertility can also be due to environmental influences. The public is particularly concerned about endocrine-disrupting contaminants, which are discussed in the reading on page 151. But thus far, it appears that a sedentary lifestyle, coupled with smoking and alcohol consumption, most often leads to male infertility. Sperm production requires a temperature that is 3°–4°C cooler than body temperature, and when males spend most of the day sitting in front of a computer or the TV or driving, the testes temperature remains too high.

Body weight appears to be the most significant factor in causing female infertility. Severely underweight women rarely ovulate and menstruate. The reason is surprising: In women of normal weight, fat cells produce a hormone called leptin that stimulates the hypothalamus to release GnRH. Being overweight is also associated with infertility. In overweight women, the ovaries often contain many small follicles, and the woman fails to ovulate. Other causes of infertility in females are blocked uterine tubes and endometriosis. Pelvic inflammatory disease (PID), discussed in Chapter 10, pages 158–59, can cause blocked uterine tubes. **Endometriosis** is the presence of uterine tissue outside the uterus, particularly in the uterine tubes and on the abdominal organs. Backward flow of menstrual fluid allows living uterine cells to establish themselves in the abdominal cavity, where they go through the usual uterine cycle, causing pain and structural abnormalities that make it more difficult for a woman to conceive.

Sometimes the causes of infertility can be corrected by medical intervention so that couples can have children. If no obstruction is apparent and body weight is normal, it is possible to give females fertility drugs, which are gonadotropic hormones that stimulate the ovaries and bring about ovulation. Such hormone treatments may cause multiple ovulations and multiple births.

When reproduction does not occur in the usual manner, many couples adopt a child. Others sometimes try one of the assisted reproductive technologies discussed in the following paragraphs.

Assisted Reproductive Technologies

Assisted reproductive technologies (ART) consist of techniques used to increase the chances of pregnancy. Often, sperm or eggs are retrieved from the testes or ovaries, and fertilization takes place in a clinical or laboratory setting.

Artificial Insemination

During **artificial insemination,** sperm are placed in the vagina by a physician. Sometimes a woman is artificially inseminated by her partner's sperm. This is especially helpful if the partner has a low sperm count, because the sperm can be collected over a period of time and concentrated so that the sperm count is sufficient to result in fertilization. Often, however, a woman is inseminated by sperm acquired from a donor who is a complete stranger to her. At times, a combination of partner and donor sperm is used.

During *intrauterine insemination (IUI)*, fertility drugs are given to stimulate the ovaries, and then the donor's sperm is placed in the uterus rather than in the vagina.

If the prospective parents wish, sperm can be sorted into those believed to be X-bearing or Y-bearing to increase the chances of having a child of the desired sex.

In Vitro Fertilization

During **in vitro fertilization (IVF),** conception occurs in laboratory glassware. Ultrasound machines can now spot follicles in the ovaries that hold immature eggs; therefore, the

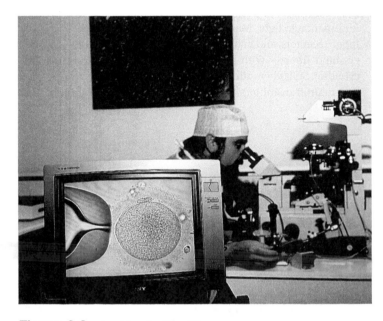

Figure 9.9   In vitro fertilization.
A researcher is using a microscope connected to a television screen (at left) to carry out in vitro fertilization. A pipette (at left of egg) holds the egg steady while a needle (not visible) introduces the sperm into the egg.

latest method is to forgo the administration of fertility drugs and retrieve immature eggs by using a needle. The immature eggs are then brought to maturity in glassware before concentrated sperm are added (Fig. 9.9). After about two to four days, the embryos are ready to be transferred to the uterus of the woman, who is now in the secretory phase of her uterine cycle. If desired, genetic analysis of the pre-embryo can be done (see page 66), so that only embryos found to be free of genetic disorders can be used. If implantation is successful, development is normal and continues to term.

Intracytoplasmic Sperm Injection

In **intracytoplasmic sperm injection (ICSI),** a highly sophisticated procedure, a single sperm is injected into an egg. This method is used effectively when a man has severe infertility problems.

Gamete Intrafallopian Transfer

Gamete intrafallopian transfer (GIFT) was devised to overcome the low success rate (15–20%) of in vitro fertilization. The method is exactly the same as in vitro fertilization, except the eggs and the sperm are placed in the uterine tubes immediately after they have been brought together. GIFT has the advantage of being a one-step procedure for the woman—the eggs are removed and reintroduced all in the same time period. A variation on this procedure is to fertilize the eggs in the laboratory and then place the zygotes in the uterine tubes.

Surrogate Mothers

In some instances, women are contracted and paid to have babies. These women are called surrogate mothers. The sperm and/or the egg can be contributed by the contracting parents.

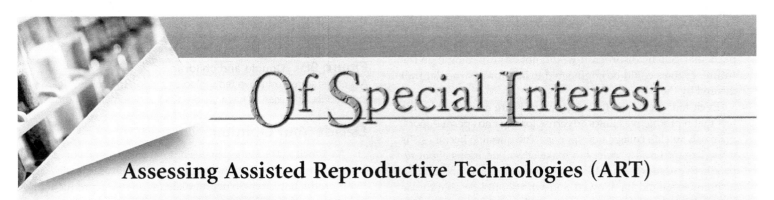

Assessing Assisted Reproductive Technologies (ART)

It's estimated that by now over a million babies have been born worldwide as a result of ART. Now that we know ART can be successful, the emphasis has shifted from perfecting the efficiency of ART to ensuring the best possible results. It is generally considered desirable to reduce the high incidence of multiple pregnancies resulting from ART. In the early days, multiple embryos, often more than three, were transferred to try to achieve a pregnancy. Some clinicians thought that, if a multiple pregnancy resulted, it was at least a way to get a complete family with one pregnancy. But since multiple births endanger both the mother and the newborns and also tax the health-care system, more and more clinicians today want to transfer only one or perhaps two embryos at a time.

There is also a concern about the effect of ART on the newborn. Available data suggest no significant differences in the scores of IQ tests among children born as a result of ART compared to children conceived in the usual way. However, there is a small but statistically significant increase in sex chromosome and autosome abnormalities following ICSI (intracytoplasmic sperm injection). There is also a slightly higher risk that ICSI male children will have a malformation of the penis.

ICSI is usually carried out when the man is infertile due to a low number and/or low quality of sperm. As discussed, such men are likely to have genetic mutations in the AZF regions of the Y chromosome. Therefore, it is not surprising that these men are more likely to father children with sex chromosome abnormalities than are men without these mutations. However, since the risk is small, many couples may be willing to bear the risk rather than remain childless.

Another approach is possible now that we know that chromosomal abnormalities in the sperm and egg often contribute to couples being infertile. Today, if ART is coupled with pre-pregnancy testing of the embryo (see Fig. 4.8), it would be possible to implant only embryos found to be free of such abnormalities. Use of pre-pregnancy testing would obviously help increase the success rate of ART and lead to implantation of only a single healthy embryo. Also, if consistently positive results could be obtained with a single embryo transfer, clinicians could collect fewer eggs from the mother. Reduction of hormonal stimulation to induce ovulation in the mother is desirable because hormonal stimulation can result in an endometrium that is not properly prepared to receive the embryo and failure of the embryo to implant.

The goal is to increase the success rate of ART both in terms of achieving pregnancy and in making sure that the pregnancy results in a genetically healthy individual.

Assisted Reproductive Technologies

The dizzying array of assisted reproductive technologies (ART) has progressed from simple in vitro fertilization to the ability to freeze eggs or sperm or even embryos for future use. Older women who never had the opportunity to freeze their eggs can still have children if they use donated eggs—perhaps today harvested from a fetus.

Legal complications abound, ranging from which mother has first claim to the child—the surrogate mother, the woman who donated the egg, or the primary caregiver—to which partner has first claim to frozen embryos following a divorce. Legal questions about who has the right to use what techniques have rarely been discussed, much less decided upon. Some clinics will help anyone, male or female, no questions asked, as long as they have the ability to pay. And most clinics are heading toward doing any type of procedure, including guaranteeing the sex of the child and making sure the child will be free from a particular genetic disorder. It would not be surprising if, in the future, zygotes could be engineered to have any particular trait desired by the parents.

Even today, eugenic (good gene) goals are evidenced by the fact that reproductive clinics advertise for egg and sperm donors, primarily in elite college newspapers. The question becomes, "Is it too late for us as a society to make ethical decisions about reproductive issues?" Should we reach a consensus about what techniques should be allowed and who should be able to use them? We all want to avoid, if possible, what happened to Jonathan Alan Austin. Jonathan, who was born to a surrogate mother, later died from injuries inflicted by his father. Perhaps if a background check were legally required, surrogate mothers would only make themselves available to individuals or couples who are known to have certain psychological characteristics.

Figure 9B   Couple and children.
Are assisted reproductive technologies a boon to society? To individuals who wish to have children? Or a detriment to both?

Decide Your Opinion

1. As a society, the United States has never been in favor of regulating reproduction. Should we regulate assisted reproduction if we do not regulate unassisted reproduction? Why or why not?
2. Should the state be the guardian of frozen embryos and make sure they all get a chance to live? Why or why not?
3. Is it appropriate for physicians and parents to select which embryos will be implanted in the uterus? On the basis of sex? On the basis of genetic inheritance? Why or why not?

Summary

9.1 Birth Control Methods

Numerous birth control methods and devices are available for those who wish to prevent pregnancy. Effectiveness varies, and research is being conducted to find new and possibly better methods.

During sterilization of males, called a vasectomy, small sections of the vasa deferentia are removed, and the cut ends are sealed. During sterilization of females, called tubal ligation, the uterine tubes are cut and then tied or sealed.

The birth control pill (composed of a combination of estrogen and progesterone) is a highly effective means of birth control if taken as directed. The primary action of the pill is to prevent the anterior pituitary from releasing FSH and LH. Also, the cervical mucus remains thick, movement of any embryo down the uterine tube is impaired, and the uterine lining does not thicken enough for implantation to occur. The pill does have side effects; the most serious is the possibility of life-threatening blood clots inside blood vessels. Today, various alternatives are available for administration of sex hormones to prevent pregnancy, including injectables, a vaginal ring, and the hormone patch.

Morning-after pills—containing progesterone, which disturbs the female reproductive cycle—are available. Intrauterine devices (IUDs) stay inside the uterus for years and release substances that prevent implantation of an embryo. PID is a possible serious side effect. A new contraceptive implant requires only one tube to be put under the skin. The diaphragm and cervical cap prevent sperm from entering the uterus; the diaphragm is used with a spermicide. The vaginal sponge relies only on a spermicide. Condoms, both male and female, prevent the penis from even touching the vagina; therefore, they prevent STDs.

Some methods of birth control are not very effective. These include coitus interruptus, which can be practiced without the need to buy a product; spermicidal jellies, creams, and foams, which are easily inserted; and natural family planning, which does indeed take a lot of planning because it restricts intercourse to days of the female reproductive cycle when it is thought pregnancy may not occur.

If an unwanted pregnancy does occur, an abortion is sometimes performed. Two types of abortions are now available: early-term abortion by surgery or the taking of medications (called the abortion pill) that bring on an abortion even earlier.

9.2 Infertility

Some couples are infertile, and if so, they may use assisted reproductive technologies (ART) in order to have a child. Artificial insemination and in vitro fertilization (IVF) have been followed by more sophisticated techniques, such as intracytoplasmic sperm injection (ICSI). Today, IVF and ICSI allow preimplantation genetic analysis to be done to assure parents that the embryo does not have a serious genetic disorder. Other methods include gamete intrafallopian transfer and the use of a surrogate mother.

Reviewing the Chapter

1. List the birth control measures discussed, and rate the effectiveness of each. 142–50
2. Which types of birth control measures require operative procedures? Why don't these operations affect the sex characteristics? 144–45
3. What is the role of a physician if a woman is taking the birth control pill or decides to use an IUD, contraceptive implants, or a diaphragm? 146–47
4. Which types of birth control devices may be purchased in a drugstore without a doctor's prescription? Of these, which is the most effective? 143, 147–49
5. Which types of birth control devices are protective against STDs if used properly? 148
6. Theoretically, how does natural family planning work? Explain its high failure rate. 149
7. What is the benefit of taking the "morning-after pill" rather than possibly needing an abortion? Name and discuss the two types of surgical abortions and the medication that is available to bring on an abortion. 146, 150
8. What are some causes of female infertility? Male infertility? 152
9. What is artificial insemination by a donor? What might be an added benefit of artificial insemination? 152
10. Describe how IVF is carried out. Describe ICSI. What is the benefit of preimplantation genetic analysis? 152

Critical Thinking Questions

1. The female birth control pill contains estrogen and progesterone. A male pill containing the normal amount of testosterone does not seem to work. Why would you have predicted this?

2. Why would you not recommend the production of a birth control pill for either males or females that contained FSH and LH antagonists—chemicals that block reception of FSH and LH?

3. Why would you expect intrauterine insemination to produce better results than the usual method of artificial insemination?

Understanding Key Terms

abortion 150
abstinence 142
artificial insemination 152
assisted reproductive
   technologies (ART) 152
birth control method 142
birth control pill 145
coitus interruptus 148
condom, female 148
condom, male 148
diaphragm 147
endometriosis 152

gamete intrafallopian transfer
   (GIFT) 153
infertility 152
intracytoplasmic sperm injection (ICSI) 153
intrauterine device (IUD) 146
in vitro fertilization (IVF) 152
miscarriage 150
natural family planning 149
sterilization 144
tubal ligation 145
vasectomy 144

Chapter 10
Sexually Transmitted Diseases

10.1 STDs of Bacterial Origin

Bacteria cause numerous diseases in humans, including the sexually transmitted diseases (STDs) chlamydia, gonorrhea, and syphilis (Table 10.1).

Bacterial cells lack a membrane-bounded nucleus and the other membranous organelles typical of human cells; therefore, they are called prokaryotic (before nucleus) cells. A nucleoid region contains their DNA, and a cytoplasm contains the enzymes of their many metabolic pathways. Bacteria are enclosed in a cell wall, and some are also surrounded by a capsule that inhibits destruction by the host. Motile bacteria often have flagella (sing., flagellum). Figure 10.1 shows the structure of a typical bacterium.

The diseases listed in Table 10.1 are caused by bacteria that are therefore called **pathogens**. Such diseases are termed *communicable* because the pathogen is transmitted from host to host. Pathogens are transferred by food and water, human or animal bites, direct contact, and aerosols (droplets in the air). Sexually transmitted diseases require intimate contact between persons for their successful transmission.

Bacterial diseases are controlled by preventing transmission, by administering vaccines, and by antibiotic therapy. **Antibiotics** are medications that kill bacteria by interfering with one of their unique metabolic pathways. Antibiotic therapy is highly successful if it is carried out in the recommended manner. Otherwise, as discussed in the reading on page 165, resistant strains can develop. Unfortunately, there are no vaccines for STDs caused by bacteria; therefore, preventing transmission becomes all the more important. Abstinence or monogamous relations (always the same partner) with someone who is free of an STD will prevent transmission. The use of a condom with a vaginal spermicide containing nonoxynol-9, and avoidance of oral/genital contact are recommended.

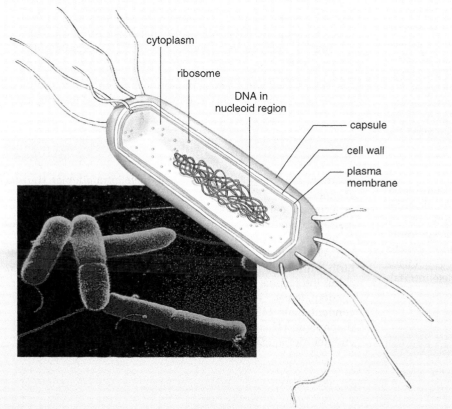

cytoplasm

ribosome

DNA in
nucleoid region

capsule

cell wall

plasma
membrane

Figure 10.1 **The structure of a bacterium.**

Table 10.1	Infectious Diseases Caused by Bacterias
Site of Infection	**Diseases**
NOT SEXUALLY TRANSMITTED	
Respiratory tract	Strep throat, pneumonia,* whooping cough,* tuberculosis*
Skin	Staph (pimples and boils)
Nervous system	Tetanus,* botulism, meningitis
Digestive tract	Food poisoning, dysentery, cholera*
Other systems	Gas gangrene* (wound infections), diphtheria,* typhoid fever*
SEXUALLY TRANSMITTED	
Reproductive system	Chlamydia, gonorrhea, syphilis (can spread to other systems)

*Vaccines are available. Tuberculosis vaccine is not used in the United States. Typhoid fever, cholera, and gas gangrene vaccines are given if the situation requires it. Others are routinely given.

Of Special Interest

Bacteria and You

The diversity of life on Earth is enormous, especially when you consider that most living things are too small to be seen with the naked eye. Scientists use microscopes to visualize bacteria and a battery of biochemical and genetic tests to study them. Bacteria are widely distributed in the environment. They cover inanimate objects and the surfaces of plants and animals; they even reside within the bodies of macroscopic organisms, including ourselves. Local environments determine where bacteria can live and what they do there. Knowing the characteristics of bacteria allows us to take advantage of their many activities.

Ecological Contributions: Nutrient Cycling

When a tree falls to the forest floor, it eventually rots because decomposers, including bacteria, break down the remains of dead organisms to inorganic nutrients, which plants then take from the soil. Without the microorganisms of decay, the work of photosynthesizing food for all living things would not continue.

Further, inorganic nutrients such as nitrogen, sulfur, and phosphorus, along with other minerals, move through biogeochemical cycles that make them available to living things. Not only plants but also animals depend on these cycles in order to have food to eat and oxygen to breathe. Without the activity of decomposing microorganisms (microbes), the biosphere, including ourselves, would cease to exist (Fig. 10A*a*).

Economic Contributions

Many of us do not realize that we eat microbial products every day (Fig. 10A*b*). Bread, beer, and wine are the products of microbial action, mainly alcohol fermentation by yeasts. Sour milk products such as yogurt, butter, and cheese are created by fermentative bacteria that produce lactic and other acids. Pickled foods such as sauerkraut and olives are made by a similar process in which bacteria produce acids and other compounds that flavor food. Low-fat salad dressings and desserts contain gels and gums derived from algae, which are photosynthetic microorganisms.

Food additives such as vitamins and citric acid are taken from large bioreactor vats where bacterial fermentation products accumulate. Nearly all of the antibiotics and many of the drugs used today are the products of microbial activity.

Contributions to Our Health

The bacteria and other organisms that routinely live on or in organs are called the normal *microflora*. The large intestine is packed full of bacteria, termed coliforms because they live in the colon. These bacteria digest compounds that would otherwise be indigestible, and thereby they provide us with additional nutrients, vitamins, and fatty acids that the body cannot synthesize. The normal microflora—the "good" bacteria—help protect us from the "bad" bacteria. For example, the normal microflora of the vagina maintain a pH that discourages the proliferation of infectious organisms.

a.

b.

Figure 10A **Services of bacteria.**
a. Bacteria and fungi of decay contribute to biogeochemical cycles, which are necessary to the continuance of ecosystems and ourselves. **b.** The growth and activity of microorganisms are used to produce foods such as those pictured here.

Chlamydia

Chlamydia is named for the tiny bacterium that causes it, *Chlamydia trachomatis.* For years, chlamydiae were considered more closely related to viruses than to bacteria, but today it is known that these organisms are cellular. Even so, like a virus, chlamydia grows within body cells. After the bacterium enters a cell by endocytosis, its life cycle occurs inside the endocytic vacuole, which eventually bursts and liberates many new infective chlamydiae.

Chlamydia is the leading sexually transmitted disease in the United States. As many as 18% of American women have vaginal chlamydial infections, and most of those cases are asymptomatic. It is estimated that the infection rate could be as high as 50% on college and university campuses. For every reported case in men, more than five cases are detected in women. This is mainly due to increased detection of asymptomatic infections through screening. The low rates in men suggest that many of the sex partners of women with chlamydia are not diagnosed or reported.

Symptoms

Chlamydial infections of the lower reproductive tract usually are mild or asymptomatic, especially in women. About 8–21 days after infection, men may experience a mild burning sensation on urination and a mucoid discharge. Women may have a vaginal discharge along with the symptoms of a urinary tract infection. Unfortunately, a physician mistakenly may diagnose these symptoms as a gonorrheal or urinary infection and prescribe the wrong type of antibiotic, or the person may never seek medical help. In these instances, there is a particular risk of the infection spreading from the cervix to the uterine tubes so that **pelvic inflammatory disease (PID)** results. This very painful condition can lead to a blockage of the uterine tubes, with the possibility of sterility or ectopic pregnancy.

Some health authorities believe that chlamydial infections increase the possibility of premature and stillborn births. If a newborn comes in contact with *Chlamydia* during delivery, pneumonia or inflammation of the eyes can result (Fig. 10.2). Erythromycin eyedrops at birth prevent this occurrence. If a chlamydial infection is detected in a pregnant woman, erythromycin should be administered during pregnancy.

Diagnosis and Treatment

New and faster laboratory tests are now available for detecting a chlamydial infection. However, their expense sometimes prevents public clinics from using them. Criteria that could help physicians decide which women should be tested include: no more than 24 years old; having had a new sex partner within the preceding two months; experiencing a cervical discharge; bleeding during parts of the vaginal

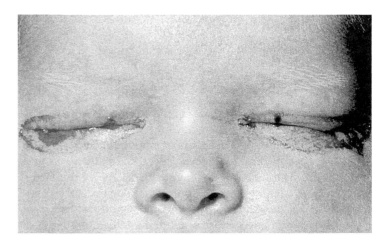

Figure 10.2   Chlamydia eye infection.
This newborn's eyes were infected after passing through the birth canal of a chlamydia-infected mother.

exam; and using a nonbarrier method of contraception. A chlamydial infection can be treated with a single dose of azithromycin, but the antibiotics tetracycline and erythromycin are less expensive alternatives.

Gonorrhea

Gonorrhea is caused by the bacterium *Neisseria gonorrhoeae,* which is a diplococcus, meaning that generally there are two spherical cells in close proximity. Reported gonorrhea rates declined steadily until the late 1990s, and then they increased by about 9% (Fig. 10.3). Rates of infection remain high among adolescents, young adults, and African Americans. Also, women using the birth control pill have a greater risk of contracting gonorrhea because hormonal contraceptives cause the genital tract to be more receptive to pathogens.

Persons with gonorrhea often have a secondary infection with chlamydia. Infection with either gonorrhea or chlamydia increases the risk of an infection with HIV.

Symptoms

The diagnosis of gonorrhea in men is not difficult as long as they display typical symptoms (as many as 20% of men may be asymptomatic). The patient complains of pain on urination and has a milky urethral discharge three to five days after contact with the pathogen. In women, the bacteria may first settle within the vagina or near the cervix, from which they may spread to the uterine tubes. Unfortunately, the majority of women are asymptomatic until they develop severe pain in the abdominal region due to PID (pelvic inflammatory disease). PID from gonorrhea is especially apt to occur in women using an IUD (intrauterine device) as a birth control measure.

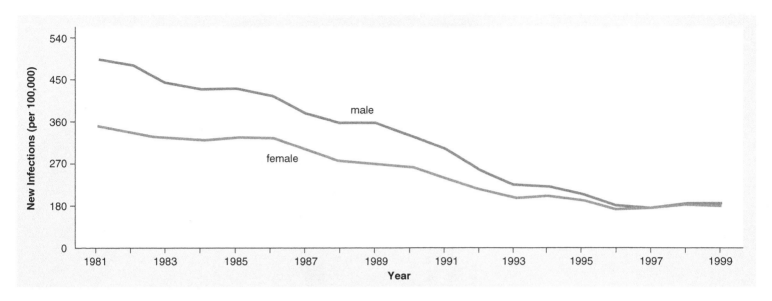

Figure 10.3   **Gonorrhea rates by gender, United States, 1981–1999.**
During the period from 1997 to 1999, epidemiologists reported an increase of 8.8% among men and 9% among women. Before then, gonorrhea was on the decline.

PID due to a chlamydial or gonorrheal infection affects many thousands of women each year in the United States. PID-induced scarring of the uterine tubes will cause infertility in about 20% of these women, ectopic pregnancy in 9%, and chronic pelvic pain in 18%.

Gonorrhea proctitis is an infection of the anus, with symptoms that include anal pain and blood or pus in the feces. Oral/genital contact can cause infection of the mouth, the throat, and the tonsils. Gonorrhea can spread to internal parts of the body, causing heart damage or arthritis. If, by chance, the person touches infected genitals and then his or her eyes, a severe eye infection can result (Fig. 10.4).

Eye infection leading to blindness can occur as a baby passes through the birth canal. Because of this, all newborns receive erythromycin eyedrops as a protective measure.

Transmission and Treatment

The chances of getting a gonorrheal infection from an infected partner are good. Women have a 50–60% risk, while men have a 20% risk of contracting the disease after even a single exposure to an infected partner. Therefore, the preventive measures described in the reading on page 167 should be followed.

Blood tests for gonorrhea are being developed, but in the meantime, it is necessary to diagnose the condition by microscopically examining the discharge of men or by growing a culture of the bacterium from either the male or the female to positively identify the organism. Because no blood test is available, it is very difficult to recognize asymptomatic carriers, who are capable of passing on the condition without realizing it. If the infection is diagnosed, gonorrhea can usually be cured using the antibiotics penicillin or tetracycline; however, resistance to antibiotic therapy is becoming more common.

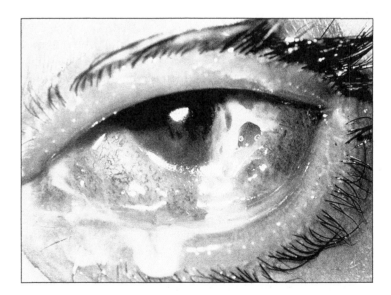

Figure 10.4   **Secondary sites for a gonorrheal infection.**
Gonorrheal infection of the eyes can happen when a newborn passes through the birth canal. Manual transfer from the genitals to the eyes is also possible.

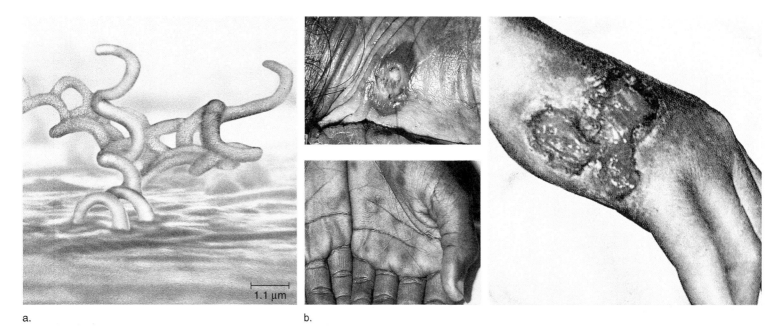

a.

b.

Figure 10.5 **Syphilis.**
a. Scanning electron micrograph of *Treponema pallidum*, the cause of syphilis. **b.** The three stages of syphilis. *Top:* The primary stage of syphilis is a chancre at the site where the bacterium enters the body. *Bottom:* The secondary stage is a body rash that occurs even on the palms of the hands and soles of the feet. *Far right:* In the tertiary stage, gummas may appear on the skin or internal organs.

Syphilis

Syphilis is caused by a bacterium called *Treponema pallidum,* an actively motile, corkscrew-like organism that is classified as a spirochete (Fig. 10.5a). The number of new cases of syphilis in 1998 was the fewest reported in the United States since 1945.

Syphilis has three stages, which can be separated by latent periods during which the bacteria are not multiplying (Fig. 10.5b). During the primary stage, a hard chancre (ulcerated sore with hard edges) indicates the site of infection. The chancre can go unnoticed, especially since it usually heals spontaneously, leaving little scarring. During the secondary stage, proof that bacteria have invaded and spread throughout the body is evident when the individual breaks out in a rash. Curiously, the rash does not itch and is seen even on the palms of the hands and the soles of the feet. Hair loss can occur, and infectious gray patches may appear on the mucous membranes, including the mouth. These symptoms disappear of their own accord.

Not all cases of secondary syphilis go on to the tertiary stage. Some spontaneously resolve the infection, and some do not progress beyond the secondary stage. During a tertiary stage, which lasts until the patient dies, syphilis may affect the cardiovascular system, and weakened arterial walls (aneurysms) are seen, particularly in the aorta. In other instances, the disease may affect the nervous system. The patient may become mentally impaired, blind, walk with a shuffle, or show signs of insanity. Gummas, large destructive ulcers, may develop on the skin or within the internal organs.

Congenital syphilis is caused by syphilitic bacteria crossing the placenta. The child is stillborn, or born blind, with many other possible anatomical malformations.

Diagnosis and Treatment

Syphilis can be diagnosed through blood tests or by microscopic examination of fluids from lesions. One blood test is based on the presence of reagin, an antibody that appears during the course of the disease. Currently, the most common test is Rapid Plasma Reagin (RPR), which is used for screening large numbers of test serums. Because the blood tests can give a false positive, they are followed by microscopic detection. Dark-field microscopic examination of fluids from lesions can detect the living organism. Alternately, test serum is added to a freeze-dried *T. pallidum* on a slide. Any antibodies present that react to *T. pallidum* are detected by fluorescent-labeled antibodies to human gamma globulin. The organism will then fluoresce when examined under a fluorescence microscope.

Syphilis is a devastating disease. Control of syphilis depends on prompt and adequate treatment of all new cases; therefore, it is crucial for all sexual contacts to be traced so that they can be treated. The cure for all stages of syphilis is some form of penicillin. To prevent transmission, the general instructions given in the reading on page 167 should be faithfully followed.

10.2 STDs of Viral Origin

Viruses cause numerous diseases in humans (Table 10.2), including AIDS, herpes, genital warts, and hepatitis B, four sexually transmitted diseases of great concern today.

Viruses are incapable of independent reproduction and reproduce only inside a living **host** cell. For this reason, viruses are called obligate intracellular parasites. To maintain viruses in the laboratory, they are injected into laboratory-bred animals, live chick embryos, or animal cells maintained in tissue culture. Viruses infect all sorts of cells—from bacterial cells to human cells—but they are very specific. For example, viruses called bacteriophages infect only bacteria, the tobacco mosaic virus infects only plants, and the rabies virus infects only mammals. Human viruses even specialize in a particular tissue. Human immunodeficiency virus (HIV) enters certain blood cells, the polio virus reproduces in spinal nerve cells, and the hepatitis viruses infect only liver cells.

Viruses are noncellular, and they have a unique construction. These tiny particles always have at least two parts: an outer capsid composed of protein subunits and an inner core of nucleic acid—either DNA or RNA (Fig. 10.6). The capsid of a virus that infects animals is often surrounded by an outer envelope, which is derived from the host-cell plasma membrane and contains viral spikes. The spikes within the envelope allow the virus to adhere to plasma membrane receptors. Then the entire virus enters the host cell. When the virus is uncoated, the envelope and capsid are removed. Once the viral genes are free inside the cell, viral components are synthesized and assembled into new

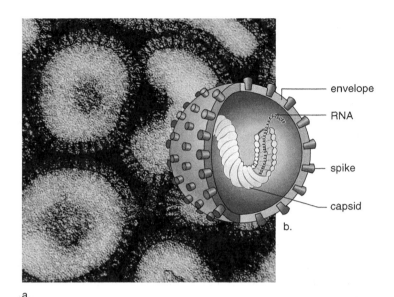

Figure 10.6   **Influenza virus.**
This RNA virus causes influenza in humans. **a.** Electron micrograph of an actual virus. **b.** Diagram of virus.

viruses. Release of the virus from the host cell occurs by *budding*. During budding, the virus gets its envelope, which consists of host plasma membrane components and spikes that were coded for by viral genes. The process of budding does not necessarily kill the host cell.

Some viruses that enter human cells—for example, the papillomaviruses, the herpesviruses, the hepatitis viruses, and the adenoviruses—can undergo a period of **latency.** While latent (in an inactive state), the viral genes are integrated into the host cell chromosome DNA, and they are copied whenever the host cell reproduces. Certain environmental factors, such as ultraviolet radiation, can induce the virus to reproduce and bud from the cell. Latent viruses are of special concern because their presence in the host cell chromosome can alter the cell and make it become cancerous.

Viral diseases are controlled by preventing transmission, by administering vaccines, and only recently by administering antiviral drugs, as discussed in the reading on page 165. Knowing how a particular pathogen is transmitted can help prevent its spread. Covering the mouth and nose when coughing or sneezing helps prevent the spread of a cold, and use of a latex condom during intercourse helps prevent the transmission of sexually transmitted diseases. Vaccines, which are antibodies administered to stimulate immunity to a pathogen so that it cannot later cause disease, are available for some viral diseases, such as polio, measles, mumps, and hepatitis B, a sexually transmitted disease (see Table 10.2). Antibiotics, which are designed to interfere with bacterial metabolism, have no effect on viral illnesses. Instead, drugs must be designed that interfere with either entry of the virus into the host cell, replication of its DNA when copies are made, or exit of the virus from the cell.

Table 10.2	Infectious Diseases Caused by Viruses
Site of Infection	**Diseases**
NOT SEXUALLY TRANSMITTED	
Respiratory tract	Common colds, flu,* viral pneumonia, hantavirus pulmonary syndrome
Skin	Measles,* German measles,* chickenpox*, shingles, warts
Nervous system	Encephalitis, polio,* rabies*
Liver	Yellow fever,* hepatitis A, C, and D
Cardiovascular	Ebola
Other systems	Mumps,* cancer
SEXUALLY TRANSMITTED	
Immune system	AIDS
Reproductive system	Genital warts, genital herpes
Liver	Hepatitis B*

*Vaccines are available. Yellow fever, rabies, and flu vaccines are given only if the situation requires them. Smallpox vaccinations are no longer required.

Herpes Infections

There are several types of herpesviruses, and only the ones called herpes simplex viruses (HSV) cause sexually transmitted diseases. The two types of herpes simplex viruses are HSV-1, which usually causes cold sores and fever blisters, and HSV-2, which more often causes **genital herpes.** Crossover infections do occur, however. That is, type 1 has been known to cause a genital infection, while type 2 has been known to cause cold sores and fever blisters.

It is estimated that 45 million persons are now infected with herpes and that one million more become infected each year, most of them teens and young adults.

Genital Herpes

Some people have no symptoms of a genital herpes infection. Others may experience a tingling or itching sensation before blisters appear on the genitals (within 2–20 days) (Fig. 10.7). Once the blisters rupture, they leave painful ulcers that may take as long as three weeks or as little as five days to heal. The blisters may be accompanied by fever, pain on urination, swollen lymph nodes in the groin, and in women, a copious vaginal discharge.

After the ulcers heal, the disease is only latent. Blisters can recur, although usually at less frequent intervals and with milder symptoms. Again, fever, stress, sunlight, and menstruation are associated with the recurrence of symptoms. When no symptoms are present, the virus primarily resides in the ganglia of sensory nerves associated with the affected skin. Although HSV-2 was formerly thought to cause cervical cancer, this is no longer believed to be the case.

Infection of the newborn can occur if the child comes in contact with a lesion in the birth canal. At worst, the infant can be gravely ill, become blind, have neurological disorders including brain damage, or die. Birth by cesarean section prevents these occurrences; therefore, all pregnant women infected with the virus should be sure to tell their healthcare provider.

Transmission

Outside a monogamous relationship, people are at risk for a herpes infection no matter how young they are. Live viruses have occasionally been cultured from the skin of infected persons with no lesions; therefore, the virus can be spread even when no lesions are visible. Persons who are infected should take extreme care to prevent the possibility of spreading the infection to other parts of their own body, such as the eyes. Certainly, sexual contact should be avoided until all lesions are completely healed, and then the general directions given on page 167 for avoiding STD transfer should be followed.

Treatment

Presently, there is no cure for genital herpes. The drugs acyclovir and vidarabine disrupt viral reproduction. The ointment form of acyclovir relieves initial symptoms, and the oral form, valaciclovir (Valtrex), is the drug of choice to prevent the recurrence of symptoms. Research is being conducted in an attempt to develop a vaccine.

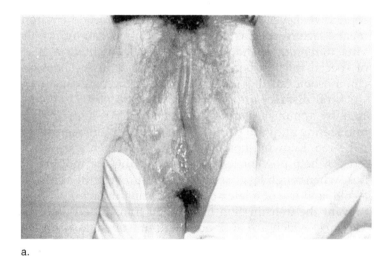

a.

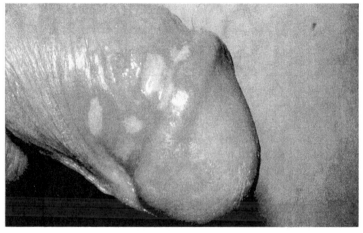

b.

Figure 10.7   Genital herpes.
Early symptoms of genital herpes include an outbreak of blisters, which can be present on the labia of females **(a)** or on the penis of males **(b)**.

Genital Warts

Human papillomaviruses (HPVs) cause warts, including common warts, plantar warts, and also genital warts, which are sexually transmitted. Over 5.5 million persons become infected each year with a form of HPV that causes **genital warts,** but only a portion seek medical help. An estimated 20 million people in the United States have an infection that can be transmitted to others. Figure 10.8 shows the incidence of genital warts, along with that of several other common STDs.

Transmission and Symptoms

Quite often, carriers of genital warts do not detect any sign of warts, although flat lesions may be present. When present, the warts commonly are seen on the penis and foreskin of men and near the vaginal opening in women. A newborn can become infected while passing through the birth canal.

Genital warts are associated with cancer of the cervix, as well as tumors of the vulva, the vagina, the anus, the penis, and the mouth. Some researchers believe that HPVs are involved in 90–95% of all cases of cancer of the cervix. Teenagers with multiple sex partners seem particularly susceptible to HPV infections. More cases of cancer of the cervix are being seen among this age group.

Treatment

Presently, there is no cure for an HPV infection, but it can be treated effectively by surgery, freezing, application of an acid, or laser burning, depending on severity. Also, even after treatment, the virus can be transmitted. Therefore, abstinence or use of a condom with a vaginal spermicide containing nonoxynol-9 is necessary to prevent the spread of genital warts. Scientists have developed a vaccine against the most common HPV and are working on developing others. Children, especially girls, should be vaccinated before they become sexually active.

Hepatitis

There are several types of **hepatitis.** Hepatitis A, caused by HAV (hepatitis A virus), is usually acquired from sewage-contaminated drinking water. Hepatitis A can also be sexually transmitted through oral/anal contact.

Hepatitis C, caused by HCV, is called the posttransfusion form of hepatitis. This type of hepatitis, which is usually acquired by contact with infected blood, is also of great concern. Infection can lead to chronic hepatitis, liver cancer, and death.

Hepatitis E, caused by HEV, is usually seen in developing countries. Only imported cases—that is, those occurring in travelers to the country or in visitors to endemic regions—have been reported in the United States.

Hepatitis B

Hepatitis B virus (HBV) is a DNA virus that is spread in the same way as HIV, the cause of AIDS—through needle-sharing by drug abusers and through sexual contact between heterosexuals or between homosexual men. Therefore, it is common for an AIDS patient to also have an HBV infection. Also, like HIV, HBV can be passed from mother to child by way of the placenta.

Only about 50% of infected persons have flu-like symptoms, including fatigue, fever, headache, nausea, vomiting, muscle aches, and a dull pain in the upper right of the abdomen. Jaundice, a yellowish cast to the skin, can also be present. Some persons have an acute infection that lasts only three to four weeks. Others have a chronic form of the disease that leads to liver failure and the need for a liver transplant.

Since no treatment is available for an HBV infection, prevention is imperative. The general directions given on page 167 should be followed, but inoculation with the HBV vaccine is the best protection. The vaccine, which is safe and does not cause any major side effects, is now on the list of recommended immunizations for children.

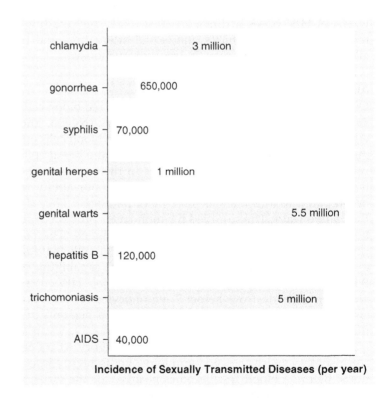

Incidence of Sexually Transmitted Diseases (per year)

Figure 10.8 Incidence of new cases of common STDs.
In the United States, more than 65 million people are living with an incurable STD. An additional 15 million people become infected with one or more STDs each year. Approximately one-fourth of these new infections occur in teenagers. Despite the fact that STDs are quite widespread, many people remain unaware of the risks and the sometimes deadly consequences of becoming infected.

HIV Infections

AIDS (acquired immunodeficiency syndrome) is caused by the human immunodeficiency virus (HIV), which infects specific blood cells. In addition to this brief discussion, more information may be found in the AIDS Supplement (see pages 171–79).

Prevalence of an HIV Infection and AIDS

Estimates vary, but as many as 64 million people worldwide may have become infected with HIV, and of these, 22 million have died of AIDS. A new HIV infection is believed to occur every 15 seconds, the majority in heterosexuals. HIV infections are not distributed equally throughout the world. Most of the infected people live in Africa (66%), where it is believed that HIV infections first began, but new infections are now occurring at the fastest rate in Southeast Asia and the Indian subcontinent.

In the United States, HIV infections have been concentrated in large cities but are now spreading to small towns and rural areas. New infections are more prevalent among particular groups; African Americans and Hispanics have a higher proportionate number of cases than do Caucasians. Even so, HIV poses a threat to all sexually active adults, regardless of their ethnicity and sexual orientation, and to all who inject themselves with drugs intravenously.

Symptoms of an HIV Infection

Our blood contains mainly two types of cells: red blood cells and white blood cells. Red blood cells carry oxygen, and white blood cells fight infections. Some white blood cells engulf pathogens, while others, such as the white blood cells called **lymphocytes,** are more specific in their actions. The lymphocytes are responsible for immunity—our ability to be prepared to attack a specific type of pathogen. They do this in two ways: The so-called B lymphocytes produce antibodies, which attach to and destroy pathogens. The so-called T lymphocytes can either be cytotoxic T cells that kill a cell directly, or helper T cells that boost the capabilities of B lymphocytes or cytotoxic T cells to do their job. HIV enters and eventually destroys helper T lymphocytes (T_h lymphocytes). In this way, HIV eventually destroys a person's immune system.

During an initial acute phase (called category A), a person usually experiences no symptoms, yet is highly infectious. Before a blood test becomes positive for the virus, a large number of viruses are present that could be passed on to another person. After the blood test becomes positive, the person remains well as long as the body stays ahead of the hordes of viruses entering the blood. Millions of T_h lymphocytes are most likely produced each day, and their count remains higher than 500 per mm^3.

Several months to several years after infection, the T_h-lymphocyte count falls below 500 per mm^3 in untreated persons, and the symptoms of a chronic infection (called category B) begin to appear. Lymph nodes are swollen, severe fatigue is common, and diarrhea and fever with night sweats are present. Indications that the virus has entered the brain may include loss of memory, inability to think clearly, loss of judgment, and/or depression.

If the individual develops non-life-threatening but recurrent infections, it most likely means that full-blown AIDS will occur shortly. One possible infection is thrush, identified by the presence of white spots and ulcers on the tongue and inside the mouth. The *Candida* infection may also spread to the vagina, resulting in a chronic infection there. Another frequent infection is oral and genital herpes, discussed on page 162.

AIDS is the final stage (called category C) of an HIV infection. In 1993, the definition of AIDS was broadened to include those persons with a severe depletion of T_h lymphocytes (less than 200 per mm^3 of blood) and/or those who have an opportunistic infection. An **opportunistic infection** is one that has the opportunity to occur because the immune system is severely weakened. Persons with AIDs die from one or more opportunistic disease—such as *P. carinii* pneumonia and Kaposi's sarcoma, a form of cancer—rather than from the HIV infection itself.

Treatment for an HIV Infection

There is no cure for AIDS, but a treatment called highly active antiretroviral therapy (HAART) is usually able to stop HIV reproduction to the extent that the virus becomes undetectable in the blood. Therapy usually consists of two drugs that inhibit reverse transcriptase and one that inhibits protease, an enzyme needed for viral assembly. This multidrug therapy, when taken as prescribed, usually seems to prevent mutation of the virus to a resistant strain. Unfortunately, mutation of the virus to an HIV strain resistant to all known drugs has been reported, and persons who become infected with this strain have no drug therapy available to them.

The sooner drug therapy begins after infection, the better are the chances that the immune system will not be destroyed by HIV. The medication must be continued indefinitely. Investigators have found that when HAART is discontinued, the virus rebounds.

Many investigators are working on an AIDS vaccine. Some are trying to develop a vaccine in the traditional way. Traditionally, vaccines are made by weakening or killing a pathogen so that it can be injected into the body without causing disease. Others are working on subunit vaccines that utilize just a single HIV protein as the vaccine. They have found that DNA for this protein can also act as a vaccine because it enters and causes cells to produce and display the protein at the plasma membrane. The immune system attacks cells that display proteins not recognized as belonging to the individual. The various vaccines are at different stages in their development. Thus far, certain vaccines have increased the immune response in the blood, but none of the vaccines has prevented future infection.

Transmission of HIV

The largest proportion of people with AIDS in the United States are homosexual men, but the proportions attributed to intravenous drug users and heterosexuals are rising. Women now account for 20% of all newly diagnosed cases of AIDS. An infected woman can pass HIV to her unborn children by way of the placenta or to a newborn through breast milk. Transmission at birth can be prevented if the mother takes AZT, and delivers by planned cesarean section.

It is clear that sexual behaviors and drug-related activities are the major means by which AIDS is transmitted in the United States. Essentially, HIV is spread by passing virus-infected T_h lymphocytes found in body fluids, such as semen or blood, from one person to another. (Blood and blood products are now tested for the presence of HIV, so the risk of contracting an infection through a blood transfusion is now considered very unlikely.) In order to prevent transmission of HIV, you should follow the general advice given on page 167.

Of Special Interest

STDs and Medical Treatment

Treatment of STDs is troublesome at best. Presently, no vaccines are available except for a hepatitis B infection, and to date, not many persons have been inoculated for HBV. Unfortunately, there is no treatment once a hepatitis B infection has occurred. The antiviral drugs acyclovir and vidarabine are helpful against genital herpes, but they do not cure herpes. Once an individual stops the therapy, the lesions are apt to recur. The current recommended therapy for AIDS includes an expensive combination of drugs that prevent HIV reproduction and curtail its ability to infect other cells.

Antibiotics are used to treat sexually transmitted diseases caused by bacteria. Antibiotics such as penicillin, streptomycin, and tetracycline interfere with metabolic pathways unique to bacteria, and therefore, they are not expected to harm host cells. Still, there are problems associated with antibiotic therapy: Some individuals are allergic to antibiotics, and the reaction may even be fatal. Antibiotics not only kill off disease-causing bacteria, but they also reduce the number of beneficial bacteria in the intestinal tract. The use of antibiotics sometimes prevents natural immunity from occurring, leading to the necessity for recurring antibiotic therapy.

Most important, perhaps, is the growing resistance of certain strains of bacteria to a particular antibiotic. Antibiotics were introduced in the 1940s, and for several decades they worked so well that infectious diseases appeared to have been brought under control. However, we now know that bacterial strains can mutate and become resistant to a particular antibiotic. Worse yet, bacteria can swap bits of DNA, and in this way, resistance can pass to other strains of bacteria. Penicillin and tetracycline, long used to cure gonorrhea, now have a failure rate of more than 20% against certain strains of gonococcus. To help prevent resistant bacteria, antibiotics should be administered only when absolutely necessary, and the prescribed therapy should be finished. Also, as a society, we have to continue to develop new antibiotics to which resistance has not yet occurred.

An alarming new concern has been the upsurge of tuberculosis in persons with weak immune systems, such as AIDS patients. Tuberculosis is a chronic lung infection caused by the bacterium *Mycobacterium tuberculosis*. This bacterium is often called the tubercle bacillus (TB) because usually the bacilli are walled off within tubercles that can sometimes be seen in X rays of the lungs. TB can pass from an HIV-infected person to a healthy person more easily than HIV. Sexual contact is not needed—only close personal contact—and thus it is possible that TB will now spread from those with STDs to the general populace. Some of the modern strains of TB are resistant to antibiotic therapy; therefore, just as with HIV, research is needed for the development of an effective vaccine.

Prevention is still the best way to manage STDs. Several STDs are primarily transmitted by infected white blood cells that penetrate the single layer of cells lining the inside of the uterine cervix and uterus. The use of a condom, along with a spermicide that contains nonoxynol-9, and the avoidance of oral/genital contact are essential unless you have a monogamous relationship (always the same partner) with someone who is free of STDs and is not an intravenous drug user.

10.3 Other Infections

Vaginal infections are caused by several different types of organisms. Pubic lice, a type of animal, can also infect the genital area as an ectoparasite (external parasite).

Vaginal Infections

Among the microflora of the vagina, lactobacilli help maintain a healthy environment. An increase in the growth of *Gardnerella vaginalis* with a decrease in lactobacilli results in the development of **bacterial vaginosis (BV).** Bacterial vaginosis is believed to account for 50% of vaginitis cases in American women. The overgrowth of the bacterium and consequent symptoms can also be due to nonsexual reasons, but males who are symptomless may pass on the bacteria to women, who then exhibit symptoms.

A woman with bacterial vaginosis usually has a thin, gray discharge that resembles flour paste and has a foul smell. The smell is particularly noticeable after sexual intercourse because the alkaline semen causes the bacteria to release the chemicals that cause the smell. Untreated BV may increase the risk of PID and an HIV infection. Both intravaginal creams and oral medications are available.

Trichomoniasis is a sexually transmitted disease caused by the protozoan *Trichomonas vaginalis* (Fig. 10.9*a*). An estimated five million new cases of trichomoniasis occur each year in the United States and account for about one-fourth of all cases of vaginitis. Trichomoniasis is characterized by an abundant, frothy, white or yellow foul-smelling vaginal discharge accompanied by itching that can be severe. Trichomoniasis is most often acquired through sexual intercourse, and an asymptomatic partner is usually the reservoir of infection. To avoid passing the condition back and forth, both partners should be treated simultaneously. If this is done, a cure rate of approximately 95% is expected.

If untreated, *Trichomonas* invades the urinary tract, and some health authorities believe *Trichomonas* can affect the cells of the cervix, eventually causing cervical cancer. Both BV and trichomoniasis in a pregnant woman can result in premature birth and/or an infant with low birth weight.

Candida albicans (Fig. 10.9*b*) is commonly found in the vagina, but the growth of this yeast is usually due to taking an antibiotic or the birth control pill. An estimated 13 million cases of **candidal vaginitis** occur annually. A woman usually notices a white, clumpy discharge that looks something like cottage cheese. Associated symptoms include intense itching and soreness of the vaginal and vulval tissues, which typically become red and dry. Over-the-counter intravaginal preparations are available, but self-treatment may not be wise because a mistake in diagnosis can have serious consequences. Treatment should continue well beyond the two days it takes for symptoms to disappear.

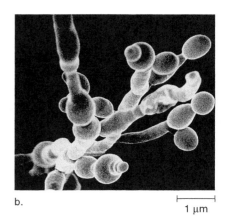

a. |⎯⎯⎯| 8 μm   b. |⎯⎯⎯| 1 μm

Figure 10.9 **Organisms that cause vaginitis.**
a. *Trichomonas vaginalis*, a protozoan. **b.** *Candida albicans*, a yeast.

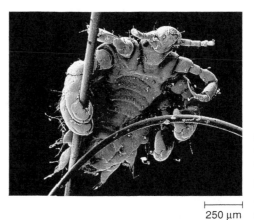

|⎯⎯⎯| 250 μm

Figure 10.10
Sexually transmitted animal.
This parasitic crab louse, *Phthirus pubis*, infests the pubic hair of humans.

Pubic Lice (Crabs)

The parasitic crab louse *Phthirus pubis* (an insect) takes its name from its resemblance to a small crab (Fig. 10.10). The louse can infest the pubic hair of humans, causing an STD commonly known as pubic lice, or crabs. The condition can be contracted by direct contact with an infested person or by contact with his or her clothing or bedding. Female lice lay their eggs around the base of the hair, and these eggs hatch within a few days to produce a larger number of animals that suck blood from their host and cause severe itching, particularly at night.

In contrast to most types of sexually transmitted diseases, self-diagnosis and self-treatment that does not require shaving are possible. Usually, an infested person finds and identifies adult lice or their numerous eggs on or near the pubic hairs. Medications such as lindane are applied to the infested area; all sexual partners need to be treated also. Undergarments, sheets, and night clothing should be washed by machine in hot water.

Of Special Interest

Preventing Transmission of STDs

It is wise to protect yourself from getting a sexually transmitted disease (STD). Some of the STDs, such as gonorrhea, syphilis, and chlamydia, can be cured by taking an antibiotic, but medication for the ones transmitted by viruses is much more problematic. In any case, it is best to prevent the passage of STDs from person to person so that treatment becomes unnecessary.

Sexual Activities Transmit STDs

Abstain from sexual intercourse or develop a long-term, monogamous (always the same partner) *sexual relationship* with a partner who is free of STDs.

Refrain from multiple sex partners or having relations with someone who has multiple sex partners. If you have sex with two other people and each of these has sex with two people and so forth, the number of people who are relating is quite large.

Remember that, although the prevalence of AIDS is presently higher among homosexuals and bisexuals, the highest rate of increase is now occurring among heterosexuals. The lining of the uterus is only one cell thick, and it does allow infected cells from a sexual partner to enter.

Be aware that having relations with an intravenous drug user is risky because the behavior of this group risks hepatitis and an HIV infection. Be aware that anyone who already has another sexually transmitted disease is more susceptible to an HIV infection.

Uncircumcised males are more likely to become infected with an STD than circumcised males because vaginal secretions can remain under the foreskin for a long period of time.

Avoid anal-rectal intercourse (in which the penis is inserted into the rectum) because the lining of the rectum is thin, and cells infected with HIV can easily enter the body there.

Unsafe Sexual Practices Transmit STDs

Always use a latex condom during sexual intercourse if you do not know for certain that your partner has been free of STDs for some time. Be sure to follow the directions supplied by the manufacturer. Use of a water-based spermicide containing nonoxynol-9 in addition to the condom can offer further protection because nonoxynol-9 immobilizes viruses and virus-infected cells.

Avoid fellatio (kissing and insertion of the penis into a partner's mouth) *and cunnilingus* (kissing and insertion of the tongue into the vagina) because they may be a means of transmission. The mouth and gums often have cuts and sores that facilitate the entrance of infected cells.

Be cautious about using alcohol or any drug that may prevent you from being able to control your behavior.

Drug Use Transmits Hepatitis and HIV

Stop, if necessary, or do not start the habit of injecting drugs into your veins. Be aware that hepatitis and HIV can be spread by blood-to-blood contact.

Always use a new sterile needle for injection or one that has been cleaned in bleach if you are a drug user and cannot stop your behavior.

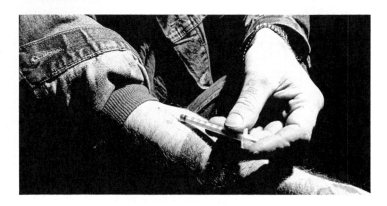

Figure 10B   **Sharing needles transmits STDs.**

Bioethical Focus

Identifying Carriers

Carriers of disease are persons who do not appear ill but can pass on an infectious disease. Carriers of sexually transmitted diseases can pass on an infection to their partners, and even sometimes to people who have never had sexual relations with them. Hepatitis C and HIV are transmitted by blood-to-blood contact, as when drug abusers share needles.

The only way society can protect itself is to identify carriers and remove them from areas or activities where transmission of the pathogen is most likely. Sometimes it's difficult to identify activities that might pass on a pathogen such as HIV. A few people believe that they have acquired HIV from their dentists, and while this is generally believed to be unlikely, medical personnel are still required to identify themselves when they are carriers of HIV. Magic Johnson, a famous basketball star, is HIV positive. When he made it known that he was a carrier, some of his teammates refused to play basketball with him, and he had no choice but to retire. Later, Johnson did play again. There are other sports in which transmission of HIV is more likely. For example, the Centers for Disease Control and Prevention did a statistical study to try to figure the odds of acquiring HIV from another football player. They figured that the odds were 1 in 85 million.

The odds might be higher for boxing, a bloody sport. When two brothers, one of whom had AIDS, got into a vicious fight, the infected brother repeatedly bashed his head against his brother's. Both men bled profusely, and soon after, the previously uninfected brother tested positive for the virus. The possibility of transmission of HIV in the boxing ring has caused several states to require boxers to undergo routine HIV testing. If they are HIV positive, they can't fight.

Figure 10C Whenever blood is shed, HIV can be transmitted.

Decide Your Opinion

1. Should all people who are HIV positive identify themselves? Why or why not? By what method would they identify themselves at school, at work, and other places?
2. What type of contact would you have with an HIV-positive individual? Would you play on the same team? Would you have sexual relations with an HIV-positive individual if a condom were used? Discuss.
3. Is it ethical to make an HIV-positive individual feel stigmatized? Discuss.

Summary

10.1 STDs of Bacterial Origin

Bacteria cause many infectious diseases in humans, from strep throat to syphilis. Chlamydia is caused by a tiny bacterium of the same name. These bacteria develop inside phagocytic vacuoles that eventually burst and liberate infective chlamydiae. Chlamydia can be asymptomatic, or it can produce symptoms of a urinary tract infection. Both chlamydia and gonorrhea can result in PID, leading to sterility or ectopic pregnancy. Gonorrhea is caused by the bacterium *Neisseria gonorrhoeae*, a diplococcus. Gonorrhea may not cause symptoms, particularly in women, but men may experience painful urination and a thick, milky discharge. Syphilis is caused by *Treponema pallidum*, an actively motile, corkscrew-like bacterium. Syphilis is a systemic disease that should be cured in its early stages before possible deterioration of the nervous system and cardiovascular system takes place.

Abstinence, a monogamous relationship, or the use of a condom with a vaginal spermicide that contains nonoxynol-9 can help prevent the transmission of viral and bacterial STDs.

10.2 STDs of Viral Origin

Viruses are the cause of many infectious diseases in humans, from common colds to cancer. Genital warts are caused by human papillomavirus (HPV), which is a cuboidal DNA virus that reproduces in the nuclei of skin cells. Genital warts is a disease characterized by warts on the penis and foreskin in men and near the vaginal opening in women. Genital herpes is caused by herpes simplex virus: Type 1 usually causes cold sores and fever blisters, while type 2 often causes genital herpes, a disease characterized by painful blisters on the genitals. Hepatitis B, which is spread in the same manner as AIDS, can lead to liver failure.

Medications have been developed to control AIDS and genital herpes, but there is no cure for these conditions, and no vaccines are available. Of all the viral STDs, only a vaccine for hepatitis B exists at the present time.

10.3 Other Infections

Significant types of vaginal infections are bacterial vaginosis, caused by a bacterium; trichomoniasis, caused by a protozoan; and candidiasis, caused by a yeast. Pubic lice is a sexually transmitted disease caused by an animal.

Reviewing the Chapter

1. Describe the symptoms and results of a chlamydial infection and gonorrhea in men and in women. What is PID, and how does it affect reproduction? 158–59
2. Describe the three stages of syphilis. 160
3. Give the cause and symptoms of genital herpes, genital warts, and a hepatitis B infection. 162–63
4. How does the newborn acquire an infection of chlamydia, gonorrhea, syphilis, herpes, or genital warts? What effects do these infections have on infants? 158–60, 163
5. How prevalent are HIV and AIDS today? 164
6. List and describe the phases of an HIV infection. 164
7. What treatment is available for an HIV infection? 164
8. What types of vaccines are being prepared to prevent an HIV infection? 165
9. Describe the symptoms of the three types of vaginitis and of pubic lice. 166

Critical Thinking Questions

1. Why wouldn't penicillin, an antibiotic that cures syphilis, be effective against AIDS? And why wouldn't a physician prescribe AZT, an AIDS treatment, for syphilis?
2. Relate the symptoms of AIDS, genital herpes, genital warts, gonorrhea, chlamydia, and syphilis to the activities of the causative agent.
3. Both HIV and *Treponema pallidum* lead to illness throughout the body. Discuss similarities and differences between the two infections.

Understanding Key Terms

AIDS (acquired immunodeficiency syndrome) 164
antibiotic 156
bacteria 156
bacterial vaginosis (BV) 166
candidal vaginitis 166
chlamydia 158
genital herpes 162
genital warts 163
gonorrhea 158
hepatitis 163
host 161
latency 161
lymphocyte 164
opportunistic infection 164
pathogen 156
pelvic inflammatory disease (PID) 158
syphilis 160
trichomoniasis 166
virus 161

AIDS Supplement

HIV (green) budding from an infected helper T lymphocyte.

White blood cells, including lymphocytes[1], help the body fight infections. The photo shows HIV budding from a helper T lymphocyte (T_h lymphocyte), the primary host for these viruses. No wonder the immune system falters in a person with AIDS. T_h lymphocytes are the very cells that orchestrate the immune response so that we can recover from a viral infection.

Will there one day be a vaccine to prevent an HIV infection? B lymphocytes would then prepare a supply of antibodies to disarm HIV before the viruses have a chance to enter T_h lymphocytes. It would be a feat. There might be something about the virus—mode of transmission or the course of the disease—that will make any type of vaccine ineffective.

The burden, it seems, is on the individual. Young and old must come to realize the importance of their T_h lymphocytes and take measures to protect them from possible destruction by HIV. The recommendations in Chapter 10, page 167, should be faithfully followed by all.

---

[1]See page 164 for a discussion of white blood cells, including lymphocytes.

S.1 Origin and Scope of AIDS

It is generally accepted that **human immunodeficiency virus (HIV)** originated in Africa and then spread to the United States and Europe by way of the Caribbean. HIV has been found in a preserved 1959 blood sample taken from a man who lived in an African country now called the Democratic Republic of the Congo. Even before this discovery, scientists speculated that an immunodeficiency virus may have evolved into HIV during the late 1950s.

Of the two types of HIV, HIV-2 corresponds to a type of immunodeficiency virus found in the green monkey, which lives in western Africa. Recently, researchers announced that they had found a virus identical to HIV-1 in a subgroup of chimpanzees once common in west-central Africa. Perhaps HIV viruses were originally found only in nonhuman primates. They could have mutated to HIV after humans ate nonhuman primates for meat.

British scientists have been able to show that **AIDS (acquired immunodeficiency syndrome)** came to their country perhaps as early as 1959. They examined the preserved tissues of a Manchester seaman who died that year and concluded that he most likely died of AIDS. Similarly, it is thought that HIV entered the United States on numerous occasions as early as the 1950s. But the first documented case is a 15-year-old male who died in Missouri in 1969 with skin lesions now known to be characteristic of an AIDS-related cancer. Doctors froze some of his tissues because they could not identify the cause of death. Researchers also want to test the preserved tissue samples of a 49-year-old Haitian who died in New York in 1959 of the type of pneumonia now known to be AIDS-related.

Throughout the 1960s, it was customary in the United States to list leukemia as the cause of death in immunodeficient patients. Most likely, some of these people actually died of AIDS. Since HIV is not extremely infectious, it took several decades for the number of AIDS cases to increase to the point that AIDS became recognizable as a specific and separate disease. The name AIDS was coined in 1982, and HIV was found to be the cause of AIDS in 1983–84.

Prevalence of AIDS

AIDS is pandemic, meaning that the disease is prevalent in the entire human population around the globe (Fig. S.1). Today, 38.6 million adults and 3.2 million children are estimated to be living with an HIV infection, and 22 million persons have died of AIDS worldwide. HIV is transmitted by sexual contact with an infected person, including vaginal or rectal intercourse and oral/genital contact. Also, needle-sharing among intravenous drug users is high-risk behavior. A less common mode of transmission (and one now rare in countries where blood is screened for HIV) is through transfusions of infected blood or blood-clotting factors. Babies born to HIV-infected women may become infected before or during birth, or through breast-feeding after birth. Table S.1 summarizes the most frequent ways by which HIV is transmitted.

The incidence of HIV infection in the more-developed countries of North America and western Europe and elsewhere is modest. The incidence ranges from 0.02% in Japan to 0.6% in the United States and 0.7% in Portugal. Further, the introduction of combination drug therapy has resulted in a drastic decrease in overall AIDS deaths since 1995. In the United States, HIV first spread through the homosexual community, and male-to-male sexual contact still accounts for the largest percentage of new AIDS cases. But the rate of new HIV infections is now rising faster among heterosexuals than homosexuals. Even now, 23% of all people with AIDS in the United States are women, and they account for 32% of all newly diagnosed cases of HIV infection. In 1986, the majority of AIDS cases occurred among Caucasians; today, this proportion has shifted to minorities. There is one more statistic to call to your attention: Most new HIV infections are occurring among teenagers and young adults; even with drug therapy, these young people will probably not escape eventually coming down with AIDS.

Table S.1	Transmission of HIV

Possible Routes

Homosexual and heterosexual contact

Intravenous drug use

Transfusion (unlikely in U.S.)

Crossing placenta during pregnancy; breast-feeding

Risk Factors

Promiscuous behavior (large number of partners, sex with a prostitute)

Drug abuse with needle-sharing

Presence of another sexually transmitted disease

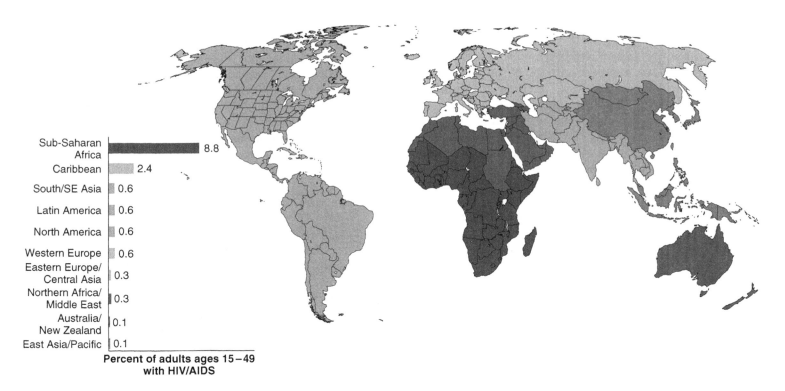

Figure S.1   **HIV prevalence rates in adults at the end of 2000.**
HIV/AIDS occurs in all continents and countries of the globe, and presently 38.6 million adults and 3.2 million children younger than 15 are infected worldwide.

In the largest countries of Latin America and the Caribbean, which have incidences of 2.0% and 0.6% respectively, the AIDS epidemic has charted a course similar to that in North America. HIV/AIDS was first seen among homosexuals and intravenous drug users. Now it is increasingly being spread by heterosexual contact.

Haiti, with an overall HIV prevalence in adults of about 5%, is the worst-affected country outside of Africa. In sub-Saharan Africa, 24.5 million people are infected with HIV. This is almost 9% of the total adult population between 15 and 49 years of age. The increasing number of deaths among young adults means that these countries will have more people in their 60s and 70s than in their 40s and 50s. Many are concerned about how families in Africa will cope when the old have to care for their grandchildren and when these grandchildren have to assume adult responsibilities much sooner than otherwise.

Some countries in Africa are affected more than others. HIV prevalence in South Africa grew from 1% of the adult population in 1990 to about 20% today. Similarly, Botswana was essentially free of the disease in 1990; now, 45–50% of young adults aged 20–30 years are infected with HIV. A certain subtype of HIV-1, namely HIV-1C, has brought about

this great devastation. HIV-1C has a greater ease of transmission, and also multiplies and mutates faster than all the other subtypes. Most likely, HIV-1C has already spread from Africa to western India, and a hybrid virus containing some HIV-1C genetic material has reached mainland China. It's quite possible that in five to twenty years the more developed countries, including the United States, will experience a new epidemic of AIDS caused by HIV-1C. Therefore, it behooves the more developed countries to do all they can to help African countries aggressively seek a solution to this new HIV epidemic.

AIDS in the United States is presently caused by HIV-1B, and drug therapy has brought the condition under control. But the drug therapy has two dangers. First, people may become lax in their efforts to avoid infection because they know that drug therapy is available. Second, the use of drugs leads to drug-resistant viruses. Even now, some HIV-1B viruses have become drug resistant when patients have failed to adhere to their drug regimens. We cannot escape the conclusion that all persons should do everything they can to avoid becoming infected. Behaviors that help prevent transmission are discussed in the reading on page 167.

S.2 Phases of an HIV Infection

The HIV viruses primarily infect T_h lymphocytes. These cells display a molecule on their surface that enables HIV to bind to them. As discussed on page 164, T_h cells ordinarily stimulate B lymphocytes to produce antibodies and cytotoxic T cells to destroy cells that are infected with a virus.

The Centers for Disease Control and Prevention now recognize three phases of an HIV-1B infection. During the acute phase (category A), no symptoms are apparent, yet the person is highly infectious. During the chronic phase (category B), the individual loses weight, suffers from diarrhea, and most likely develops infections such as thrush or genital herpes. The final phase of an HIV infection is AIDS (category C), when the person comes down with pneumonia, cancer, and other serious conditions.

Category A: Acute Phase

A normal T_h-lymphocyte count is at least 800 cells per cubic millimeter of blood. This first phase of an HIV infection is characterized by a T_h-lymphocyte count of 500 per mm^3 or greater (*blue line*, Fig. S.2). This count is sufficient for the immune system to function normally to protect us from disease.

Today, investigators are able to track not only the blood level of T_h lymphocytes, but also the viral load. The viral load is the number of HIV particles in the blood (*red line*, Fig. S.2).

At the start of an HIV-1B infection, the virus is replicating ferociously, and the killing of T_h lymphocytes is evident because the blood level of these cells drops dramatically. For a few weeks, however, people don't usually have any symptoms at all. Then, a few (1–2%) do have mononucleosis-like symptoms that may include fever, chills, aches, swollen lymph nodes, and an itchy rash. These symptoms disappear, and no other symptoms appear for quite some time. The HIV blood test commonly used at clinics is not yet positive because it tests for the presence of antibodies, not for the presence of HIV itself. This means that the person is highly infectious, even though the HIV blood test is negative.

After a period of time, the body responds to the infection by increased activity of immune cells, and the HIV blood test becomes positive. During this phase, the number of T_h lymphocytes is greater than the viral load (see Fig. S.2). But some investigators believe that a great unseen battle is going on. The body is staying ahead of the hordes of viruses entering the blood by producing as many as one to two billion new T_h lymphocytes each day. This is called the "kitchen sink model". The sink's faucet (production of new T_h lymphocytes) and the sink's drain (destruction of T_h lymphocytes) are wide open. As long as the body can produce enough new T_h lymphocytes to keep pace with the destruction of these cells by HIV and by cytotoxic T cells, the person has a healthy immune system that can deal with the infection.

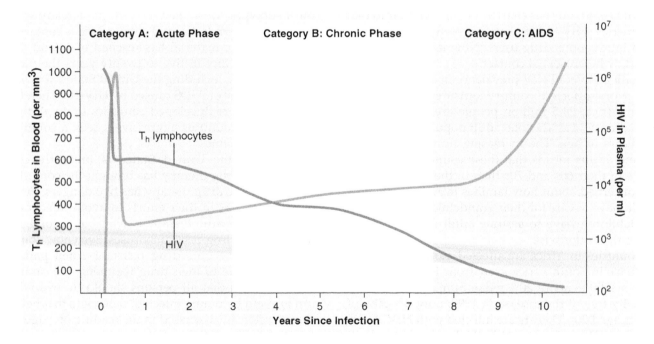

Figure S.2 **Phases of an HIV infection.**
In category A individuals, the number of HIV in plasma (*red line*) rises upon infection and then falls. The number of T_h lymphocytes (*blue line*) falls, but stays above 400 per mm^3. In category B individuals, the number of HIV in plasma is slowly rising, and the number of T_h lymphocytes is decreasing. In category C individuals, the number of HIV in plasma rises dramatically as the number of T_h lymphocytes falls below 200 per mm^3.

Category B: Chronic Phase

Several months to several years after infection, an untreated individual will probably progress to category B. During this stage, the T_h-lymphocyte count is 200 to 499 per mm^3 of blood, and the number of HIV is on the rise (see Fig. S.2). Most likely, symptoms will begin to appear, including swollen lymph nodes in the neck, armpits, or groin that persist for three months or more; severe fatigue not related to exercise or drug use; unexplained persistent or recurrent fevers, often with night sweats; persistent cough not associated with smoking, a cold, or the flu; and persistent diarrhea. Also possible are signs of nervous system impairment, including loss of memory, inability to think clearly, loss of judgment, and/or depression.

The development of non-life-threatening but recurrent infections is a signal that full-blown AIDS will occur shortly. One possible infection is thrush, a *Candida albicans* infection that is identified by the presence of white spots and ulcers on the tongue and inside the mouth. The fungus may also spread to the vagina, resulting in a chronic infection there. Another frequent infection is herpes simplex, with painful and persistent sores on the skin surrounding the anus, the genital area, and/or the mouth.

Category C: AIDS

When a person has AIDS, the T_h-lymphocyte count has fallen below 200 per mm^3, and the lymph nodes have degenerated. The patient is extremely thin and weak due to persistent di-arrhea and coughing, and will most likely develop an opportunistic infection. An **opportunistic infection** is one that has the *opportunity* to occur only because the immune system is severely weakened. Persons with AIDS die from one or more of the following diseases rather than from the HIV infection itself:

- *Pneumocystis carinii* pneumonia. The lungs become useless as they fill with fluid and debris due to an infection with a protozoan.
- *Mycobacterium tuberculosis.* This bacterial infection, usually of the lungs, is seen more often as an infection of the lymph nodes and other organs in patients with AIDS.
- Toxoplasmic encephalitis is caused by a protozoan parasite that ordinarily lives in cats and other animals. Many people harbor a latent infection in the brain or muscle, but in AIDS patients, the infection leads to loss of brain cells, seizures, and weakness.
- Kaposi's sarcoma is an unusual cancer of the blood vessels, which gives rise to reddish-purple, coin-sized spots and lesions on the skin.
- Invasive cervical cancer. This cancer of the cervix spreads to nearby tissues. This condition was added to the list when AIDS became more common in women.

Although newly developed drugs can deal with opportunistic diseases, most AIDS patients are repeatedly hospitalized due to weight loss, constant fatigue, and multiple infections (Fig. S.3). Death usually follows in two to four years.

a. AIDS patient Tom Moran, July 1987

b. AIDS patient Tom Moran, early January 1988

c. AIDS patient Tom Moran, late January 1988

Figure S.3   A patient with AIDS.
These photos show how the health of a patient with AIDS deteriorates.

S.3 HIV Structure and Life Cycle

HIV is a **retrovirus**, a type of RNA virus that has a DNA stage in its replication. A retrovirus contains a special enzyme called reverse transcriptase that carries out RNA–DNA transcription. During a period of latency, viral DNA is integrated into host DNA until it becomes active during viral replication. The various events that occur in the life cycle of an HIV virus are shown in Figure S.4. Note the structure of HIV. Inside an HIV capsid are RNA and three enzymes of interest: reverse transcriptase (already mentioned), integrase, and protease. The HIV particle has an envelope that it acquires when it buds from an infected cell.

These are the steps in the life cycle of HIV:

1. *Attachment.* During attachment, the HIV virus binds to the plasma membrane.
2. *Fusion.* After attachment occurs, the HIV virus fuses with the plasma membrane, and the virus enters the cell.
3. *Uncoating.* A process called uncoating removes the capsid, and RNA is released.

4. *Reverse transcription.* This event in the reproductive cycle is unique to retroviruses. The enzyme called **reverse transcriptase** makes a DNA copy of the retroviruses' RNA genetic material. Usually in cells, DNA is transcribed into RNA. Retroviruses can do the opposite only because they have a unique enzyme, from which they take their name. (*Retro* in Latin means reverse.)
5. *Replication.* The DNA copy of viral genetic material now undergoes replication, and the result is double-stranded DNA.
6. *Integration.* The viral enzyme called **integrase** now splices viral DNA into a host chromosome. The term **HIV provirus** refers to viral DNA integrated into host DNA. HIV is usually transmitted to another person by means of cells that contain proviruses. Also, proviruses serve as a latent reservoir for HIV during drug treatment. Even if drug therapy results in an undetectable viral load, investigators know that there are still proviruses inside infected lymphocytes.

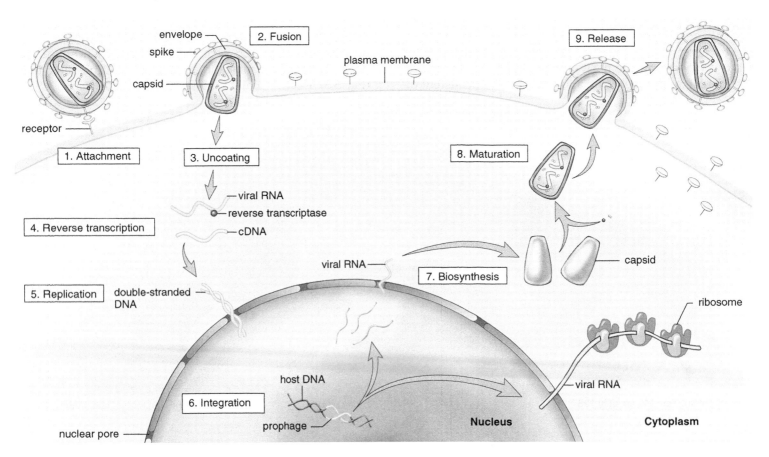

Figure S.4   Reproduction of HIV.
HIV is a retrovirus that utilizes reverse transcription to produce viral DNA. Viral DNA integrates into the cell's chromosomes before it reproduces and buds from the cell.

7. *Biosynthesis.* When the provirus is activated, perhaps by a new and different infection, the normal cell machinery directs the production of more viral RNA. Some of this RNA becomes the genetic material for new virus particles. The rest of viral RNA brings about the synthesis of viral proteins (including capsid proteins, viral enzymes, and the envelope marker) at host ribosomes.

8. *Maturation.* Capsid proteins, viral enzymes, and RNA are assembled to form new viral particles. The viral enzyme called **protease** cleaves viral proteins so that they are a size suitable for viral assembly. Reproduction of the virus has now taken place.

9. *Release.* During budding, the virus gets its envelope and envelope marker coded for by the viral genetic material.

The life cycle of an HIV virus includes transmission to a new host. Body secretions, such as semen from an infected male, contain proviruses inside T_h lymphocytes. When this semen is discharged into the vagina, rectum, or mouth, infected T_h lymphocytes migrate through the organ's lining and enter the body. The receptive partner in anal-rectal intercourse appears to be most at risk because the lining of the rectum is a thin, single-cell layer. When infected white blood cells move to the lymph nodes, HIV begins to infect more T_h lymphocytes. HIV can hide out in local lymph nodes for some time, but eventually the lymph nodes degenerate, and large numbers of HIV enter the general bloodstream. Now the viral load begins to increase; when it exceeds the T_h-lymphocyte count, the individual progresses to the final stage of an HIV infection.

S.4 Drug Therapy for HIV Infection

There is no cure for AIDS, but a treatment called highly active antiretroviral therapy (HAART) is usually able to stop HIV replication to the extent that the viral load becomes undetectable. Even so, investigators know that about one million viruses are still present, including those that exist only as inactive proviruses.

HAART utilizes a combination of two types of drugs: reverse transcriptase and protease inhibitors. The well-publicized drug called AZT and several others are reverse transcriptase inhibitors, which prevent viral DNA from being produced. When HIV protease is blocked, the resulting viruses lack the capacity to cause infection. It is important to realize that these drugs are very expensive; that they cause side effects such as diarrhea, neuropathy (painful or numb feet), hepatitis, and possibly diabetes; and that the regimen of pill-taking throughout the day is very demanding. If the drugs are not taken as prescribed or if therapy is stopped, resistance may occur. Researchers are trying to develop new drugs that might be helpful against resistant strains. A new class of drugs, called fusion inhibitors, seems to block HIV's entry into cells. Even more experimental is the discovery of compounds that sabotage integrase, the enzyme that splices viral RNA into host-cell DNA.

Investigators have found that when HAART is discontinued, the virus rebounds. It may then be possible to help the immune system counter the virus by injecting the patient with a stimulatory cytokine such as interferon or interleukin-2.

A pregnant woman who is infected with HIV and takes reverse transcriptase inhibitors during her pregnancy reduces the chances of HIV transmission to her newborn by nearly 66%. If possible, drug therapy should be delayed until the tenth to twelfth week of pregnancy to minimize any adverse effects of AZT on fetal development. Treatment with reverse transcriptase inhibitors during only the last few weeks of a pregnancy cuts the chance of transmitting HIV to the offspring by half.

Vaccines

The general consensus is that the AIDS epidemic will not be controlled until a vaccine that prevents an HIV infection is developed. Traditionally, vaccines are made by weakening a pathogen so that it will not cause disease when it is injected into the body. One group of investigators using this approach announced that they have found a way to expose hidden parts of the viral envelope marker so that the immune system can better learn to recognize this antigen. It will be several years before this vaccine is ready for clinical trials.

Another group has developed a pill that might keep HIV from ever entering the body by turning on cytotoxic T_h lymphocytes, the type of T_h lymphocyte that kills cells outright.[2] This vaccine has been tested in Uganda, an African country. Other researchers have been working on subunit vaccines that utilize just a single HIV protein, such as a viral envelope protein, as the vaccine. So far, this approach has not resulted in sufficient antibodies to keep an infection at bay. After many clinical trials, none too successful, most investigators now agree that a combination of various vaccines may be the best strategy to bring about a response in both B lymphocytes and cytotoxic T cells.

There might be something about the HIV virus—its mode of transmission or the course of the disease—that will make any type of vaccine ineffective. The burden, it seems, is on the individual. We all must come to realize the importance of our T_h lymphocytes and take measures to protect them from possible destruction by HIV. The various ways to prevent infection discussed in the reading on page 167 should be followed faithfully.

---

[2]See page 164 for a discussion of white blood cells, including lymphocytes.

Bioethical Focus

HIV Vaccine Testing in Africa

The United Nations estimates that 16,000 people become newly infected with the human immunodeficiency virus (HIV) each day, or 5.8 million per year. Ninety percent of these infections occur in sub-Saharan Africa, where infected persons do not have access to antiviral therapy. In Uganda, for example, there is only one physician per 100,000 people, and only $6 per person is spent annually on health care. In the United States, $12,000–$15,000 is usually spent on treating an HIV-infected person per year.

The only methodology presently available to prevent the spread of HIV in a less-developed country* is counseling against behaviors that increase the risk of infection. Clearly, an effective vaccine would be most beneficial to these countries. Several HIV vaccines are in various stages of development, and all need to be clinically tested to see if they are effective. It seems reasonable to carry out such trials in less-developed countries, but many ethical questions arise.

A possible way to carry out the trial is this: Vaccinate the uninfected sexual partners of HIV-infected individuals. After all, if the uninfected partner remains free of the disease, the vaccine is effective. But is it ethical to allow a partner identified as having an HIV infection to remain untreated for the sake of the trial?

And should there be a placebo group—a group that does not get the vaccine? After all, if a greater number of persons in the placebo group become infected than those in the vaccine group, the vaccine is effective. But if members of the placebo group become infected, shouldn't they be given effective treatment? For that matter, even participants in the vaccine group might become infected. Shouldn't all participants in the trial be given proper treatment if they become infected? Who would pay for such treatment when the trial could involve thousands of persons?

*Country in which the population is expanding rapidly and the majority of people live in poverty.

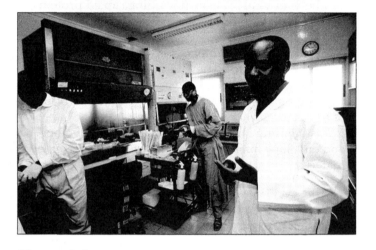

Figure S.A   **AIDS in Africa.**
Performing clinical trials and treating HIV infections in Africa raises many ethical questions.

Decide Your Opinion

1. Should HIV vaccine trials be done in less-developed countries, which stand to gain the most from an effective vaccine? Why or why not?
2. Should the trial be carried out using the same standards as in more-developed countries? Why or why not?
3. Who should pay for the trial—the drug company, the participants, or the country of the participants?

Summary

S.1 Origin and Scope of AIDS

AIDS most likely originated in the 1950s, but it wasn't until 1983 that HIV was recognized as the cause of AIDS.

New HIV infections are increasing faster among heterosexuals than homosexuals; women in the United States now account for nearly 25% of AIDS cases.

S.2 Phases of an HIV Infection

During the acute phase of an HIV infection, the person is highly infectious although no symptoms may be present; during the chronic phase, the person may experience swollen lymph nodes and various infections; during the last phase, which is called AIDS, the patient usually succumbs to an opportunistic infection.

S.3 HIV Structure and Life Cycle

HIV is a retrovirus that infects immune cells, such as T_h lymphocytes, carrying a receptor. HIV is transmitted as a provirus inside infected T_h lymphocytes.

S.4 Drug Therapy for HIV Infection

Combination drug therapy has met with encouraging success against HIV infection. Development of a vaccine is also being pursued.

Reviewing the Chapter

1. How did AIDS arise, and how prevalent is it today? 172–73
2. List and describe the phases of an HIV infection. 174–75
3. Describe the life cycle of HIV, and tell how the life cycle relates to drug therapy for an HIV infection. 176–77
4. What types of vaccines are being prepared to prevent an HIV infection? 177–78

Critical Thinking Questions

1. Why is a person with AIDS particularly subject to infection by other pathogens?

2. Why is HIV able to enter T_h lymphocytes and not other types of lymphocytes?

3. Why doesn't the drug therapy for an HIV infection kill T_h lymphocytes?

Understanding Key Terms

AIDS (acquired immunodeficiency syndrome) 172
HIV provirus 176
human immunodeficiency virus (HIV) 172

integrase 176
opportunistic infection 175
protease 177
retrovirus 176
reverse transcriptase 176

A natural environment contrasted with a human-impacted environment.

III

Evolution, Behavior, and Population Concerns

Human reproduction is intimately involved in human evolution, which proceeds when individuals who are better adapted to the environment have more children than those who are not as well adapted. In turn, human evolution shapes behavior, especially sexual behavior. It is clear that human sexual behavior, like other human characteristics, is guided by natural selection.

Human reproduction has resulted in a very large population that is just now leveling off after a period of rapid expansion. Resource consumption by the growing population has resulted in pollution and other practices that threaten the health of the ecosystems on which humans depend. Many environmentalists recommend that energy be used more efficiently and that raw materials be recycled to ensure a continued supply and improved environmental conditions for future generations.

Chapter 11

Evolution

11.1 Origin of Life

Many scientists believe that a **chemical evolution** produced the first cell(s) on the primitive Earth.

The Primitive Earth

We know that the solar system was in place about 4.6 billion years ago (BYA) and that the gravitational field of the Earth allowed it to have an atmosphere. The Earth's primitive atmosphere was not the same as today's atmosphere. Most likely, the primitive atmosphere was formed by gases escaping from volcanoes. If so, the primitive atmosphere would have consisted mostly of water vapor (H_2O), nitrogen (N_2), and carbon dioxide (CO_2), with only small amounts of hydrogen (H_2) and carbon monoxide (CO). The primitive atmosphere had little, if any, free oxygen.

At first, the Earth and its atmosphere were extremely hot, and water, existing only as a gas, formed dense, thick clouds. Then, as the Earth cooled, water vapor condensed to liquid water, and rain began to fall. It rained in such enormous quantities over hundreds of millions of years that the oceans of the world were produced.

Small Organic Molecules

The rain washed the other gases, such as nitrogen and carbon dioxide, into the oceans (Fig. 11.1a). The primitive Earth had many sources of energy, including volcanoes, meteorites, radioactive isotopes, lightning, and ultraviolet radiation. In the presence of so much available energy, the primitive gases may have reacted with one another and produced small organic compounds, such as nucleotides and amino acids (Fig. 11.1b). In 1953, Stanley Miller performed an experiment to see whether it would be possible for organic molecules to result from these conditions. He placed a mixture of primitive gases in a closed system, heated the mixture, and circulated it past an electric spark. After cooling, Miller discovered a variety of small organic molecules in the resulting liquid. Other investigators have achieved the same results using various mixtures of gases.

Macromolecules

The newly formed small organic molecules likely joined to produce organic macromolecules (Fig. 11.1c). Two hypotheses of special interest have arisen concerning this stage in the origin of life. One is the **RNA-first hypothesis,** which suggests that only the macromolecule RNA (ribonucleic acid) was needed at this time to progress toward formation of the first cell(s). This hypothesis was formulated after the discovery that RNA can sometimes be both a substrate and an enzyme. Such RNA molecules are called ribozymes. Perhaps RNA could have carried out the processes of life commonly associated today with DNA (deoxyribonucleic acid) and proteins. Scientists who support this hypothesis say that it was an "RNA world" some 3.5 billion years ago.

Another hypothesis is termed the **protein-first hypothesis.** Sidney Fox has shown that amino acids join together when exposed to dry heat. He suggests that amino acids collected in shallow puddles along the rocky shore, and the heat of the sun then caused them to form proteinoids, small polypeptides that have some catalytic properties. When proteinoids are returned to water, they form microspheres, structures composed only of protein that have many of the properties of a cell.

The Protocell

A cell has a lipid-protein membrane. Fox has shown that if lipids are made available to microspheres, the two tend to become associated, producing a lipid-protein membrane. A **protocell,** which could carry on metabolism but could not reproduce, would have come into existence in this manner.

The protocell would have been able to use the still-abundant small organic molecules in the ocean as food. Therefore, the protocell is believed to have been a **heterotroph,** an organism that takes in preformed food. Further, the protocell would have been a fermenter because no free oxygen was available.

The True Cell

A true cell can reproduce, and in today's cells, DNA replicates before the cell divides. Enzymatic proteins carry out the replication process.

How did the first cell acquire both DNA and enzymatic proteins? Scientists who support the RNA-first hypothesis propose a series of steps. According to this hypothesis, the first cell had RNA genes that, like messenger RNA, could have specified protein synthesis. Some of the proteins formed would have been enzymes. Perhaps one of these enzymes, such as reverse transcriptase found in retroviruses, could use RNA as a template to form DNA. Replication of DNA would then proceed normally.

By contrast, supporters of the protein-first hypothesis suggest that some of the proteins in the protocell would have evolved the enzymatic ability to synthesize DNA from nucleotides in the ocean. Then DNA would have gone on to specify protein synthesis, and in this way the cell could have acquired all its enzymes, even the ones that replicate DNA.

11.2 Biological Evolution

The first true cells were the simplest of life-forms; therefore, they must have been **prokaryotic cells,** which lack a nucleus. Later, **eukaryotic cells** (protists), which have nuclei, evolved. Eventually, multicellularity and the other kingdoms (fungi, plants, and animals) evolved. Obviously, all these types of organisms—even prokaryotic cells—are alive today. Each type of organism has its own evolutionary history that is traceable back to the first cell(s).

Biological evolution is a change in life-forms that has taken place in the past and will take place in the future. Biological evolution has two important aspects: descent from a common ancestor and adaptation to the environment. Descent from the original cell(s) explains why all living things have a common chemistry and a cellular structure. An **adaptation** is a characteristic that makes an organism able to survive and reproduce in its environment. Adaptations to different environments explain the diversity of life—why there are so many different types of living things.

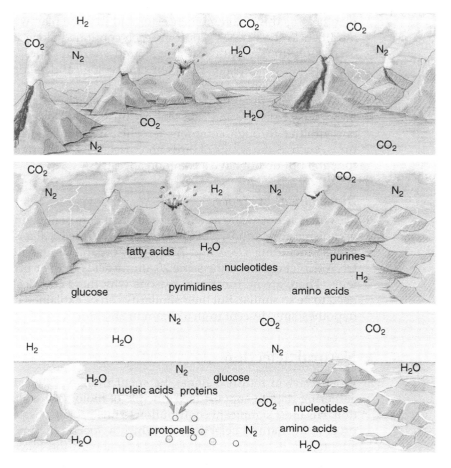

a. The primitive atmosphere contained gases, including H_2O, CO_2, and N_2, that escaped from volcanoes. As the water vapor cooled, some gases were washed into the oceans by rain.

b. The availability of energy from volcanic eruption and lightning allowed gases to form small organic molecules, such as nucleotides and amino acids.

c. Small organic molecules could have joined to form proteins and nucleic acids, which became incorporated into membrane-bounded spheres. The spheres became the first cells, called protocells. Later protocells became true cells that could reproduce.

Figure 11.1   Chemical evolution.
A chemical evolution is believed to have produced the protocell which became a true cell once it had genes composed of DNA and could reproduce.

Common Descent

Charles Darwin was the English naturalist who first formulated the theory of evolution that has since been supported by so much independent data. At the age of 22, Darwin sailed around the world as the naturalist on board the HMS *Beagle.* Between 1831 and 1836, the ship sailed in the tropics of the Southern Hemisphere, where life-forms are more abundant and varied than in Darwin's native England.

Even though it was not his original intent, Darwin began to realize and to gather evidence that life-forms change over time and from place to place. Three types of evidence convinced Darwin that common descent occurs: fossil, biogeographical, and anatomical.

Fossil Evidence

Fossils are the remains and traces of past life, or any other direct evidence of past life. Traces include trails, footprints, burrows, worm casts, or even preserved droppings. Most fossils consist only of hard parts, such as shells, bones, or teeth, because these parts are usually not consumed or destroyed.

The **fossil record** is the history of life recorded by remains from the past. The fossil record supports common descent because similarity of form allows fossils to be linked over time despite observed changes. Darwin found the fossil remains of a sloth and an armadillo, and the similarity of the fossils to the living animals made him realize that the fossils were related to the modern animals. The fossil record offers evidence of human evolution as well; Figure 11.2 shows the similarities between an australopithecine and ourselves.

Biogeographical Evidence

Biogeography is the study of the distribution of plants and animals throughout the world. Darwin noted that South

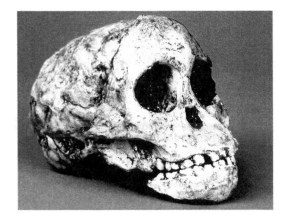

Figure 11.2 **Fossil evidence.**
Our ancestors, even those not classified as humans, look remarkably like ourselves.

America had no rabbits, even though the environment was quite suitable for them. He concluded that there are no rabbits in South America because rabbits originated somewhere else and had no means of reaching South America.

Instead of rabbits, the Patagonian hare exists in the grasslands of South America. This hare has long legs and ears but the face of a guinea pig. Both rabbits and Patagonian hares eat grass, hide in bushes, and move rapidly using long hind legs. Darwin began to think that the Patagonian hare was related to a guinea pig through common descent and that rabbits and Patagonian hares share the same characteristics because they are both adapted to the same type of environment.

Anatomical Evidence

Darwin was able to show that a common descent hypothesis offers a plausible explanation for anatomical similarities among living organisms. Vertebrate forelimbs are used for flight (birds and bats), orientation during swimming (whales and seals), running (horses), climbing (arboreal lizards), or swinging from tree branches (monkeys). Despite dissimilar functions, all vertebrate forelimbs contain the same sets of bones organized in similar ways. The most plausible explanation for this unity is that the basic forelimb plan belonged to a common ancestor and that the plan was modified in the various groups as each continued along its own evolutionary pathway. The shared characteristics of vertebrates also explain why their embryological development is so similar.

Vertebrate forelimbs are **homologous structures.** Homologous structures indicate that organisms are related to one another through common descent. **Analogous structures,** such as the wings of birds and insects, have the same function but do not have a common ancestry.

Biochemical Evidence

Darwin was not aware as we are today that almost all living organisms are composed of the same basic biochemical molecules, including DNA and ATP. Also, organisms use the DNA triplet code and the same 20 amino acids in their proteins. There are no functional reasons why these chemicals need to be so similar. But their similarity can be explained by hypothesizing descent from a common ancestor.

Natural Selection

When Darwin returned home, he spent the next 20 years gathering data to support the principle of biological evolution. His most significant contribution to this principle was a process for **natural selection,** by which a species becomes adapted to its environment. On his trip aboard the *Beagle,* Darwin had visited the Galápagos Islands. There he had seen a number of finches that resembled one another but had different ways of life. Some were seed-eating ground finches, some cactus-eating ground finches, and some insect-eating tree finches. A warbler-type finch had a beak that could take honey from a flower. A woodpecker-type finch lacked the long tongue of a woodpecker but could use a cactus spine or twig to ferret out insects from the bark of a tree. Darwin thought the finches were all descended from a mainland ancestor whose offspring had spread out among the islands and become adapted to different environments. Darwin believed that organisms do not strive to adapt themselves to the environment; instead, the environment selects for survival and reproduction those organisms that happen to have a characteristic that gives them an advantage in a particular environment.

In order to emphasize the nature of Darwin's natural selection process, it is often contrasted with a process espoused by Jean-Baptiste Lamarck, another nineteenth-century naturalist. Lamarck's explanation for the long neck of the giraffe was based on the assumption that the ancestors of the modern giraffe were trying to reach into the trees to browse on high-growing vegetation (Fig. 11.3a). Continual stretching of the neck caused it to become longer, and this acquired characteristic was passed on to the next generation. Lamarck's process is **teleological** because, according to him, the desired outcome is known ahead of time. This type of explanation has not stood the test of time. Darwin's process of natural selection, on the other hand, is nonteleological and has been fully substantiated by later investigators (Fig. 11.3b).

Here are the critical elements of the process of natural selection:

- *Variation.* Individual members of a species vary in physical characteristics. Physical variations can be passed from generation to generation. (Darwin was never aware of genes, but we know today that the inheritance of the genotype determines the phenotype.)
- *Struggle for existence.* Even though each individual could eventually produce many descendants, the number in each generation usually stays about the same. Why? Because resources are limited, and only certain individuals survive and reproduce.
- *Survival of the fittest.* Some members of a species are able to capture more resources in a particular environment because they have a characteristic that gives them an advantage over other members of the species. The environment "selects" these better-adapted members to have offspring and therefore to pass on this characteristic.
- *Adaptation.* Each subsequent generation includes more individuals that are adapted in the same way to the environment.

Can natural selection account for the great diversity of life? Yes, if we are aware that environments differ widely and that life has been evolving for a very long time.

Early giraffes probably had short necks that they stretched to reach food.

Early giraffes probably had necks of various lengths.

Their offspring had longer necks that they stretched to reach food.

Natural selection due to competition led to survival of the longer-necked giraffes and their offspring.

Eventually, the continued stretching of the neck resulted in today's giraffe.

Eventually, only long-necked giraffes survived the competition.

a. Lamarck's proposal   b. Darwin's proposal

Figure 11.3   Mechanism of evolution.
This diagram contrasts Jean-Baptiste Lamarck's process of acquired characteristics with Charles Darwin's process of natural selection. Only natural selection is supported by data.

Prosimians

Ring-tailed lemur, *Lemus catta*

a.

Tarsier, *Tarsius bancanus*

New World Monkeys

White-faced monkey,
Cebus capucinus

Old World Monkeys

Anubis baboon, *Papio anubis*

b.

Asian Apes

African Apes

Western lowland gorilla,
Gorilla gorilla

White-handed gibbon,
Hylobates lar

c.

Orangutan, *Pongo pygmaeus*

Chimpanzee, *Pan troglodytes*

Humans, *Homo sapiens*

d.

Figure 11.4   Primate diversity.

a. Today's prosimians are related to the first group of primates to evolve. **b.** Today's monkeys are divided into the New World monkeys and the Old World monkeys. **c.** Today's apes can be divided into the Asian apes (gibbons and orangutans) and the African apes (chimpanzees and gorillas). **d.** Humans are also classified as primates.

11.3 Humans Are Primates

Primates [L. *primus,* first] include prosimians, monkeys, apes, and humans. In contrast to other types of mammals, primates are adapted for an **arboreal** life—that is, for living in trees (Fig. 11.4). The evolution of primates is characterized by trends toward mobile limbs, grasping hands, a flattened face, binocular vision, a large, complex brain, and a reduced reproductive rate. These traits are particularly useful for living in trees.

Mobile Forelimbs and Hindlimbs

In primates, the limbs are mobile, and the hands and feet have five digits each. In most primates, flat nails have replaced the claws of ancestral primates, and sensitive pads on the undersides of fingers and toes assist the grasping of objects. Many primates have both an opposable big toe and thumb—that is, the big toe or thumb can touch each of the other toes or fingers. Humans don't have an opposable big toe, but the thumb is opposable, and this results in a grip that is both powerful and precise. Figure 11.5 contrasts the human hand with that of other primates.

How are these features adaptive for a life in trees? Mobile limbs with clawless opposable digits allow primates to freely grasp and release tree limbs. They also allow primates to easily reach out and bring food, such as fruit, to the mouth.

Binocular Vision

A foreshortened snout and a relatively flat face are evolutionary trends in primates. These may be associated with a general decline in the importance of smell and an increased reliance on vision, leading eventually to binocular vision. In most primates, the eyes are located in the front where they can focus on the same object from slightly different angles (Fig. 11.6). The stereoscopic (three-dimensional) vision and good depth perception that result permit primates to make accurate judgments about the distance and position of adjoining tree limbs.

Some primates, humans in particular, have color vision and greater visual acuity because the retina contains cone cells in addition to rod cells. Rod cells are activated in dim light, but the blurry image is in shades of gray. Cone cells require bright light, but the image is sharp and in color. The lens of the eye focuses light directly on the fovea, a region of the retina where cone cells are concentrated.

Large, Complex Brain

Sense organs are only as beneficial as the brain that processes their input. The evolutionary trend among primates is toward a larger and more complex brain—the brain size is smallest in prosimians and largest in modern humans. The portion of the brain devoted to smell has gotten smaller, and the portions devoted to sight have increased in size and complexity. Also, more of the brain of modern humans is devoted to controlling and processing information received from the hands and the thumb. The result is good hand-eye coordination.

Reduced Reproductive Rate

One other trend in primate evolution is a general reduction in the rate of reproduction, which is associated with increased age of sexual maturity and extended life spans. Gestation is lengthy, allowing time for forebrain development. One birth at a time is the norm in primates; it is difficult to care for several offspring while moving from limb to limb. The juvenile period of dependency is extended, and learned behavior and complex social interactions are emphasized.

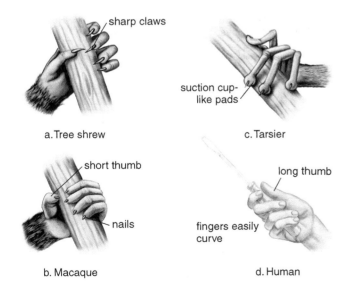

Figure 11.5 Evolution of primate hand.
Comparison of **(a)** the claw of a tree shrew to the hands of primates: **(b–d)** a macaque, a tarsier, and a human.

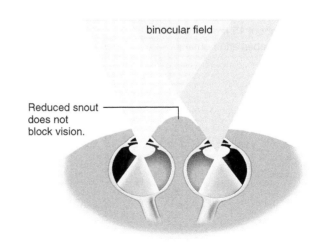

Figure 11.6 Binocular vision.
In primates, the snout is reduced, and the eyes are at the front of the head. The result is a binocular field that aids depth perception.

Relationships Among Primates

The **evolutionary tree** in Figure 11.7 shows that all primates share one common ancestor and that the other types of primates diverged from the human line of descent over time. Notice that humans are most closely related to African apes, specifically the chimpanzee. One of the most unfortunate misconceptions concerning human evolution is that Darwin and others suggested that humans evolved from apes. On the contrary, humans and apes are believed to have shared a common apelike ancestor. Today's apes are our distant cousins, and we couldn't have evolved from our cousins because we are contemporaries—living on Earth at the same time. Presently, scientists believe that this common ancestor existed about 6 million years ago (MYA).

Biologists have not been able to agree on which extinct form known only by the fossil record is our common ancestor with apes. Molecular data have therefore been used to determine the date of the split between **hominids** (immediate ancestors to humans) and apes. When two lines of descent, called a **lineage,** first diverge from a common ancestor, the genes and proteins of the two lineages are nearly identical. But as time goes by, each lineage accumulates genetic and protein changes. Such changes can be used as a kind of **molecular clock** to indicate the relatedness of two groups and when they diverged from one another.

Biologists suggest that the first hominid began to develop bipedalism and walk upright even while it lived in trees. Why? Because they cannot find evidence of a dramatic shift in vegetation about 6 MYA. The first hominid's environment is now thought to have included some forest, some woodland, and some grassland. While still living in trees, the first hominids may have walked upright on large branches as they collected fruit from overhead. Then, when they began to forage on the ground among bushes, it would have been easier to shuffle along on their hind limbs. Bipedalism would also have prevented them from getting heatstroke because an upright stance exposes more of the body to breezes. Bipedalism may have been an advantage in still another way. Males may have acquired food far afield, and if they could carry it back to females, they would have been more assured of sex.

Figure 11.7 **Primate evolutionary tree.**
The ancestor to all primates climbed into one of the first fruit-bearing forests about 66 MYA. The descendants of this ancestor adapted to the new way of life and developed traits such as a shortened snout and nails instead of claws. The time when the other primates diverged from the human line of descent is largely known from the fossil record. A common ancestor was living at each point of divergence; for example, there was a common ancestor for monkeys, apes, and humans about 33 MYA; one for all apes and humans about 15 MYA; and one for just African apes and humans about 6 MYA.

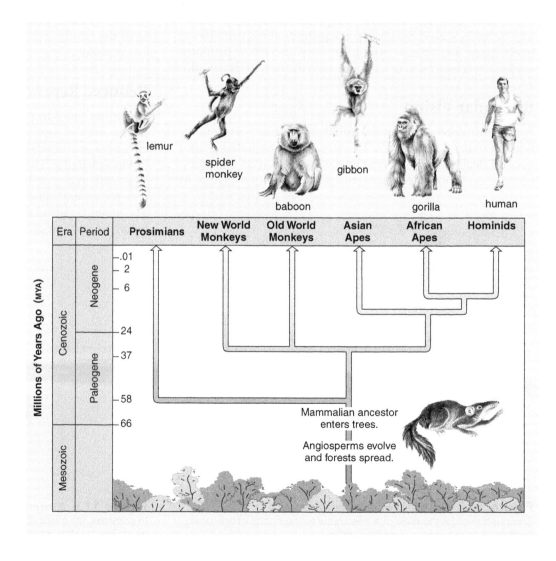

11.4 Evolution of Australopithecines

The hominid line of descent begins in earnest with the **australopithecines,** a group of individuals that evolved and diversified in Africa. Some australopithecines were slight of frame and termed gracile (slender) types. Some were robust (powerful) and tended to have strong upper bodies and especially massive jaws, with chewing muscles anchored to a prominent bony crest along the top of the skull. The gracile types most likely fed on soft fruits and leaves, while the robust types had a more fibrous diet that may have included hard nuts.

Southern Africa

The first australopithecine to be discovered was unearthed in southern Africa by Raymond Dart in the 1920s. This hominid, named *Australopithecus africanus*, is a gracile type dated about 2.8 MYA. *A. robustus*, dated from 2 to 1.5 MYA, is a robust type from southern Africa. Both *A. africanus* and *A. robustus* had a brain size of about 500 cc; their skull differences are essentially due to dental and facial adaptations to different diets.

These hominids are believed to have walked upright. Nevertheless, the proportions of their limbs are apelike: The forelimbs are longer than the hindlimbs. Some argue that *A. africanus,* with its relatively large brain, is the best ancestral candidate for early *Homo,* whose limb proportions are similar to those of this fossil.

Eastern Africa

More than 20 years ago, a team led by Donald Johanson unearthed nearly 250 fossils of a hominid called *A. afarensis.* This now-famous female skeleton, dated at 3.18 MYA, is known worldwide by its field name, Lucy. (The name derives from the Beatles song "Lucy in the Sky with Diamonds.") Although her brain was quite small (400 cc), the shapes and relative proportions of her limbs indicate that Lucy stood upright and walked bipedally (Fig. 11.8*a*). Even better evidence of bipedal locomotion comes from a trail of footprints in Laetoli dated about 3.7 MYA. The larger prints are double, as though a smaller-sized being was stepping in the footfalls of another—and there are additional small prints off to the side, within hand-holding distance (Fig. 11.8*b*).

Since the australopithecines were apelike above the waist (small brain) and humanlike below the waist (walked erect), it seems that human characteristics did not evolve all at one time. The term **mosaic evolution** is applied when different body parts change at different rates and therefore at different times.

A. afarensis, a gracile type, is believed to be ancestral to the robust types found in eastern Africa: *A. aethiopicus* and *A. boisei. A. boisei* had a powerful upper body and the largest molars of any hominid. These robust types died out, and therefore, it is possible that *A. afarensis* is ancestral to both *A. africanus* and early *Homo.*

a.

b.

Figure 11.8   *Australopithecus afarensis.*
a. A reconstruction of Lucy on display at the St. Louis Zoo. **b.** These fossilized footprints occur in ash from a volcanic eruption some 3.7 million years ago. The larger footprints are double (one individual followed behind the other), and a third, smaller individual was walking to the side. (A female holding the hand of a youngster may have been walking in the footprints of a male.) These footprints suggest that *A. afarensis* walked bipedally.

11.5 Evolution of Humans

Fossils are assigned to the genus *Homo* if (1) the brain size is 600 cc or greater, (2) the jaw and teeth resemble those of humans, and (3) tool use is evident (Fig. 11.9).

Early *Homo*

Homo habilis, dated between 2.0 and 1.9 MYA, may be ancestral to modern humans. Some of these fossils have a brain size as large as 775 cc, which is about 45% larger than that of *A. afarensis.* The cheek teeth are smaller than even those of the gracile australopithecines. Therefore, it is likely that these early *Homos* were omnivores who ate meat in addition to plant material. Bones at their campsites bear cut marks, indicating that they used tools to strip them of meat.

The stone tools made by *H. habilis,* whose name means "handy man," are rather crude. It's possible that these are the cores from which they took flakes sharp enough to scrape away hide, cut tendons, and easily remove meat from bones.

The skulls of early *Homos* suggest that the portions of the brain associated with speech areas were enlarged. We can speculate that the ability to speak may have led to hunting cooperatively. Other members of the group may have remained plant gatherers, and if so, both hunters and gatherers most likely ate together and shared their food. In this way, society and culture could have begun. **Culture,** which encompasses human behavior and products (such as technology and the arts), is dependent upon the capacity to speak and transmit knowledge. We can further speculate that the advantages of a culture to *H. habilis* may have hastened the extinction of the australopithecines.

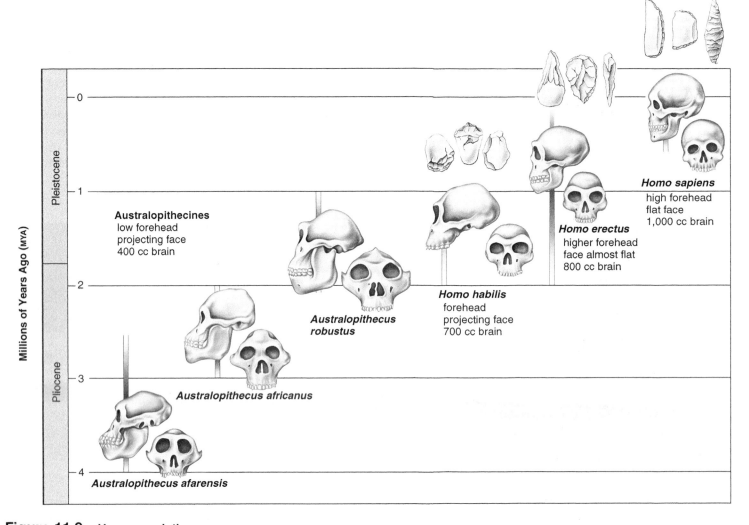

Figure 11.9   Human evolution.
The length of time each species existed is indicated by the vertical gray lines. Notice that two or more hominids have existed at some of the same times. Therefore, human evolution resembles a "bush" rather than a single branch.

Homo erectus

Homo erectus and like fossils are found in Africa, Asia, and Europe and dated between 1.9 and 0.3 MYA. A Dutch anatomist named Eugene Dubois was the first to unearth *H. erectus* bones in Java in 1891, and since that time many other fossils have been found in the same area. Although all fossils assigned the name *H. erectus* are similar in appearance, enough discrepancy exists to suggest that several different species have been included in this group. In particular, some experts believe that the African and Asian forms are two different species.

Compared to *H. habilis, H. erectus* had a larger brain (about 1,000 cc) and a flatter face. The nose projected, however. This type of nose is adaptive for a hot, dry climate because it permits water to be removed before air leaves the body. The recovery of the almost complete skeleton of a 10-year-old boy indicates that *H. erectus* was much taller than the hominids discussed thus far (Fig. 11.10). Males were 1.8 m tall (about 6 ft), and females were 1.55 m (approaching 5 ft). Indeed, these hominids were erect and most likely had a striding gait like ours. The robust and probably heavily muscled skeleton still retained some australopithecine features. Even so, the size of the birth canal indicates that infants were born in an immature state that required an extended period of care.

It is believed that *H. erectus* first appeared in Africa and then migrated into Asia and Europe. At one time, the migration was thought to have occurred about 1 MYA, but recently *H. erectus* fossil remains in Java and the Republic of Georgia have been dated at 1.9 and 1.6 MYA, respectively. These remains push the evolution of *H. erectus* in Africa to an earlier date than had previously been determined. In any case, such an extensive population movement is a first in the history of humankind and a tribute to the intellectual and physical skills of the species.

H. erectus was the first hominid to use fire, and also fashioned more advanced tools than early *Homo*s. These hominids used heavy, teardrop-shaped axes and cleavers as well as flakes, which were probably used for cutting and scraping. Some believe that *H. erectus* was a systematic hunter who brought kills to the same site over and over again. In one location, researchers have found over 40,000 bones and 2,647 stones. These sites could have been "home bases" where social interaction occurred and a prolonged childhood allowed time for learning. Perhaps a language evolved and a culture more like our own developed.

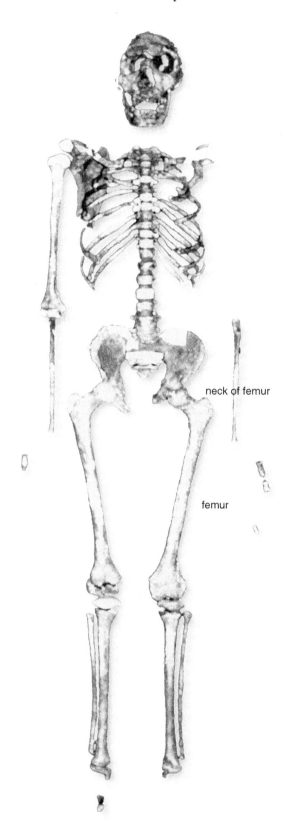

neck of femur

femur

Figure 11.10 *Homo erectus.*
This skeleton of a 10-year-old boy who lived 1.6 MYA in eastern Africa shows femurs that are angled, with femur necks much longer than in the femurs of modern humans.

Evolution of Modern Humans

Most researchers believe that **Homo sapiens** (modern humans) evolved from *H. erectus,* but they differ as to the details. Perhaps *Homo sapiens* evolved from *H. erectus* separately in Asia, Africa, and Europe. The hypothesis that *Homo sapiens* evolved in several different locations is called the **multiregional continuity hypothesis** (Fig. 11.11*a*). This hypothesis proposes that evolution to modern humans was essentially similar in several different places. If so, each region should show a continuity of its own anatomical characteristics from the time when *H. erectus* first arrived in Europe and Asia.

Opponents argue that it seems highly unlikely for evolution to have produced essentially the same result in these different places. They suggest, instead, the **out-of-Africa hypothesis,** which proposes that *H. sapiens* evolved from *H. erectus* only in Africa, and thereafter *H. sapiens* migrated to Europe and Asia about 100,000 years BP (before present) (Fig. 11.11*b*). If so, there would be no continuity of characteristics between fossils dated 200,000 BP and 100,000 BP in Europe and Asia.

According to which hypothesis would modern humans be most genetically alike? The multiregional continuity hypothesis states that human populations have been evolving separately for a long time, and therefore genetic differences are expected. The out-of-Africa hypothesis states that we are all descended from a few individuals from about 100,000 years BP. Therefore, the out-of-Africa hypothesis suggests that we are more genetically similar.

A few years ago, a study attempted to show that all the people of Europe (and the world, for that matter) have essentially the same mitochondrial DNA. Called the "mitochondrial Eve" hypothesis by the press (note that this is a misnomer because no single ancestor is proposed), the statistics that calculated the date of the African migration were found to be flawed. Still, the raw data—which indicate a close genetic relationship among all Europeans—support the out-of-Africa hypothesis.

Recent fossil finds from Ethiopia dated about 160,000 years show many modern human characteristics. These fossils may very well provide a transition between ancient African forms and more modern ones. Still, despite the presence of some primitive features, these new finds are probably the oldest definitive record of what we currently think of as modern *H. sapiens.* They also lend support to the out-of-Africa hypothesis.

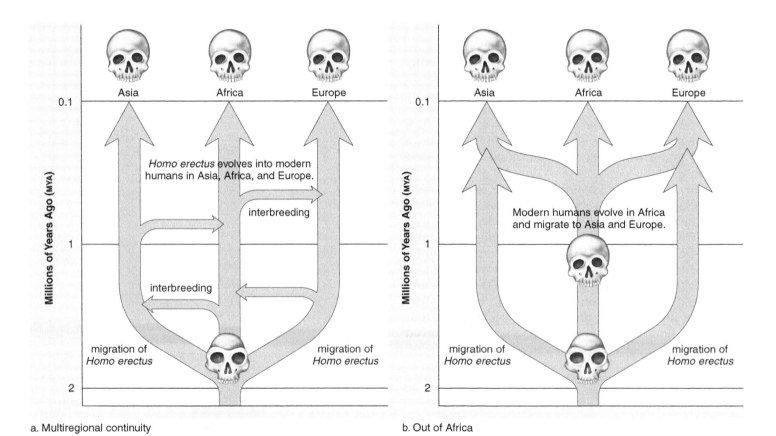

a. Multiregional continuity

b. Out of Africa

Figure 11.11   **Evolution of modern humans.**

a. The multiregional continuity hypothesis proposes that *Homo sapiens* evolved separately in at least three different places: Asia, Africa, and Europe. Therefore, continuity of genotypes and phenotypes is expected in these regions. **b.** The out-of-Africa hypothesis proposes that *Homo sapiens* evolved only in Africa; then this species migrated and supplanted populations of *Homo* in Asia and Europe about 100,000 years ago.

Neanderthals

Neanderthals *(H. neanderthalensis)* take their name from Germany's Neander Valley, where one of the first Neanderthal skeletons, dated some 200,000 years ago, was discovered. The Neanderthals had massive brow ridges, and their nose, jaws, and teeth protruded far forward. The forehead was low and sloping, and the lower jaw lacked a chin. New fossils show that the pubic bone was long compared to ours.

According to the out-of-Africa hypothesis, Neanderthals were eventually supplanted by modern humans. Surprisingly, however, the Neanderthal brain was, on the average, slightly larger than that of *Homo sapiens* (1,400 cc, compared to 1,360 cc in most modern humans). The Neanderthals were heavily muscled, especially in the shoulders and neck (Fig. 11.12). The bones of their limbs were shorter and thicker than those of modern humans. It is hypothesized that a larger brain than that of modern humans was required to control the extra musculature. The Neanderthals lived in Europe and Asia during the last Ice Age, and their sturdy build could have helped conserve heat.

The Neanderthals give evidence of being culturally advanced. Most lived in caves, but those living in the open may have built houses. They manufactured a variety of stone tools, including spear points, which could have been used for hunting, and scrapers and knives, which would have helped in food preparation. They most likely successfully hunted bears, woolly mammoths, rhinoceroses, reindeer, and other contemporary animals. They used and could control fire, which probably helped them cook frozen meat and keep themselves warm. They even buried their dead with flowers and tools and may have had a religion.

Cro-Magnons

Cro-Magnons are the oldest fossils to be designated *Homo sapiens*. In keeping with the out-of-Africa hypothesis, the Cro-Magnons, who are named after a fossil location in France, were the modern humans who entered Asia and Europe from Africa 100,000 years ago or even earlier. Cro-Magnons had a thoroughly modern appearance (Fig. 11.13). They made advanced stone tools, including compound tools, as when stone flakes were fitted to a wooden handle. They may have been the first to throw spears, enabling them to kill animals from a distance, and to make knifelike blades. They were such accomplished hunters that some researchers believe they were responsible for the extinction of many larger mammals, such as the giant sloth, the mammoth, the saber-toothed tiger, and the giant ox, during the late Pleistocene epoch.

Cro-Magnons hunted cooperatively, and perhaps they were the first to have a language. They are believed to have lived in small groups, with the men hunting by day while the women remained at home with the children. It's quite possible that this hunting way of life among prehistoric people influences our behavior even today. The Cro-Magnon culture included art. They sculpted small figurines out of reindeer bones and antlers. They also painted beautiful drawings of animals on cave walls in Spain and France (Fig. 11.13).

Figure 11.12   Neanderthals.
This drawing shows that the nose and the mouth of the Neanderthals protruded from their faces, and their muscles were massive. They made stone tools and were most likely excellent hunters.

Figure 11.13   Cro-Magnons.
Cro-Magnon people are the first to be designated *Homo sapiens*. Their toolmaking ability and other cultural attributes, including artistic talents, are legendary.

Human Variation

Human beings have been widely distributed about the globe ever since they evolved. As with any other species that has a wide geographical distribution, phenotypic and genotypic variations are noticeable between populations. Today, we say that people have different ethnicities (Fig. 11.14a).

It has been hypothesized that human variations evolved as adaptations to local environmental conditions. One obvious difference among people is skin color. A darker skin protects against the high UV intensity of bright sunlight. On the other hand, a white skin ensures vitamin D production in the skin when the UV intensity is low. As the Harvard University geneticist Richard Lewontin points out, however, this hypothesis concerning the survival value of dark and light skin has never been tested.

Two correlations between body shape and environmental conditions have been noted since the nineteenth century. The first, known as Bergmann's rule, states that animals in colder regions of their range have a bulkier body build. The second, known as Allen's rule, states that animals in colder regions of their range have shorter limbs, digits, and ears. Both of these effects help regulate body temperature by increasing the surface-area-to-volume ratio in hot climates and decreasing the ratio in cold climates. For example, Figure 11.14b,c shows that the Massai of East Africa tend to be slightly built, with elongated limbs, while the Eskimos, who live in northern regions, are bulky and have short limbs.

Other anatomical differences among ethnic groups, including hair texture, a fold on the upper eyelid (common in Asian peoples), or the shape of lips, cannot be explained as adaptations to the environment. Perhaps these features became fixed in different populations due simply to genetic drift. As far as intelligence is concerned, no significant disparities have been found among different ethnic groups.

Genetic Evidence for a Common Ancestry

The two hypotheses regarding the evolution of humans, discussed on page 192, pertain to the origin of ethnic groups. The multiregional hypothesis suggests that different human populations came into existence as long as one million years ago, giving time for significant ethnic differences to accumulate despite some gene flow. The out-of-Africa hypothesis, on the other hand, proposes that all modern humans have a relatively recent common ancestor who evolved in Africa and then spread into other regions. Paleontologists tell us that the variation among modern populations is considerably less than that existing among archaic human populations some 250,000 years ago. This would mean that all ethnic groups evolved from the same single, ancestral population.

A comparative study of mitochondrial DNA shows that the differences among human populations are consistent with their having a common ancestor no more than a

a.

b.   c.

Figure 11.14   Ethnic groups.
a. Some of the differences between three prevalent ethnic groups in the United States may be due to adaptations to the original environment. **b.** The Massai live in East Africa. **c.** Eskimos live near the Arctic Circle.

million years ago. Lewontin has also found that the genotypes of different modern populations are extremely similar. He examined variations in 17 genes, including blood groups and various enzymes, among seven major geographic groups: Caucasians, Black Africans, Mongoloids, South Asian Aborigines, Amerinds, Oceanians, and Australian Aborigines. He found that the great majority of genetic variation—85%—occurs *within* ethnic groups, not among them. In other words, the amount of genetic variation between individuals of the same ethnic group is greater than the variation between ethnic groups.

Bioethical Focus

The Theory of Evolution

The term "theory" in science is reserved for those ideas that scientists have found to be all-encompassing because they are based on data collected in a number of different fields. Evolution is a scientific theory. So is the cell theory, which states that all organisms are composed of cells, and so is the atomic theory, which states that all matter is composed of atoms. No one argues that schools should teach alternatives to the cell theory or the atomic theory. Yet controversy reigns over the use of the expression "the theory of evolution."

No wonder most scientists in the United States are dismayed when state legislatures or school boards rule that teachers must put forward a variety of "theories" on the origin of life, including one that runs contrary to the mass of data that supports the theory of evolution. An organization in California called the Institute for Creation Research advocates that students be taught an "intelligent-design theory," which states that DNA could never have arisen without the involvement of an "intelligent agent," and that gaps in the fossil record mean that species arose fully developed with no antecedents.

Since our country forbids the mingling of church and state—that is, no purely religious ideas can be taught in the schools—the advocates for an intelligent-design theory are careful not to mention the Bible or any strictly religious ideas (i.e., God created the world in seven days). Still, teachers who have a solid scientific background do not feel comfortable teaching an intelligent-design theory because it does not meet the test of a scientific theory. Science is based on hypotheses that have been tested by observation and/or experimentation. A scientific theory has stood the test of time—that is, no hypotheses that run contrary to the theory have been supported by observation and/or experimentation. Consistent with that definition, the theory of evolution is supported by data collected in such wide-ranging fields as development, anatomy, geology, and biochemistry.

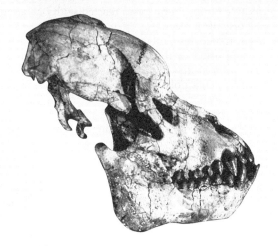

Figure 11A   *Proconsul* **skull.**
Proconsul, which may have been an intermediate form between the monkeys and the apes, shows similarities to modern humans.

Polls consistently show that nearly half of all Americans prefer to believe the Old Testament account of creation. That, of course, is their right, but should schools be required to teach an intelligent-design theory that traces its roots back to the Old Testament and is not supported by observation and experimentation?

Decide Your Opinion

1. Should teachers be required to teach an intelligent-design theory of the origin of life? Why or why not?
2. Should schools rightly teach that science is based on data collected by testing hypotheses through observation and experimentation? Why or why not?
3. Should schools be required to show that the intelligent-design theory does not meet the test of being scientific? Why or why not?

Summary

11.1 Origin of Life

A chemical evolution is believed to have produced the first cell. In the presence of an outside energy source, such as ultraviolet radiation, the primitive atmospheric gases reacted with one another to produce small organic molecules.

Next, macromolecules evolved and interacted. The RNA-first hypothesis is supported by the discovery of RNA enzymes called ribozymes. The protein-first hypothesis is supported by the observation that amino acids polymerize abiotically when exposed to dry heat. The protocell must have been a heterotrophic fermenter living on the preformed organic molecules in the ocean. Eventually, the DNA → RNA → protein self-replicating system evolved, and a true cell that could reproduce came into being.

11.2 Biological Evolution

Descent from a common ancestor explains the unity of living things—for example, why all living things have a cellular structure and a common chemistry. Adaptation to different environments explains the great diversity of living things.

Darwin discovered much evidence for common descent. The fossil record gives us the history of life in general and allows us to trace the descent of a particular group. Biogeography shows that the distribution of organisms on Earth is explainable by assuming that organisms evolved in one locale. The common anatomies and development of a group of organisms adapted to different environments are explainable by descent from a common ancestor. All organisms have similar biochemical molecules, and this supports the concept of common descent.

Darwin developed a mechanism for adaptation known as natural selection. Members of a population exhibit inherited variations and compete with one another for limited resources. The members with variations that help them survive and reproduce have more offspring, and in this way the adaptive characteristics become widespread in the next generation. The process of natural selection is nonteleological.

11.3 Humans Are Primates

The classification of humans can be used to trace their ancestry. Humans are primates, mammals adapted to living in trees. An evolutionary diagram of primates based on anatomical, molecular, and fossil evidence shows that we share a common ancestor with African apes. This common ancestor lived about 6 MYA. Researchers are trying to find environmental reasons why hominids came down out of trees and walked erect.

11.4 Evolution of Australopithecines

The first hominid (humans are in this family) was an australopithecine that lived about 3 MYA. Australopithecines could walk erect, but they had a small brain. This testifies to a mosaic evolution for humans—that is, not all of the advanced features evolved at the same time. It is uncertain which australopithecine is ancestral to early *Homo*.

11.5 Evolution of Humans

H. habilis made tools, but fossil evidence shows that *H. erectus* was the first *Homo* to have a brain size of more than 1,000 cc. *H. erectus* migrated from Africa into Europe and Asia. They used fire and may have been big-game hunters.

Whereas the multiregional continuity hypothesis suggests that modern humans evolved separately in Europe, Africa, and Asia, the out-of-Africa hypothesis says that *H. sapiens* evolved in Africa but then migrated to Asia and Europe. The Neanderthals were already living in Europe and Asia before modern humans arrived. The Neanderthals did not have the physical traits of modern humans, but they did have a culture. Cro-Magnon is a name often given to the first *H. sapiens*. Their tools were sophisticated, and they definitely had a culture, as shown by their paintings on the walls of caves.

Reviewing the Chapter

1. List and discuss the steps by which a chemical evolution could have produced a protocell. 182
2. What is a true cell? How might DNA replication have come about? 183
3. Biological evolution explains what two general observations about living things? 183
4. Show that the fossil record, biogeography, comparative anatomy, and biochemistry all give evidence of evolution. 184
5. Explain Darwin's mechanism of natural selection. How does natural selection result in adaptation to the environment? 184–85
6. In general, primates are adapted to what type of life? List and discuss several primate characteristics. 187
7. Describe an evolutionary tree. What can we learn from the primate evolutionary tree? 188
8. Describe the characteristics of australopithecines, early *Homo*, *Homo erectus*, Neanderthals, and Cro-Magnons. 189–93
9. Give evidence that human evolution resembles a bush rather than a single branch. 190
10. Which of our ancestors first walked erect? Used tools? Used fire? Drew pictures? 189–93
11. Contrast the multiregional continuity hypothesis with the out-of-Africa hypothesis. 192

Critical Thinking Questions

1. Despite the continued development of the human brain after birth, a human being has a larger head than other primates at birth. This makes birth more difficult and death of the mother and/or child more likely than otherwise. How do you explain the selection of a trait that is both positive and negative?
2. Human beings undergo both biological evolution and cultural evolution. Provide evidence for this statement from this chapter.
3. Despite having a small brain, australopithecines are considered the first hominids. Why?

Understanding Key Terms

adaptation 183
analogous structure 184
arboreal 187
australopithecine 189
biogeography 184
biological evolution 183
chemical evolution 182
Cro-Magnon 193
culture 190
eukaryotic cell 183
evolutionary tree 188
fossil 184
fossil record 184
heterotroph 182
hominid 188
Homo erectus 191
Homo habilis 190

homologous structure 184
Homo sapiens 192
lineage 188
molecular clock 188
mosaic evolution 189
multiregional continuity hypothesis 192
natural selection 184
Neanderthal 193
out-of-Africa hypothesis 192
primate 187
prokaryotic cell 183
protein-first hypothesis 182
protocell 182
RNA-first hypothesis 182
teleological 185

Chapter 12

Behavior

12.1 Genetic Basis of Behavior

The **behavior** of animals is any action that can be observed and described. *Sexual behavior* includes mating, reproducing, and caring for offspring. All forms of behavior have a genetic basis because an animal inherits the anatomy and physiology suitable to performing a behavior. Specific behaviors also have a genetic basis, as various experiments have shown.

Lovebirds are small, green and pink African parrots that nest in tree hollows. There are several closely related species of lovebirds, whose behavior differs by the way they build nests. Fischer lovebirds pick up a large leaf (or in the laboratory, a piece of paper) with their bills, perforate it with a series of bites along its length, and then cut out long strips. They carry the strips in their bills to the nest (Fig. 12.1a) and weave them in with others to make a deep cup. Peach-faced lovebirds cut somewhat shorter strips in a similar manner, but then carry them to the nest in a very unusual way. They pick up the strips in their bills and insert them deep into their rump feathers (Fig. 12.1b). In this way, they can carry several of these short strips with each trip to the nest, while Fischer lovebirds can carry only one of the longer strips at a time.

Researchers hypothesized that, if the behavior for obtaining and carrying nesting material is inherited, then hybrids might show intermediate behavior. When the two species of birds were mated, it was observed that the hybrid birds have difficulty carrying nesting materials. They cut strips of intermediate length and then attempt to tuck the strips into their rump feathers. However, they do not push the strips far enough into the feathers, and when they walk or fly, the strips always come out. After a long period of time (about three years), a hybrid learns to carry the cut strips in its beak, but still briefly turns its head toward its rump before flying off. Therefore, these studies support the hypothesis that behavior has a genetic basis.

Figure 12.1 **Nest-building behavior in lovebirds.**
a. Fischer lovebirds carry strips of nest material in their beaks, as do most other birds. **b.** Peach-faced lovebirds tuck strips of nest material into their rump feathers before flying back to the nest.

Nervous and Endocrine Systems

Genes determine the phenotype, which includes certain characteristics of the nervous system and the endocrine system. Various studies have been done to show the role of these systems in sexual behavior. For example, the egg-laying behavior in *Aplysia,* a marine snail, involves a set sequence of movements. Following copulation, the animal extrudes long strings of more than a million egg cases. The snail then takes the egg case string in its mouth, covers it with mucus, waves its head back and forth to wind the string into an irregular mass, and attaches the mass to a solid object, such as a rock. Several years ago, scientists isolated and analyzed an egg-laying hormone (ELH) that causes the snail to lay eggs even if it has not mated. ELH was found to be a small protein composed of 36 amino acids that diffuses into the circulatory system and excites the smooth muscle cells of the reproductive duct, causing them to contract and expel the egg string. Using recombinant DNA (deoxyribonucleic acid) techniques, the investigators isolated the ELH gene. The gene's product turned out to be a protein composed of 271 amino acids. The protein can be cleaved into as many as 11 possible products, and ELH is one of these. ELH alone, or in conjunction with these other products, is thought to control all the components of egg-laying behavior.

The roles of the nervous system and hormones in animal behavior are exemplified very well by a study of ringdove reproductive behavior. When male and female ringdoves are put together in a cage, the male begins courting by repeatedly bowing and cooing (Fig. 12.2). Because castrated males do not do this, it can be reasoned that the hormone testosterone readies the male for this behavior. The sight of the male courting causes the pituitary gland in the female to release FSH. Then her ovaries produce eggs and release estrogen into the bloodstream. Now both the male and the female construct a nest, during which time copulation takes place. The hormone progesterone causes birds of either sex to incubate the eggs; the hormone prolactin causes crop growth so that both parents are capable of feeding their young crop milk.

To determine whether the incubation behavior of the female is actually controlled by this sequence of events, investigators studied three experimental groups: (1) females housed alone, (2) females housed with males only, and (3) females housed with a male and nesting material. Each group of females was presented with a nest containing eggs. All females that were housed with a male and nesting material incubated eggs, but the other two groups did not. In another study, male ringdoves were allowed to court and mate with females and to participate in nest construction. After the eggs had been laid and incubation had begun, each male was placed behind a partition so that he could see his mate sitting on the eggs. Only this visual experience was then needed for the male to undergo normal crop development.

a.

b.

c.

d.

Figure 12.2 Ringdove mating behavior.
a. Male and female responding to one another.
b. Copulation takes place. **c.** Male and female create a nest. **d.** Chicks are fed crop milk.

12.2 Development of Behavior

Given that all behaviors have a genetic basis, we can go on to ask if environmental experiences after hatching or birth also shape the behavior. Some behaviors seem to be stereotyped—that is, they are performed the same way each time. These have been called fixed action patterns (FAPs), and it was originally assumed that FAPs are elicited by a sign stimulus, a cue that sets the behavior in motion. For example, human babies will smile when a flat, face-sized mask with two dark spots for eyes is brought near them. Although it's possible that some behaviors are FAPs, investigators are increasingly finding that many behaviors, formerly thought to be FAPs, develop after practice.

Laughing gull chicks' begging behavior is always performed the same way in response to the parent's red beak. A chick directs a pecking motion toward the parent's beak, grasps it, and strokes it downward (Fig. 12.3a). Sometimes a parent stimulates the begging behavior by swinging its beak gently from side to side. After the chick responds, the parent regurgitates food onto the floor of the nest. If need be, the parent then encourages the chick to eat. This interaction between the chicks and their parents suggests that the begging behavior involves learning. (**Learning** is defined as a durable change in behavior brought about by experience.) To test this hypothesis, diagrammatic pictures of gull heads were painted on small cards, and then eggs were collected in the field. The eggs were hatched in a dark incubator to eliminate visual stimuli before the test. On the day of hatching,

each chick was allowed to make about a dozen pecks at the model. The chicks were returned to the nest, and then each was retested. The tests showed that on the average, only one-third of the pecks by a newly hatched chick strike the model. But one day after hatching, more than half of the pecks are accurate, and two days after hatching, the accuracy reaches a level of more than 75%. Figure 12.3b graphs these results. Investigators concluded that improvement in motor skills, as well as visual experience, strongly affect development of chick begging behavior.

The Phenomenon of Learning

Newly hatched chicks peck equally at any model as long as it has a red beak. Chicks a week old, however, peck only at models that closely resemble the parent. Factors that could account for this change in behavior are operant conditioning with a food reward or imprinting.

Operant Conditioning and Imprinting

Operant conditioning, which is one of many forms of learning, is often defined as the gradual strengthening of stimulus-response connections. In everyday life, most people know that animals can be taught tricks by being given rewards such as food or affection. The trainer presents the stimulus, say a hoop, and then gives a reward (food) for the proper response (jumping through the hoop). B. F. Skinner is well known for studying this type of learning in the laboratory. In the simplest type of experiment performed by Skinner, a

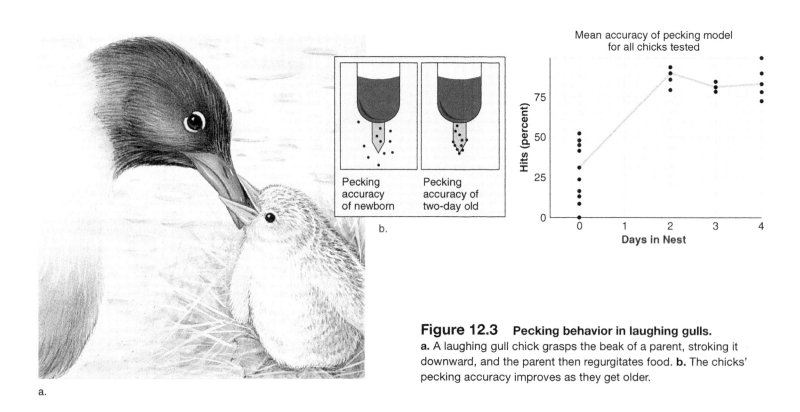

Figure 12.3   Pecking behavior in laughing gulls.
a. A laughing gull chick grasps the beak of a parent, stroking it downward, and the parent then regurgitates food. **b.** The chicks' pecking accuracy improves as they get older.

caged rat happens to press a lever and is rewarded with sugar pellets, which it avidly consumes. Thereafter, the rat regularly presses the lever whenever it is hungry. In more sophisticated experiments, Skinner even taught pigeons to play Ping-Pong by reinforcing desired responses to stimuli.

In **imprinting,** another form of learning, chicks, ducklings, and goslings will follow the first moving object they see after hatching. This object is ordinarily their mother, but they seemingly can be imprinted on any object—a human or a red ball—if it is the first moving object they see during a sensitive period of two to three days after hatching. The term *sensitive period* means that the behavior only develops during this time.

Although the Englishman Douglas Spalding first observed imprinting, the Austrian Konrad Lorenz is well known for investigating it. He found that imprinting not only served the useful purpose of keeping chicks near their mother, but it also caused male birds to court a member of the correct species—someone who looks like mother! The goslings who had been imprinted on Lorenz courted human beings later in life. In-depth studies on imprinting have shown that the process is more complicated than originally thought.

Eckhard Hess found that mallard ducklings imprinted on humans in the laboratory would switch to a female mallard that had hatched a clutch of ducklings several hours before. He found that vocalization before and after hatching was an important element in the imprinting process. Female mallards cluck during the entire time imprinting is occurring. Do social interactions influence other forms of learning? Patterns of song learning in birds suggest that they can.

Song Learning in Birds

During the past several decades, an increasing number of investigators have studied song learning in birds. White-crowned sparrows sing a species-specific song, but males of a particular region have their own dialect. Birds were caged in order to test the hypothesis that young white-crowned sparrows learn how to sing from older members of their species. Three groups of birds were tested (Fig. 12.4):

1. Birds in the first group *heard no songs at all.* When grown, these birds sang a song, but it was not fully developed.
2. Birds in the second group *heard tapes of white-crowns singing.* When grown, they sang in that dialect, as long as the tapes had been played during a sensitive period from about age 10 to 50 days. White-crowned sparrows' dialects (or other species' songs) played before or after this sensitive period had no effect on their song.
3. Birds in a third group did not hear tapes and instead were *given a social tutor.* These birds sang a song of even a different species—no matter when the tutoring began!

Neurons that are critical for song production have been located, and they fire when the bird's own song is played or when a song of the same dialect is played. Apparently, however, the brain of a bird is especially primed to respond to acoustical stimuli during a sensitive period. It would appear also that social experience has an even stronger influence on the development of singing.

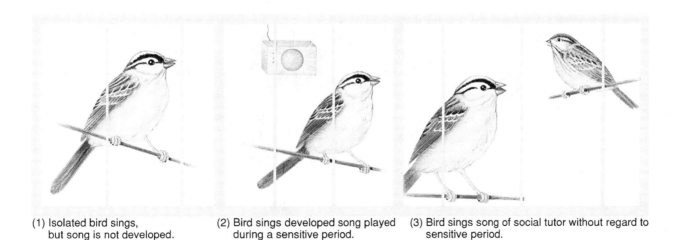

(1) Isolated bird sings, but song is not developed.
(2) Bird sings developed song played during a sensitive period.
(3) Bird sings song of social tutor without regard to sensitive period.

Figure 12.4   Song learning by white-crowned sparrows.
Three different experimental procedures are depicted, and the results noted. These results suggest both a genetic basis and a social basis for song learning in white-crowned sparrows.

Human Culture

The **culture** of a human society includes a wide spectrum of customs, from how to dress to whom to marry, as well as various rituals such as the marriage ceremony. Learning is absolutely necessary to the perpetuation of culture, which defines for us the proper modes of behavior that are both understood and passed on by all members of a society. Language and the use of tools are essential to human culture. Indeed, language is used to socialize children and to teach them how to use or make tools for various purposes. Technological skills, such as knowing how to use a computer, and knowledge of possible careers are also taught from an early age.

It is easier to trace our biological evolution than to trace our cultural evolution. However, we can assume that cultural traits do undergo evolution and that, like all behavioral traits, they have a genetic component in addition to an environmental component. In other words, those cultural traits that were the most adaptive to the environment and led to the greatest number of surviving offspring were the ones that became the norm among humans. Cultural traits that are common to a number of different societies must have arisen before those that are unique to a particular group of people. For example, incest—marriage between close relatives—is taboo in most cultures. Because incest tends to bring out recessive disorders such as albinism and hemophilia, obviously those individuals who chose not to marry close relatives were more likely to have surviving offspring than those who did.

Division of Labor Among Humans

Which of our ancestors were or were not hunters is a matter of debate among paleontologists (biologists who study fossils). Still, we can speculate that a predatory lifestyle would have encouraged the evolution of intelligence and the development of language. When people prey on animals larger than themselves (Fig. 12.5), they are required to use tools, to cooperate, and to signal one another. Cooperative hunting may help explain why the human brain became larger over time.

In any case, the human brain develops further after birth, and the human infant is born largely helpless. Consider that women are the ones who bear children, and therefore they are always certain that a child is their own. This may be why women generally invest more than men in taking care of children. But the extended dependency of children means that women have a greater need for a lasting relationship with a partner who is willing to provide the necessary resources for child rearing. Most mammalian females—but not some primates, including humans—experience estrus (heat), a regularly occurring period of sexual receptivity during which ovulation occurs and copulation takes place. Pair bonding became more likely when human females became sexually receptive all the time and ovulation was no longer a detectable event. The sexual and behavioral differences between the sexes may have led to a division of labor that did not necessarily involve child rearing. It was the task of men to bring home resources and the task of women to be homemakers.

Figure 12.5   Primitive men hunting for food.
To what degree large-game hunting contributed to the evolution of human behavior is not known. However, group hunting requires cooperation, signaling between hunters, and intelligence.

12.3 Adaptive Mating Behavior

Animals usually go through some sort of mating behavior in order to secure a mate. **Sexual selection** refers to adaptive changes in males and females that lead to an increased ability to secure a mate. Sexual selection in males often results in an increased ability to compete with other males for a mate, while it allows females the ability to better select a mate with the best fitness. **Fitness** is a measure of an organism's ability to produce fertile offspring.

In this section, we discuss sexual selection and also touch on two survival issues—capturing resources and avoiding predators—that help an animal survive, because without survival, reproduction is impossible. Investigators studying survival issues also test hypotheses that specify how a given trait might improve fitness.

Female Choice

Females produce few eggs, so the choice of a mate becomes a serious consideration. In a study of satin bowerbirds, two opposing hypotheses regarding female choice were tested:

Good genes hypothesis: Females choose mates on the basis of traits that improve the chance of survival.

Run-away hypothesis: Females choose mates on the basis of traits that improve appearance. The term "run-away" pertains to the possibility that the trait will be exaggerated in the male until its reproductively favorable benefit is checked by the trait's unfavorable survival cost.

Investigators watched a certain species of bowerbird that is blue-black in color and that also has a preference for blue objects. As they observed these birds at feeding stations and also monitored the bowers, they discovered that the more aggressive and vigorous males were able to keep their bowers in good condition despite the habit of most males to steal blue feathers and/or to actively destroy a neighbor's bower. Aggressive males were usually chosen as mates by females. It could be that aggressiveness, if inherited, does improve the chance of survival, or it could be that females simply prefer bowers with the most blue feathers. Therefore, the data do not clearly support either hypothesis. Another study involving bowerbirds is discussed in the reading on pages 204–5.

The raggiana bird of paradise is remarkably *dimorphic*, meaning that males and females differ in size and other traits. The males are larger than the females and have beautiful orange flank plumes. In contrast, the females are drab (Fig. 12.6). First, courting males gather, and then they all begin to call. (The gathering of courting males is called a lek.) If a female joins them, the males raise their orange display plumes, shake their wings, and hop from side to side, while continuing to call. They then stop calling and lean upside down, with their wings projected forward to show off their beautiful feathers.

Female choice can explain why male birds are so much more showy than females, even if we do not know which of the two hypotheses applies. It is possible that the remarkable plumes of the male signify health and vigor. Or it's possible that females choose the flamboyant males on the basis that their sons will have an increased chance of being selected by females. Some investigators have hypothesized that extravagant male features could indicate that they are relatively parasite-free. In a study of barn swallows, females also chose those with the longest tails, and investigators have shown that males that are relatively free of parasites have longer tails than otherwise.

Is a difference in reproductive behavior related to a particular food source? Raggiana birds forage far and wide for their food (nutritious, complex fruits), and lekking is one way for males to attract the wide-ranging females. The male raggiana is polygynous (has more than one mate) and does not help raise the offspring. On the other hand, a related species, the trumpet manucode, *Manucodia keraudrenit,* feeds on figs, which are more prevalent but not as nutritious as complex fruits. These birds are monogamous—the pair bonds perhaps for life—and the males are not as colorful as raggiana males. Both sexes are needed to successfully raise the young, and this relaxes pressure on the male to be showy.

male

female

Figure 12.6   Raggiana bird of paradise.
Raggiana males have resplendent plumage brought about by sexual selection. The drab females tend to choose flamboyant males as mates.

Courtship Display of Male Bowerbirds

At the start of the breeding season, male bowerbirds use small sticks and twigs to build elaborate display areas called bowers. They clear the space around the bower and decorate the area with fresh flowers, fruits, pebbles, shells, bits of glass, tinfoil, and any bright baubles they can find. The satin bowerbird, *Ptilonorhynchus violaceus*, of eastern Australia prefers blue objects, a color that harmonizes with the male's glossy blue-black plumage (Fig. 12A). Males collect blue parrot feathers, flowers, berries, ballpoint pens, clothespins, and even toothbrushes from researchers' cabins.

After the bower is complete, a male bowerbird spends most of his time near this bower, calling to females, renewing his decorations, and guarding his work against possible raids by other males. After inspecting many bowers and their owners, a female approaches one, and the male begins a display. He faces her, fluffs up his feathers, and flaps his wings to the beat of a call. The female enters the bower, and if she crouches, the two mate.

Female bowerbirds build their own nests and raise the young without help from their mates, so attractive males can mate with multiple females. The reproductive advantage gained by attractive male bowerbirds is quite large; the most attractive males may mate with up to 25 females per year, but most males mate rarely or not

Figure 12A   Male and female bowerbird.
This male bowerbird *(left)* has prepared this bower and decorated its platform with objects, particularly blue ones. A female bowerbird *(right)* has entered the bower, and the male's courtship display will now begin.

at all. As already discussed, the males most often chosen by females have well-built bowers with well-decorated platforms. In addition, it is possible that the ability of a male bowerbird to respond appropriately to the female during courtship might influence his success. I [Gail Patricelli] and my colleagues studied this interactive component of satin bowerbird mating behavior as part of my doctoral dissertation research at the University of Maryland, in collaboration with Dr. Borgia, my graduate advisor.

Male bowerbirds are not gaudy in appearance, but their displays are highly intense and aggressive. Their courting displays are similar to those used by males to intimidate each other in aggressive encounters—with males puffing their feathers, rapidly extending their wings, and running, while making a loud, buzzing vocalization. Analysis of natural courtships has shown that males must display intensely to be attractive, but males that are too intense too soon can startle females. Females may benefit from preferentially mating with the most intensely display-

ing males (for example, if these displays indicate male health or vigor), but when females are startled repeatedly by male displays, they may not be able to efficiently assess male traits. Thus, both sexes can maximize the potential benefits of intense male courtship displays—and minimize the potential costs—by communicating. Indeed, a female behavior (degree of crouching) reflects the level of display intensity that the female will tolerate without being startled. By giving higher-intensity displays only when females increase their crouching, males could increase their courtship success by displaying intensely enough to be attractive without threatening females with displays more intense than they are ready to tolerate.

With this information in mind, we specifically tested the hypothesis that males respond to female crouching signals by adjusting their intensity, and that a particular male's ability to respond to female signals is related to his success in courtship. A male's ability to modify his courtship display according to the

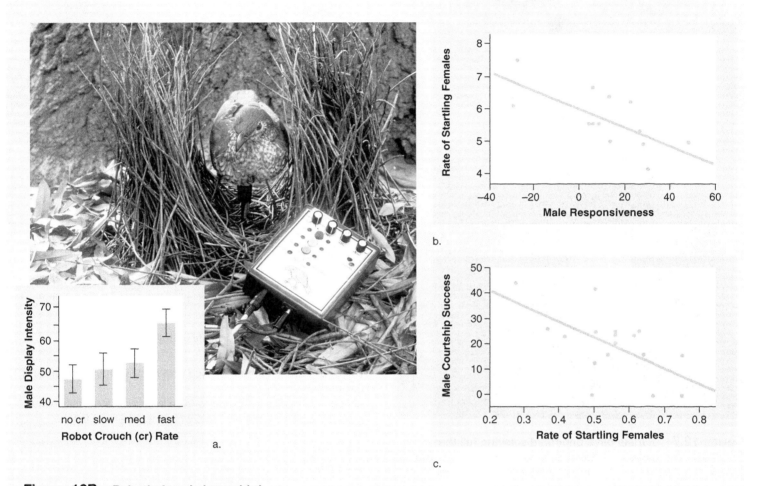

Figure 12B **Robotic female bowerbird.**
a. Robots were placed in the bower of the male being tested and controlled from a blind using the remote controller shown in the foreground. The faster the robot crouch rate, the more intense was the male display. Males that were more responsive to varying robotic signals **(b)** were less likely to startle live females and more likely to enjoy courtship success **(c).**

rapidity with which the female crouches was difficult to measure in natural courtships, since it was not clear whether males were responding to females, or vice versa. To solve this problem, we collaborated with an engineer to develop robotic female bowerbirds, which used tiny servo motors to mimic female movements (Fig. 12B*a*).

Using these "fembots," we were able to control female signals and measure male response in experimental courtships. During the bowerbird mating season at our field site in Wallaby Creek, Australia, we worked with student volunteers to test each male in our population with robots that crouched at four different rates: no crouch, slow, moderate, and fast. These experiments showed that male satin bowerbirds in general modulate their displays in response to robotic female crouching (see graph, Fig. 12B*a*). This supports the prediction that males are able to respond to female signals by giving their highest-intensity courtship displays for females who crouched the fastest and are least likely to be startled.

Utilizing automatically triggered video cameras that monitor behaviors at bowers, it was possible to measure each male's courtship/mating success with no difficulty. We found that males who modulate their displays more effectively in response

to robotic female signals startle real females less often in natural courtships (Fig. 12B*b*), and are thus more successful in courting females (Fig. 12B*c*).

Our results suggest that females prefer intensely displaying males as mates, but that successful males do not always display at maximum intensity; they modulate their intensity in response to female signals, thus producing displays attractive to females without threatening them.

Male responsiveness to female signals may be an important part of successful courtship in many species—even if males do not dance aggressively during courtship as male bowerbirds do. For instance, when females choose their mates based on bright coloration, successful males may respond to female signals by altering their position relative to the sun, their distance from the female, or the way they shake their tail when displaying their colors. So, along with extreme male traits—such as gaudy colors and aggressive dances—sexual selection may favor the ability of males to read female signals and adjust courtship displays accordingly.

Courtesy of Gail Patricelli
University of Maryland

Figure 12.7   A male olive baboon displaying full threat.
In olive baboons, males are larger than females and have enlarged canines. Competition between males establishes a dominance hierarchy for the distribution of resources.

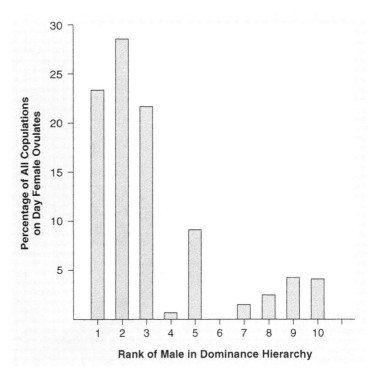

Figure 12.8   Female choice and male dominance among baboons.
Although females may appear to mate indiscriminately, they mate more often with a dominant male when they are most fertile.

Male Competition

Males can father many offspring because they continuously produce sperm in great quantity. We expect males to compete in order to inseminate as many females as possible. Studies have been done to determine if the benefit of access to mating is worth the cost of competition among males. Only if the positive effects outweigh the negative effects will a behavior continue.

Dominance Hierarchy

Baboons, a type of Old World monkey, live together in a troop. Males and females have separate **dominance hierarchies** in which a higher-ranking animal has greater access to resources than a lower-ranking animal. Dominance is decided by confrontations, resulting in one animal giving way to the other.

Baboons are dimorphic; the males are larger than the females, and they can threaten other members of the troop with their long, sharp canines (Fig. 12.7). One or more males become dominant by frightening the other males. However, the male baboon pays a cost for his dominant position.

Being larger means that he needs more food, and being willing and able to fight predators means that he may get hurt, and so forth. Is there a reproductive benefit to his behavior? Yes, in that dominant males do indeed monopolize females when they are most fertile (Fig. 12.8). Females undergo a period known as estrus, during which they ovulate and are willing to mate. At this time, a female approaches a dominant male, and they form a mating pair for several hours or days.

Nevertheless, there may be other ways to father offspring. A male may act as a helper to a female and her offspring; then, the next time she is in estrus, she may mate preferentially with him instead of a dominant male. Or subordinate males may form a friendship group that opposes a dominant male, making him give up a receptive female.

Territoriality

A **territory** is an area that is defended against competitors. Scientists are able to track an animal in the wild in order to determine its home range or territory. **Territoriality** includes the type of defensive behavior needed to defend a territory. Baboons travel within a home range, foraging for food each day and sleeping in trees at night. Dominant males decide where and when the troop will move. If the troop is threatened, dominant males protect the troop as it retreats and attack intruders when necessary. Vocalization and displays, rather than outright fighting, may be sufficient to defend a territory. In songbirds, for example, males use singing to announce their willingness to defend a territory. Other males of the species then become reluctant to use the same area.

Red deer stags (males) on the Scottish island of Rhum compete to be the harem master of a group of hinds (females) that mate only with them. The reproductive group occupies a territory that the harem master defends against other stags. Harem masters first attempt to repel challengers by roaring. If the challenger remains, the two lock antlers

and push against one another (Fig. 12.9). If the challenger then withdraws, the master pursues him for a short distance, roaring the whole time. If the challenger wins, he becomes the harem master.

A harem master can father two dozen offspring at most, because he is at the peak of his fighting ability for only a short time. And there is a cost to being a harem master. Stags must be large and powerful in order to fight; therefore, they grow faster and have less body fat. During bad times, they are more likely to die of starvation, and in general, they have shorter lives. Harem master behavior will only persist in the population if its cost (reduction in the potential number of offspring because of a shorter life) is less than its benefit (increased number of offspring due to harem access).

a.

b.

Figure 12.9 **Competition between male red deer.**
Male red deer compete for a harem within a particular territory. **a.** Roaring alone may frighten off a challenger, but **(b)** outright fighting may be necessary, and the victor is most likely the stronger of the two animals.

Mating in Humans

A study of human mating behavior shows that the concepts of female choice and male competition apply to humans as well as to the animals we have been discussing.

Human Males Compete

Consider that women necessarily must invest more in having a child than men have to invest. After all, it takes nine months to have a child, and pregnancy is followed by lactation when a woman may nurse her infant. Men, on the other hand, need only contribute sperm during a sex act that may require only a few minutes. The result is that men are generally more available for mating than are women; therefore, they usually compete for mates.

Like many other animals, humans are dimorphic. Males tend to be larger and more aggressive than females, perhaps as a result of past sexual selection by females. As in other animals also, males pay a price for their physical attractiveness to females. Male humans live on the average seven years less than females do.

Females Choose

Today, females are more likely to choose to mate with a male who is wealthy and has a successful career because they will be assured of the resources needed to raise their children (Fig. 12.10). A study in modern Quebec sampled a large number of respondents on how often they had copulated with different sexual partners in the preceding year. Male mating success correlated best with income—those males who had both wealth and status were much more successful in acquiring mates than those who lacked these attributes.

The desire of women for just certain types of men has led to the practice of polygamy in many primitive human societies and even in some modern societies. Women would rather share a husband who can provide resources than to have a one-on-one relationship with a poor man, because the resources provided by the wealthy man make it all the more certain that her children will live to reproduce. On the other hand, polygamy works for wealthy men because having more than one wife will undoubtedly increase his fitness as well. As an alternative to polygamy, modern societies stress monogamy in which the male plays a prominent role in helping to raise the children.

Men Also Have a Choice

Just as women choose men who can provide resources, men who are expected to provide resources prefer women who are most likely to present them with children. It has been shown that the "hourglass figure" so touted by men actually correlates with the best distribution of body fat for reproductive purposes! Men responding to questionnaires list attributes that biologists associate with a strong immune system, good health, high estrogen levels, and especially with youthfulness. Young males prefer partners who are their own age, give or take five years, but as men age they prefer women who are many years younger than themselves. Men can reproduce for many more years than women can. Therefore, by choosing younger women, older men increase their fitness as judged by the number of children they have.

Men, unlike women, do not have the same assurance that a child is their own. Therefore, men put a strong emphasis on having a wife who is faithful to them. Both men and women respondents to questionnaires view adultery in women as more offensive than adultery in men.

Figure 12.10   King Hussein and family.
The tendency of men to mate with fertile younger women is exemplified by King Hussein of Jordan, who was about 16 years older than his wife, Queen Noor. This photo shows some of their children.

12.4 Animal Societies

Animals exhibit a wide diversity of social behaviors. Some animals are largely solitary and join with a member of the opposite sex only for the purpose of reproduction. Others pair, bond, and cooperate in raising offspring. Still others form a **society,** in which members of species are organized in a cooperative manner, extending beyond sexual and parental behavior. We have already mentioned the social groups of baboons and red deer. Social behavior in these and other animals requires that they communicate with one another.

Communicative Behavior

Communication is an action by a sender that influences the behavior of a receiver. The communication can be purposeful, but it does not have to be. Bats send out a series of sound pulses and listen for the corresponding echoes in order to find their way through dark caves and locate food at night. Some moths have an ability to hear these sound pulses, and they begin evasive tactics when they sense that a bat is near. Are the bats purposefully communicating with the moths? No, bat sounds are simply a cue to the moths that danger is near.

Tactile Communication

Tactile communication occurs when one animal touches another. For example, gull chicks peck at the parent's beak in order to induce the parent to feed them (see Fig. 12.3). A male leopard nuzzles the female's neck to calm her and to stimulate her willingness to mate. In primates, grooming—one animal cleaning the coat and skin of another—helps cement social bonds within a group.

Honeybees use a combination of communication methods, but especially tactile ones, to impart information about the environment. When a foraging bee returns to the hive, it performs a waggle dance that indicates the distance and the direction to a food source (Fig. 12.11). As the bee moves between the two loops of a figure 8, it buzzes noisily and shakes its entire body in so-called waggles. Outside the hive, the dance is done on a horizontal surface, and the straight run indicates the direction of the food. Inside the hive, the angle of the straight run to that of the direction of gravity is the same as the angle of the food source to the sun. In other words, a 40° angle to the left of vertical means that food is 40° to the left of the sun. Bees can use the sun as a compass to located food because they have biological clocks, which allow them to compensate for the movement of the sun in the sky.

a. Waggle dance

b. Components of dance

Figure 12.11   Communication among bees.
a. Honeybees do a waggle dance to indicate in what direction food is located. **b.** If the dance is done outside the hive on a horizontal surface, the straight run of the dance will point to the food source. If the dance is done inside the hive on a vertical surface, the angle of the straightaway to that of the direction of gravity is the same as the angle of the food source to the sun.

Auditory Communication

Auditory (sound) communication has some advantages over other kinds of communication. It is faster than chemical communication, and it too is effective both night and day. Further, auditory communication can be modified not only by loudness but also by pattern, duration, and repetition. In an experiment with rats, a researcher discovered that an intruder can avoid attack by increasing the frequency with which it makes an appeasement sound.

Male crickets have calls, and male birds have songs for a number of different occasions. For example, birds may have one song for distress, another for courting, and still another for marking territories. Sailors have long heard the songs of humpback whales transmitted through the hull of a ship. But only recently has it been shown that the song has six basic themes, each with its own phrases, that can vary in length and be interspersed with sundry cries and chirps. The purpose of the song is probably sexual, serving to advertise the availability of the singer. Language is the ultimate auditory communication, but only humans have the biological ability to produce a large number of different sounds and to put them together in many different ways. Nonhuman primates have at most only 40 different vocalizations, each having a definite meaning, such as the one meaning "baby on the ground," which is uttered by a baboon when a baby baboon falls out of a tree. Although chimpanzees can be taught to use an artificial language, they never progress beyond the capability of a 2-year-old child. It has also been difficult to prove that chimps understand the concept of grammar or can use their language to reason. It still seems that humans possess a communication ability unparalleled in other animals.

Chemical Communication

Chemical signals have the advantage of being effective both night and day. The term **pheromone** designates chemical signals in low concentration that are passed between members of the same species. For example, female moths secrete chemicals from special abdominal glands, which are detected downwind by receptors on male antennae. The antennae are especially sensitive, and this ensures that only male moths of the correct species (not predators) will be able to detect them.

Cheetahs and other cats mark their territories by depositing urine, feces, and anal gland secretions at the boundaries (Fig. 12.12). Klipspringers (small antelope) use secretions from a gland below the eye to mark twigs and grasses in their territory.

Visual Communication

Visual signals are most often used by species that are active during the day (Fig. 12.13). Contests between males make use of threat postures and possibly prevent outright fighting, a behavior that might result in reduced fitness. A male baboon displaying full threat is an awesome sight that establishes his dominance and keeps peace within the baboon troop (see Fig. 12.7). Hippopotamuses perform territorial displays that include mouth opening.

The plumage of a male raggiana bird of paradise allows him to put on a spectacular courtship dance to attract a female and to give her a basis on which to select a mate (see Fig. 12.6). Defense and courtship displays are exaggerated and always performed in the same way so that their meaning is clear.

Figure 12.12   **Use of a pheromone.**
This male cheetah is spraying a pheromone onto a tree in order to mark his territory.

Figure 12.13   **A chimpanzee with a researcher.**
Chimpanzees are unable to speak but can learn to use a visual language consisting of symbols. Some researchers believe chimps only mimic their teachers and never understand the cognitive use of language. Here the experimenter shows Nim the sign for "drink." Nim copies.

12.5 Sociobiology and Animal Behavior

Sociobiology applies the principles of evolutionary biology to the study of social behavior in animals, including humans. Among other hypotheses, sociobiologists test whether the reproductive benefit of living in a society is greater than the reproductive cost. Then they perform a cost-benefit analysis to see if this hypothesis is supported.

Group living does have its benefits. It can help an animal avoid predators, rear offspring, and find food. A group of impalas is more likely to hear an approaching predator than a solitary one. Many fish moving rapidly in many directions might distract a would-be predator. Pair bonding of trumpet manucodes helps the birds raise their young. Due to their particular food source, the female cannot rear as many offspring alone as she can with the male's help. Weaver birds form giant colonies that help protect them from predators, but the birds may also share information about food sources. Primate members of the same troop signal to one another when they have found an especially bountiful fruit tree. Lions working together are able to capture large prey, such as zebras and buffalo.

Group living also has its disadvantages. When animals are crowded together into a small area, disputes can arise over access to the best feeding places and sleeping sites. Dominance hierarchies are one way to apportion resources, but this puts subordinates at a disadvantage. Among red deer, the ability of a hind to rear sons is dependent on her dominance. Only large, dominant females can successfully rear sons; small, subordinate females tend to rear daughters. From an evolutionary point of view, sons are preferable because, as a harem master, a son will produce a greater number of grandchildren. However, sons, which tend to be larger than daughters, need to be nursed more frequently and for a longer period of time. Subordinate females do not have access to enough food resources to adequately nurse sons, and therefore they tend to rear daughters. Still, like the subordinate males in a baboon troop, subordinate females in a red deer harem may be better off in terms of fitness if they stay with a group, despite the cost involved.

Living in close quarters means that illness and parasites can pass from one animal to another more rapidly. Baboons and other types of social primates invest much time in grooming one another, and this most likely helps them remain healthy.

Altruism Versus Self-Interest

Altruism is behavior that has the potential to decrease the lifetime reproductive success of the altruist while benefiting the reproductive success of another member of the society. In insect societies especially, reproduction is limited to only one pair, the queen and her mate. For example, among army ants, the queen is inseminated only during her nuptial flight, and thereafter she spends her time reproducing. The society has three different sizes of sterile female workers. The smallest workers (3 mm), called the nurses, take care of the queen and larvae, feeding them and keeping them clean. The intermediate-sized workers, constituting most of the population, go out on raids to collect food. The soldiers (14 mm), with huge heads and powerful jaws, run along the sides and rear of raiding parties where they can best attack any intruders.

Can the altruistic behavior of sterile workers be explained in terms of fitness, which is judged by reproductive success? Genes are passed from one generation to the next in two quite different ways. The first way is direct: A parent can pass a gene directly to an offspring. The second way is indirect: A relative that reproduces can pass the gene to the next generation. *Direct selection* is adaptation to the environment due to the reproductive success of an individual. *Indirect selection* is adaptation to the environment due to the reproductive success of the individual's relatives. The **inclusive fitness** of an individual includes personal reproductive success and the reproductive success of relatives.

Among social bees, social wasps, and ants, the queen is diploid, but her mate is haploid. If the queen has had only one mate, sister workers are more closely related to each other (sharing on average 75% of their genes) than they are to their potential offspring (with which they would share on average only 50% of their genes). Therefore, a worker can achieve a greater inclusive fitness benefit by helping her mother (the queen) produce additional sisters than by directly reproducing herself. Under these circumstances, behavior that appears altruistic is more likely to evolve.

Indirect selection can also occur among animals whose offspring receive only a half set of genes from both parents. Consider that your brother or sister shares 50% of your genes, your niece or nephew shares 25%, and so forth. This means that the survival of two nieces (or nephews) is worth the survival of one sibling, assuming they both go on to reproduce.

Among chimpanzees in Africa, a female in estrus frequently copulates with several members of the same group, and the males make no attempt to interfere with each other's matings. How can they be acting in their own self-interest? Genetic relatedness appears to underlie their apparent altruism; members of a group share more than 50% of their genes in common because members never leave the territory in which they are born.

Figure 12.14   **Inclusive fitness.**
A meerkat is acting as a baby-sitter for its young sisters and brothers while their mother is away. Could this helpful behavior contribute to the baby-sitter's inclusive fitness?

Helpers at the Nest

In some bird species, offspring from one clutch of eggs may stay at the nest, helping parents rear the next batch of offspring. In a study of Florida scrub jays, the number of fledglings produced by an adult pair doubled when they had helpers. Mammalian offspring are also observed to help their parents (Fig. 12.14). Among jackals in Africa, pairs alone managed to rear an average of 1.4 pups, whereas pairs with helpers reared 3.6 pups.

Is the reproductive success of the helpers increased by their apparent altruistic behavior? This could be the case if the chance of their reproducing on their own is limited. David and Sandra Ligon studied the breeding behavior of green wood-hoopoes (*Phoeniculus purpurens*), an insect-eating bird of Africa. A flock may have as many as 16 members but only one breeding pair; the other sexually mature members help feed and protect the fledglings and protect the home territory from invasion by other green wood-hoopoes. The Ligons found that nest sites are rare, since acacia trees with cavities are relatively rare and the cavities are

often occupied by other species. Moreover, predation by snakes within the cavities can be intense; even if a pair of birds were to acquire an appropriate cavity, they would be unable to protect their offspring by themselves. Therefore, the cost of trying to establish a territory is clearly very high.

What are the benefits of staying behind to help? First, a helper is contributing to the survival of its own kin. Therefore, the helper actually gains a fitness benefit (albeit a smaller benefit than it would achieve were it a breeder). Second, a helper is more likely than a nonhelper to inherit a parental territory—including other helpers. Helping, then, involves making a minimal, short-term reproductive sacrifice in order to maximize future reproductive potential. Once again, an apparently altruistic behavior turns out to be an adaptation.

Application to Humans

Sociobiologists interpret human behavior according to these same principles. Human infants are born helpless and have a much better chance of developing properly if both parents contribute to the effort. Perhaps this explains why the human female has evolved to be continuously amenable to sexual intercourse. Under these circumstances, the male is more likely to remain and help care for offspring. In any case, parental love is clearly selfish in that it promotes the likelihood that an individual's genes will be present in the next generation's gene pool.

Studies of other human cultures lend themselves to sociobiological interpretations. For example, among African tribes, one man may have several wives. This is reproductively advantageous to the male, but it is also advantageous to the woman. By this arrangement, she has more surviving children because they are assured of a more nutritious diet. If she married a monogamous man too poor to support her offspring to adulthood, she would end up with fewer surviving children. In Africa, sources of protein are scarce, and early weaning poses a threat to the health of the child. In contrast, among the Bihari hill people of India, brothers have the same wife. There the environment is hostile, and it takes two men to provide the everyday necessities for one family. Since the men are brothers, they are actually helping each other look after common genes.

Some people object to an interpretation of human behavior based on evolutionary fitness, preferring to stress that humans have the ability to control their behavior, and that therefore it need not be determined by relatedness to others. And it is certainly possible to find examples that do not support the principles of sociobiology, as when people adopt and care for children who are not related to them.

Bioethical Focus

Animals in Zoos

Is it ethical to keep animals in zoos where they are not free to behave as they do in the wild? If we keep animals in zoos, are we depriving them of their freedom? Some people point out that freedom is never absolute. Even an animal in the wild is restricted in various ways by its abiotic and biotic environment. The so-called five freedoms are to be free of starvation, cold, injury, and fear, and to be free to wander and express one's natural behavior. Perhaps it's worth giving up a bit of that last freedom to achieve the first four? Many modern zoos keep animals in habitats that nearly match their natural one so that they do have some freedom to roam and behave naturally. Perhaps, too, we should consider the education and enjoyment of the many thousands of human visitors to a zoo compared to the loss of freedom to a much smaller number of animals kept in a zoo.

Today, reputable zoos rarely go out and capture animals in the wild—they usually get their animals from other zoos. Most people feel it is never a good idea to take animals from the wild except for very serious reasons. Certainly, zoos should not be involved in the commercial and often illegal trade in wild animals that still goes on today. When animals are captured, it should be done by skilled biologists or naturalists who know how to care for and transport the animal.

Many zoos today are involved in the conservation of animals. They provide the best home possible while the animals are recovering from injury or until their numbers are increased so that they can be released to the wild. Perhaps we can look upon zoos favorably if they show that they are keeping their animals under good conditions, and that they are also involved in preserving animals.

Figure 12C A chimpanzee and offspring.
Do chimpanzees feel motherly love, as this photograph seems to suggest?

Decide Your Opinion

1. Do you think it is ethical to keep animals in zoos? Under particular circumstances? Explain.
2. Do the animals that are descended from zoo animals have the right to be protected as their parents were? Why or why not?
3. Do the same concerns about zoos also apply to aquariums? Why or why not?

Summary

12.1 Genetic Basis of Behavior
Hybrid studies with lovebirds produce results consistent with the hypothesis that behavior has a genetic basis. DNA studies in a marine snail indicate that the endocrine system directly controls the egg-laying behavior of this animal. The roles of the nervous system and endocrine system are exemplified by a study of ringdove reproductive behavior.

12.2 Development of Behavior
The environment influences the development of behavioral responses, as exemplified by an improvement in laughing gull chick begging behavior and an increased ability of chicks to recognize their parents. Modern studies suggest that most behaviors improve with experience. Even behaviors formerly thought to be fixed action patterns (FAPs) or otherwise inflexible can sometimes be modified.

Song learning in birds involves various elements—including the existence of a sensitive period during which an animal is primed to learn—and the effect of social interactions.

Humans learn types of behavior that are appropriate to their culture. A hunting way of life may have led to a division of labor between the sexes.

12.3 Adaptive Mating Behavior
Traits that promote reproductive success are expected to be advantageous overall, despite any possible disadvantage. Males who produce many sperm are expected to compete to inseminate females. Females who produce few eggs are expected to be selective about their mates. Experiments with satin bowerbirds and birds of paradise support these bases for sexual selection.

The raggiana bird of paradise males gather in a lek—most likely because females are widely scattered, as is their customary food source. The food source for a related species, the trumpet manucode, is readily available but less nutritious. These birds are monogamous, and it takes two parents to rear the young.

A cost-benefit analysis can be applied to competition between males for mates in reference to a dominance hierarchy (e.g., baboons) and territoriality (e.g., red deer).

Male competition and female choice also guide human sexual behavior. Men are constantly available for reproduction, but women are not. This leads to competition between males for women to reproduce with. Because females invest so much time and energy in raising children, they prefer men who can provide the necessary resources. In turn, men want women who can reproduce and will stay faithful to them.

12.4 Animal Societies
Animals that form social groups communicate with one another. Chemical, auditory, visual, and tactile signals foster cooperation that benefits both the sender and the receiver.

There are both benefits and costs to living in a social group. If animals live in a social group, it is expected that the advantages (e.g., help to avoid predators, raise young, and find food) will outweigh the disadvantages (e.g., tension between members, spread of illness and parasites, and reduced reproductive potential). This expectation can sometimes be tested.

12.5 Sociobiology and Animal Behavior
In most instances, the individuals of a society act to increase their own reproductive success. Sometimes animals perform altruistic acts, as when individuals help their parents rear siblings. Social insects help their mother reproduce, but this behavior seems reasonable when we consider that siblings share 75% of their genes. Among mammals, a parental helper may be likely to inherit the parent's territory.

These examples of altruistic behavior show that it has a benefit in terms of inclusive fitness, which involves both direct selection and indirect selection.

These principles also apply to human societies, which may vary according to the environmental circumstances.

Reviewing the Chapter

1. Describe an experiment with lovebirds, and explain how it shows that behavior has a genetic basis. 198
2. Studies of *Aplysia* DNA show that the endocrine system is involved in behavior. Explain. 199
3. Describe the roles of the nervous system and the endocrine system in the reproductive behavior of ringdoves. 199
4. Some behaviors require practice before developing completely. How does the experiment with laughing gull chicks support this statement? 200
5. An argument can be made that social contact is an important element in learning. Explain this with reference to imprinting in mallard ducks and song learning in white-crowned sparrows. 200–201
6. What type of behavior may have led to the beginning of human culture? How might it have influenced human behavior? 202
7. Why would you expect mating behavior to be adaptive and subject to natural selection? 203

8. Reproductive behavior sometimes seems tied to how an animal acquires food. Explain with reference to the raggiana bird of paradise and the trumpet manucode discussed in this chapter. 203
9. Explain how the anatomy and behavior of dominant male baboons is both a benefit and a drawback. 206
10. How have male competition and female choice influenced human mating behavior? 208
11. Give examples of the different types of communication among members of a social group. 209–10
12. What is a cost-benefit analysis, and how does it apply to living in a social group? Give examples. 211
13. How can altruism be explained on the basis of self-interest? 211–12
14. Explain the variation in mating systems in human societies on the basis of sociobiology. 212

Critical Thinking Questions

1. You are testing the hypothesis that human infants instinctively respond to higher-pitched voices. Your design is to record head turns toward speakers placed on opposite sides of a month-old infant. The speakers would play voices (all making the same noises) in different pitches, and you would see if the infants turned toward some voices more often than others. Criticize the methodology
2. Meerkats sometimes act as sentries. Sentries stand on rocks or other high places and serve as lookouts while others feed. However, sentries are the first ones to reach safety when a predator is spotted, and sentries only serve after they have eaten. Should the behavior of sentries be considered altruistic?

Understanding Key Terms

altruism 211
behavior 198
communication 209
culture 202
dominance hierarchy 206
fitness 203
imprinting 201
inclusive fitness 211

learning 200
operant conditioning 200
pheromone 210
sexual selection 203
society 209
sociobiology 211
territoriality 206
territory 206

Chapter **13**

Population Concerns

13.1 Human Population Growth

The world's human population has risen steadily (Fig. 13.1). Prior to 1750, the growth of the human population was relatively slow, but as more reproducing individuals were added, growth increased, until the curve began to slope steeply upward, indicating that the population was undergoing **exponential growth.** The number of people added annually to the world population peaked at about 87 million around 1990, and currently it is a little over 79 million per year. That is roughly the population of Germany, the Philippines, or Vietnam.

The **growth rate** of a population is determined by considering the difference between the number of persons born per year (birthrate, or natality) and the number of persons who die per year (death rate, or mortality). It is customary to

record these rates per 1,000 persons. For example, the world at the present time has a birthrate of 22 per 1,000 per year, but it has a death rate of 9 per 1,000 per year. This means that the world's population growth, or simply its growth rate, is

$$\frac{22 - 9}{1,000} = \frac{13}{1,000} = 0.013 \times 100 = 1.3\%$$

(Notice that while the birthrate and death rate are expressed in terms of 1,000 persons, the growth rate is expressed per 100 persons, or as a percentage.) After 1750, the world population growth rate steadily increased, until it peaked at 2% in 1965. It has fallen since to its present 1.3%. Yet, the world population is still steadily growing because of its past exponential growth.

In the wild, exponential growth indicates that a population is enjoying its **biotic potential**—that is, the maximum growth rate under ideal conditions. Growth begins to decline because of **environmental resistance,** which includes limiting factors such as food and space. Finally, the population levels off at the carrying capacity. The **carrying capacity** is the maximum population that the environment can support for an indefinite period. The carrying capacity of the Earth for humans has not been determined. Some authorities think the Earth is potentially capable of supporting 50 to 100 billion people. Others think we already have more humans than the Earth can adequately support.

The MDCs Versus the LDCs

The countries of the world today can be divided into two groups. The *more-developed countries (MDCs)*, typified by countries in North America and Europe, are those in which population growth is modest and the people enjoy a good standard of living. The *less-developed countries (LDCs)*, typified by some countries in Asia, Africa, and Latin America, are those in which population growth is dramatic and the majority of people live in poverty.

The MDCs

The MDCs did not always have low population increases. Between 1850 and 1950, they doubled their populations, largely because of a decline in the death rate due to development of modern medicine and improved socioeconomic conditions. The decline in the death rate was followed shortly thereafter

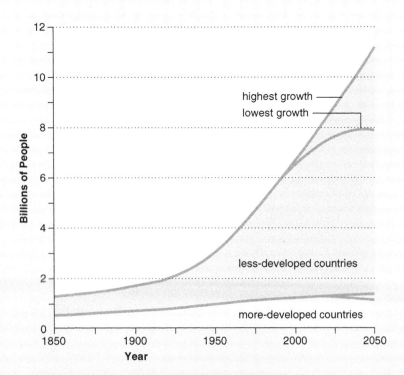

Figure 13.1 **Human population growth.**
It is predicted that the world's population size may level off at 8 billion or increase to as much as 11 billion by 2050, depending on the speed with which the growth rate declines.

by a decline in the birthrate, so that populations in the MDCs have experienced only modest growth since 1950.

The growth rate for the MDCs as a whole is now about 0.1%, but several are not growing at all or are actually decreasing in size. The MDCs are expected to increase by 52 million between 2002 and 2050, but this amount will still keep their total population at just about 1.2 billion. In contrast to these MDCs, there is no leveling off and no end in sight to U.S. population growth. The United States has a growth rate of 0.6%, and many people immigrate to this country each year. In addition, a baby boom between 1947 and 1964 means that a large number of U.S. women are still of reproductive age.

The LDCs

The death rate began to decline steeply in the LDCs following World War II with the introduction of modern medicine, but the birthrate remained high. The growth rate of the LDCs peaked at 2.5% between 1960 and 1965. Since that time, the collective growth rate for the LDCs has declined to 1.6%, but some 46 countries have not participated in this decline. Thirty-five of these countries are in sub-Saharan Africa, where women on the average are presently having more than five children each.

The LDCs are experiencing a population momentum because they have more women entering the reproductive years than older women leaving them. Between 2002 and 2050, the population of the LDCs may jump from 5 billion to at least 8 billion. Some of this increase will occur in Africa, but most will occur in Asia because the many deaths from AIDS are slowing the growth of the African population. Asia already has 56% of the world's population living on 31% of its arable (farmable) land. Therefore, Asia is expected to experience acute water scarcity, a significant loss of biodiversity, and more urban pollution. Twelve of the world's 15 most polluted cities are in Asia.

Comparing Age Structure

Populations have three age groups: dependent, reproductive, and postreproductive. This is best visualized by plotting the proportion of individuals in each group on a bar graph, thereby producing an age-structure diagram (Fig. 13.2).

Most MDCs—not including the United States—have a stabilized age-structure diagram. Therefore, their populations are expected to remain just about the same or decline if couples are having fewer than two children each.

Laypeople are sometimes under the impression that if each couple has two children, zero population growth will take place immediately. However, **replacement reproduction,** as this practice is called, will still cause most LDCs today to have a positive growth rate due to the age structure of the population. Because there are more young women entering the reproductive years than there are older women leaving them, the population continues to increase.

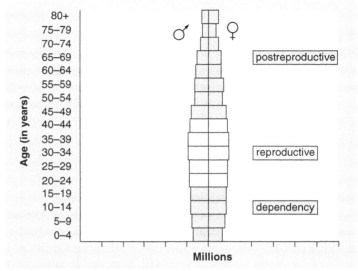

a. More-developed countries (MDCs)

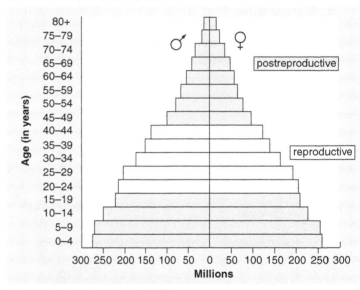

b. Less-developed countries (LDCs)

c.

Figure 13.2   Age-structure diagrams (1998).
The shapes of these age-structure diagrams allow us to predict that **(a)** the populations of MDCs are approaching stabilization, and **(b)** the populations of LDCs will continue to increase for some time. **c.** Improved women's rights and increasing use of contraceptives could change this scenario. Here a community health worker is instructing some women of Bangladesh about the use of contraceptives.

13.2 Resources and Pollution

A **resource** is anything needed from the biotic or abiotic environment for human life and civilization. Land, water, food, energy, and minerals are the maximally used resources that will be discussed in this chapter.

Some resources are nonrenewable, and others are renewable. **Nonrenewable resources** are limited in supply. For example, the amount of land, fossil fuels, and minerals is finite and can be exhausted. Better extraction methods can make more fossil fuels and minerals available. Efficient use, recycling, or substitution can make the supply last longer, but eventually these resources will run out.

Renewable resources are not limited in supply. We can use water and certain forms of energy (e.g., solar energy) or harvest plants and animals for food, and more supply will always be forthcoming. Even with renewable resources, though, we have to be careful not to squander them. Consider, for example, that most species have population thresholds below which they cannot recover, as when the huge herds of buffalo that once roamed the plains of the United States disappeared after being overexploited.

Unfortunately, a side effect of resource consumption can be pollution. **Pollution** is any alteration of the environment in an undesirable way. Pollution is often caused by human activities. The impact of humans on the environment is proportional to the size of the population. As the population grows, so do the need for resources and the amount of pollution caused by using these resources. Consider that six people adding waste to the ocean may not be alarming, but six billion people doing so would certainly affect its cleanliness. Actually, in modern times, the consumption of mineral and energy resources has grown faster than population size, most likely because people in the LDCs have increased their use of them.

Land

People need a place to live. Worldwide, there are currently more than 32 persons for each square kilometer (83 persons per square mile) of all available land, including Antarctica, mountain ranges, jungles, and deserts. Naturally, land is also needed for a variety of uses aside from homes, such as agriculture, electric power plants, manufacturing plants, highways, hospitals, and schools.

Beaches and Human Habitation

At least 40% of the world population lives within 100 km (60 mi) of a coastline, and this number is expected to increase. In the United States today, over one-half of the population lives within 80 km (50 mi) of the coasts (including the Great Lakes). Living right on the coast is an unfortunate choice because it leads to beach erosion and loss of habitat for marine organisms.

Beach Erosion An estimated 70% of the world's beaches are eroding; Figure 13.3 shows how extensive the problem is in the United States. The seas have been rising for the past 12,000 years, ever since the climate turned warmer after the last Ice Age! Authorities are concerned that global warming, discussed later in this chapter (see page 224) is also contributing to the melting of ice caps and glaciers and therefore to an increase in sea level.

Humans carry on other activities that divert more water to the oceans, and this contributes to the seas rising and beach erosion. For example, humans have filled in coastal wetlands, such as mangrove swamps in the southern United States and saltwater marshes in the northern United States. With growing recognition of the services provided by wetlands, the tide of wetland loss has been stemmed in the United States during the past 40 years, but it is just starting in South America, where a project to straighten the Parana River will drain the world's largest wetland. One reason to protect coastal wetlands is that they are spawning areas for fish and other forms of marine life. They are also habitats for certain terrestrial species, including many types of birds.

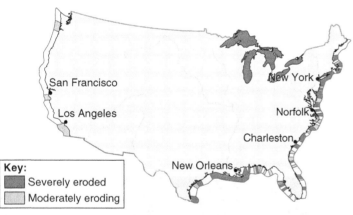

a.

b.

Figure 13.3 **Beach erosion.**
a. The map shows that most of the U.S. coastline is subject to beach erosion. **b.** Therefore, people who choose to live near the coast may eventually lose their homes.

Humans often try to stabilize beaches by building groins (structures that extend from the beach into the water) and seawalls. Groins trap sand on one side, but erosion is worse on the other side. Seawalls, in the end, also increase erosion because ocean waves remove sand from in front of and to the side of the seawalls. Importing sand is a better solution, but it is very costly and can disturb plant and animal populations. It's estimated that today the U.S. shoreline loses 40% more sediment than it receives, especially because the building of dams prevents sediment from reaching the coast.

Coastal Pollution   The coast is particularly subject to pollution because toxic substances placed in freshwater lakes, rivers, and streams may eventually find their way to the coast. Oil spills at sea cause localized harmful effects also.

Semiarid Lands and Human Habitation

Forty percent of the Earth's lands are already deserts, and land adjacent to a desert is in danger of becoming unable to support human life if it is improperly managed by humans (Fig. 13.4). **Desertification** is the conversion of semiarid land to desertlike conditions.

Quite often, desertification begins when humans allow animals to overgraze the land. The soil can no longer hold rainwater, and it runs off instead of keeping the remaining plants alive or recharging wells. Humans then remove whatever vegetation they can find to use as fuel or fodder for their animals. The result is a lifeless desert, which is then abandoned as people move on to continue the process someplace else. Some estimate that nearly three-quarters of all rangelands worldwide are in danger of desertification. The recent famine in Ethiopia was due at least in part to degradation of the land to the point that it can no longer support human beings and their livestock.

Tropical Rain Forests and Human Habitation

Deforestation, the removal of trees, has long allowed humans to live in areas where forests once covered the land. The concern of late has been that people are settling in tropical rain forests, such as the Amazon, following the building of roads (Fig. 13.5). This land, too, is subject to desertification. Soil in the tropics is often thin and nutrient-poor because all the nutrients are tied up in the trees and other vegetation. When the trees are felled and the land is used for agriculture or grazing, it quickly loses its fertility and becomes subject to desertification.

a.

b.

Figure 13.4   Desertification.
a. Desertification is a worldwide occurrence that **(b)** reduces the amount of land suitable for human habitation.

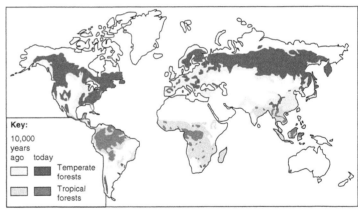

a.

b.

Figure 13.5   Deforestation.
a. Nearly half of the world's forest lands have been cleared for farming, logging, and urbanization. **b.** The soil of tropical rain forests is not suitable for long-term farming.

Water

The surface of our planet is 70% water. Most of this is seawater, of course, and only about 3% is fresh water. Most of the fresh water is tied up in ice caps, ice sheets, and glaciers. Less than 1% of fresh water is readily available, mainly in lakes and rivers, and the remainder (30%) is groundwater, which can be withdrawn (Table 13.1).

Freshwater resources differ among major areas of the globe and even within these areas (Fig. 13.6). In the water-poor areas of the world, some people do not have ready access to drinking water, and if they do, the water may be impure. It's estimated that 1.2 billion people worldwide drink impure water. More than 5 million people die each year from water-related diseases such as cholera and dysentery. In addition, pesticides and fertilizers taint waters in agricultural areas.

It's considered a human right for people to have clean drinking water, but actually most fresh water is utilized by industry and agriculture (Fig 13.7). Worldwide, 70% of all fresh water is used to irrigate crops! Consider that water demand in 1995 was six times that of 1900, even though the global population only tripled during the same period.

Much of the surge in demand stems from increased industrial activity and irrigation-intensive agriculture, the type of agriculture that now supplies about 40% of the world's food crops. Domestically in the MDCs, more water is usually used for bathing, flushing toilets, and watering lawns than for drinking and cooking.

Increasing Water Supplies

The readily available sources of water—primarily rivers and lakes—are renewable supplies. In the water cycle, evaporation from bodies of water and land leads to precipitation that, when adequate, refills lakes and rivers. Although the needs of the human population overall do not exceed the renewable supply, this is not the case in certain regions of the United States and the world. As illustrated in Figure 13.4, about 40% of the world's land is desert, and deserts are bordered by semiarid land. When needed, humans increase the supply of fresh water by damming rivers and withdrawing water from aquifers.

Dams   The world's 45,000 large dams catch 14% of all precipitation runoff, provide water for up to 40% of irrigated land, and give some 65 countries more than half their electricity. Damming of certain rivers has been so extensive that they no longer flow as they once did. The Yellow River in China fails to reach the sea most years; the Colorado River

Table 13.1	Water Resources
Salt water (e.g., oceans)	96.5% of Earth's water
Fresh water	3.5% of Earth's water
Ice and snow	Nearly 70%
Groundwater (e.g., aquifers)	Nearly 30%
Lakes and rivers	Less than 1%

	Fresh Water (cubic meters)
Oceania	53,711
South America	36,988
Middle Africa	20,899
North America	16,801
Eastern Europe	14,818
	Regions with most fresh water
Western Europe	2,215
Western Asia	1,771
South-Central Asia	1,465
Southern Africa	1,289
Northern Africa	495
	Regions with least fresh water

Figure 13.6   Freshwater resources.
Countries and regions within continents differ in the amount of fresh water available. The amounts given here are average annual cubic meters per capita.

a. Agriculture uses most of the freshwater consumed.

b. Industrial use of water is about half that of agricultural use.

c. Domestic use of water is about half that of industrial use.

Figure 13.7   Global water use.
a. Agriculture primarily uses water for irrigation. **b.** Industry uses water in various ways. **c.** Households use water to drink, shower, flush toilets, and water lawns.

barely makes it to the Gulf of California; and even the Rio Grande dries up before it can merge with the Gulf of Mexico. The Nile in Egypt and the Ganges in India are also so over-exploited that at some times of the year, they hardly make it to the ocean.

Dams have other drawbacks: (1) They lose water due to evaporation and seepage into underlying rock beds. The amount of water lost sometimes equals the amount they made available! (2) The salt left behind by evaporation and agricultural runoff increases salinity and can make a river's water unusable farther downstream. (3) Dams hold back less water with time because of sediment buildup. Some-times a reservoir becomes so full of silt that it is no longer useful for storing water.

Aquifers   To meet their freshwater needs, people are pump-ing vast amounts of water from **aquifers,** which are reser-voirs just below or as much as 1 km below the surface. This water accumulates from rain that fell in far-off regions even hundreds of thousands of years ago. Aquifers hold about 1,000 times the amount of water that falls on land as precip-itation each year. Deep aquifers are slow to recharge, and therefore their reservoirs are essentially a nonrenewable re-source that is being mined. In the past 50 years, ground-water depletion has become a problem in many areas of the world. In substantial portions of the High Plains Aquifer, which stretches from South Dakota to the Texas Panhandle, more than half of the water has been pumped out. In the 1950s, India had 100,000 motorized pumps in operation; today, India has 20 million pumps, a huge increase in groundwater pumping.

Environmental Consequences   Removal of water is caus-ing **land subsidence,** a settling of the soil as it dries out. In California's San Joaquin valley, an area of more than 13,000 square km has subsided at least 30 cm due to groundwater depletion, and in the worst spot, the surface of the ground has dropped more than 9 m! In some parts of Gujarat, India, the water table has dropped as much as 7 m. Subsidence damages canals, buildings, and underground pipes. With-drawal of groundwater can cause **sinkholes,** in which an underground cavern collapses when water no longer holds up its roof. Sinkholes that develop quickly can cause trees, houses, and cars to drop out of sight with no warning into a crater that may be hundreds of meters wide.

Saltwater intrusion is another consequence of aquifer depletion. The flow of water from streams and aquifers usu-ally keeps them fairly free of seawater. But as water is with-drawn, the water table can lower to the point that seawater backs up into streams and aquifers. Saltwater intrusion reduces the supply of fresh water along the coast.

Conservation of Water

By 2025, two-thirds of the world's population may be living in countries that are facing serious water shortages. Figure 13.8 offers some solutions for conserving water and expand-ing water supplies. Planting drought- and salt-tolerant crops would help a lot. Using drip irrigation delivers more water to crops and saves about 50% over traditional methods while increasing crop yields as well. Although the first drip systems were developed in 1960, they are only being used on less that 1% of irrigated land. Most governments subsi-dize irrigation so heavily that farmers have little incentive to invest in drip systems or other water-saving methods. Reusing water and adopting conservation measures could help the world's industries cut their water demands by more than half.

a. Drought-resistant plants

b. Drip irrigation

tubing

drop of water

c. Wastewater (not sewage) treatment plant

Figure 13.8   Conservation measures to save water.
a. Planting drought-resistant crops in the field and drought-resistant plants in parks and gardens cuts down on the need to irrigate. **b.** When irrigation is necessary, drip irrigation is preferable to using sprinklers. **c.** Wastewater can be treated and reused instead of withdrawing more water from a river or aquifer.

Food

The world food supply has been able to expand as population has increased. With 6 billion people on Earth, the world food supply provides more than 2,500 calories per person per day. Generally speaking, food comes from three activities: growing crops, raising animals, and fishing the seas. The increase in the food supply has largely been possible because of modern farming methods, which unfortunately include some harmful practices:

1. **Planting of a few genetic varieties.** The majority of farmers specialize in growing only one variety of a crop. For example, a wheat farmer plants the same type of wheat, and a corn farmer plants the same type of corn. Unfortunately, this so-called monoculture means that a single type of parasite can cause much devastation.
2. **Heavy use of fertilizers, pesticides, and herbicides.** Fertilizer production is energy-intensive, and fertilizer runoff contributes to water pollution. Pesticides reduce soil fertility because they kill off beneficial soil organisms as well as pests, and some pesticides are linked to the development of cancer.
3. **Generous irrigation.** As already discussed, water is sometimes taken from aquifers whose water content may in the future become so reduced that it could be too expensive to pump out any more.
4. **Excessive fuel consumption.** Irrigation pumps remove water from aquifers, and large farming machines are used to spread fertilizers, pesticides, and herbicides, as well as to sow and harvest the crops. In effect, modern farming methods transform fossil fuel energy into food energy.

Figure 13.9 shows ways to minimize the harmful effects of modern farming practices.

Soil Loss and Degradation

Land suitable for farming and grazing animals is being degraded worldwide. Topsoil, the topmost portion of the soil, is the richest in organic matter and the most capable of supporting grass and crops. When bare soil is acted on by water and wind, soil erosion occurs and topsoil is lost. As a result, marginal rangeland becomes desertized, and farmland loses its productivity.

The custom of planting the same crop in straight rows that facilitate the use of large farming machines has caused the United States and Canada to have one of the highest rates of soil erosion in the world. Conserving the nutrients now being lost could save farmers $20 billion annually in fertilizer costs. Much of the eroded sediment ends up in lakes and streams, where it reduces the ability of aquatic species to survive.

Another side effect of modern farming practices is **salinization,** an accumulation of mineral salts on the land due to the evaporation of excess irrigation water. Salinization also makes the land unsuitable for growing crops. Between 25% and 35% of the irrigated western croplands are thought to have excessive salinity.

The Green Revolution

About 50 years ago, research scientists began to breed tropical wheat and rice varieties specifically for farmers in the LDCs. The dramatic increase in yield resulting from the introduction of these new varieties around the world was called "the green revolution." These plants helped the world food supply keep pace with the rapid increase in world population. Most green revolution plants are called "high responders" because they need high levels of fertilizer, water, and pesticides in order to produce a high yield. In other words, they require the same subsidies and create the same ecological problems as do modern farming methods.

a. Polyculture

b. Contour and no-till farming

c. Biological pest control

Figure 13.9   Improved farming practices.
a. Polyculture reduces the ability of one parasite to wipe out an entire crop and reduces the need to use a herbicide to kill weeds. **b.** Contour farming with no-till conserves topsoil because water has less tendency to run off. Instead of adding fertilizer, this farmer has planted alfalfa between strips of corn in order to replenish the nitrogen content of the soil. Alfalfa, a legume, has root nodules that contain nitrogen-fixing bacteria. **c.** Instead of pesticides, it is sometimes possible to use a natural predator. Here ladybugs are feeding on cottony-cushion scale insects on citrus trees.

Genetic Engineering As we discussed in Chapter 3, genetic engineering can produce transgenic plants with new and different traits, among them, resistance to both insects and herbicides. When herbicide-resistant crops are planted, weeds are easily controlled, less tillage is needed, and soil erosion is minimized. Researchers also want to produce crops that tolerate salt, drought, and cold. Some progress has also been made in increasing the food quality of crops so that they will supply the proteins, vitamins, and minerals people need. Genetically engineered crops could result in still another green revolution.

Nevertheless, some citizens are opposed to the use of genetically engineered crops, fearing that they will damage the environment and lead to health problems in humans.

Domestic Livestock

A low-protein, high-carbohydrate diet consisting only of grains such as wheat, rice, or corn can lead to malnutrition. In the LDCs, kwashiorkor, caused by a severe protein deficiency, is seen in infants and children ages 1–3, usually after a new baby arrives in the family and the older children are no longer breast-fed. Such children are lethargic, irritable, and have bloated abdomens. Mental retardation is expected.

In the MDCs, many people tend to have more than enough protein in their diet. Almost two-thirds of U.S. cropland is devoted to producing livestock feed. This means that a large percentage of the fossil fuel, fertilizer, water, herbicides, and pesticides we use are actually for the purpose of raising livestock. Typically, cattle are range-fed for about four months, and then they are brought to crowded feedlots, where they receive growth hormone and antibiotics while feeding on grain or corn. Most pigs and chickens spend their entire lives cooped up in crowded pens and cages.

If livestock eat a large proportion of the crops in the United States, then raising livestock accounts for much of the pollution associated with farming. Consider, also, that fossil fuel energy is presently needed not just to produce herbicides and pesticides and to grow food but also to make the food available to the livestock. Raising livestock is extremely energy-intensive in the MDCs. In addition, water is used to wash livestock wastes into nearby bodies of water, where they add significantly to water pollution. Whereas human wastes are sent to sewage treatment plants, raw animal wastes are not.

As a rule of thumb, for every 10 calories of energy from a plant, only 1 calorie is available for the production of animal tissue. In other words, it is extremely wasteful for the human diet to contain more protein than is needed to maintain good health. It is possible to feed 10 times as many people on grain as on meat.

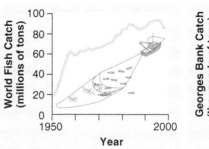

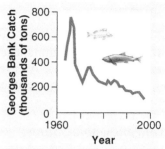

a. World fish catch   b. Groundfish, Georges Bank

	Atlantic Ocean			Pacific Ocean	
Area	Year	Change (%)	Area	Year	Change (%)
NW	1973	−42	NW	1988	−10
NE	1976	−16	NE	1987	−9
SW	1987	−11	SW	1991	−2
SE	1973	−53	SE	1989	−9

c. Changes in fishing catch between the years listed and 1992

Figure 13.10   **Fisheries.**
The world fish catch **(a)** is now declining because fish catches in specific areas have declined **(b)**. **c.** The percentage of fish caught has continued to decline in both the Atlantic and the Pacific Oceans since 1973.

Fishing

Worldwide, between 1970 and 1990, the number of large boats devoted to fishing doubled to 1.2 million. The U.S. fishing fleet participated in this growth due to the availability of federal loans for building fishing boats. The new boats have sonar and depth recorders, and their computers remember the sites of previous catches so that the boats can go there again. Helicopters, planes, and even satellite data are used to help find fish. The result of the increased number and efficiency of fishing boats is a severe reduction in the fish catch (Fig. 13.10). For example, the number of North Atlantic swordfish caught in the United States declined 70% from 1980 to 1990, and the average weight of a swordfish fell from 115 to 60 pounds. Many believe that the Atlantic bluefin tuna is so overfished that it will never recover and will instead become extinct.

Modern fishing practices negatively impact biodiversity because a large number of marine animals are caught by chance in the huge nets that some fishing boats use. These animals are discarded. The world's shrimp fishery has an annual catch of 1.8 million tons, but the other animals caught and discarded in the process amount to 9.5 million tons.

Energy

Modern society uses energy sources to produce electricity, provide transportation, heat buildings, and perform numerous other functions. As previously stated (see page 218), some of these energy sources are nonrenewable, and others are renewable.

Nonrenewable Sources

Presently, about 6% of the world's energy supply comes from nuclear power and 75% comes from fossil fuels; both of these are finite, nonrenewable sources. Today, nuclear power comes from fission power plants, which split ^{235}uranium. Although it was once predicted that the nuclear power industry would fulfill a significant portion of the world's energy needs, this has not happened for two reasons: (1) People are very concerned about nuclear power dangers, such as the meltdown that occurred in 1986 at the Chernobyl nuclear power plant in Russia. (2) Radioactive wastes from nuclear power plants remain a threat to the environment for thousands of years, and we still have not decided how to store them most safely.

Fossil fuels (oil, natural gas, and coal) are so named because they are derived from the compressed remains of plants and animals that died many thousands of years ago. Although the U. S. population makes up less than one-fifth of the world's population, it uses more than one-half of the fossil fuel energy supply. Comparatively speaking, each person in the MDCs uses approximately as much energy in one day as a person in an LDC does in one year.

Among the fossil fuels, oil burns more cleanly than coal, which may contain a considerable amount of sulfur. So despite the fact that the United States has a substantial supply of coal, imported oil is our preferred fossil fuel today. Even so, the burning of any fossil fuel causes environmental problems because as it burns, pollutants are emitted into the air.

Fossil Fuels and Global Climate Change   Many environmentalists are concerned that the global climate will continue to warm and that this global warming will occur at a rate 10 times faster than at any time in the past, due to our use of fossil fuels. In 1850, the level of carbon dioxide in the atmosphere was about 280 parts per million (ppm), and today it is about 350 ppm. This increase is largely due to the burning of fossil fuels and the burning and clearing of forests to make way for farmland and pasture. Human activities are causing the emission of other gases as well. For example, the amount of methane given off by oil and gas wells, rice paddies, and all sorts of organisms, including domesticated cows, is increasing by about 1% a year. These gases are known as **greenhouse gases** because, just like the panes of a greenhouse, they allow solar radiation to pass through but hinder the escape of infrared heat back into space.

Today, data collected around the world show a steady rise in the concentration of the various greenhouse gases. These data are used to generate computer models that predict the Earth's future temperatures. The global climate has already warmed about 0.6°C since the Industrial Revolution. Computer models are unable to consider all possible variables, but the Earth's temperature may rise 1.5°–4.5°C by 2060 if greenhouse emissions continue at the current rates (Fig. 13.11). The Earth may warm to temperatures never before experienced by living things.

As the oceans warm due to global warming, it is predicted that temperatures in the polar regions will rise to a greater degree than in other regions. If so, glaciers will melt, and sea levels will rise, not only due to this melting but also because water expands as it warms. Water evaporation will increase, and most likely precipitation will increase along the coasts while conditions inland become dryer. The occurrence of droughts will reduce agricultural yields and also cause trees to die off. The expansion of forests into arctic areas will most likely not offset the loss of forests in the temperate zones. Coastal agricultural lands, such as the deltas of Bangladesh, India, and China, will be inundated, and billions will have to be spent to keep coastal cities, such as New York, Boston, Miami, and Galveston in the United States, from disappearing into the sea.

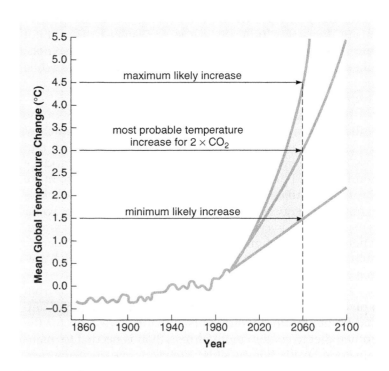

Figure 13.11   Global warming.
The mean global temperature is expected to rise due to the introduction of greenhouse gases into the atmosphere.

Renewable Energy Sources

Renewable types of energy include hydropower, geothermal energy, wind power, and solar energy. These sources do not lead to the same environmental problems as fossil fuel does, but they do have other detrimental effects.

Hydropower   Hydroelectric plants convert the energy of falling water into electricity (Fig. 13.12*a*). Hydropower accounts for about 10% of the electric power generated in the United States and almost 98% of the total renewable energy used in the United States. Brazil, New Zealand, and Switzerland produce at least 75% of their electricity with water power, but Canada is the world's leading producer. Worldwide, hydropower presently generates 19% of all the electricity utilized, but this percentage is expected to rise because of increased use in certain countries. For example, Iceland has an ambitious hydropower project under way because presently it uses only 10% of its potential capacity.

Much of the hydropower development in recent years has been due to the construction of enormous dams, which are known to have detrimental environmental effects. The better choice is believed to be small-scale dams that generate less power per dam but do not have the same environmental impact.

Geothermal Energy   The Earth has an internal source of heat that has been put to use in scattered instances about the globe. Elements such as uranium, thorium, radium, and plutonium undergo radioactive decay below the Earth's surface and then heat the surrounding rocks to hundreds of degrees Centigrade. When the rocks are in contact with underground streams or lakes, huge amounts of steam and hot water are produced. This steam can be piped up to the surface to supply hot water for home heating or to run steam-driven turbogenerators. The California's Geysers project is the world's largest geothermal electricity-generating complex.

Wind Power   Wind power is expected to account for a significant percentage of our energy needs in the future (Fig. 13.12*b*). Despite the common belief that a huge amount of land is required for the "wind farms" that produce commercial electricity, the actual amount of space for a wind farm compares favorably to the amount of land required by a coal-fired power plant or a solar thermal energy system.

A community that generates its own electricity by using wind power can solve the problem of uneven energy production by selling electricity to a local public utility when an excess is available and buying electricity from the same facility when wind power is in short supply.

a.

b.

c.

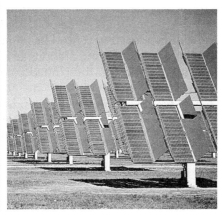

d.

Figure 13.12   Renewable energy sources.
a. Hydropower dams provide a clean form of energy but can be ecologically disastrous in other ways. **b.** Wind power requires land on which to place enough windmills to generate energy. **c.** Photovoltaic cells on rooftops and **(d)** sun-tracking mirrors on land can collect diffuse solar energy more cheaply than was formerly possible.

The Solar-Hydrogen Revolution

Solar energy is diffuse energy that must be (1) collected, (2) converted to another form, and (3) stored if it is to compete with other available forms of energy. Passive solar heating of a house is successful when the windows of the house face the sun, the building is well insulated, and heat can be stored in water tanks, rocks, bricks, or some other suitable material.

In a **photovoltaic (solar) cell,** a wafer of the electron-emitting metal is in contact with another metal that collects the electrons and passes them along into wires in a steady stream. Spurred by the oil shocks of the 1970s, the U.S. government has been supporting the development of photovoltaics ever since. As a result, the price of buying one has dropped from about $100 per watt to around $4. The photovoltaic cells placed on roofs, for example, generate electricity that can be used inside a building and/or sold back to a power company (Fig. 13.12c).

Several types of solar power plants are now operational in California. In one type, huge reflectors focus sunlight on a pipe containing oil. The heated pipes boil water, generating steam that drives a conventional turbogenerator. In another type, 1,800 sun-tracking mirrors focus sunlight onto a molten salt receiver mounted on a tower (Fig. 13.12d). The hot salt generates steam that drives a turbogenerator.

Hydrogen, the Fuel of the Future Now that better methods are being developed to capture solar energy and the price of solar energy has become more competitive, scientists are seriously considering using solar energy to extract hydrogen from water via electrolysis. It has been known for some time that hydrogen is a clean-burning fuel. When it burns, water is produced.

Presently, cars have internal combustion engines that run on gasoline. In the future, vehicles are expected to be powered by fuel cells, which use hydrogen to produce electricity. The electricity runs a motor that propels the vehicle. Fuel cells are now powering buses in Vancouver and Chicago, and more buses are planned. The conversion to a world that runs on solar-hydrogen power may have begun!

Hydrogen fuel can be produced locally by photovoltaic cells or produced in central locations. If the latter, hydrogen can be piped to filling stations using the natural gas pipes already plentiful in the United States. The advantages of a solar-hydrogen revolution are at least twofold: (1) The world would no longer be dependent on the Middle East for oil, and (2) environmental problems such as global warming, acid rain, and smog would begin to lessen.

Minerals

Minerals are nonrenewable raw materials in the Earth's crust that can be mined (extracted) and used by humans. Nonrenewable minerals include fossil fuels; nonmetallic raw materials such as sand, gravel, and phosphate; and metals such as aluminum, copper, iron, lead, and gold.

Nonrenewable resources are subject to *depletion;* that is, the supply that is mineable will eventually run out. A depletion curve is dependent on how fast the resource is used, whether new reserves can be found, and whether recycling and reuse are possible. We can extend our supply of fossil fuels if we conserve our use and if we find new reserves. In addition to these possibilities, metals can be recycled.

One of the greatest threats to the maintenance of ecosystems and biodiversity is a type of surface mining called strip mining. In the United States, huge machines can go so far as to remove mountaintops in order to reach a mineral (Fig. 13.13). The land, devoid of vegetation, takes on a surreal appearance, and rain washes toxic waste deposits into nearby streams and rivers. Legislation now requires strip miners to reclaim the land to its original condition, a process that can take years to complete.

The most dangerous metals to human health are the heavy metals: lead, mercury, arsenic, cadmium, tin, chromium, zinc, and copper. They are used to produce batteries, electronics, pesticides, medicines, paints, inks, and dyes. In the ionic form, they enter the body and inhibit vital enzymes. That's why these items should be discarded carefully and taken to hazardous waste sites.

Figure 13.13   Modern mining capabilities.
Giant mining machines—some as tall as a 20-story building—can remove an enormous amount of the Earth's crust in one scoop in order to mine for coal or a metal.

Synthetic Organic Compounds

Thus far, we have concentrated on our use of metals, but synthetic organic compounds are another area of considerable ecological concern because of their detrimental effects on the health of living things, including humans. Synthetic organic compounds play a role in the production of plastics, pesticides, herbicides, cosmetics, coatings, solvents, wood preservatives, and hundreds of other products.

Synthetic organic compounds include halogenated hydrocarbons, in which halogens (chlorine, bromine, fluorine) have replaced certain hydrogens. One such molecule comprises the **CFCs (chlorofluorocarbons),** a type of halogenated hydrocarbon in which both chlorine and fluorine atoms replace some of the hydrogen atoms. CFCs have brought about a thinning of the Earth's **ozone shield,** which protects terrestrial life from the dangerous effects of ultraviolet radiation. In most MDCs, legislation has been passed to prevent the production of any more CFCs. Hydrofluorocarbons, which contain no chlorine, are expected to take their place in coolants and other products. The ozone shield is predicted to recover by 2050; in the meantime, many more cases of skin cancer are expected to occur.

Other synthetic organic chemicals pose a direct and serious threat to the health of living things, including humans. Rachel Carson's book *Silent Spring,* published in 1962, made the public aware of the deleterious effects of pesticides.

Wastes

Every year, the countries of the world discard billions of tons of solid wastes, some on land and some in fresh and marine waters. Such pollution comes from many sources, and it results in both cultural eutrophication (overabundance of organic nutrients leading to a depleted oxygen supply) and health hazards to humans (Fig. 13.14).

Wastes are generated during the mining and production of a product. Clean water and clean air legislation in the early 1970s prevented venting wastes into the atmosphere and flushing them into waterways. Thus, industries turned to land disposal, which was unregulated at the time. Their utilization of deep-well injection, pits with plastic liners, and landfills led to much water pollution and human illness, including cancer.

An estimated 5 billion metric tons of highly toxic chemicals were improperly discarded in the United States between 1950 and 1975. The public's concern was so great that the Environmental Protection Agency (EPA) came into existence. Using an allocation of monies called the superfund, the EPA oversees the cleanup of hazardous waste disposal sites in the United States.

The 10 most commonly found contaminants are heavy metals (lead, arsenic, cadmium, chromium) and organic compounds (trichloroethylene, toluene, benzene, polychlorinated biphenyls [PCBs], chloroform, and toluene). Some of these are endocrine-disrupting contaminants.

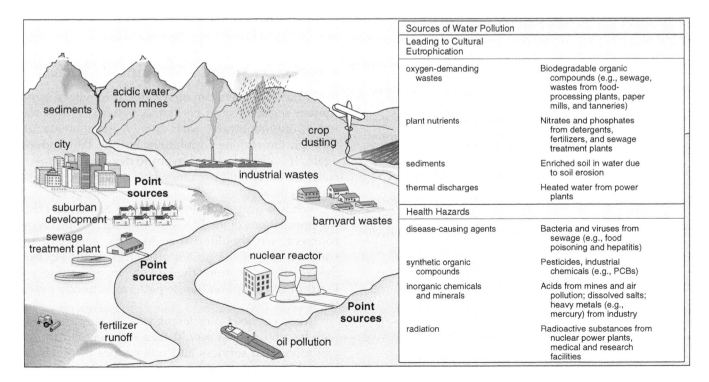

Figure 13.14   **Sources of surface water pollution.**
Many bodies of water are dying due to the introduction of pollutants from point sources, which are easily identifiable, and from nonpoint sources, which cannot be specifically identified.

Endocrine-Disrupting Contaminants

Recently, we have become aware of the subtle hormonal effects of pollutants, as discussed in the reading on page 151. At first, the altered reproductive traits in wildlife seemed to indicate only the estrogen-like effects of certain contaminants, but now we know that pollutants can have all sorts of hormonal effects. Therefore, *endocrine-disrupting contaminants (EDCs)* is the preferred term for chemicals used in pesticides, herbicides, plastics, food additives, and personal hygiene products that can affect the endocrine system. These pollutants occur at a level one thousand times greater than the hormone levels in human blood.

Sewage

Sewage treatment can help degrade human wastes, which otherwise can cause oxygen depletion in lakes and rivers. As the oxygen level decreases, the diversity of life is greatly reduced. Also, human feces can contain pathogenic microorganisms that cause cholera, typhoid fever, and dysentery. In regions of the LDCs where sewage treatment is practically nonexistent, many children die each year from these diseases.

Typically, sewage treatment plants use bacteria to break down organic matter to inorganic nutrients, such as nitrates and phosphates, which then enter surface waters. The end result of this treatment can be cultural eutrophication; first there is an algal bloom, and when the algae die off, decomposition robs the water of oxygen, often resulting in a massive fish kill.

Industrial Wastes

Industrial wastes can include heavy metals and chlorinated hydrocarbons, such as those in some pesticides. Sometimes, they accumulate in the mud of deltas and estuaries of highly polluted rivers and cause environmental problems if disturbed. When these wastes enter bodies of water, they are subject to **biological magnification.** Decomposers are unable to break down these wastes. They enter and remain in the bodies of organisms because they are not excreted. Therefore, they become more concentrated as they pass along a food chain. Biological magnification is most apt to occur in aquatic food chains, which have more links than terrestrial food chains. Humans are the final consumers in both types of food chains, and in some areas, human milk contains detectable amounts of DDT and PCBs, which are polychlorinated hydrocarbons. Industrial pollution is being addressed in many MDCs but usually has low priority in LDCs.

13.3 Working Toward a Sustainable Society

A **sustainable** society, like a sustainable ecosystem, would be able to provide the same goods and services for future generations of human beings as it does now.

Today's Society

Current evidence indicates that human society is most likely not sustainable. The following characteristics make the present human society unsustainable:

- A considerable proportion of land, and therefore natural ecosystems, is being used for human purposes (homes, agriculture, factories, etc.).
- Agriculture requires large inputs of nonrenewable fossil fuel energy, fertilizer, and pesticides, which create much pollution.
- At least half of the agricultural yield in the United States goes toward feeding animals. It is wasteful for citizens in MDCs to eat as much meat as they do. Also, animal sewage pollutes water.
- Even though fresh water is a renewable resource, we are running out of the available supply within a given time frame.
- Our society primarily utilizes nonrenewable fossil fuel energy, which leads to global warming, acid precipitation, and smog.
- Minerals are nonrenewable, and humans' mining, manufacture, and use of products are responsible for much environmental pollution.

Characteristics of a Sustainable Society

A natural ecosystem can offer clues as to what a sustainable human society would be like. A natural ecosystem makes use of only renewable solar energy, and its materials cycle through the various populations back to the producer once again. It is clear that if we want to develop a sustainable society, we too should use renewable energy sources and recycle materials.

While we are sometimes quick to realize that the growing populations of the LDCs are putting a strain on the environment, we should realize that the excessive resource consumption of the MDCs also stresses the environment. Sustainability is more than likely incompatible with the kinds of consumption/waste patterns currently practiced in the MDCs.

Also, we need a different way of indicating economic well-being, one that would take into account the value of environmental services and other types of goods and services that are not presently considered.

Oil Drilling in the Arctic

The Arctic National Wildlife Refuge is home to a diverse array of wildlife, including migratory birds, caribou, grizzly bears, Dall sheep, polar bears, and musk oxen. The nearby continental shelf provides the coastal waters with a rich nutrient base that supports a wide variety of marine mammals during the summer months.

People who favor oil drilling in the Arctic National Wildlife Refuge suggest that it would affect only an area the size of an airport within a state. And the effect would mainly be underground because new techniques allow us to drill lower and then spread out beneath the surface to get the oil. Acquiring the oil, advocates say, would also protect jobs and security in the United States by lessening our dependence on foreign countries for oil. If these countries were to stop supplying us with oil, it would cause economic hardships, including high gasoline prices.

Those who do not favor oil drilling in the Arctic National Wildlife Refuge believe that we can reduce our need for energy by adopting simple efficiency measures. They suggest that this would save many times the oil that could come from drilling in the refuge and that, by using a renewable energy resource, we would protect the environment here at home in addition to protecting the wildlife in the Arctic National Wildlife Refuge.

Should citizens decide this matter on the basis of party politics? If not, how should they go about making a decision?

Figure 13A Caribou in the Arctic National Wildlife Refuge.

Decide Your Opinion

1. Are you in favor of oil drilling in the Arctic National Wildlife Refuge? If so, discuss your support for this measure of increasing our oil supply.
2. Are you against drilling in the Arctic National Wildlife Refuge? If so, give the reasons you feel this way.
3. Do you feel citizens should go along with their political parties' stand on oil drilling in the Arctic National Wildlife Refuge, or do you feel that all citizens should decide for themselves? Why or why not?

Summary

13.1 Human Population Growth

The present growth rate for the world's human population has decreased to 1.3%, and if it keeps on decreasing, the population could level off at 8 billion by 2050. Populations have a biotic potential for increase in size. Biotic potential is normally held in check by environmental resistance, and a population size usually levels off at the carrying capacity of the environment.

The MDCs have experienced only modest growth since 1950; their rate of growth is around 0.1%. In contrast, the LDCs have experienced a population explosion. Their growth rate peaked at 2.5% in the early 1960s, and it is now 1.6%. Although the worldwide growth rate is decreasing, the population will increase considerably because there are more women entering their reproductive years than leaving them.

13.2 Resources and Pollution

People need a place to live, and sometimes they make poor choices. Beach erosion is common along coasts; the seas are rising, and people often fill in wetlands. They also build dams that retard sediment so that it never reaches the coast. Desertification is a possibility when people overuse semiarid lands and also after they remove trees from tropical rain forests where the soil is thin and nutrient-poor.

Fresh water is available as surface water in rivers and lakes and also in underground sources called aquifers. To increase the supply of fresh water, people build dams, which may not be useful for long because of sediment buildup. Many rivers around the world now run dry and carry a heavy burden of salt. People also remove water from aquifers at a rate that cannot be sustained. Land subsidence, sinkholes, and saltwater intrusion are environmental consequences to withdrawing too much water from aquifers.

Food production has kept pace with population growth. Modern farming is characterized by the use of few genetic varieties; heavy use of fertilizers, pesticides, and herbicides; generous irrigation; and excessive fuel consumption. Soil erosion and salinization are side effects of modern farming methods. The green revolution gave the LDCs hybrid plants called "high responders" that produce well as long as they have the subsidies already mentioned. Genetically engineered crops might usher in a second green revolution. Much of the grain grown in the MDCs goes toward feeding domesticated animals, which produce much sewage that gets washed into waterways. Also, it takes 10 grain calories to produce one meat calorie, thus it would be possible to feed 10 times as many people on grain as on meat. Modern fishing methods have decimated fisheries, and the catch of the past may never be seen again.

Some types of energy are nonrenewable (e.g., fossil fuels and ^{235}uranium), and some are renewable (e.g., hydropower, wind, geothermal energy, and solar energy). The burning of fossil fuels has environmental consequences. Like the panes of a greenhouse, carbon dioxide and other gases allow the sun's rays to pass through but impede the release of infrared wavelengths. It is predicted that a buildup of these "greenhouse gases" will lead to global warming. The effects of global warming could include a rise in sea level and a change in climate patterns. An effect on agriculture could follow.

With regard to renewable energy supplies, only hydropower (dams) and geothermal energy are routinely utilized. However, wind and solar energy are expected to be utilized more in the future. Some predict a solar-hydrogen revolution, in which solar energy replaces fossil fuel energy and cars run on hydrogen fuel instead of gasoline. This would eventually do away with the environmental problems associated with using fossil fuel energy.

Minerals are a nonrenewable resource that we are using up at a rapid rate because, at present, we do not recycle at any of the steps involved in the production process. Rather, each step in the process creates waste and pollution. Some synthetic organic chemicals are involved in the production of plastics, pesticides, and herbicides as well as all sorts of other products. Ozone shield destruction is particularly associated with CFCs.

The countries of the world discard billions of tons of solid wastes, some on land and some in fresh and marine waters. The sources of surface water pollution, which are many and varied, include human sewage, agricultural wastes, and industrial wastes.

13.3 Working Toward a Sustainable Society
Our present-day society is not sustainable. If we were to pattern our society after natural ecosystems, solar energy would supply our energy needs, and materials would be recycled.

Reviewing the Chapter

1. Explain why today's world population is still increasing even though the growth rate is decreasing. What are some predictions regarding at what size and when the human population will level off? 216
2. Distinguish between MDCs and LDCs. Why did the LDCs recently experience a huge increase in population, whereas the MDCs did not? 216–17
3. Discuss three locales where humans have settled with unfortunate environmental consequences. What are those consequences? 218–19
4. From where do people get fresh water? What environmental problems are associated with damming rivers and taking water from aquifers? What can be done to conserve water? 220–21
5. Discuss four characteristics of modern farming methods and the drawbacks of each. What is happening to the soil around the world? What was the green revolution, and why might there be another one? 222–23
6. What environmental problems are associated with eating meat? What has happened to the fisheries of the seas? 223
7. What are the types of fossil fuels, and what environmental problems are associated with burning fossil fuels? 224
8. What renewable energy sources are available? Discuss the possible solar-hydrogen revolution that is expected to be under way. What are the benefits of this revolution? 225–26
9. What are minerals, and what are the drawbacks of mining them? What are synthetic organic compounds, and what are the drawbacks of using halogenated hydrocarbons? 226–27
10. What are the characteristics of the present unsustainable human society? Of a sustainable society? 228

Critical Thinking Questions

1. What factors might cause the human population to increase more than expected? Decrease more than expected?

2. The Mexican government at one time encouraged large families because it believed that the greater the number of people, the greater the workforce and the greater the prosperity. What is wrong with this thinking?

Understanding Key Terms

aquifer 221
biological magnification 228
biotic potential 216
carrying capacity 216
CFCs (chlorofluorocarbons) 227
deforestation 219
desertification 219
environmental resistance 216
exponential growth 216
fossil fuel 224
greenhouse gases 224
growth rate 216

land subsidence 221
mineral 226
nonrenewable resources 218
ozone shield 227
photovoltaic (solar) cell 226
pollution 218
renewable resources 218
replacement reproduction 217
resource 218
salinization 222
saltwater intrusion 221
sinkhole 221
sustainable 228

Appendix A
Testing Yourself

Choose the best answer for each question.

Chapter 1

In questions 1–5, match each syndrome in the key to its chromosomal makeup.

Key:
a. Down syndrome
b. Turner syndrome
c. Klinefelter syndrome
d. cri du chat syndrome
e. Jacobs syndrome

1. Deletion in chromosome 5

2. Extra chromosome 21

3. XO

4. XXY

5. XYY

6. The diploid number of chromosomes
   a. is the 2n number.
   b. is in a parental cell and therefore in the two daughter cells following mitosis.
   c. in humans is 46.
   d. is in every somatic cell.
   e. All of these are correct.

In questions 7–9, match each description to a term in the key.

Key:
a. centriole
b. chromatid
c. chromosome
d. centromere

7. Point of attachment for sister chromatids

8. Found at a pole in the center of an aster

9. Coiled and condensed chromatin

10. If a parental cell has 14 chromosomes prior to mitosis, how many chromosomes will each daughter cell have?
   a. 28 because each chromatid is a chromosome
   b. 14 because the chromatids separate
   c. only 7 after mitosis is finished
   d. any number between 7 and 28
   e. 7 in the nucleus and 7 in the cytoplasm, for a total of 14

11. In which phase of mitosis are the chromosomes moving toward the poles?
   a. prophase   d. anaphase
   b. prometaphase   e. telophase
   c. metaphase

12. Interphase
   a. is the same as prophase, metaphase, anaphase, and telophase.
   b. includes stages G_1, S, and G_2.
   c. requires the use of spindle fibers.
   d. is a stage in the cell cycle.
   e. Both b and d are correct.

13. Which is not a characteristic of meiosis?
   a. two rounds of cell division
   b. production of four daughter cells
   c. reduction in chromosome number
   d. functions in growth and the healing of wounds
   e. All of these are characteristics of meiosis.

14. During which mitotic phases are duplicated chromosomes present?
   a. all but telophase
   b. prophase and anaphase
   c. all but anaphase and telophase
   d. only during metaphase at the metaphase plate
   e. Both a and b are correct.

15. If a parental cell has 12 chromosomes, then each of the daughter cells following meiosis will have
   a. 48 chromosomes.
   b. 24 chromosomes.
   c. 12 chromosomes.
   d. 6 chromosomes.
   e. Any one of these could be correct.

16. At the equator during metaphase I of meiosis, there are
   a. chromosomes consisting of one chromatid.
   b. unpaired duplicated chromosomes.
   c. tetrads.
   d. homologous pairs of chromosomes.
   e. Both c and d are correct.

17. At the equator during metaphase II of meiosis, there are
   a. chromosomes consisting of one chromatid.
   b. unpaired duplicated chromosomes.
   c. dyads.
   d. homologous pairs of chromosomes.
   e. Both b and c are correct.

18. Gametes contain one of each kind of chromosome because
   a. the homologous chromosomes separate during meiosis.
   b. the chromatids separate during meiosis.
   c. only one replication of DNA occurs during meiosis.
   d. crossing-over occurs during prophase I.
   e. the parental cell contains only one of each kind of chromosome.

19. Crossing-over occurs between
    a. sister chromatids of the same chromosome.
    b. two different kinds of dyads.
    c. two different kinds of chromosomes.
    d. nonsister chromatids of a tetrad.
    e. two daughter nuclei.

20. During which phase of meiosis do homologous chromosomes separate?
    a. prophase II
    b. telophase I
    c. metaphase I
    d. anaphase I
    e. anaphase II

21. Which of the following associations is not a difference between spermatogenesis and oogenesis in humans?

Spermatogenesis	Oogenesis
a. Occurs in males.	Occurs in females.
b. Produces four sperm per meiosis.	Produces one egg per meiosis.
c. Produces haploid cells.	Produces diploid cells.
d. Always goes to completion.	Does not always go to completion.

22. An abnormal number of chromosomes could result during meiosis because of
    a. recombination.
    b. a carrier.
    c. nondisjunction.
    d. inversion.
    e. translocation.

Chapter 2

In questions 1–4, match each genetics problem with an answer in the key.
Key:
a. 0%
b. 25%
c. 50%
d. 100%

1. A woman heterozygous for polydactyly (6 fingers and toes) reproduces with a man without the condition. Polydactyly is dominant; what are the chances a child will have the condition?

2. Parents who do not have Tay-Sachs disease produce a child who has Tay-Sachs disease (recessive). What are the chances the next child will have Tay-Sachs?

3. One parent has sickle-cell disease (incompletely dominant), and the other is perfectly normal. What are the chances a child will have sickle-cell trait?

4. Unattached earlobes are dominant over attached earlobes. What are the chances a homozygous dominant man will have children with attached earlobes?

5. A Punnett square can be used to determine
    a. the phenotype of a parent.
    b. the genotype of an offspring.
    c. the phenotype of an offspring.
    d. whether independent assortment occurred.
    e. the number of offspring.

6. Which of these could be a normal gamete?
    a. Gg
    b. GG
    c. G
    d. None of these is correct.

7. In humans, pointed eyebrows (B) are dominant over smooth eyebrows (b). Mary's father has pointed eyebrows, but she and her mother have smooth. What is the genotype of the father?
    a. BB
    b. Bb
    c. bb
    d. BBbb
    e. Any one of these is correct.

8. Parents who do not have cystic fibrosis (recessive) produce a child who has cystic fibrosis. What are the chances that each child born to this couple will have cystic fibrosis?
    a. 100%
    b. 75%
    c. 25%
    d. 0%
    e. All of these are correct.

9. A man has type AB blood. If he has a child with type B blood, what blood type could the child's mother have?
    a. type A   d. type O
    b. type B   e. All of these are correct.
    c. type AB

10. Two affected parents have an unaffected child. The trait involved is
    a. autosomal recessive.
    b. incompletely dominant.
    c. controlled by multiple alleles.
    d. autosomal dominant.

11. Alice and Henry are at the opposite extremes for a polygenic trait. Their children will
    a. be bell-shaped.
    b. be a phenotype typical of a 3:1 ratio.
    c. have the middle phenotype between their two parents.
    d. look like one parent or the other.

12. Which of the following statements is not true regarding sex-linked traits?
    a. Women can be carriers because they can be heterozygous for the trait.
    b. X-linked traits are more common in men.

c. Males inherit X-linked traits from their fathers.
d. Males are never carriers since they only receive one X chromosome.
e. Both c and d are incorrect.

13. If a man has an X-linked recessive disorder, which of the following statements is not likely?
    a. Both parents are unaffected.
    b. Only the males in a pedigree chart have the disorder.
    c. Only females in previous generations have the disorder.
    d. Both a and c are not likely.

14. John has hemophilia, but his parents do not. Using H for normal and h for hemophilia, give the genotype of his father, mother, and John in that order.
    a. Hh, Hh, hh
    b. $X^H Y, hh, X^H Y$
    c. $X^H Y, X^H X^h, X^h Y$
    d. $X^h Y, X^H X^H, X^h Y$
    e. $X^H Y, X^h Y, X^h Y$

15. Identify each of these genetic disorders.
    a. Mucus in lungs and digestive tract is thick and viscous. _____
    b. Neurological impairment and psychomotor difficulties develop early. _____
    c. Benign tumors occur under the skin or deeper. _____
    d. Minor disturbances in balance and coordination develop in middle age and progress toward severe mental disturbances. _____

Chapter 3

1. The double-helix model of DNA resembles a twisted ladder in which the rungs of the ladder are
   a. complementary base pairs.
   b. A paired with G and C paired with T.
   c. A paired with T and G paired with C.
   d. a sugar-phosphate paired with a sugar-phosphate.
   e. Both a and c are correct.

2. In a DNA molecule, the
   a. backbone is sugar and phosphate molecules.
   b. bases are bonded to the sugars.
   c. sugars are bonded to the phosphates.
   d. bases are hydrogen-bonded to one another.
   e. All of these are correct.

3. If the sequence of bases in DNA is TAGCCT, then the sequence of bases in RNA will be
   a. TCCGAT.
   b. ATCGGA.
   c. TAGCCT.
   d. AUCGGA.
   e. Both a and b are correct.

4. mRNA processing
   a. takes place in the cytoplasm.
   b. is the same as transcription.
   c. is an event that occurs after DNA is transcribed.
   d. is the rejection of old, worn-out RNA.
   e. Both a and c are correct.

5. During protein synthesis, an anticodon of a transfer RNA (tRNA) pairs with
   a. amino acids in the polypeptide.
   b. DNA nucleotide bases.
   c. ribosomal RNA (rRNA) nucleotide bases.
   d. messenger RNA (mRNA) nucleotide bases.
   e. other tRNA nucleotide bases.

6. Which of these associations does not correctly compare DNA and RNA?

DNA	RNA
a. Contains the base thymine.	Contains the base uracil.
b. Is double stranded.	Is also double stranded.
c. Is a helix.	Is not a helix.
d. The sugar is deoxyribose.	The sugar is ribose.

7. The process of converting the information contained in the nucleotide sequence of RNA into a sequence of amino acids is called
   a. transcription.
   b. translation.
   c. translocation.
   d. replication.

8. Complementary base pairing
   a. involves T, A, G, C.
   b. is necessary to replication.
   c. utilizes hydrogen bonds.
   d. occurs when ribose binds with deoxyribose.
   e. All but d are correct.

9. Which one or more of the following does not characterize the process of transcription?
   a. RNA is made with one strand of the DNA.
   b. In making RNA, the base uracil of RNA pairs with the base adenine of DNA.
   c. The enzyme RNA polymerase synthesizes RNA.
   d. RNA is made in the cytoplasm.

10. Translation can be defined as
    a. the making of protein using mRNA and tRNA.
    b. the making of RNA from a DNA template.
    c. the gathering of amino acids by tRNA molecules in the cytoplasm.
    d. the removal of introns from mRNA.

11. The polymerase chain reaction
    a. utilizes RNA polymerase.
    b. takes place in huge bioreactors.
    c. utilizes a temperature-insensitive enzyme.
    d. makes lots of nonidentical copies of DNA.
    e. All of these are correct.

12. DNA fingerprinting can be used for which of the following?
    a. identifying human remains
    b. identifying infectious diseases
    c. finding evolutionary links between organisms
    d. solving crimes
    e. All of these are correct.

13. DNA amplified by PCR and then used for fingerprinting could come from
    a. any diploid or haploid cell.
    b. only white blood cells that have been karyotyped.
    c. only skin cells after they are dead.
    d. only purified animal cells.
    e. Both b and d are correct.

14. Which of the following is not a proper association with regard to genetic engineering?
    a. plasmid as a vector—bacteria
    b. protoplast as a vector—plant
    c. RNA retrovirus as a vector—human stem cells
    d. All of these are correct.

15. Restriction enzymes found in bacterial cells are ordinarily used
    a. during DNA replication.
    b. to degrade the bacterial cell's DNA.
    c. to cut up viral DNA that enters the cell.
    d. to attach pieces of DNA together.

16. Which of the following is not needed in order to clone an animal?
    a. sperm from a donor animal
    b. nucleus from an adult animal cell
    c. enucleated egg from a donor animal
    d. host female to develop the embryo
    e. All of these are needed.

17. Because of the Human Genome Project, we know the
    a. sequence of the base pairs of human DNA.
    b. sequence of genes along the human chromosomes.
    c. mutations that lead to genetic disorders.
    d. All of these are correct.
    e. Only a and c are correct.

18. Which of the following is a benefit to having insulin produced by biotechnology?
    a. It is just as effective.
    b. It can be mass-produced.
    c. It is nonallergenic.
    d. It is less expensive.
    e. All of these are correct.

19. Gene therapy
    a. is still an investigative procedure.
    b. has met with no success.
    c. is only used to cure genetic disorders such as SCID and cystic fibrosis.
    d. uses viruses to carry foreign genes into human cells.
    e. Both a and d are correct.

Chapter 4

1. In a karyotype, the chromosomes are arranged
   a. in no particular order.
   b. according to numbered pairs.
   c. according to those inherited from the mother and those inherited from the father.
   d. from the smallest to the largest.
   e. Both b and d are correct.

2. From this pedigree chart, it is evident that the gene for normal pigment is

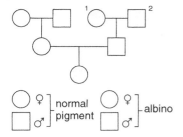

   a. dominant.
   b. recessive.
   c. sex-linked.
   d. None of these is correct.

3. In the pedigree chart in question 2, the genotype for parents 1 and 2 will be
   a. homozygous dominant.
   b. homozygous recessive.
   c. heterozygous.
   d. homozygous dominant or homozygous recessive.

4. It is evident from this pedigree chart that myopia is

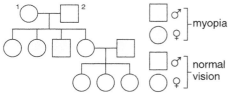

   a. recessive.
   b. dominant.
   c. X-linked.
   d. None of these is correct.

5. In the pedigree chart in question 4, the genotype of parents 1 and 2 will be
   a. homozygous recessive.
   b. heterozygous.
   c. homozygous dominant.
   d. Insufficient data make it impossible to determine the genotype.

6. In a pedigree chart, it is noted that both parents have the characteristic and all the children have it. Under these circumstances, the characteristic
   a. must be autosomal dominant.
   b. must be autosomal recessive.
   c. could be either autosomal dominant or recessive.
   d. can only be X-linked.

7. The trait in this pedigree chart is

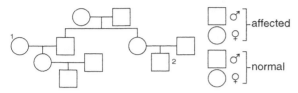

   a.   a dominant X-linked trait.
   b.   a recessive X-linked trait.
   c.   a recessive Y-linked trait.
   d.   an autosomal dominant trait.

8. Identify each pedigree chart as one of the following: X-linked recessive, autosomal dominant, or autosomal recessive.

   a.

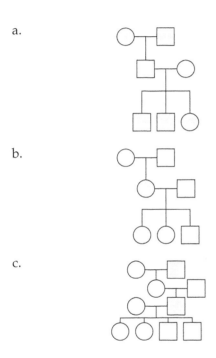

   b.

   c.

9. Which disease can be diagnosed by a genetic marker?
   a.   Huntington disease
   b.   sickle-cell disease
   c.   Duchenne muscular dystrophy
   d.   All of these choices are correct.

10. Genetic testing can be done on a(n)
   a.   egg.
   b.   embryo.
   c.   fetus.
   d.   newborn.
   e.   All of these are correct.

11. What's the difference between testing for a protein and testing for DNA?
   a.   no difference
   b.   testing for an enzyme versus testing the genes
   c.   One is done in a doctor's office, and the other is done in the laboratory.
   d.   Both b and c are correct.

12. Tests utilizing genetic markers look for
   a.   abnormal cleavage sites.
   b.   abnormal sequence of bases.
   c.   a DNA probe.
   d.   Both a and b are correct.

13. One advantage of DNA probes is
   a.   a DNA chip can identify several mutations at one time.
   b.   no fluorescent dye is needed.
   c.   its use of genetic markers.
   d.   All of these are correct.

14. Testing fetal cells from the mother's blood is better than amniocentesis because
   a.   it can be done at 9 weeks compared to 12 weeks.
   b.   it is noninvasive.
   c.   PCR is not required.
   d.   Both a and b are correct.
   e.   All of these choices are correct.

15. What advantage does testing the egg for genetic abnormalities have over testing the embryo?
   a.   no advantage
   b.   If the embryo is tested, it might not survive.
   c.   Only normal eggs are used for IVF, but all embryos are implanted in the uterus whether they are normal or not.
   d.   Embryos are already living, whereas an egg is not yet a living human being.

Chapter 5

1. Put the following events in the correct sequence.
   a.   accelerated synthesis of mRNA
   b.   hormone combines with receptor
   c.   binding with a portion of DNA
   d.   protein synthesis

2. Which gland produces sex hormones?
   a.   anterior pituitary
   b.   posterior pituitary
   c.   adrenal cortex
   d.   All of these choices are correct.

3. GnRH
   a.   is produced by the hypothalamus.
   b.   stimulates the anterior pituitary.
   c.   stimulates the production of FSH and LH.
   d.   All of these choices are correct.

4. FSH and LH stimulate the
   a.   ovaries.
   b.   anterior pituitary.
   c.   posterior pituitary.
   d.   anterior and posterior pituitary.

5. GnRH production is regulated by
   a.   sex hormone levels.
   b.   gonadotropic hormone levels.
   c.   FSH and LH levels.
   d.   All of these choices are correct.

6. The hypothalamic-pituitary-gonad system starts functioning
   a. long before puberty.
   b. before puberty.
   c. after the development of the secondary sex characteristics.
   d. when the umbilical cord is cut.

7. Which is responsible for a greater accumulation of fat beneath the skin?
   a. androgens
   b. testosterone
   c. estrogen
   d. androgens and testosterone

8. The pelvic girdle is wider in females
   a. to accommodate the baby's head during birth.
   b. to give more support during gestation.
   c. to accommodate the baby's head during birth and to give more support during gestation.
   d. The female pelvic cavity is about the same relative size as that of males.

9. Which hormones are needed for breast development and lactation?
   a. estrogen
   b. progesterone
   c. prolactin
   d. All of these are correct.

10. Gonadotropic hormones
    a. are produced by the testes and ovaries.
    b. stimulate the testes and ovaries.
    c. are produced by the hypothalamus.
    d. stimulate the anterior pituitary.

11. Which anterior pituitary hormone is involved with lactation?
    a. oxytocin
    b. prolactin
    c. LH
    d. oxytocin and prolactin

12. Feedback control involves the
    a. hypothalamus.
    b. anterior pituitary.
    c. gonads.
    d. All of these are correct.

13. Masculinization of a female might be due to
    a. an overactive anterior pituitary.
    b. an overactive adrenal cortex.
    c. an overactive hypothalamus.
    d. an overactive ovary.

14. What determines the gender of an individual?
    a. sex chromosomes
    b. sex hormones
    c. gonadotropic hormone
    d. sex chromosomes and sex hormones

15. Gonadotropic hormones are produced by the
    a. testes.
    b. pituitary.

c. ovaries.
d. All of these are correct.

16. The ovaries are under direct control of the
    a. hypothalamus.
    b. anterior pituitary gland.
    c. brain.
    d. posterior pituitary gland.

17. Which is the primary male hormone?
    a. LH
    b. testosterone
    c. FSH
    d. progesterone

18. Testosterone is released into the
    a. male ducts.
    b. female ducts.
    c. blood.
    d. male and female ducts.

19. Which hormone(s) play(s) a direct role in lactation?
    a. estrogen
    b. oxytocin
    c. prolactin
    d. prostaglandins
    e. Both b and c are correct.

Chapter 6

1. Semen
   a. provides nourishment for sperm.
   b. helps regulate pH.
   c. provides liquid medium for sperm motility.
   d. All of these are correct.

2. The testes are under direct control of which structure?
   a. hypothalamus
   b. pituitary gland
   c. brain
   d. semen

3. The seminiferous tubules
   a. are where spermatogenesis occurs.
   b. are where testosterone is produced.
   c. are stimulated by LH.
   d. All of these are correct.

4. Another name for sperm cell is
   a. spermatogonia.
   b. spermatozoa.
   c. spermatid.
   d. spermatocyte.

5. The acrosome
   a. is in the sperm tail.
   b. contains an enzyme needed for fertilization.
   c. contains energy-producing organelles.
   d. All of these are correct.

6. The interstitial cells
   a. produce testosterone.
   b. are stimulated by LH.

c.   are stimulated by FSH.

d.   produce testosterone and are stimulated by LH.

7.   Sperm mature in the
   a.   vas deferens.
   b.   epididymis.
   c.   interstitial cells.
   d.   ejaculatory duct.

8.   Prostaglandins
   a.   nourish sperm.
   b.   regulate pH.
   c.   cause the uterus to contract.
   d.   nourish sperm and regulate pH.

9.   A swelling of the _____ may block the urethra.
   a.   seminal vesicle
   b.   prostate gland
   c.   Cowper glands
   d.   All of these are correct.

10.   Which is the first phase of ejaculation?
   a.   emission
   b.   expulsion
   c.   myotonia
   d.   refractory period

11.   What ovarian hormone is mainly active in the luteal phase?
   a.   FSH
   b.   LH
   c.   estrogen
   d.   progesterone

12.   Arrange the following organs in correct sequence, from exterior to interior.
   a.   ovary
   b.   uterine tube
   c.   uterus
   d.   vagina

13.   Which contains an oocyte?
   a.   a corpus
   b.   a luteum
   c.   a follicle
   d.   a corpus and a luteum

14.   When the endometrium doubles in thickness,
   a.   it is influenced by progesterone.
   b.   it produces a thick, mucoid secretion.
   c.   it is in the secretory phase.
   d.   All of these are correct.

15.   FSH stimulates the production of
   a.   androgens.
   b.   sperm.
   c.   egg.
   d.   sperm and egg.

16.   LH stimulates the production of (directly)
   a.   progesterone.
   b.   sperm.
   c.   egg.
   d.   sperm and egg.

17.   During menstruation,
   a.   the endometrium breaks down.
   b.   the endometrium builds up.
   c.   bleeding occurs.
   d.   the egg is fertilized.
   e.   the endometrium breaks down and bleeding occurs.

18.   The urethra joins the
   a.   vagina.
   b.   uterus.
   c.   uterine tube.
   d.   None of these is correct.

Chapter 7

1.   Western culture often
   a.   places sexual response in a more goal-oriented context.
   b.   perceives sexual response as an expression of spiritual energies.
   c.   associates sexuality with concepts of creativity and unity.
   d.   believes in preparing the mind with sensual thoughts before sensual touching begins.

2.   The excitement phase of Masters and Johnson's model is characterized by
   a.   blood being routed to the pelvic region.
   b.   erection of the penis.
   c.   vaginal lubrication.
   d.   All of these are correct.

3.   The phase at which sexual arousal builds and is maintained is called
   a.   climax.
   b.   plateau.
   c.   resolution.
   d.   None of these is correct.

4.   An (A) _____ is the sexual release after the buildup of sensual enjoyment.
   a.   excitement
   b.   resolution
   c.   orgasm
   d.   None of these is correct.

5.   During resolution, the body
   a.   is closer to climax.
   b.   returns to the unexcited state.
   c.   is aroused.
   d.   None of these is correct.

6.   The human motivation theory states that sexual desire is triggered by
   a.   interpretations of reactions, sensations, and memories.
   b.   social rules that regulate sexual activity.
   c.   feeling valued by others and oneself.
   d.   All of these are correct.

7. The central arousal system refers to the _____ factors of activating sexual response.
   a. external
   b. internal
   c. stimulus
   d. None of these is correct.

8. External factors that affect the peripheral arousal system include
   a. spinal cord reflexes.
   b. stimuli from senses.
   c. sensations from genitals.
   d. All of these are correct.

9. Contemporary theorists believe that sexual arousal can include physiological responses as well as
   a. emotions.
   b. environment.
   c. experiences.
   d. All of these are correct.

10. Women, in general, romanticize the goals of sexual desire, seeing them as
    a. leading to marriage.
    b. emotional intimacy.
    c. control over their partner.
    d. None of these is correct.

11. During the female excitement phase, the vagina
    a. walls darken.
    b. becomes lubricated with slippery, alkaline fluid.
    c. lengthens, and distention of the inner one-third begins.
    d. All of these are correct.

12. During the _____ phase in the female, the vagina, labia minora, and breasts become engorged and swollen while the nipples stay erect.
    a. excitement
    b. resolution
    c. plateau
    d. orgasm

13. During the female orgasm, most women experience
    a. a suffusion of warmth through the pelvic region.
    b. muscle contraction throughout the body.
    c. quickening pulse rate.
    d. All of these are correct.

14. Kegel exercises can help
    a. increase the ability to experience orgasms.
    b. tone the vagina and uterus after childbirth.
    c. stop leaking urine from the bladder.
    d. All of these are correct.

15. During the male excitement phase, the
    a. penis is erect.
    b. urethra doubles in diameter.
    c. scrotum pulls upward toward the body.
    d. All of these are correct.

16. The length of time that the refractory period lasts depends on
    a. age.
    b. mood.
    c. sexual stimulation.
    d. All of these are correct.

17. The organizing effect refers to ways in which hormones
    a. control patterns of early development in the body.
    b. affect sexual arousal.
    c. play a crucial role in the structure and function of particular organs.
    d. Both a and c are correct.

18. The effects of age on the female sexual response include
    a. reduction of vaginal lubrication.
    b. thinning of the vaginal lining.
    c. increase in time needed to experience sexual arousal.
    d. All of these are correct.

19. Male sexual response undergoes change due to age, such as by
    a. taking two to three times longer to achieve erection.
    b. taking longer to reach orgasm.
    c. the lengthening of the refractory period.
    d. All of these are correct.

Chapter 8

1. When all three germ layers are present (ectoderm, endoderm, and mesoderm), the embryo is termed a
   a. blastula.   d. morula.
   b. archenteron.   e. blastopore.
   c. gastrula.

2. Which of these associations is mismatched?
   a. morula—ball of cells
   b. blastocyst—gut formation
   c. gastrula—three germ layers
   d. Both b and c are mismatched.

3. Which of these is a process of development?
   a. morphogenesis
   b. growth
   c. cleavage
   d. differentiation
   e. All of these are correct.

4. In human development, which part of the blastocyst will develop into a fetus?
   a. morula
   b. trophoblast
   c. inner cell mass
   d. chorion
   e. yolk sac

5. In humans, the fetus
   a. has four extraembryonic membranes.
   b. has developed organs and is recognizably human.
   c. is dependent upon the placenta for excretion of wastes and acquisition of nutrients.
   d. All of these are correct.

6. The placenta does not
   a. produce estrogen and progesterone.
   b. exchange dissolved gases.
   c. supply nutrients.
   d. cause the embryo to implant itself.

7. Which of these organs cannot be traced back to the germ layers?
   a. brain
   b. intestine
   c. bones
   d. All organs can be traced to germ layers.

8. Which hormone can be administered to begin the process of childbirth?
   a. estrogen
   b. oxytocin
   c. prolactin
   d. testosterone
   e. Both b and d are correct.

9. Only one sperm enters an egg because
   a. sperm have an acrosome.
   b. the corona radiata gets larger.
   c. of chemical changes in the egg's surface.
   d. the plasma membrane hardens.
   e. All of these are correct.

10. Which is a correct sequence that ends with the stage that implants?
    a. morula, blastocyst, embryonic disk, gastrula
    b. ovulation, fertilization, cleavage, morula, early blastocyst
    c. embryonic disk, gastrula, primitive streak, neurula
    d. primitive streak, neurula, extraembryonic membranes, chorion
    e. cleavage, neurula, early blastocyst, morula

11. Differentiation is equivalent to which term?
    a. morphogenesis
    b. growth
    c. specialization
    d. gastrulation
    e. induction

12. Two germ layers, not three, are present in the
    a. morula.
    b. blastocyst.
    c. embryonic disk.
    d. gastrula.
    e. neurula.

13. Which process refers to the shaping of the embryo and involves cell migration?
    a. cleavage
    b. differentiation
    c. growth
    d. induction
    e. morphogenesis

14. At 25 days, the embryo has
    a. become a fetus.
    b. all the extraembryonic membranes.
    c. a nervous system and a digestive system.
    d. already undergone gastrulation.
    e. Both b and d are correct.

15. At two months, the embryo has
    a. become a fetus.
    b. body systems, but they don't function yet.
    c. a head, arms, and legs.
    d. a nose and eyes.
    e. All but b are correct.

16. Which of these statements is correct?
    a. The head starts out big but then gets smaller.
    b. The hands and feet begin as paddlelike structures.
    c. The heart is at first tubular.
    d. The placenta functions until birth occurs.
    e. All of these are correct statements.

17. Which length can be best associated with the embryo at the end of two months when it becomes a fetus?
    a. less than one millimeter, which is microscopic
    b. 38 millimeters, which is about 1½ inches
    c. one foot, which is about one-third meter
    d. same length as a fetus at birth, which is about 20 inches
    e. Length varies too much to say.

18. Male/female gender of the fetus can be accurately determined as soon as the
    a. embryo is a zygote.
    b. germ layers have appeared.
    c. vertebrae have appeared.
    d. embryo is a fetus.
    e. embryo is about three months.

Chapter 9

1. In a vasectomy, the _____ are cut.
   a. epididymides
   b. seminiferous tubules
   c. vasa deferentia
   d. urethra

2. Which hormone is involved with uterine contractions and lactation?
   a. oxytocin
   b. HCG
   c. prostaglandins
   d. prolactin

3. An episiotomy is an incision to
   a. expand the vaginal opening.
   b. expand the uterus.
   c. cut the umbilical cord.
   d. rupture the amniotic membrane.

4. Which may occur during pregnancy?
   a. overeating
   b. increased urination
   c. increased energy levels
   d. All of these are correct.

5. Which hormone does the birth control pill contain?
   a. FSH
   b. LH
   c. estrogen
   d. All of these are correct.

6. The hormones of the birth control pill shut down (directly) the
   a. anterior pituitary.
   b. posterior pituitary.
   c. ovary.
   d. corpus luteum.

7. The birth control pill also prevents a pregnancy by secondary methods such as
   a. slowing down the transport of the embryo to the uterus.
   b. keeping the cervical mucus thick and impenetrable by sperm.
   c. preventing normal buildup of the uterine lining.
   d. All of these are correct.

8. The primary action of the birth control pill is to prevent
   a. fertilization.
   b. ovulation.
   c. implantation.
   d. All of these are correct.

9. Who should use an IUD?
   a. women who have had a child
   b. women of middle to older reproductive age
   c. young women
   d. middle-aged to older women who have had a child

10. An IUD prevents pregnancy by preventing
    a. fertilization.
    b. ovulation.
    c. implantation.
    d. both fertilization and ovulation.

11. What are possible side effects of an IUD?
    a. expulsion
    b. perforation of the uterus
    c. uterine infection
    d. All of these are correct.

12. The diaphragm, cervical cap, and sponge all prevent pregnancy by preventing
    a. fertilization.
    b. ovulation.

    c. implantation.
    d. All of these are correct.

13. Which means of birth control offers possible protection against sexually transmitted diseases?
    a. IUD
    b. diaphragm
    c. condom
    d. sponge

14. Mifepristone is administered
    a. before intercourse if menstruation is late.
    b. after intercourse if menstruation is late.
    c. at ovulation if pregnancy is desired.
    d. at regular times, as is done with the birth control pill.

15. Uterine aspiration is performed
    a. during the first three months of pregnancy.
    b. during the fourth and fifth months of pregnancy.
    c. during the sixth month of pregnancy.
    d. any time.

16. With GIFT, fertilization occurs in
    a. a test tube.
    b. the uterine tubes.
    c. the uterus.
    d. the ovary.

17. A surrogate mother is a woman who
    a. adopts a baby.
    b. is paid to have a baby.
    c. puts a baby up for adoption.
    d. donates an egg.

18. The sperm used in artificial insemination are from
    a. the woman's husband.
    b. a stranger.
    c. a mixture of her husband's sperm and those of a stranger.
    d. All of these are possible.

19. During regular artificial insemination, sperm are placed in the
    a. vagina.
    b. uterus.
    c. uterine tube.
    d. ovary.

Chapter 10 and AIDS Supplement

1. AIDS patients generally die due to which of the following causes?
   a. opportunistic infections
   b. HIV virus
   c. papillomaviruses
   d. heart attacks
   e. cancer

2. Which of the following statements is not true about genital warts?
   a. They are implicated in many cases of cervical cancer.

b.   They are caused by a different class of viruses than common warts.
c.   They often go undetected.
d.   There is no cure.
e.   They occur on the genitals.

3.   When the herpesvirus is latent, it resides in which area?
a.   ganglia of sensory nerves
b.   ganglia of motor neurons
c.   muscle cells
d.   skin cells
e.   adipose cells

4.   Which of the following is true about STDs?
a.   They cannot be transmitted without sexual intercourse.
b.   They cannot be transmitted through oral sex.
c.   They can be transmitted through toilet seats.
d.   They can be transmitted through handshakes.
e.   They can be transmitted by simply touching lesions.

5.   Which of the following is prescribed to treat herpes?
a.   herpicin
b.   penicillin
c.   erythromycin
d.   simplex cream
e.   acyclovir

6.   Hepatitis C is generally transmitted through which of the following mechanisms?
a.   contact with blood
b.   sexual contact
c.   drinking water
d.   airborne particles
e.   sputum

7.   Hepatitis B is generally transmitted through which of the following mechanisms?
a.   contact with blood
b.   sexual contact
c.   drinking water
d.   airborne particles
e.   sputum

8.   Hepatitis affects which organ?
a.   brain   d.   liver
b.   spleen   e.   kidney
c.   heart

9.   Which of the following is the causative agent of *Chlamydia* infections?
a.   bacterium
b.   virus
c.   phage
d.   fungus
e.   protozoan

10. *Chlamydia* infections can lead to which of the following?
a.   gummas
b.   pelvic inflammatory disease
c.   heart murmurs

d.   neonatalis
e.   erythema

11. Gonorrhea is caused by which of the following?
a.   bacterium   d.   fungus
b.   virus   e.   protozoan
c.   phage

12. Which of the following areas cannot be infected with gonorrhea?
a.   eye
b.   urethra
c.   vagina
d.   anus
e.   All of these areas can be infected.

13. Which of the following is indicative of the first stage of a syphilis infection?
a.   chancre
b.   rash
c.   gumma
d.   erythema
e.   generalized edema

14. Syphilis is diagnosed by a blood test that determines the presence of which of the following?
a.   hematonin
b.   syphilin
c.   gumma protein
d.   reagin
e.   globulin

15. Pubic lice fall into which class of infectious agent?
a.   fungi
b.   protozoans
c.   viruses
d.   animals
e.   bacteria

16. Which of the following is not a possible route for transmission of HIV?
a.   homosexual contact
b.   heterosexual contact
c.   blood transfusions
d.   breast-feeding
e.   sharing utensils

17. Which of the following is the least likely route for HIV transmission?
a.   vaginal intercourse
b.   rectal intercourse
c.   French kissing
d.   oral/penile contact
e.   oral/vaginal contact

18. Which continent has the greatest prevalence of HIV infection?
a.   Asia
b.   Africa
c.   North America
d.   Europe
e.   South America

19. Which of the following is generally not true of the acute phase of HIV infection?
    a. Viral loads can be high.
    b. Patients show acute symptoms.
    c. CD4 cell numbers drop.
    d. It can last for several years.
    e. The patient may have a positive HIV blood test.

20. Which of the following is not an opportunistic infection observed in AIDS patients?
    a. pneumocystis pneumonia
    b. tuberculosis
    c. toxoplasmic encephalitis
    d. choriogenic aplasia
    e. All of these are correct.

21. Which of the following terms is used to describe the remaining viral sequence after the genome of HIV integrates into the host cell chromosome?
    a. provirus
    b. integrin
    c. silent gene
    d. transfusion
    e. prion

22. Which of the following is the most successful AIDS drug?
    a. ABC
    b. AGT
    c. AZT
    d. ART
    e. ARC

23. Which of the following is the primary host for the HIV virus?
    a. T lymphocytes
    b. B lymphocytes
    c. H lymphocytes
    d. thrombocytes
    e. neutrocytes

Chapter 11

1. Which of these did Stanley Miller place in his experimental system to show that organic molecules could have arisen from inorganic molecules on the primitive Earth?
    a. microspheres
    b. purines and pyrimidines
    c. primitive gases
    d. only RNA
    e. All of these are correct.

2. Which of these is the chief reason the protocell was probably a fermenter?
    a. The protocell didn't have any enzymes.
    b. The atmosphere didn't have any oxygen.
    c. Fermentation provides the most energy.
    d. There was no ATP yet.
    e. All of these are correct.

3. Evolution of the DNA → RNA → protein system was a milestone because the protocell could now
    a. be a heterotrophic fermenter.
    b. pass on genetic information.
    c. use energy to grow.
    d. take in preformed molecules.
    e. All of these are correct.

4. According to Lamarck,
    a. if a man loses his hand, then his children will also be missing a hand.
    b. changes in phenotype are passed on by way of the genotype to the next generation.
    c. organisms are able to bring about a change in their phenotype.
    d. evolution is striving toward particular traits.
    e. All of these are correct.

5. Organisms
    a. compete with other members of their species.
    b. vary in physical characteristics.
    c. are adapted to their environment.
    d. are related by descent from common ancestors.
    e. All of these are correct.

6. If evolution occurs, we would expect different biogeographical regions with similar environments to
    a. all contain the same mix of plants and animals.
    b. each have its own specific mix of plants and animals.
    c. have plants and animals with similar adaptations.
    d. have plants and animals with different adaptations.
    e. Both b and c are correct.

7. The fossil record offers direct evidence for evolution because you can
    a. see that the types of fossils change over time.
    b. sometimes find common ancestors.
    c. trace the ancestry of a particular group.
    d. trace the biological history of living things.
    e. All of these are correct.

8. Organisms such as whales and sea turtles that are adapted to an aquatic way of life
    a. will probably have homologous structures.
    b. will have similar adaptations but not necessarily homologous structures.
    c. may very well have analogous structures.
    d. will have the same degree of fitness.
    e. Both b and c are correct.

9. Which of these gives the correct order of divergence from the main line of descent leading to humans?
    a. prosimians, monkeys, Asian apes, African apes, humans
    b. gibbons, baboons, prosimians, monkeys, African apes, humans
    c. monkeys, gibbons, prosimians, African apes, baboons, humans

  d. African apes, gibbons, monkeys, baboons, prosimi-
      ans, humans
  e. *H. habilis, H. erectus, H. neanderthalensis,*
      Cro-Magnon

10. Lucy is a member of what species?
    a. *Homo erectus*
    b. *Australopithecus afarensis*
    c. *H. habilis*
    d. *A. robustus*
    e. *A. anamensis* and *A. afarensis* are alternate forms
        of Lucy.

11. What possibly may have influenced the evolution of
    bipedalism?
    a. A larger brain   d. Both b and c are
        developed.   correct.
    b. Gathering of food   e. Both a and c are
        was easier.   correct.
    c. The climate became
        colder.

12. *H. erectus* could have been the first to
    a. use and control fire.
    b. migrate out of Africa.
    c. make tools.
    d. a and b are correct, but c is not.
    e. a, b, and c are correct.

13. Which of these characteristics is not consistent with the
    others?
    a. opposable thumb   d. well-developed
    b. learned behavior   brain
    c. multiple births   e. stereoscopic vision

14. The last common ancestor for African apes and hom-
    inids
    a. has been found, and it resembles a gibbon.
    b. has not been found, but it is expected to be dated
        from about 6 MYA.
    c. has been found, and it has been dated at 30 MYA.
    d. is not expected to be found because there was no
        such common ancestor.
    e. is now believed to have lived in Asia, not Africa.

15. If the multiregional continuity hypothesis is correct, then
    a. hominid fossils in China after 100,000 BP are not
        expected to resemble earlier fossils.
    b. hominid fossils in China after 100,000 BP are ex-
        pected to resemble earlier fossils.
    c. the mitochondrial Eve study must be invalid.
    d. Both a and c are correct.
    e. Both b and c are correct.

In questions 16–19, match each description to a type of evolutionary evidence in the key.
Key:
    a. biogeography
    b. fossil record
    c. comparative biochemistry

  d. comparative anatomy

16. Species change over time.

17. Forms of life are variously distributed.

18. A group of related species have homologous structures.

19. The same types of molecules are found in all living
    things.

Chapter 12

1. Which question is least likely to interest a behaviorist?
    a. How do genes control the development of the
        nervous system?
    b. Why do animals living in the tundra have white
        coats?
    c. Does aggression have a genetic basis?
    d. Why do some animals feed in groups and others
        feed singly?
    e. Behaviorists only study specific animals.

2. Which results illustrate that behavior has a genetic basis?
    a. Chicks have more accurate pecks a day or two af-
        ter hatching.
    b. Matings between two snake types who preferred
        different diets resulted in offspring that would ac-
        cept the same diet.
    c. Rats press a lever to obtain a piece of food.
    d. Birds learn songs from other birds in their area.

3. Female sage grouse are widely scattered throughout
    the prairie, where food is plentiful. Which of these
    would you expect?
    a. A male maintains a territory large enough to con-
        tain at least one female.
    b. Male and female birds are monogamous, and both
        help feed the young.
    c. Males form a lek from which females choose a
        mate.
    d. Males form a dominance hierarchy for the pur-
        pose of distributing resources.
    e. All of these are correct.

4. White-crowned sparrows from two different areas sing
    with a different dialect. If the behavior is primarily ge-
    netic, newly hatched birds from each area will
    a. sing with their own dialect.
    b. need tutors in order to sing in their dialect.
    c. sing only when a female is nearby.
    d. learn to sing later.
    e. Both a and c are correct.

5. Orangutans are solitary but territorial. This would mean
    orangutans defend their territory's boundaries against
    a. other male orangutans.
    b. female orangutans.
    c. all types of animals, whether orangutans or not.
    d. animals that prey on them.
    e. Both a and b are correct.

6. The resplendent plumes of a raggiana bird of paradise are due to the fact that birds with the best display
   a. are dominant over other birds.
   b. have the best territories.
   c. are chosen by females as mates.
   d. are chosen by males and females as companions.
   e. All of these are correct.

7. Subordinate females in a baboon troop do not produce offspring as often as dominant females. It is clear that
   a. the cost of being in the troop is too high.
   b. the dominant males do not mate with subordinate females.
   c. subordinate females must benefit in some way from being in the troop.
   d. Subordinate females should leave the troop.
   e. Both a and b are correct.

8. Which answer is based on anatomy? Males compete because
   a. they have the size and weapons with which to compete.
   b. they produce many sperm for a long time.
   c. the testes produce the hormone testosterone.
   d. only then do females respond to them.
   e. Both a and c are correct.

9. German blackcaps migrate southeast to Africa, and Austrian blackcaps fly southwest to Africa. The fact that hybrids of these two are intermediate shows that
   a. the trait is controlled by the nervous system.
   b. nesting is controlled by hormones.
   c. the behavior is at least partially genetic.
   d. behavior is according to the sex of animals.
   e. Both a and c are correct.

10. At first, laughing gull chicks peck at any model that looks like a red beak; later, they will not peck at any model that does not look like a parent. This shows that the behavior
    a. is a fixed action pattern.
    b. undergoes development after birth.
    c. is controlled by the nervous system.
    d. is under hormonal control.
    e. All of these are correct.

11. Which answer is in keeping with evolutionary theory? When females are choosy,
    a. they do not have the size and weapons with which to compete.
    b. they invest heavily in their offspring.
    c. the ovaries produce the hormones estrogen and progesterone.
    d. they need time to get ready to respond.
    e. All of these are correct.

12. Which is the benefit of being a large, aggressive, dominant male within a group?
    a. access to receptive females
    b. requiring more resources, such as food
    c. having the responsibility to fight off predators
    d. being able to defend against other challenging males

13. Which is a form of communication?
    a. the waggle dance of bees
    b. grooming
    c. a male peacock displaying his brilliant tail feathers
    d. a baboon in full threat
    e. All of these are correct.

14. Which of the following is an advantage of group living?
    a. competition for resources
    b. increased fitness of the group
    c. easier spread of disease
    d. parasites more common

15. Which statement shows that behavior is likely subject to natural selection?
    a. Certain behaviors can result in increased fitness.
    b. Reproductive behavior often involves sexual selection.
    c. Behavior has a genetic basis.
    d. Altruistic behaviors increase reproductive success.
    e. All of these are correct.

16. Which of these statements is correct?
    a. Behavior involves distinct actions with a genetic basis, and learning is a change in behavior due to experience.
    b. Most behaviors are fixed action patterns, and therefore predictable, while learning behaviors are unpredictable.
    c. Most behaviors seem to be learned actions, produced long after the birth of an individual.
    d. All of these are correct.
    e. None of these is correct.

Chapter 13

1. Exponential growth is best described by
   a. steep, unrestricted growth.
   b. an S-shaped growth curve.
   c. a constant rate of growth.
   d. growth that levels off after rapid growth.
   e. Both b and d are correct.

2. Decreased death rate followed by decreased birthrate has occurred in
   a. MDCs.
   b. LDCs.
   c. MDCs and LDCs.
   d. neither MDCs nor LDCs.

3. A renewable energy source is
   a. natural gas.
   b. coal.
   c. water.
   d. nuclear power.

4. A nonrenewable energy source is
   a. wind.
   b. geothermal energy.
   c. solar energy.
   d. land.

5. A transition to hydrogen fuel technology will
   a. be long coming and not likely to be of major significance.
   b. lessen many current environmental problems.
   c. not be likely since it will always be expensive and just as polluting as natural gas.
   d. be of major consequence, but resource limitations for obtaining hydrogen will hinder its progress.

6. Human societies at present are characterized by
   a. ever-increasing population growth.
   b. unsustainable practices.
   c. over-reliance on fossil fuels.
   d. All of these are correct.

7. GNP measures all but
   a. total costs of all manufacturing and production.
   b. costs of services.
   c. cost of environmental degradation through waste costs.
   d. profit.
   e. All of these are correct.

8. A population's maximum growth rate is also called its
   a. carrying capacity.
   b. biotic potential.
   c. growth curve.
   d. replacement rate.

9. Environmental resistance causes
   a. extinction of species.
   b. exponential growth.
   c. population decline.
   d. a decrease in the carrying capacity.
   e. Both c and d are correct.

10. The term "green revolution" refers to
    a. the application of fertilizer to increase crop yields.
    b. the use of artificial fertilizers rather than animal manure.
    c. the introduction of research-developed, high-yield monoculture crops.
    d. the introduction of new planting techniques in poor farming soil.

11. Which of the following is not usually involved in the process of desertification?
    a. conversion of semiarid land to desert
    b. overgrazing of land by farm animals
    c. land becoming unable to support human life
    d. removal of trees from forests

12. Most fresh water is held in
    a. groundwater.
    b. lakes.
    c. rivers.
    d. ice and snow.
    e. oceans.

13. Subsidence involves
    a. the overexploitation of land.
    b. the removal of water from land.
    c. the removal of plant life.
    d. desertification or deforestation.

14. Which of the following farming practices is capable of producing harmful environmental effects?
    a. fuel consumption
    b. fertilizer usage
    c. monoculture
    d. irrigation
    e. All of these can cause harmful environmental effects.

15. Evaporation of excess water from irrigation of farmland causes
    a. salinization.
    b. accumulation of mineral salts.
    c. loss of topsoil.
    d. a and b are correct, but c is not.
    e. a, b, and c are all correct.

16. In general, how many calories of plant material are needed to produce 1 calorie of animal material?
    a. 1
    b. 10
    c. 100
    d. 1,000

17. Endocrine-disrupting contaminants
    a. contribute to global warming.
    b. deplete the ozone shield.
    c. contribute to deforestation.
    d. produce hormonal effects in wildlife.
    e. All of these are correct.

18. In which of the following is biological magnification most pronounced?
    a. aquatic food chains
    b. terrestrial food chains
    c. long food chains
    d. energy pyramids
    e. a and c are both correct.

19. The ozone shield is
    a. depleted by CFCs.
    b. required for protection from ultraviolet radiation.
    c. predicted to recover.
    d. a and b are correct, but c is not.
    e. a, b, and c are all correct.

20. Which is not a possible consequence of aquifer depletion?
    a. saltwater intrusion
    b. sinkhole development
    c. subsidence
    d. cultural eutrophication
    e. All of these may result from aquifer depletion.

Answers to Testing Yourself

Chapter 1
1. d; 2. a; 3. b; 4. c; 5. e; 6. e; 7. d; 8. a; 9. c; 10. b; 11. d; 12. e; 13. d; 14. c; 15. d; 16. e; 17. e; 18. a; 19. d; 20. d; 21. c; 22. c

Chapter 2
1. c; 2. b; 3. d; 4. a; 5. b; 6. c; 7. b; 8. c; 9. e; 10. d; 11. c; 12. c; 13. c; 14. c; 15. a. cystic fibrosis; b. Tay-Sachs disease; c. neurofibromatosis; d. Huntington disease

Chapter 3
1. e; 2. e; 3. d; 4. c; 5. d; 6. b; 7. b; 8. e; 9. d; 10. a; 11. c; 12. e; 13. a; 14. b; 15. c; 16. a; 17. d; 18. e; 19. e

Chapter 4
1. b; 2. a; 3. c; 4. a; 5. b; 6. c; 7. b; 8. a. autosomal dominant; b. autosomal recessive; c. X-linked recessive; 9. d; 10. e; 11. b; 12. d; 13. a; 14. d; 15. d

Chapter 5
1. b,c,a,d; 2. c; 3. d; 4. a; 5. d; 6. b; 7. c; 8. a; 9. d; 10. b; 11. b; 12. d; 13. b; 14. d; 15. b; 16. b; 17. b; 18. c; 19. e

Chapter 6
1. d; 2. b; 3. a; 4. b; 5. b; 6. d; 7. b; 8. c; 9. b; 10. a; 11. d; 12. d,c,b,a; 13. c; 14. d; 15. d; 16. a; 17. e; 18. d

Chapter 7
1. a; 2. d; 3. b; 4. c; 5. b; 6. d; 7. b; 8. d; 9. d; 10. b; 11. d; 12. c; 13. d; 14. d; 15. d; 16. d; 17. d; 18. d; 19. d

Chapter 8
1. c; 2. b; 3. e; 4. c; 5. d; 6. d; 7. d; 8. b; 9. c; 10. b; 11. c; 12. c; 13. e; 14. e; 15. e; 16. e; 17. b; 18. e

Chapter 9
1. c; 2. a; 3. a; 4. d; 5. c; 6. a; 7. d; 8. b; 9. d; 10. c; 11. d; 12. a; 13. c; 14. b; 15. a; 16. b; 17. b; 18. d; 19. a

Chapter 10
1. a; 2. c; 3. a; 4. e; 5. e; 6. a; 7. b; 8. d; 9. a; 10. b; 11. a; 12. e; 13. a; 14. d; 15. d; 16. e; 17. c; 18. b; 19. b; 20. d; 21. a; 22. c; 23. a

Chapter 11
1. c; 2. b; 3. b; 4. e; 5. e; 6. e; 7. e; 8. e; 9. a; 10. b; 11. b; 12. d; 13. c; 14. b; 15. e; 16. b; 17. a; 18. d; 19. c

Chapter 12
1. b; 2. b; 3. c; 4. a; 5. e; 6. c; 7. c; 8. e; 9. c; 10. b; 11. b; 12. a; 13. e; 14. b; 15. e; 16. a

Chapter 13
1. a; 2. a; 3. c; 4. d; 5. b; 6. d; 7. c; 8. b; 9. c; 10. c; 11. d; 12. d; 13. b; 14. e; 15. d; 16. b; 17. d; 18. e; 19. e; 20. d

Appendix B
Answer Key

This appendix contains the answers to the additional genetics questions (Chapters 2 and 4) and to the critical thinking questions that appear at the end of each chapter.

Chapter 1

Critical Thinking Questions

1. The cell on the right represents metaphase I. The cell on the left represents metaphase II. This is known because homologous pairs at the equator only occur during metaphase I. The chromosomes of the two cells differ in number whether they are paired or not. **2.** A cell that has undergone meiosis will contain only one allele, either *A* or *a*. Since the genes are part of the chromosomes, they go with the chromosomes. The chromosomes separate during meiosis, and so the alleles also separate during meiosis. (You might want to expand on similarities between genes and chromosomes—i.e., they both are paired, they both separate during meiosis, only one of each is in the gamete, fertilization restores the full number.) **3.** Both alleles will be in one daughter cell because they are part of the chromosome and must go where the chromosome goes.

Chapter 2

Additional Genetics Questions

1. 50%; **2.** 50%; **3.** No. Only homozygous recessives cannot curl the tongue, and persons with this genotype cannot pass on the ability to curl the tongue. **4.** 50% (most likely, father is heterozygous); **5.** None; **6.** *Aa*, 25%; **7.** Child: *aa*, parents: *Aa*; **8.** 50%; **9.** father: *Wwcc*, mother: *wwCc*, child: *wwcc*; **10.** 75%; **11.** X^bYCc; **12.** *BO* (type B blood), *AO* (type A blood), *AB* (type AB blood), *OO* (type O blood); **13.** AB. He could be the father of a child with type B if mother is *BB*, *BO*, or *OO*. **14.** Father could be *BB*, *BO*, or *AB*. **15.** 100%; **16.** sickle-cell trait; **17.** *Aa*; **18.** 25%; **19.** Darkest skin possible is light; lightest skin possible is very light; **20.** Males 3/4, females 1/4.

Critical Thinking Questions

1. This is a 3:1 ratio; therefore, the parent flies were heterozygous. Most likely, about 100 of the 300 long-winged flies are homozygous dominant and 200 are heterozygous. A 1:2 genotype ratio is seen among those who have the dominant phenotype in Figure 2.4. **2.** Sickle-cell disease will always appear in each generation, because persons with sickle-cell trait reproduce with one another. **3.** This couple

can have children with all possible blood types (B^+, B^-, A^+, A^-, AB^+ AB^-, O^+, O^-). The best way to arrive at the answer is to first decide the ABO blood types by figuring every possible combination when the parents are AO × BO. Then figure the Rh factor outcome by observing that the *Dd* parent can either give the dominant or recessive allele to each child. **4.** The genotype is wwX^bY.

Chapter 3

Critical Thinking Questions

1. The piece of furniture is the organism, the cards are the cells, and the letters on the cards are the bases of the DNA code. DNA stores the information for the synthesis of proteins, which is passed on from parent to offspring in the chromosomes. **2.** DNA mutations lead to the variety of life that we see about us. **3.** Yes, DNA controls protein synthesis in plant cells just as it does in animal cells.

Chapter 4

Figure 4.2

The disorder is recessive. This female does not have the disorder; therefore, she has to have at least one dominant allele. She has two affected children; therefore, she also has to have a recessive allele.

Figure 4.3

The disorder is dominant. This male has the disorder; therefore, he has to have at least one dominant allele. He has an unaffected child; therefore, he also has to have a recessive allele.

Critical Thinking Questions

1. The expression "blood test for genetic diseases" is slightly misleading because DNA from lymphocytes is used for testing, and whole blood is not needed for the test. **2.** You would expect testing of DNA to be more accurate than biochemical testing because DNA is the genetic material. **3.** A genetic counselor bothers to do pedigrees because a pedigree can indicate which persons should be tested.

Chapter 5

Critical Thinking Questions

1. Testosterone combines with a cellular receptor just inside the plasma membrane, and the complex enters the nucleus, where it activates the genes that direct the synthesis of actin and myosin. Messenger RNA travels out of the nucleus to the ribosomes, where actin and myosin synthesis occurs. The result is increased muscle mass. **2. a.** You would expect this individual to have ovaries because there is no Y to bring about the development of testes. **b.** The individual cannot respond to estrogen because there are no functioning receptors. The primary sex characteristics cannot mature, and female secondary sex characteristics cannot appear. **c.** Assuming that the individual has receptors for testosterone, it's possible that there will be some masculinization. **d.** This individual will not be fertile; the female sex organs never mature, and there are no male sex organs.

Chapter 6
Critical Thinking Questions

1. The penis would have to have two separate tubes—one for urine and one for sperm. The ejaculatory duct could continue on rather than joining up with the urethra. **2.** The penis allows the sperm to pass directly into the body of the female so that the sperm do not dry out. The penis has to become erect to serve its function, and some males are sexually dysfunctional. **3.** The uterus would have to lead to two tubes. One of these would be the vagina, which would be used only for sexual intercourse. The sperm would travel from vagina to uterus to uterine tube as before. The other would be the birth canal, which would be used only for birth. The vagina would have to constrict just before birth so that the only opening from the uterus would be the birth canal. **4.** Females bear offspring, and originally females devoted more energy to raising them. This being the case, it was advantageous for a female to bear and raise offspring only when her body was young and strong.

Chapter 7
Critical Thinking Questions

1. Individuals learn to be sexually aroused by certain stimuli, and the learning experiences of people differ. **2.** Yes, it is consistent with the role of the female in bearing children that she desire love, emotional intimacy, and physical closeness. A relationship characterized in this way is more likely to be a lasting one, in which the male will help raise the children. **3.** This answer will vary according to the student.

Chapter 8
Critical Thinking Questions

1. See the reading, Preventing Birth Defects, on page 134. **2.** Most likely, the egg was fertilized in the uterine tube and then expelled into the abdominal cavity. One place of attachment could be the intestine where a placenta could develop—there are blood vessels in the intestine as well as in the uterus. The baby could be delivered by cesarean section.

Chapter 9
Critical Thinking Questions

1. In the female, rising levels of estrogen and progesterone normally shut down the hypothalamus and pituitary so that FSH and LH are not produced for a limited time. No such cycle exists in the male—a male always produces sperm—and the normal level of testosterone does not shut down the hypothalamus and pituitary. **2.** A pill containing FSH and LH antagonists would result in the absence of either the ovarian or testicular sex hormones in the body. The result would be feminization of males and masculinization of females due to production of both male and female hormones by the adrenal cortex. **3.** Placing the sperm in the uterus means that (1) there is less distance for the sperm to travel to get to the egg, and (2) the uterus is a more benign environment for sperm than the vagina. Therefore, you would expect more sperm to reach the egg, giving a better chance of fertilization.

Chapter 10
Critical Thinking Questions

1. Syphilis is caused by a bacterium, and AIDS is caused by a virus. Antibiotics interfere with bacterial enzymes. Viruses don't usually have enzymes because they use the enzymes of a host cell. A drug such as AZT interferes with viral replication of DNA, a necessary step in the viral reproductive cycle that takes place inside a host cell. It's possible that AZT might be somewhat effective against syphilis, but an antibiotic acts specifically against bacteria. **2.** HIV attacks helper T cells; as their number declines, the patient becomes ill with other diseases. Herpes simplex virus causes blisters that occur on the genitals. HPVs reproduce in skin cells, and this leads to warts. *Neisseria gonorrhoeae* and *Chlamydia* live and reproduce in the cavities and tubes of the urogenital system. These infections may lead to a discharge. *Treponema pallidum* invades the blood; therefore, the illness affects various organs and systems of the body. **3.** Both HIV and *Treponema pallidum* enter the blood; however, HIV is a virus and *Treponema pallidum* is a bacterium. HIV infection leads to an ever-decreasing number of helper T cells so that other infections set in. *Treponema pallidum* itself infects various organs in the body.

AIDS Supplement
Critical Thinking Questions

1. A person with AIDS is particularly subject to infection by other pathogens because the immune system has been compromised. **2.** HIV will enter T lymphocytes because the virus fits into a receptor on the cell surface of T lymphocytes like a key fits a lock. **3.** The drug therapy for an HIV infection does not kill T lymphocytes because the drugs are specific to the production of HIV.

Chapter 11

Critical Thinking Questions

1. As long as the positive benefits are greater than the negative benefits, a trait can be selected because of its advantageous nature. **2.** During the course of human evolution, we see certain traits arising that would be considered cultural, such as the use of fire; the use of language, which would foster cooperation among members of a social group; the arts, such as drawing on cave walls; and even an indication of a primitive type of religion. **3.** Australopithecines are considered the first hominids, even though they had a small brain, because they walked erect.

Chapter 12

Critical Thinking Questions

1. The investigator has not taken into account that an infant is more apt to turn toward a caretaker's voice. A better methodology would be to have the caretaker's voice played at different pitches to see if the infant turns more readily to a higher pitch of that voice. **2.** To be an altruistic behavior, the animal has to be giving up something for the good of the whole. It does not appear, in this instance, that the meerkats are giving up anything when they serve as sentries.

Chapter 13

Critical Thinking Questions

1. Factors that would cause the human population to increase more than expected would be when women have children at a younger age, when they are socially disadvantaged, when they lack birth control, and when the children are a benefit to the family. Factors related to a decrease are when women have children at a later age, when they have social advantages, when birth control is available, and when children are not necessarily helpful to the family unit. **2.** A greater number of people does not necessarily lead to a greater workforce. It can simply lead to a greater number of people unemployed. So, the Mexican government should have planned ahead in order to create jobs for the greater number of people expected.

Appendix C
Further Readings

Chapter 1

Alberts, B., et al. 1997. *Essential cell biology: An introduction to the molecular biology of the cell.* New York: Garland Publishing, Inc. Excellent student text for the easy understanding of the cell and its functions.

Berns, M. W. April 1998. Laser scissors and tweezers. *Scientific American* 278(62):4. New laser techniques allow manipulation of chromosomes and other structures inside cells.

Mader, S. 2004. *Human biology,* 8th ed. Dubuque, IA: McGraw-Hill Publishing. Covers the principles of biology with applications to humans, including a sound survey of the body's systems.

Miller, O., and Therman, E. 2001. *Human chromosomes, 4th ed.* New York: Springer Verlag Publishing. Concise, understandable introduction to the structure and behavior of human chromosomes.

Shashidhar Pai, G., et al. 2002. *Handbook of chromosomal syndromes.* St. Louis: Wiley-Liss Publishing. An overview of the syndromes caused by chromosomal mutations.

Tobin, R., and Morrow, A. 1997. *Asking about cells.* Philadelphia: Saunders College Publishing. Good introduction to the cell.

Chapter 2

Barkley, R. A. September 1998. Attention-deficit hyperactivity disorder. *Scientific American* 279(3):66. ADHD may result from neurological abnormalities with a genetic basis.

Cummings, M. 2002. *Human heredity: Principles and issues.* New York: West Publishing Co. The Principles of heredity in humans as well as the genetic disorders that arise are discussed.

Hopkin, K. March 1999. Death to sperm mitochondria. *Scientific American* 280(3):21. Article discusses why mitochondrial DNA only comes from the mother.

Lewis, R. 2001. *Human genetics: Concepts and applications.* Dubuque, IA: McGraw-Hill Publishing. A good introduction to genetics.

Mader, S. 2004. *Human biology,* 8th ed. Dubuque, IA: McGraw-Hill Publishing. Covers the principles of biology with applications to humans, including a sound survey of the body's systems.

Mirsky, S. August 2001. Sticky situation. *Scientific American* 285(2):22. The great hope for curing sickle-cell disease continues to be gene therapy.

Plomerin, R., and DeFries, J. C. May 1998. The genetics of cognitive abilities and disabilities. *Scientific American* 278(5):62. The search is under way for the genes involved in cognitive abilities and disabilities, including dyslexia.

Swartz, C., et al. 1999. *X-linked mental retardation.* New York: Oxford University Press. Comprehensive survey of mental retardation caused by genes on the X chromosome.

Thompson, M., et al. 1991. *Thompson & Thompson genetics in medicine,* 5th ed. Philadelphia: W.B. Saunders Publ. Introduction to the fundamental principles of human genetics with an emphasis on genes and molecular mechanisms operating in human diseases.

Weiner, D. B., and Kennedy, R. C. July 1999. Genetic vaccines. *Scientific American* 281(1):50. Bits of DNA or RNA, if introduced into cells, can stimulate powerful immune responses against viruses, bacteria, and some cancers. These techniques could be used as genetic vaccines.

Chapter 3

Ezzell, C. July 2000. Beyond the human genome. *Scientific American* 283(1):64. A new field called proteonomics will try to make use of the information learned from the Human Genome Project.

Friedmann, T., et. al. June 1997. Making gene therapy work. *Scientific American* 276(6):95. Article discusses the obstacles that must still be overcome before gene therapy is ready for widespread use.

Friend, S., and Stoughton, R. February 2002. The magic of microarrays. *Scientific American* 286(2):44. DNA microarray tools are clarifying the molecular roots of health and disease and speeding drug discovery.

Lau, N., and Bartel, D. August 2003. Censors of the genome. *Scientific American* 289(2):34–41. Biologists have been surprised to discover that most animal cells contain a built-in system to silence individual genes by shredding the RNA they produce.

Mader, S. 2004. *Human biology*, 8th ed. Dubuque, IA: McGraw-Hill Publishing. Covers the principles of biology with applications to humans, including a sound survey of the body's systems.

Martindale, D. October 2001. Genes are not enough. *Scientific American* 285(4):22. Switching genes on and off sometimes depends on the addition of methyl groups to DNA.

Mirsky, S. August 2001. Sticky situation. *Scientific American* 285(2):22. The great hope for curing sickle-cell disease continues to be gene therapy. Another important aspect of the disease has been found—a protein is largely responsible for the cellular stickiness.

O'Brochta, D. A., and Atkinson, P. W. December 1998. Building a better bug. *Scientific American* 279(6):90. Article discusses the production of a transgenic insect. Transgenic insect technology could decrease pesticide use and prevent certain infectious diseases.

Pinon, R., Jr. 2002. *Biology of human reproduction*. Sausalito, CA: University Science Books. A systematic overview of the biology of human reproduction at the intermediate level.

Scientific American editors. June 1997. Special report: Making gene therapy work. 276(6):95. Obstacles must be overcome before gene therapy is ready for widespread use.

Scientific American editors. April 1999. The promise of tissue engineering. 280(4):59–89. Much of the issue examines the hopes and challenges of tissue engineering for use in gene therapy and for the growth of new organs.

Chapter 4

Baker, D. 1998. *A guide to genetic counseling*. New York: John Wiley and Sons Publ. Devoted to the principles and practice of genetic counseling.

Gardner, R. J., and Sutherland, G. R. 1996. *Chromosome abnormalities and genetic counseling*, 2nd ed. New York: Oxford University Press. An important introduction to genetic counseling and interpretation of cytogenetic results.

Harper, P. 1998. *Practical genetic counseling*, 5th ed. New York: Oxford University Press. Updated guide to new information and emerging psychosocial and ethical concerns connected to genetic counseling.

Jones, R. E. 1997. *Human reproductive biology*. San Diego, CA: Academic Press. Introduction to the human reproductive systems.

Mader, S. 2004. *Human biology*, 8th ed. Dubuque, IA: McGraw-Hill Publishing. Covers the principles of biology with applications to humans, including a sound survey of the body's systems.

Nemecek, S. December 2000. The second abortion pill. *Scientific American* 283(6):16. Article examines the anticipated usage of Mifepristone (RU486) as a means of abortion.

Thompson, M., et al. 1991. *Thompson & Thompson genetics in medicine*, 5th ed. Philadelphia: W. B. Saunders Publ. Introduction to the fundamental principles of human genetics with an emphasis on genes and molecular mechanisms operating in human diseases.

Chapter 5

Crowley, L. 2001. *An introduction to human disease: Pathology and pathophysiology correlations.* Boston: Jones & Bartlett Publishers. This well-illustrated text for study in the allied health fields describes diseases and their symptoms, diagnoses, and treatments.

Jones, R. E. 1997. *Human reproductive biology.* San Diego, CA: Academic Press. An accurate and up-to-date presentation of the reproductive systems and related topics.

Jordan, V. C. October 1998. Designer estrogens. *Scientific American* 279(4):60. Selective estrogen receptor modulators may protect against breast and endometrial cancers, osteoporosis, and heart disease.

Litwack, G., and Norman, A. 1997. *Hormones.* San Diego, CA: Academic Press. This is an extensive reference about human hormone interactions with organ physiology.

Mader, S. 2004. *Understanding human anatomy and physiology,* 5th ed. Dubuque, IA: McGraw-Hill Publishing. A text that emphasizes the basics for beginning allied health students.

Pinon, R., Jr. 2002. *Biology of human reproduction.* Sausalito, CA: University Science Books. A systematic overview of the biology of human reproduction at the intermediate level.

Porterfield, S. 2000. *Endocrine physiology,* 2d ed. St. Louis: Mosby, Inc. Text explains in a clear and concise manner the workings of the endocrine system.

Smith, R. March 1999. The timing of birth. *Scientific American* 280(3):68. A hormone in the human placenta that influences the timing of delivery could yield ways to predict and prevent premature labor.

Chapter 6

Garnick, M. B., and Fair, W. R. December 1998. Combating prostate cancer. *Scientific American* 279(6):74. Article details the recent developments in the diagnosis and treatment of prostate cancer.

Jones, R. E. 1997. *Human reproductive biology.* San Diego, CA: Academic Press. An accurate and up-to-date presentation of the reproductive systems and related topics.

Mader, S. 2004. *Understanding human anatomy and physiology,* 5th ed. Dubuque, IA: McGraw-Hill Publishing. A text that emphasizes the basics for beginning allied health students.

Pinon, R., Jr. 2002. *Biology of human reproduction.* Sausalito, CA: University Science Books. A systematic overview of the biology of human reproduction at the intermediate level.

Sloane, E. 2002. *Biology of women.* Albany, NY: Delmar. Overview of the reproductive system of women.

Chapter 7

Byer, C. O., et al. 2002. *Dimensions of human sexuality.* New York: McGraw-Hill Higher Education. An in-depth look at human sexual response.

Crooks, R., and Baur, K. 2001. *Our sexuality*, 8th ed. Redwood City, CA: Thompson International Publishing. Introduction to the biological, psychosocial, behavioral, and cultural aspects of sexuality.

Hyde, J. S., and DeLamanter, J. D. 2003. *Understanding human sexuality.* Dubuque, IA: McGraw-Hill Companies, Inc. Introductory text covering the basics of human sexuality and responses.

Jones, R. E. 1997. *Human reproductive biology.* San Diego, CA: Academic Press. An accurate and up-to-date presentation of the reproductive systems and related topics.

Kelly, G. F. 1998. *Notable selections in human sexuality.* Guilford, CT: McGraw-Hill Companies, Inc. A look into the research behind human sexuality studies.

Kelly, G. F. 2001. *Sexuality today.* New York: McGraw-Hill Companies, Inc. An up-to-date look at the current aspects of sexual responses.

Mader, S. 2004. *Understanding human anatomy and physiology*, 5th ed. Dubuque, IA: McGraw-Hill Publishing. A text that emphasizes the basics for beginning allied health students.

Masters, W., and Johnson, V. 1996. *Human sexual response.* Baltimore, MD: Lippincott Williams & Wilkens Publ. A report on clinical findings about human sexual response patterns and orgasmic expression.

Pomeroy, M., and Kinsey, A. 1998. *Sexual response in the human male.* Bloomington, IN: Indiana University Press. The first research by Alfred Kinsey into human sexuality to be published.

Chapter 8

Carlson, B. M. 1999. *Human embryology and developmental biology*, 2nd ed. St. Louis: Mosby. Concise introductory text covering human development from fertilization to death.

Jones, R. E. 1997. *Human reproductive biology.* San Diego, CA: Academic Press. An accurate and up-to-date presentation of the reproductive systems and related topics.

MacDonald, P. C., and Casey, M. L. March/April 1996. Preterm birth. *Scientific American Science & Medicine* 3(2):42. Article discusses the role of oxytocin, prostaglandins, and infections in the initiation of human labor.

Mader, S. 2004. *Understanding human anatomy and physiology*, 5th ed. Dubuque, IA: McGraw-Hill Publishing. A text that emphasizes the basics for beginning allied health students.

Moore, K., and Persaud, T. 2002. *Before we are born: Essentials of embryology and birth defects*, 6th ed. Philadelphia: W. B. Saunders and Co. For medical and associated health students, this text presents the essentials of normal and abnormal human embryological development.

Nilsson, L. 1990. *A child is born.* New York: Delacorte Press. Human-interest overview of development from fertilization to birth.

O'Rahilly, R., and Muller, F. 2001. *Human embryology and teratology,* 3rd ed. New York: Wiley-Liss Publishing. This is an exceptional reference on normal and abnormal human prenatal development.

Pinon, R., Jr. 2002. *Biology of human reproduction.* Sausalito, CA: University Science Books. A systematic overview of the biology of human reproduction at the intermediate level.

Smith, B. March 1999. Visualizing human embryos. *Scientific American* 280(3):77. Magnetic resonance microscopy is revealing the secrets of early human development.

Smith, R. March 1999. The timing of birth. *Scientific American* 280(3):68. A hormone in the human placenta that influences the timing of delivery could yield ways to predict and prevent premature labor.

Chapter 9

American College of Obstetricians. 2003. *Birth control: A woman's choice.* Up-to-date information on methods of birth control: how it works, how to use it, and the health benefits and effectiveness rates.

Healey, D. L. 2001. *Reproductive medicine in the twenty-first century.* London: CRC Press-Parthenon Publ. Overview of procedures available to infertile couples.

Henig, R. June 2003. Pandora's baby. *Scientific American* 288(6):63–67. In vitro fertilization was once considered by some to be a threat to our humanity.

Jegalian, K., and Lahn, B. T. February 2001. Why the Y is so weird. *Scientific American* 284(2):56. Article examines the differences in the Y chromosome; the evolutionary history of the Y chromosome may provide answers in treating male infertility.

Jones, R. E. 1997. *Human reproductive biology.* San Diego, CA: Academic Press. An accurate and up-to-date presentation of the reproductive systems and related topics.

MacDonald, P. C., and Casey, M. L. March/April 1996. Preterm birth. *Scientific American Science & Medicine* 3(2):42. Article discusses the role of oxytocin, prostaglandins, and infections in the initiation of human labor.

Mader, S. 2004. *Understanding human anatomy and physiology,* 5th ed. Dubuque, IA: McGraw-Hill Publishing. A text that emphasizes the basics for beginning allied health students.

Nemecek, S. December 2000. The second abortion pill. *Scientific American* 283(6):16. Article examines the anticipated usage of mifepristone (RU486) as a means of abortion.

Pinon, R., Jr. 2002. *Biology of human reproduction.* Sausalito, CA: University Science Books. A systematic overview of the biology of human reproduction at the intermediate level.

Smith, R. March 1999. The timing of birth. *Scientific American* 280(3):68. A hormone in the human placenta that influences the timing of delivery could yield ways to predict and prevent premature labor.

Sutcliffe, A. 2002. *IVF children: The first generation: Assisted reproduction and child development.* London: CRC Press-Parthenon Publ. Relevant studies of the development and well-being of IVF children as well as outcomes of ICSI, cryopreservation, standard IVF, and other recent technologies.

Chapter 10

Cox, F. 2000. *The AIDS booklet.* Dubuque, IA: McGraw-Hill Publishing. This reference guide explains the transmission, characteristics, and causes of the HIV virus and AIDS.

Handsfield, H. 2000. *Genital herpes,* 2nd ed. Dubuque, IA: McGraw-Hill Publishing. Succinct coverage on the clinical presentation of primary, nonprimary, and recurrent herpes.

Holmes, P. 1999. *Sexually transmitted disease.* Dubuque, IA: McGraw-Hill Publishers. Comprehensive resource on sexually transmitted diseases.

Jones, R. E. 1997. *Human reproductive biology.* San Diego, CA: Academic Press. An accurate and up-to-date presentation of the reproductive systems and related topics.

Mader, S. 2004. *Understanding human anatomy and physiology,* 5th ed. Dubuque, IA: McGraw-Hill Publishing. A text that emphasizes the basics for beginning allied health students.

Pinon, R., Jr. 2002. *Biology of human reproduction.* Sausalito, CA: University Science Books. A systematic overview of the biology of human reproduction at the intermediate level.

Stine, G. 2002. *AIDS update 2003.* San Francisco: Benjamin/Cummings Publishers. Overview of AIDS including causes, characteristics, therapy, transmission, and prevalence.

AIDS Supplement

Cox, F. 2000. *The AIDS booklet.* Dubuque, IA: McGraw-Hill Publishing. This reference guide explains the transmission, characteristics, and causes of the HIV virus and AIDS.

Stine, G. 2002. *AIDS update 2003.* San Francisco: Benjamin/Cummings Publishers. Overview of AIDS including causes, characteristics, therapy, transmission, and prevalence.

Chapter 11

Agnew, N., and Demas, M. September 1998. Preserving the Laetoli footprints. *Scientific American* 279(3):44. This article recaps the discovery of hominid footprints in eastern Africa, and explains steps taken to preserve them.

Boyd, R., and Silk, J. B. 2002. *How humans evolved*, 3rd ed. New York: W. W. Norton & Co., Inc. This introductory text integrates evolutionary theory, population genetics, and behavioral ecology with evidence from the hominid fossil record to emphasize the processes of human evolution.

Leakey, M., and Walker, A. June 1997. Early hominid fossils from Africa. *Scientific American* 276(6):74. A bone unearthed in 1965 recently proved the existence of a new species of *Australopithecus,* showing that ancestral humans existed 4 million years ago.

Levin, H. L. 1998. *The Earth through time*, 6th ed. Fort Worth, TX: Saunders College Publishing. This introductory text provides background information on such topics as the geologic timescale, plate tectonics, the fossil record, and human origins.

Mader, S. 2003. *Biology*, 8th ed. Dubuque, IA: McGraw-Hill Companies, Inc. Text covering topics from anatomy of the cell to human development and physiology as well as plant biology.

Tattersall, I. April 1997. Out of Africa again . . . and again? *Scientific American* 276(4):60. Hominids may have migrated out of Africa several times, with each emigration sending a different species.

Tattersall, I. January 2000. Once we were not alone. *Scientific American* 282(1):56. This article discusses *Paranthropus boisei, H. rudolfensis, H. habilis, H. ergaster,* and others. A speculative family tree is presented; the question "Why are *H. sapiens* the only ones to remain?" is posed.

Wong, K. December 2000. Paleolithic pit stop. *Scientific American* 283(6):18. Findings at an archeological site in France suggest that Neanderthals and early humans behaved similarly.

Chapter 12

Alcock, J. 2001. *Animal behavior: An evolutionary approach.* Sunderland, MA: Sinauer Assoc. Excellent resource for an in-depth understanding of animal behavior with a chapter on human behavior.

Boyd, R., and Silk, J. B. 2002. *How humans evolved*, 3rd ed. New York: W. W. Norton & Co., Inc. This introductory text integrates evolutionary theory, population genetics, and behavioral ecology with evidence from the hominid fossil record to emphasize the processes of human evolution.

Cunningham, W. P., and Saigo, B. W. 2001. *Environmental science: A global concern*, 7th ed. Dubuque, IA: McGraw-Hill Publishing. Provides scientific principles plus insights into the social, political, and economic systems impacting the environment.

deWaal, F. B. M. December 1999. The end of nature-versus-nurture. *Scientific American* 281(6):56. Article presents arguments about whether our behavior is shaped more by genetics or environment.

Dugatkin, L. A., and Godin, J. J. April 1998. How females choose their mates. *Scientific American* 278(4):56. Female choice is studied in relation to a number of fish and bird species.

Weiss, M. 1990. *Human biology and behavior: An anthropological perspective.* Glenview, IL: Scott Foresman & Co. Although a dated text, this is an excellent resource book.

Whiten, A., and Boesch, C. January 2001. The culture of chimpanzees. *Scientific American* 284(1):60. Wild chimpanzees display social customs in group settings.

Chapter 13

Cox, G. 1997. *Conservation ecology,* 2nd ed. Dubuque, IA: McGraw-Hill Publishing. Discusses the nature of the biosphere, the threats to its integrity, and ecologically sound responses.

Cunningham, W. P., and Saigo, B. W. 2001. *Environmental science: A global concern,* 7th ed. Dubuque, IA: McGraw-Hill Publishing. Provides scientific principles plus insights into the social, political, and economic systems impacting the environment.

Enger, E., and Smith, B. 2002. *Environmental science.* Boston: McGraw-Hill Publishers. Overview of ecology, conservation, pollution, botany, and the human impact.

Goldfarb, T. 2000. *Taking sides: Clashing views on controversial environmental issues,* 9th ed. Guilford, CT: Dushkin/McGraw-Hill. This text examines the pros and cons and gives the history of 18 current environmental controversies.

Miller, G. T. 2002. *Living in the environment.* San Francisco: Thomson Learning. Human impact on the environment.

Molles, M. C., Jr. 2002. *Ecology: Concepts and applications,* 2nd ed. Boston: McGraw-Hill Higher Education. An evolutionary perspective forms the foundation for this introductory ecology text.

Rice, R. E., et al. April 1997. Can sustainable management save tropical forests? *Scientific American* 276(4):44. The strategy of replacing harvested trees in rain forests often fails.

Safina, C. November 1995. The world's imperiled fish. *Scientific American* 273(5):46. Article discusses the decline of fish populations due to the commercial fishing industry.

Schmidt, M. J. January 1996. Working elephants. *Scientific American* 274(1):82. In Asia, teams of elephants serve as an alternative to destructive logging equipment.

Smil, V. July 1997. Global population and the nitrogen cycle. *Scientific American* 277(1):76. One-third of all the nitrogen in people's bodies comes from artificial sources rather than natural sources. Article asks what this is doing to the environment.

Glossary

A

abortion Termination of pregnancy before the fetus is capable of survival.   150

abstinence Method of birth control; the practice of not engaging in sexual intercourse.   142

acrosome (ak-ruh-sohm) Cap at the anterior end of a sperm that partially covers the nucleus and contains enzymes that help the sperm penetrate the egg.   90

activating effect Direct influence some hormones can have on activating or deactivating sexual behavior.   120

adaptation Organism's modification in structure, function, or behavior suitable to the environment.   183

adenine (A) (ad-uh-neen) One of four nitrogen-containing bases in nucleotides comprising the structure of DNA and RNA; pairs with thymine or uracil.   41

adrenal cortex (uh-dree-nul kor-teks) Outer portion of the adrenal gland; secretes mineralocorticoids such as aldosterone and glucocorticoids such as cortisol.   77

adrenal gland (uh-dree-nul) Endocrine gland that lies atop a kidney, consisting of the inner adrenal medulla and the outer adrenal cortex.   77

adrenal medulla (uh-dree-nul muh-dul-uh) Inner portion of the adrenal gland; secretes the hormones epinephrine and norepinephrine.   77

afterbirth Placenta and the extraembryonic membranes, which are delivered (expelled) during the third stage of parturition.   137

AIDS (acquired immunodeficiency syndrome) (im-yuh-noh-dih-fish-un-see) Disease caused by HIV and transmitted via body fluids; characterized by failure of the immune system.   164, 172

allantois (uh-lan-toh-is) Extraembryonic membrane that contributes to the formation of umbilical blood vessels in humans.   127

allele (uh-leel) Alternative form of a gene; alleles occur at the same locus on homologous chromosomes.   22

altruism Social interaction that has the potential to decrease the lifetime reproductive success of the member exhibiting the behavior.   211

amniocentesis Procedure in which a sample of amniotic fluid is removed through the abdominal wall of a pregnant woman. Fetal cells in it are cultured before doing a karyotype of the chromosomes.   58

amnion (am-nee-ahn) Extraembryonic membrane that forms an enclosing, fluid-filled sac.   127

analogous structure Structure that has a similar function in separate lineages but differs in anatomy and ancestry.   184

anaphase Mitotic phase during which daughter chromosomes move toward the poles of the spindle.   9

androgen (an-druh-jun) Male sex hormone (e.g., testosterone).   77, 88, 120

anencephaly Congenital absence of the cranial vault, with cerebral hemispheres completely missing or reduced to small masses attached to the base of the skull.   134

anterior pituitary (pih-too-ih-tair-ee) Portion of the pituitary gland that is controlled by the hypothalamus and produces six types of hormones, some of which control other endocrine glands.   77

antibiotic Medications that kill bacteria by interfering with one of their unique metabolic pathways.   156

anticodon (an-tih-koh-dahn) Three-base sequence in a transfer RNA molecule base that pairs with a complementary codon in mRNA.   46

apoptosis (ap-uh-toh-sis, ahp-) Programmed cell death involving a cascade of specific cellular events leading to death and destruction of the cell.   7

aquifer (ahk-wuh-fur) Rock layers that contain water and will release it in appreciable quantities to wells or springs.   221

arboreal Living in trees.   187

artificial insemination Placement of donated sperm in the vagina so that fertilization followed by pregnancy might occur.   152

assisted reproductive technologies (ART) Medical techniques, sometimes performed in vitro, that are done to increase the chances of pregnancy.   152

aster Short, radiating fibers about the centrioles at the poles of a spindle.   8

australopithecine (aw-stray-loh-pith-uh-syn) Any of the first evolved hominids; classified into several species of *Australopithecus*.   189

autosome (aw-tuh-sohm) Any chromosome other than the sex chromosomes.   16

B

bacteria One of three domains of life; prokaryotic cells other than archaea with unique genetic, biochemical, and physiological characteristics.   166

bacterial vaginosis (BV) Sexually transmitted disease caused by *Gardnerella vaginalis, Mobiluncus* spp., *Mycoplasma hominis,* and various anaerobic bacteria. Although a mild disease, it is a risk factor for obstetric infections and pelvic inflammatory disease.   166

Barr body Dark-staining body (discovered by M. Barr) in the nuclei of female mammals that contains a condensed, inactive X chromosome.   18, 32

behavior Observable, coordinated responses to environmental stimuli.   198

benign prostatic hyperplasia (BPH) Enlargement of the prostate gland that is not caused by malignancy.   93

biogeography Study of the geographical distribution of organisms.   184

biological evolution Change in life-forms that has taken place in the past and will take place in the future; includes descent from a common ancestor and adaptation to the environment.   183

biological magnification Process by which substances become more concentrated in organisms in the higher trophic levels of a food web.   228

biotechnology Term that encompasses genetic engineering and other techniques that make use of natural biological systems to create a product or achieve a particular result desired by humans.   50

biotic potential Maximum reproductive rate of an organism, given unlimited resources and ideal environmental conditions. Compare with *environmental resistance.*   216

birth control method Method used to prevent either fertilization or implantation of an embryo in the uterine lining.   142

birth control pill Oral contraceptive containing estrogen and progesterone.   146

blastocyst (blas-tuh-sist) Early stage of human embryonic development that consists of a hollow, fluid-filled ball of cells.   129

Braxton Hicks contractions Strong, late-term uterine contractions prior to cervical dilation; also called false labor.   136

breech birth Birth in which the baby is positioned rump first.   133

bulbourethral gland (bul-boh-yoo-ree-thrul) Either of two small structures located below the prostate gland in males; each adds secretions to semen.   88

C

candidal vaginitis Vaginitis caused by *Candida albicans*.   166

carrier Heterozygous individual who has no apparent abnormality but can pass on an allele for a recessively inherited genetic disorder.   60

carrying capacity Maximum number of individuals of any species that can be supported by a particular ecosystem on a long-term basis.   216

cell Structural and functional unit of an organism; smallest structure capable of performing all the functions necessary for life.   4

cell cycle Repeating sequence of cellular events that consists of interphase, mitosis, and cytokinesis.   6

central arousal system Internal components of sexual arousal that come from the cognitive and emotional centers of the brain, forming the foundations for sexual response.   108

centriole Short, cylindrical organelle that contains microtubules in a $9 + 0$ pattern and is associated with the formation of the spindle during cell division.   5

centromere (sen-truh-meer) Constriction where sister chromatids of a chromosome are held together.   7

cervix (sur-viks) Narrow end of the uterus, which projects into the vagina.   95

cesarean section Birth by surgical incision of the abdomen and uterus.   133

CFCs (chlorofluorocarbons) (klor-oh-floor-oh-kar-buns) Organic compounds containing carbon, chlorine, and fluorine atoms. CFCs such as Freon can deplete the ozone shield by releasing chlorine atoms into the upper atmosphere.   227

chemical evolution Increase in the complexity of chemicals over time that could have led to the first cells.   182

chlamydia (kluh-mid-ee-uh) Sexually transmitted disease, caused by the bacterium *Chlamydia trachomatis;* can lead to pelvic inflammatory disease.   158

chorion (kor-ee-ahn) Extraembryonic membrane that contributes to placenta formation.   127

chorionic villi (kor-ee-ahn-ik vil-eye) Treelike extensions of the chorion that project into the maternal tissues at the placenta.   131

chorionic villi sampling (CVS) Removal of cells from the chorionic villi portion of the placenta. Karyotyping is done to determine if the fetus has a chromosomal abnormality.   58

chromatid One of the two side-by-side replicas in a duplicated chromosome.   7

chromosome (kroh-muh-som) Chromatin condensed into a compact structure.   4

circumcision Removal of the foreskin of the penis.   92

cleavage Cell division without cytoplasmic addition or enlargement; occurs during the first stage of animal development.   127

cleavage furrow Indentation that begins the process of cleavage, by which human cells undergo cytokinesis.   9

climax Another term for orgasm.   105

clitoris Small, erectile female organ located in the vulva and homologous to the penis.   99

cocaine babies Babies born to mothers who use cocaine; usually have visual problems, lack coordination, and are mentally retarded due to oxygen deprivation in the developing brain.   134

codominance Inheritance pattern in which both alleles of a gene are equally expressed.   31

codon Three-base sequence in messenger RNA that causes the insertion of a particular amino acid into a protein or termination of translation.   44

coitus interruptus Birth control method in which the penis is withdrawn prior to ejaculation of semen.   148

colostrum (kuh-lahs-trum) Thin, milky fluid rich in proteins, including antibodies, that is secreted by the mammary glands a few days prior to or after delivery of the fetus before true milk is secreted.   138

communication Signal by a sender that influences the behavior of a receiver.   209

complementary base pairing Hydrogen bonding between particular bases. In DNA, thymine (T) pairs with adenine (A), and guanine (G) pairs with cytosine (C); in RNA, uracil (U) pairs with A, and G pairs with C.   41

condom, female Polyurethane tube that covers external genitals and has a flexible ring that fits onto cervix; used during sexual intercourse as a contraceptive, and also helps protect against STDs.   148

condom, male Sheath used to cover the penis during sexual intercourse; used as a contraceptive and, if latex, helps protect against STDs.   148

congenital birth defect Body abnormality arising due to hereditary factors.   134

corpus albicans White, fibrous tissue that replaces the regressing corpus luteum in the ovary in the latter half of pregnancy.   97

corpus luteum (kor-pus loot-ee-um) Yellow body that forms in the ovary from a follicle that has discharged its secondary oocyte; it secretes progesterone and some estrogen.   97

Cro-Magnon (kroh-mag-nun) Common name for first fossils to be designated *Homo sapiens*.   193

crossing-over Exchange of segments between nonsister chromatids of a tetrad during meiosis.   10

culture Total pattern of human behavior; includes technology and the arts, and is dependent upon the capacity to speak and transmit knowledge.   190, 202

cytokinesis (sy-tuh-kyn-ee-sus) Division of the cytoplasm following mitosis and meiosis.   6, 9

cytoplasm Ground substance of cells that is located between the nucleus and the plasma membrane.   5

cytosine (C) (sy-tuh-seen) One of four nitrogen-containing bases in nucleotides comprising the structure of DNA and RNA; pairs with guanine.   41

D

deforestation (dee-for-eh-stay-shun) Removal of trees from a forest in a way that forever reduces the size of the forest.   219

delirium tremens Alcohol withdrawal.   134

desertification Denuding and degrading a once-fertile land, initiating a desert-producing cycle that feeds on itself and causes long-term changes in the soil, climate, and biota of an area.   219

desire phase Kaplan's term for the psychological interest in sex that precedes physiological sexual arousal.   107

diaphragm (dy-uh-fram) Birth control device consisting of a soft rubber or latex cup that fits over the cervix.   147

differentiation Cell specialization.   127

dihybrid An individual heterozygous for two pairs of genes.   25

diploid (2n) Cell condition in which two of each type of chromosome are present in the nucleus.   6

DNA (deoxyribonucleic acid) Nucleic acid polymer produced from covalent bonding of nucleotide monomers that contain the sugar deoxyribose; the genetic material of nearly all organisms.   3, 40

DNA fingerprinting Using DNA fragment lengths, resulting from restriction enzyme cleavage, to identify particular individuals.   51

DNA ligase (ly-gays) Enzyme that links DNA fragments; used during production of recombinant DNA to join foreign DNA to vector DNA.   50

DNA polymerase During replication, an enzyme that joins the nucleotides complementary to a DNA template.   42

DNA probe A piece of single-stranded DNA that will bind to a complementary piece of DNA.   63

dominance hierarchy Organization of animals in a group that determines the order in which the animals have access to resources.   206

dominant allele (uh-leel) Allele that exerts its phenotypic effect in the heterozygote; it masks the expression of the recessive allele.   22

dyad Duplicated chromosome having two sister chromatids.   11

E

ectopic pregnancy Implantation of the embryo in a location other than the uterus, most often in a uterine tube.   98

ejaculation Ejection of semen (seminal fluid).   88

ejaculatory duct Tube, formed by the joining of the vas deferens and the tube from the seminal vesicle, that transports sperm to the urethra.   88

ejaculatory inevitability Sensation in the male that ejaculation is imminent.   118

embryo (em-bree-oh) Immature developmental stage that is not recognizable as a human being.   129

embryonic development Period of development from the second through the eighth weeks.   130

embryonic disk Stage of embryonic development following the blastocyst stage that has two layers; one layer will be endoderm, and the other will be ectoderm.   130

endocrine gland (en-duh-krin) Ductless organ that secretes (a) hormone(s) into the bloodstream.   72

endocrine system Organ system involved in the coordination of body activities; uses hormones as chemical signals secreted into the bloodstream.   72

endometriosis (en-doh-mee-tree-oh-sus) Presence of uterine tissue outside the uterus, which can contribute to infertility; possibly the result of irregular menstrual flow.   152

endometrium Mucous membrane lining the interior surface of the uterus.   95

endoplasmic reticulum (ER) Complex system of tubules, vesicles, and sacs in cells; sometimes has attached ribosomes.   5

environmental resistance All the limiting factors that tend to reduce population growth rates and set the maximum allowable population size or carrying capacity of an ecosystem.   216

epididymis (ep-uh-did-uh-mus) Coiled tubule next to the testes where sperm mature and may be stored for a short time.   88

episiotomy (ih-pee-zee-aht-uh-mee) Surgical procedure performed during childbirth in which the opening of the vagina is enlarged to avoid tearing.   137

epistasis Inheritance pattern in which one gene masks the expression of another gene that is at a different locus and is independently inherited.   27

erectile dysfunction Failure of the penis to achieve erection.   92

estrogen (es-truh-jun) Female sex hormone that helps maintain the sex organs and secondary sex characteristics.   77

eukaryotic cell Type of cell that has a membrane-bounded nucleus and membranous organelles.   183

evolutionary tree Diagram that describes the evolutionary relationship of groups of organisms; a common ancestor is presumed to have been present at points of divergence.   188

excitement Arousal phase of Masters and Johnson's four-phase model of the sexual response cycle.   105

exponential growth Growth at a constant rate of increase per unit of time; can be expressed as a constant fraction or exponent.   216

external genitals Sex organs that occur outside the body in the groin.   92

extraembryonic membrane (ek-struh-em-bree-ahn-ik) Membrane that is not a part of the embryo but is necessary to the continued existence and health of the embryo.   127

ex vivo gene therapy Cells are altered outside the body and then returned to the body.   52

F

female condom Birth control method that blocks the entrance of sperm to the uterus; also prevents STDs.   148

fertilization Union of a sperm nucleus and an egg nucleus, which creates a zygote.   126

fetal alcohol syndrome (FAS) Baby born with decreased weight, height, and head size and with malformation of the head and face due to the mother's consumption of alcohol during pregnancy.   134

fetal development Period of development from the ninth week through birth.   133

fimbria (pl., fimbriae) (fim-bree-uh) Fingerlike extension from the uterine tube near the ovary.   98

first messenger Chemical signal such as a peptide hormone that binds to a plasma membrane receptor protein and alters the metabolism of a cell because a second messenger is activated.   74

fitness Ability of an organism to reproduce and pass its genes to the next fertile generation; measured against the ability of other organisms to reproduce in the same environment.   203

follicle (fahl-ih-kul) Structure in the ovary that produces a secondary oocyte and the hormones estrogen and progesterone.   97

follicle-stimulating hormone (FSH) Hormone secreted by the anterior pituitary gland that stimulates the development of an ovarian follicle in a female or the production of sperm in a male.   77

fontanel (fahn-tun-el) Membranous region located between certain cranial bones in the skull of a fetus or infant.   133

fossil Any past evidence of an organism that has been preserved in the Earth's crust.   184

fossil fuel Fuels such as oil, coal, and natural gas that are the result of partial decomposition of plants and animals coupled with exposure to heat and pressure for millions of years.   224

fossil record History of life recorded from remains of the past.   184

frameshift mutation Insertion or deletion of at least one base so that the reading frame of the corresponding mRNA changes.   49

G

gamete (ga-meet, guh-meet) Haploid sex cell; the egg or a sperm, which join in fertilization to form a zygote.   6

gamete intrafallopian transfer (GIFT) Method of achieving pregnancy in which eggs retrieved from the ovary are mixed with sperm and immediately placed into a uterine tube.   153

gastrulation Formation of a gastrula from a blastula; characterized by an invagination of the cell layers to form a caplike structure.   131

gene Unit of heredity located on a chromosome.   5

gene therapy Correction of a detrimental mutation by adding normal DNA and inserting it into a genome.   52

genetic counseling Prospective parents consult a counselor who determines the genotype of each and whether an unborn child will have a genetic disorder.   58

genetic engineering Alteration of DNA for medical or industrial purposes.   50

genetic marker Abnormality in the sequence of a base at a particular location on a chromosome signifying a disorder.   63

genetic mutation Altered gene whose sequence of bases differs from the previous sequence.   49

genital herpes (jen-ih-tul hur-peez) Sexually transmitted disease caused by herpes simplex virus and sometimes accompanied by painful ulcers on the genitals.   162

genital warts Sexually transmitted disease caused by human papillomavirus, resulting in raised growths on the external genitals.   163

genome Full set of genetic information within an organism or a virus.   54

genotype (jee-nuh-typ) Genes of an individual for a particular trait or traits; often designated by letters, for example, *BB* or *Aa*.   22

gestation Period of development, from the start of the last menstrual cycle until birth; in humans, typically 280 days.   129

Golgi apparatus Organelle consisting of concentrically folded membranes that functions in the packaging and secretion of cellular products.   5

gonad (goh-nad) Organ that produces gametes; the ovary produces eggs, and the testis produces sperm.   6

gonadotropic hormone (goh-nad-uh-trahp-ic, -troh-pic) Chemical signal secreted by anterior pituitary that regulates the activity of the ovaries and testes; principally, follicle-stimulating hormone (FSH) and luteinizing hormone (LH).   77

gonadotropin-releasing hormone (GnRH) Hormone secreted by the hypothalamus that stimulates the anterior pituitary to secrete follicle-stimulating hormone and luteinizing hormone.   77

gonorrhea (gahn-nuh-ree-uh) Sexually transmitted disease caused by the bacterium *Neisseria gonorrhoeae* that can lead to pelvic inflammatory disease.   158

greenhouse gases Gases, such as carbon dioxide and methane, that are involved in the greenhouse effect.   224

growth Increase in the number of cells and/or the size of these cells.   127, 224

growth hormone (GH) Substance secreted by the anterior pituitary; controls size of individual by promoting cell division, protein synthesis, and bone growth.   77

growth rate Percentage that reflects the difference between the number of persons in a population who are born each year and the number of persons who die each year.   216

G spot Vaginal area that some researchers feel is particularly sensitive to sexual stimulation when its underlying spongy tissues are engorged with blood.   113

guanine (G) (gwah-neen) One of four nitrogen-containing bases in nucleotides comprising the structure of DNA and RNA; pairs with cytosine.   41

H

haploid (n) (hap-loyd) The n number of chromosomes—half the diploid number; the number characteristic of gametes, which contain only one set of chromosomes.   6

hepatitis (hep-uh-ty-tis) Inflammation of the liver. Viral hepatitis occurs in several forms.   163

hernia Protrusion of an organ through an abnormal opening, such as the intestine through the abdominal wall near the scrotum (inguinal hernia) or the stomach through the diaphragm (hiatal hernia).   91

heterotroph Organism that cannot synthesize organic molecules from inorganic nutrients and therefore must take in organic nutrients (food).   182

heterozygous Possessing unlike alleles for a particular trait.   22

HIV provirus Viral DNA that has been integrated into host cell DNA.   176

hominid (hahm-uh-nid) Member of the family Hominidae, which contains australopithecines and humans.   188

Homo erectus (hoh-moh ih-rek-tus) Hominid who used fire and migrated out of Africa to Europe and Asia.   191

Homo habilis (hoh-moh hab-uh-lus) Hominid of 2 million years ago who is believed to have been the first tool user.   190

homologous chromosomes (hoh-mahl-uh-gus, huh-mahl-uh-gus) Pair of chromosomes that are alike and come together in synapsis during prophase of the first meiotic division.   10

homologous structure Structure that is similar in two or more species because of common ancestry.   184

Homo sapiens (hoh-moh say-pe-nz) Modern humans.   192

homozygous dominant Possessing two identical alleles, such as *AA*, for a particular trait.   22

homozygous recessive Possessing two identical alleles, such as *aa*, for a particular trait.   22

hormone (hor-mohn) Chemical signal produced in one part of the body that controls the activity of other parts.   74

host Organism that provides nourishment and/or shelter for a parasite.   161

human chorionic gonadotropin (HCG) (kor-ee-ahn-ik goh-nad-uh-trahp-in, -troh-pin) Hormone produced by the chorion that functions to maintain the uterine lining.   100, 130

human immunodeficiency virus (HIV) Virus responsible for AIDS.   172

hypothalamus (hy-poh-thal-uh-mus) Part of the brain located below the thalamus that helps regulate the internal environment of the body and produces releasing factors that control the anterior pituitary.   77

I

implantation Attachment and penetration of the embryo into the lining of the uterus (endometrium).   95, 130

imprinting Learning to make a particular response to only one type of animal or object.   201

inclusive fitness Fitness that results from personal reproduction and from helping nondescendant relatives reproduce.   211

incomplete dominance Inheritance pattern in which the offspring has an intermediate phenotype compared to those of its parents; for example, a normal individual and an individual with sickle-cell disease can produce a child with sickle-cell trait.   31

infertility Inability to have as many children as desired.   152

inner cell mass Aggregation of cells at one pole of the blastocyst that is destined to form the embryo proper.   129

integrase Viral enzyme that splices viral DNA into a host chromosome.   176

interphase Cell cycle stage during which growth and DNA synthesis occur when the nucleus is not actively dividing.   6

interstitial cell (in-tur-stish-ul) Hormone-secreting cell located between the seminiferous tubules of the testes.   90

intracytoplasmic sperm injection (ICSI) Infertility procedure in which a single sperm is injected into an egg to produce a pregnancy.   153

intrauterine device (IUD) (in-truh-yoo-tur-in) Birth control device consisting of a small piece of molded plastic inserted into the uterus, and believed to alter the uterine environment so that fertilization does not occur.   146

in vitro fertilization (IVF) Process of achieving pregnancy in which eggs retrieved from an ovary are fertilized in a laboratory; viable embryos are then placed into the woman's uterus.   65, 152

in vivo gene therapy Either a vector carrying the gene or the gene itself is introduced directly into the body.   52

K

karyotype (kar-ee-uh-typ) Duplicated chromosomes arranged by pairs according to their size, shape, and general appearance.   58

L

labia majora Two large, hairy folds of skin of the female external genitalia.   99

labia minora Two small folds of skin inside the labia majora and encircling the clitoris.   99

land subsidence Occurs when a portion of the Earth's surface gradually settles downward.   221

lanugo (luh-noo-goh) Short, fine hair that is present during the later portion of fetal development.   133

latency State of seeming inactivity or dormancy.   161

learning Relatively permanent change in behavior that results from practice and experience.   200

lineage Evolutionary line of descent.   188

luteinizing hormone (LH) Hormone that controls the production of testosterone by interstitial cells in males and promotes the development of the corpus luteum in females.   77

lymphocyte Specialized white blood cell that functions in specific defense—T lymphocyte and B lymphocyte.   164

lysosome Organelle involved in intracellular digestion; contains powerful digestive enzymes.   5

M

Marfan syndrome Congenital disorder of connective tissue characterized by abnormal length of the extremities.   30

meiosis (my-oh-sis) Type of nuclear division that occurs as part of sexual reproduction in which the daughter cells receive the haploid number of chromosomes in varied combinations.   6, 10

melatonin Hormone, secreted by the pineal gland, that is involved in biorhythms.   81

menopause (men-uh-pawz) Termination of the ovarian and uterine cycles in older women.   100

menstrual cycle Recurring changes in the uterine lining of a woman of reproductive age.   100

messenger RNA (mRNA) Type of RNA formed from a DNA template that bears coded information for the amino acid sequence of a polypeptide.   43

metaphase Mitotic phase during which chromosomes are aligned at the equator of the mitotic spindle.   9

mineral Naturally occurring inorganic substance containing two or more elements; certain minerals are needed in the diet.   226

miscarriage Spontaneous abortion occurring naturally.   150

mitochondrion Organelle in which cellular respiration produces the energy molecule ATP.   5

mitosis (my-toh-sis) Type of cell division in which daughter cells receive the exact chromosomal and genetic makeup of the parent cell; occurs during growth and repair.   6, 7

molecular clock Mutational changes that accumulate at a presumed constant rate in regions of DNA not involved in adaptation to the environment.   188

mons pubis Rounded, fleshy prominence over the pubic symphysis.   99

morphogenesis Emergence of shape in tissues, organs, or entire embryo during development.   127

morula Spherical mass of cells resulting from cleavage during animal development prior to the blastula stage.   129

mosaic evolution Concept that human characteristics did not evolve at the same rate; for example, some body parts are more humanlike than others in early hominids.   189

multifactorial trait Interaction of several genes and usually, to some extent, nongenetic factors.   28

multiple alleles (uh-leelz) Inheritance pattern in which there are more than two alleles for a particular trait; each individual has only two of all the possible alleles.   30

multiregional continuity hypothesis Proposal that modern humans evolved independently in at least three different places: Asia, Africa, and Europe.   192

mutation Alteration in chromosome structure or number and also an alteration in a gene due to a change in DNA composition.   26, 42

N

natural family planning Method of birth control in which ovulation is tracked by record keeping and intercourse is avoided during ovulation.   149

natural selection Mechanism resulting in adaptation to the environment.   184

Neanderthal (nee-an-dur-thahl, -tahl) Hominid with a sturdy build who lived during the last Ice Age in Europe and the Middle East; hunted large game and has left evidence of being culturally advanced.   193

negative feedback system Mechanism of homeostatic response in which a stimulus initiates reactions that reduce the stimulus.   78

nondisjunction Failure of homologous chromosomes or daughter chromosomes to separate during meiosis I and meiosis II, respectively.   16

nonrenewable resources Minerals, fossil fuels, and other materials present in essentially fixed amounts (within human timescales) in our environment.   218

nucleolus Organelle found inside the nucleus and composed largely of RNA for ribosome formation (pl., nucleoli).   5

nucleus Large organelle that contains the chromosomes and acts as a cell control center.   4

O

oocyte Developing female gamete.   97

oogenesis (oh-uh-jen-uh-sis) Production of an egg in females by the process of meiosis and maturation.   14, 97

operant conditioning Learning that results from rewarding or reinforcing a particular behavior.   200

opportunistic infection Infection that has an opportunity to occur because the immune system has been weakened.   164, 175

organizing effect Manner in which hormones control patterns of early development in the body.   120

orgasm Pleasurable sensation and series of contractions that release sexual tension, usually accompanied by ejaculation in men.   105

orgasmic release Reversal of the vasocongestion and muscular tension of sexual arousal, triggered by orgasm.   107

out-of-Africa hypothesis Proposal that modern humans originated only in Africa; then they migrated out of Africa and supplanted populations of early *Homo* in Asia and Europe about 100,000 years ago.   192

ovariohysterectomy Surgical removal of the ovaries and uterus.   95

ovary Female gonad that produces eggs and the female sex hormones.   95

ovulation (ahv-yuh-lay-shun, ohv-) Release of a secondary oocyte from the ovary; if fertilization occurs, the secondary oocyte becomes an egg.   97

oxytocin (ahk-sih-toh-sin) Hormone released by the posterior pituitary that causes contraction of the uterus and milk letdown.   77

ozone shield Accumulation of O_3, formed from oxygen in the upper atmosphere; a filtering layer that protects the Earth from ultraviolet radiation.   227

P

Pap smear Analysis done on cervical cells for detection of cancer.   99

parturition (par-tyoo-rish-un, par-chuh-) Processes that lead to and include birth and the expulsion of the afterbirth.   136

pathogen (path-uh-jun) Disease-causing agent.   156

pedigree Chart showing the relationships of relatives and which ones have a particular trait.   60

pelvic inflammatory disease (PID) Disease state of the reproductive organs caused by a sexually transmitted disease that can result in scarring and infertility.   158

penis External organ in males through which the urethra passes; also serves as the organ of sexual intercourse.   92

peripheral arousal system External components of sexual arousal that reach the brain and spinal cord from the skin, genitals, and sense organs.   108

phenotype (fee-nuh-typ) Visible expression of a genotype—for example, brown eyes or attached earlobes.   22

pheromone Chemical signal released by an organism that affects the metabolism or influences the behavior of another individual of the same species.   75, 210

photovoltaic (solar) cell Energy-conversion device that captures solar energy and directly converts it to electrical current.   226

pineal gland (pin-ee-ul, py-nee-ul) Endocrine gland located in the third ventricle of the brain; produces melatonin.   81

pituitary gland Endocrine gland that lies just inferior to the hypothalamus; consists of the anterior pituitary and posterior pituitary.   77

placenta (pluh-sen-tuh) Structure that forms from the chorion and the uterine wall and allows the embryo, and then the fetus, to acquire nutrients and rid itself of wastes.   127

placental membrane Semipermeable membrane that separates the fetal from the maternal blood in the placenta.   132

plasmid (plaz-mid) Self-replicating ring of accessory DNA in the cytoplasm of bacteria.   50

plateau Stable, leveled-off phase of Masters and Johnson's four-phase model of the sexual response cycle.   105

point mutation Change of only one base in the sequence of bases in a gene.   49

polar body In oogenesis, a nonfunctional product; two to three meiotic products are of this type.   14, 97

pollution Any environmental change that adversely affects the lives and health of living things.   218

polygenic inheritance (pahl-ee-jen-ik) Inheritance pattern in which a trait is controlled by several allelic pairs; each dominant allele contributes to the phenotype in an additive and like manner.   28

polymerase chain reaction (PCR) (pahl-uh-muh-rays, -rayz) Technique that uses the enzyme DNA polymerase to produce millions of copies of a particular piece of DNA.   51

polyribosome (pahl-ih-ry-buh-sohm) String of ribosomes simultaneously translating regions of the same mRNA strand during protein synthesis.   46

porphyria Chemical insufficiency in the production of hemoglobin.   30

positive feedback mechanism Reaction in which the stimulus initiates reactions that lead to an increase in the stimulus.   77

posterior pituitary Portion of the pituitary gland that stores and secretes oxytocin and antidiuretic hormone, which are produced by the hypothalamus.   77

pre-embryonic development Development of the zygote in the first week, including fertilization, the beginning of cell division, and the appearance of the chorion.   129

primary germ layer Three layers (endoderm, mesoderm, and ectoderm) of embryonic cells that develop into specific tissues and organs.   131

primary spermatocyte A cell dividing into two secondary spermatocytes.   90

primate (pry-mayt) Animal that belongs to the order Primate; includes prosimians, monkeys, apes, and humans, all of whom have adaptations for living in trees.   187

progesterone (proh-jes-tuh-rohn) Female sex hormone that helps maintain sex organs and secondary sex characteristics.   77

prokaryotic cell Type of cell that lacks a membrane-bounded nucleus and organelles.   183

prolactin (PRL) (proh-lak-tin) Hormone secreted by the anterior pituitary that stimulates the production of milk from the mammary glands.   77

prophase (proh-fayz) Mitotic phase during which chromatin condenses so that chromosomes appear; chromosomes are scattered.   8

prostate gland (prahs-tayt) Gland located around the male urethra below the urinary bladder; adds secretions to semen.   88

protease Viral enzyme that cleaves viral proteins so that virus reproduction can take place.   177

protein Macromolecule composed of amino acids.   5

protein-first hypothesis In chemical evolution, the proposal that protein originated before other macromolecules and allowed the formation of protocells.   182

protocell In biological evolution, a possible cell forerunner that became a cell once it could reproduce.   182

Punnett square (pun-ut) Gridlike device used to calculate the expected results of simple genetic crosses.   24

R

recessive allele (uh-leel) Allele that exerts its phenotypic effect only in the homozygote; its expression is masked by a dominant allele.   22

recombinant DNA (rDNA) DNA that contains genes from more than one source.   50

refractory period Time following orgasm during which a man cannot be restimulated to orgasm.   119

renewable resources Resources normally replaced or replenished by natural processes; resources not depleted by moderate use. Examples include solar energy, biological resources such as forests and fisheries, biological organisms, and some biogeochemical cycles.   218

replacement reproduction Population in which each person is replaced by only one child.   217

replication Making an exact copy, as when one copy of DNA is duplicated by a complementary base-pairing process.   42

resolution Term for the return of the body to its unexcited state following orgasm.   105

resource In economic terms, anything with potential use in creating wealth or giving satisfaction.   218

restriction enzyme Bacterial enzyme that stops viral reproduction by cleaving viral DNA; used to cut DNA at specific points during production of recombinant DNA.   50

retrovirus RNA virus containing the enzyme reverse transcriptase that carries out RNA and DNA transcription.   176

reverse transcriptase Enzyme unique to retroviruses; enables a retrovirus to make a DNA copy of retroviruses' RNA genetic material.   176

ribosomal RNA (rRNA) (ry-buh-soh-mul) Type of RNA found in ribosomes, where protein synthesis occurs.   43

ribosome Minute particle, found attached to the endoplasmic reticulum or loose in the cytoplasm, that is the site of protein synthesis.   5

RNA (ribonucleic acid) (ry-boh-noo-klee-ik) Nucleic acid produced from covalent bonding of nucleotide monomers that contain the sugar ribose; occurs in three forms: messenger RNA, ribosomal RNA, and transfer RNA.   43

RNA-first hypothesis In chemical evolution, the proposal that RNA originated before other macromolecules and allowed the formation of the first cell(s).   182

RNA polymerase (pahl-uh-muh-rays) During transcription, an enzyme that joins nucleotides complementary to a DNA template.   45

rubella (German measles) Acute, infectious disease affecting children and nonimmune young adults; affects the respiratory tract; characterized by a slight cold, sore throat, and fever, and the appearance of a fine, pink rash.   134

S

salinization Process in which mineral salts accumulate in the soil, killing plants; occurs when soils in dry climates are irrigated profusely.   222

saltwater intrusion Movement of salt water into freshwater aquifers in coastal areas where groundwater is withdrawn faster than it is replenished.   221

scrotum (skroh-tum) Pouch of skin that encloses the testes.   88

secondary sex characteristic Trait that is sometimes helpful but not absolutely necessary for reproduction and is maintained by the sex hormones in males and females.   82

secondary spermatocyte One of the two cells into which a primary spermatocyte divides, and which in turn gives origin to spermatids.   90

second messenger Chemical signal such as cyclic AMP that causes the cell to respond to the first messenger—a hormone bound to a plasma membrane receptor.   74

semen (see-mun) Thick, whitish fluid consisting of sperm and secretions from several glands of the male reproductive tract; also called seminal fluid.   88

seminal vesicle (sem-uh-nul) Convoluted, saclike structure attached to the vas deferens near the base of the urinary bladder in males; adds secretions to semen.   88

seminiferous tubule (sem-uh-nif-ur-us) Long, coiled structure contained within chambers of the testis; site where sperm are produced.   89

sex chromosome Chromosome that determines the sex of an individual; in humans, females have two X chromosomes, and males have an X and a Y chromosome.   16, 33

sex-influenced trait Autosomal phenotype controlled by an allele that is expressed differently in the two sexes; for example, the possibility of pattern baldness is increased by the presence of testosterone in human males.   36

sex-limited trait Transmission of a trait that is expressed in one sex only.   36

sex-linked Allele that occurs on the sex chromosomes but may control a trait that has nothing to do with the sex characteristics of an individual.   33

sexual dysfunction Difficulties people have in achieving sexual arousal and in other stages of sexual response.   107

sexual selection Changes in males and females, often due to male competition and female selectivity, that lead to increased fitness.   203

sinkhole Large surface crater caused by the collapse of an underground channel or cavern; often triggered by groundwater withdrawal.   221

Skene glands Secretory cells located inside the female urethra.   113

society Group in which members of a species are organized in a cooperative manner, extending beyond sexual and parental behavior.   209

sociobiology Application of evolutionary principles to the study of the social behavior of animals, including humans.   211

somatic cell (soh-mat-ik) Body cell; excludes cells that undergo meiosis and become a sperm or an egg.   3

sperm Male gamete having a haploid number of chromosomes and the ability to fertilize an egg, the female gamete.   90

spermatid Intermediate stage in the formation of sperm cells.   90

spermatogenesis (spur-mat-uh-jen-ih-sis) Production of sperm in males by the process of meiosis and maturation.   14, 90

spina bifida Disorder characterized by defective closure of the bony encasement of the spinal cord, through which the cord and meninges may or may not protrude.   134

spindle Microtubule structure that brings about chromosomal movement during nuclear division.   8

SRY (sex-determining region of the Y) One of the sex-determining genes on the Y chromosome that does not have a copy on the X chromosome.   80

sterilization Surgical procedure that renders an individual incapable of reproduction; vasectomy in males and tubal ligation in females.   144

striae gravidarum Linear, depressed, scarlike lesions occurring on the abdomen, breasts, buttocks, and thighs due to the weakening of the elastic tissues during pregnancy.   138

sustainable Ability of a society or ecosystem to maintain itself while also providing services to human beings.   228

synapsis (sih-nap-sis) Pairing of homologous chromosomes during prophase I of meiosis I.   10

syndrome Group of symptoms that appear together and tend to indicate the presence of a particular disorder.   16

syphilis (sif-uh-lis) Sexually transmitted disease caused by the bacterium *Treponema pallidum* that, if untreated, can lead to cardiac and central nervous system disorders.   160

T

teleological Belief that the outcome is known ahead of time because the outcome is influenced by the need to progress in a certain direction.   185

telophase (tel-uh-fayz) Mitotic phase during which daughter chromosomes are located at each pole.   9

template (tem-plit) Pattern or guide used to make copies; parental strand of DNA serves as a guide for the production of daughter DNA strands, and DNA also serves as a guide for the production of messenger RNA.   42

teratogen Any substance that produces abnormalities during human development.   134

territoriality Marking and/or defending a particular area against invasion by another species member; area often used for the purpose of feeding, mating, and caring for young.   206

territory An area an animal defends against intruders.   206

testis (pl., testes) (tes-tus, tes-teez) Male gonad that produces sperm and the male sex hormones.   88

testosterone (tes-tahs-tuh-rohn) Male sex hormone that helps maintain sexual organs and secondary sex characteristics.   77, 90

tetrad Four chromatids that result when homologous chromosomes pair during meiosis I.   10

thymine (T) (thy-meen) One of four nitrogen-containing bases in nucleotides comprising the structure of DNA; pairs with adenine.   41

transcription Process whereby a DNA strand serves as a template for the formation of mRNA.   45

transfer RNA (tRNA) Type of RNA that transfers a particular amino acid to a ribosome during protein synthesis; at one end, it binds to the amino acid, and at the other end, it has an anticodon that binds to an mRNA codon.   43

translation Process whereby ribosomes use the sequence of codons in mRNA to produce a polypeptide with a particular sequence of amino acids.   46

trichomoniasis Sexually transmitted disease caused by the parasitic protozoan *Trichomonas vaginalis*.   166

triplet code Each sequence of three nucleotide bases in the DNA of genes stands for a particular amino acid.   45

trophoblast Outer cells of a blastocyst that help form the placenta and other extraembryonic membranes.   129

tubal ligation Method for preventing pregnancy in which the uterine tubes are cut and sealed.   146

U

umbilical cord Cord connecting the fetus to the placenta through which blood vessels pass.   131

uracil (U) (yoor-uh-sil) Nitrogen-containing base in RNA that replaces thymine found in DNA; pairs with adenine.   43

urethra (yoo-ree-thruh) Tubular structure that receives urine from the bladder and carries it to the outside of the body.   88

uterine tube Tube that extends from the uterus on each side toward an ovary and transports sex cells; also called fallopian tube or oviduct.   95

uterus (yoo-tur-us) Organ located in the female pelvis where the fetus develops; also called the womb.   95

V

vagina Organ that leads from the uterus to the vestibule and serves as the birth canal and organ of sexual intercourse in females.   95

vas deferens (vas def-ur-unz, -uh-renz) Tube that leads from the epididymis to the urethra in males.   88

vasectomy Method for preventing pregnancy in which the vasa deferentia are cut and sealed.   144

vector (vek-tur) In genetic engineering, a means to transfer foreign genetic material into a cell (e.g., a plasmid).   50

vernix caseosa (vur-niks kay-see-oh-suh) Cheeselike substance covering the skin of the fetus.   133

vesicle Small, membranous sac that stores substances within a cell.   5

vesicular (Graafian) follicle Mature follicle within the ovaries that houses a developing egg.   97

vestibule (ves-tuh-byool) Space or cavity at the entrance of a canal, such as the cavity that lies between the semicircular canals and the cochlea.   99

virus Noncellular parasitic agent consisting of an outer capsid and an inner core of nucleic acid.   161

vulva External genitals of the female that surround the opening of the vagina.   95

X

X-linked Allele located on an X chromosome, but may control a trait that has nothing to do with the sex characteristics of an individual.   33

Y

yolk sac Extraembryonic membrane that encloses the yolk of birds; in humans, it is the first site of blood cell formation.   127

Z

zygote (zy-goht) Diploid cell formed by the union of sperm and egg; the product of fertilization.   6, 126

Credits

Photographs

Part Openers

One: © Brenda Fitzsimons/Sportsfile; Two: © George Shelley/Corbis; Three(left): © William M. Smithy Jr./Masterfile; Three(right): © Don and Pat Valenti/DRK.

Chapter 1

Figure 1.2b: © Barry F. King/Biological Photo Service; 1.7(all): © Michael Abbey/ Photo Researchers, Inc.; 1.14: © Jill Cannefax/EKM-Nepenthe; 1.15a,b: Courtesy of G.H. Valentine; 1.16a,b: Photograph by Earl Plunkett. Courtesy of G.H. Valentine; p. 20: © Corbis Royalty-Free.

Chapter 2

Figure 2.3a: © Superstock; 2.3b: © Michael Grecco/Stock Boston; 2.3c-f: © The McGraw-Hill Companies, Inc./Bob Coyle, photographer; 2.3g: Courtesy of Mary L. Drapeau; 2.3h: © The McGraw-Hill Companies, Inc./Bob Coyle, photographer; Fig. 2.7: © Steve Uzzell; 2.8: Courtesy PathoGenesis; 2.9a: © Kevin Fleming/ Corbis; p. 29: © Julie Houck/Corbis; 2.12a,b: © Bill Longcore/Photo Researchres, Inc.; 2.14: Courtesy Muscular Dystrophy; p. 37: © Jerry Cooke/Photo Researchers, Inc.

Chapter 3

Figure 3.14: Courtesy Dr. Howard Jones, Eastern VA Medical School; 3.17(Decker): © AP/Photo/Muscular Dystrophy Association/Jay LaPrete; 3.17(Cutshall): © Elizabeth Fulford/AP Photo 1994; 3.17(Sa'ad): © David Silverman/Getty News Service; 3.17(Conradi): © AP Photo/Peter Dejong; p. 55: © Ron Chapple/FPG/Getty; p. 56: © Hank Morgan/ Science Source/Photo Researchers, Inc.

Chapter 4

Figure.4.1c-e: © CNRI/SPL/Photo Researchers, Inc.; p. 62: © David M. Phillips/Visuals Unlimited; 4.6: Courtesy Affymetrix; p. 64: © 2000 Howard Hughes Medical Institute, photo: Paul Fetters; p. 68: © Carroll Weiss/Camera M.D. Studios.

Chapter 5

Figure 5.6a: © Biophoto Associates/Photo Researchers, Inc.; 5.6b(center): © Vol. 161/Corbis; 5.6b(right): © Vol. 178/Corbis; p. 81: © James Darell/Stone; p. 86: © Corbis/Royalty-Free.

Chapter 6

Figure 6.2b: © Secchi-Leaque/CNRI/SPL/ Photo Researchers, Inc.; 6.7: © Ed Reschke/ Peter Arnold, Inc.; p. 102: © Corbis Royalty-Free Website.

Chapter 7

Figure. 7.2: © Vol. 209/Corbis; 7.4: © Corbis/Royalty-Free; pp. 114,115: © Corbis Royalty-Free; 7.8: © Corbis Royalty-Free; p. 119: © Vol. 62/Corbis; Fig. 7 page 120 : © Bill Lai/The Image Works; 7.11: © Corbis/ Royalty Free; p. 123: © Jeff Greenberg/Peter Arnold, Inc.

Chapter 8

Figure 8.1a: © David M. Phillips/Photo Researchers, Inc.; 8.5a: Lennart Nilsson, "A Child is Born, "Dell Publishing Company; 8.7: © James Stevenson/SPL/Photo Researchers, Inc.; p. 135: Streissguth, AP., Landesman-Dwyer, S., Martin, J.C., and Smith, D.W. (1980). Teratogenic effects of alcohol in humans and laboratory animals. Science 209(18): 353-361; p. 140: © Bob Daemmrich/Stock Boston.

Chapter 9

Figure 9.1a: © The McGraw-Hill Companies, Inc./Bob Coyle, photographer; 9.1b: © The McGraw-Hill Companies, Inc./Vincent Ho, photographer; 9.1c,d: © The McGraw-Hill Companies, Inc./Bob Coyle, photographer; 9.1e: © Population Council/Karen Tweedy-Holmes; 9.1f: © The McGraw-Hill Companies, Inc./Bob Coyle, photographer; 9A(left): © J. Brian Alker/Getty; 9A(center top): © Norbert Wu; 9A(center lower): © Alan Barnes/ Getty; 9A(right): © Steven Peters/Stone/ Getty Images; 9.9: © CC Studio/SPL/Photo Researchers, Inc.; p. 154: © Myrleen Ferguson Cate/PhotoEdit.

Chapter 10

Figure 10.1: © David M. Phillips/Visuals Unlimited; 10Aa: © Inga Spence/Visuals Unlimited; 10Ab: © Paul Webster/Getty; 10.2: Courtesy STD Training Center, Harborview Medical Center, Seattle, WA; 10.4: Courtesy of Dr. Ira Abrahamson; 10.5a: © Science VU/CDC/Visuals Unlimited; 10.5b: © Carroll Weiss/Camera M.D.; 10.5c: © Science VU/Visuals Unlimited; 10.6: © K.G. Murti/Visuals Unlimited; 10.7a,b: Courtesy of the Centers for Disease Control, Atlanta, GA; 10.9a,b: © David Phillips/Photo Researchers, Inc.; 10.10:

© Oliver Meckes/Photo Researchers, Inc.; p. 167: © Argus Fotoarchiv/Peter Arnold, Inc.; p. 168: © Corbis/Royalty Free.

AIDS Supplement

Page 171: © NIBSC/SPL/Photo Researchers, Inc.; p. 175: © Nicholas Nixon; p. 178: © Malcolm Linton/Liaison Agency.

Chapter 11

Figure 11.2: © CABISCO/Visuals Unlimited; 11.4(lemur): © Frans Lanting/ Minden Pictures; 11.4(tarsier): © Doug Wechsler; 11.4(white-faced): © C.C. Lockwod/DRK Photo; 11.4(anubis): © St. Meyers/Okapia/Photo Researchers, Inc.; 11.4(gibbon): © Hans & Judy Beste/ Animals Animals/Earth Scenes; 11.4(orangutan): © Evelyn Gallardo/Peter Arnold, Inc.; 11.4(chimp): © Martin Harvey/Peter Arnold, Inc.; 11.4(gorilla): © Martin Harvey/Peter Arnold, Inc.; 11.4(humans): © Tim Davis/Photo Researchers, Inc.; 11.8a: © Dan Dreyfus and Associates; 11.8b: © John Reader/Photo Researchers, Inc.; 11.10: © National Museum of Kenya; 11.12: Courtesy of The Field Museum; 11.13: Transp. #608 Courtesy Department of Library Services, American Museum of Natural History; 11.14a: © Vol. 136/Corbis; 11.14b: Sylvia Mader; 11.14c: © B & C Alexander/Photo Researchers, Inc.; p. 195: © National Museum of Kenya.

Chapter 12

Figure 12.1a: © Joseph Scherschel/TimePix; 12.1b: © Joseph Scherschel/TimePix; 12.2a-d: Dr. Rae Silver; 12.5: © The Natural History Museum, London; p. 204: © T & P Gardner/Bruce Coleman, Inc.; p. 205: Courtesy Gail Patricelli/University of Maryland; 12.7: © Frans Lanting/Minden Pictures; 12.9a: © Y. Arthus-Bertrand/Peter Arnold, Inc.; 12.9b: © FPG International; 12.10: © National Geographic, Jodi Cobb, photographer; 12.11: © OSF/Animals Animals/Earth Sciences; 12.12: © Gregory G. Dimijian/Photo Researchers, Inc.; 12.13: © Susan Kuklin/Photo Researchers, Inc.; 12.14: © J & B Photo/Animals Animals/Earth Scenes; p. 213: © Tom McHugh/Photo Researchers, Inc.

Chapter 13

Figure 13.2: © Mark Edwards/Peter Arnold, Inc.; 13.3: © Melvin B. Zucker/Visuals Unlimited; 13.4: William P. Cunningham; 13.5: Carla Montgomery; 13.7a: © Greg Vaughn/Tom Stack & Associates; 13.7b: © Food Pix/Getty Images; 13.7c: © Greg Vaughn/Tom Stack & Associates; 13.8a: © Jodi Jacobson/Peter Arnold, Inc.; 13.8b: © Peter Essick/AURORA; 13.8c: © Peter Essick/AURORA; 13.9a: © Mitch Kezar/Phototake; 13.9b: © Laish Brtistol/Visuals Unlimited; 13.9c: Courtesy V. Jane Windsor, Division of Plant Industry, Florida Department of Agriculture & Consumer Services; 13.12a: © David L. Pearson/Visuals Unlimited; 13.12b: © S.K. Patrick/Visuals Unlimited; 13.12c: © Mike Schroder/Peter Arnold, Inc.; 13.12d: © Gerald & Buff Corsi/Visuals Unlimited; 13.13: © James P. Blair/National Geographic Image Collection; p. 229: © Ted Kerasote/Photo Researchers, Inc.

Index

Note: Page numbers followed by f refer to figures; page numbers followed by t refer to tables.